Building Change-of-Use

Building Change-of-Use:

Renovating, Adapting, and Altering Commercial, Institutional, and Industrial Properties

Dorothy Henehan

R. Dodge Woodson

McGraw -Hill

New York Chicago San Francisco Lisbon London Madrid
Mexico City Milan New Delhi San Juan Seoul
Singapore Sydney Toronto

The McGraw-Hill Companies

Cataloging-in-Publication Data is on file with the Library of Congress

1 2 3 4 5 6 7 8 9 0 DOC/DOC 0 9 8 7 6 5 4 3

ISBN 0-07-138481-2

The sponsoring editor for this book was Cary Sullivan and the production supervisor was Pamela Pelton. It was set in Century Schoolbook by Lone Wolf Enterprises, Ltd.

Printed and bound by RR Donnelley

ACKNOWLEDGMENTS

We'd like to thank the following individuals for their contributions to this book.

For contributions, editing, guidance, and their tireless belief in this project: Victoria Roberts of Lone Wolf Enterprises, Ltd., ReNae Grant of PageCrafters, Wendy Lochner, editor, and Cary Sullivan, sponsoring editor at McGraw-Hill.

For photographs and images: Stephen Culbert, P.E., Nick Fredericks, Stan Palma, AIA, and Luther Mock, RA

Others who have contributed to this effort by offering inspiration, suggestions, project references, and interviews include: Damon Adams, ICBO; Bruce Anderson, AIA; Pet Baker, CSI, CCPR; Cynthia Bowen, AICP; Stephen Culbert, PE; Vera Dordick; Harry Drake, AIA; Hon. William H. Hudnut, III; Harol Dungan, PE, DEE; Jeff Durham; Steve Easley; Bob Erikson, CSI, AIA; Nick Fredericks; Glenn Garies, AIA; Gloria Geiger; Ralph Gerdes, RA, ICBO, BOCA, NFPA, Assoc. AIA; Glendale Branch Library; The Greater Broad Ripple Community Coalition; David Halvorsen, AIA; Harley Ellis (Southfield, Michigan); James Kienle, AIA; Gene King, CSI; Kelly King; Laura Parrot, CSI, CCPR, DHI; Butch Lockhart; William McDonough Partners; Michael Mills, AIA; Luther Mock, RRC; Louis Morales, RA; David Nieh, AIA, AICP; Stan Palma, AIA; Ed Rensink, ICBO, NFPA; Re-View; John Rigsbee, AIA; Steve Schultz, ICBO; John Speweik, CSI; Robert Stern, AIA; Brian Stumphf, ASLA, AICP; Ron Taylor, ASLA; Troy Thompson, AIA; Urban Land Institute; Anne Walker, AIA; Edith Washington, FCSI; Janet Weins; and Dan Wienheimer, AIA, ULI.

CONTENTS

INTRODUCTION

The purpose in writing this book is to the illuminate the Change-Of-Use process. This book will examine the context and scale in which adaptive re-use occurs. It will identify the key players and convey enough about each of their agendas to create a common vocabulary from which each can draw for constructive dialogue with one another. In doing so, the reader may use this knowledge to better cultivate beneficial relationships and develop successful projects. The Change-Of-Use process, and the practice of architecture for that matter, derives a measure of its intellectual and aesthetic challenge from asking questions, identifying the vital issues, seeking answers, and making difficult choices. The relationships among owner (developer), contractor, and design professional are central to the process. The timely involvement of and clear communication with other players can be critical to project success.

Players in the process are diverse and include owners, tenants, property managers, city planners and reviewers, code consultants, inspectors, testing agencies, construction managers, contractors, material suppliers, manufacturers, lenders, engineers, attorneys, insurers, redevelopment authorities, neighborhood associations, preservationists, utilities, environmental engineers and hygienists, realtors, architects, space planners, and designers.

Actual projects, both built and un-built, will be used to exemplify the process and illustrate concepts and situations typical to a variety of project situations. Product information and resources will be shared so that the reader can explore his interest in specific areas presented. Although a few award-winning project examples are included, the authors have also provided many examples of ordinary projects that were successful chiefly by the client's standards. And, because there is something to be learned with every new venture, they have also included a few that may be characterized as learning experiences.

Professional tools such as code analysis, zoning review, and facility evaluation of existing buildings can be used together to identify new uses for existing buildings that will maximize the potential profit and/or benefit to be realized from owning them. Building owners might begin with the question, "What can this building become?" Business owners or agency operators might ask, "Where can I locate that will create the best advantage for my enterprise?" This book discusses the answers to those questions and suggests how design professionals can use their understanding of re-development analysis and renovation to offer a greater and more valuable service to these clients.

In renovation, designers and owners must choose what elements will stay and what will go. Once the program is set, the designer will select the most effective materials and systems to fit the program and budget. Using examples that are easy to grasp, Roger clarifies approaches to setting budget priorities and completing renovations on time and within budget.

Renovation accounts for nearly a third of all construction and as much as a quarter of all design work. The smart economics of this trend are undeniable, if not sometimes inscrutable. Renovation and Change-of-Use trends are likely to develop as urban redevelopment and sustainability become supported planks in the platform of each major political party in this country and savvy citizens think of new ways to participate in that growth. We hope this book will open some doors.

CHAPTER 1
URBAN SPRAWL

America's cities have undergone a profound transformation in the past 150 years. Social changes combined with economic development have shifted the focus of growth from urban to suburban areas. Cities and the people who live there have suffered from neglect in many ways. Planners and developers can address these issues and, as a result, infuse cities with a new vitality.

WHY CHANGE-OF-USE?

Change-of-use is a term used both in the context of zoning, as applied to functional and characteristic changes in allowable land use, and as a term used in construction plan review (code enforcement). The term describes an existing building or structure that alters the level of risk associated with a building. A change-of-use in terms of zoning won't necessarily trigger alterations to the site or existing structures. A change-of-use in terms of the building code may, especially if a building has moved to a riskier use. This section identifies issues broader than the site scale. These issues define the context in which change-of-use and redevelopment occur. They include identifying certain problems:

- The urban core
- Edge cities
- Sprawl

The response could be in the following forms:

- Economic development
- Planning
- Zoning
- Development
- Citizen action that fosters regional sustainability
- Urban and suburban forms that positively contribute to the quality of life

Why change-of-use? Ultimately it's about economics and quality of life. Communities can sustain and revitalize their existing fabric by finding a new use for existing buildings that have become obsolete. This is readily achieved if their primary structural integrity is intact. Such buildings can be a wonderful resource to a community.

For the community, re-used buildings are a source of historic, cultural, and visual fabric. Re-use keeps existing neighborhoods intact, occupied and vital. Newly occupied existing buildings are increasingly valuable assets to cities because they raise the tax base and allow cities to improve and extend infrastructure that serves the whole community. On a larger scale, they help to mitigate urban and suburban sprawl.

Newly occupied existing buildings are increasingly valuable assets to cities because they raise the tax base and allow cities to improve and extend infrastructure that serves the whole community. On a larger scale, they help to mitigate urban and suburban sprawl.

For environmentally conscious builders, they can be an energy efficient source of building shells for almost any proposed use. Reduced urban sprawl leads to energy conservation in transportation required to support business activity.

For businesses, organizations, and developers in search of space for a project, unused structures form a ready supply of spaces that might be quickly and affordably occupied. Often there are incentives for re-use of existing structures in the form of infrastructure improvements and tax abatements. Architecturally, an existing building and its context can be a foil or fabric to work with in designing the spaces for a new user to occupy. If the building is historic, it may have details worth preserving that cannot be affordably replicated with modern construction techniques.

For owners with empty buildings, a little creative thinking and application of code and zoning optimization can increase the value of a property and attract groups of tenants or purchasers that might be otherwise untapped.

> A little creative thinking and application of code and zoning optimization can increase the value of a property and attract groups of tenants or purchasers that might have been otherwise untapped.

What is Urban Sprawl?

Urban sprawl describes the growth of metropolises and urban areas into adjacent hinterlands. Sprawl often paves over farmland and rural communities. The negative images associated with urban sprawl remind us of traffic congestion, pollution, inconvenience, commuting, social isolation, and place isolation. The words "Urban Sprawl" also call to mind its ugly companion, deterioration. It brings to mind images of central business districts decorated with litter and graffiti and dotted with fringe businesses and empty storefronts. Urban sprawl reminds us of the social and economic cost of unkempt and minimally maintained infrastructure in the form of abandoned businesses and institutions that blight urban neighborhoods. It reminds us of the poverty, idleness and social inequity endured by those who are left behind, and generates a public burden in the form of higher taxes, more police, and increased need for social services.

Sprawl has made a sense of community more difficult to achieve. Physical distance between the blighted areas of the city and the newer, more affluent residential communities allows people to avoid visually confronting blight or even perceiving core urban districts as part of their community.

While not exclusively the problem of older cities, sprawl is perpetuated by the desire of those who have the means to leave, doing so. Figure 1.1 illustrates this point. Wouldn't we all like to live better? But can we continue to discard our timeworn structures and environment because we can move a little farther down the road into something new? How do we build a better environment for living?

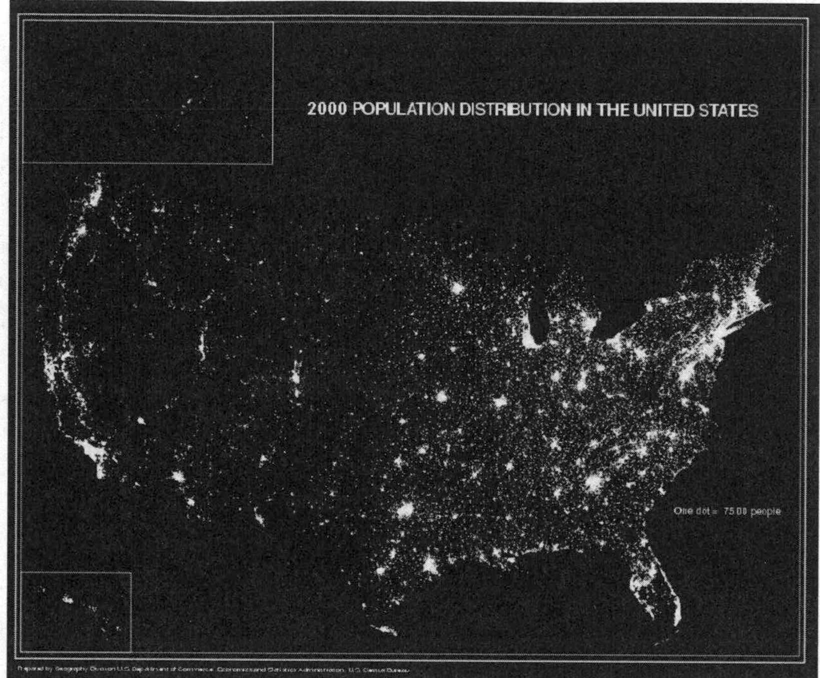

FIGURE 1.1 Population Distribution US 2000, US Dept. of Commerce

Causes of Urban Sprawl

Urban sprawl came about for several reasons. For example, traffic congestion and long commutes for suburban residents, as shown in Figure 1.2, triggered support for increased taxes. These taxes were earmarked for development of additional roads. To support the tax base required for constructing roads and providing services for bedroom communities, residents sought clean businesses and industries for their community. It had the effect of "cannibalizing" the most prosperous and agile businesses from the major city and giving them economic incentive to move where land is cheaper and taxes are lower. The "doughnut" expands outward like a supernova, depleting the economically viable businesses and population from the center, from the edge cities, and from the older suburbs.

Zoning regulations and lending practices required large lot sizes and encouraged single use zoning. This stratified neighborhoods economically by reducing density. It also indirectly supported biased racial policies. Reactive development of highways and infrastructure exacerbated suburban growth by making the suburbs more accessible and temporarily less congested.

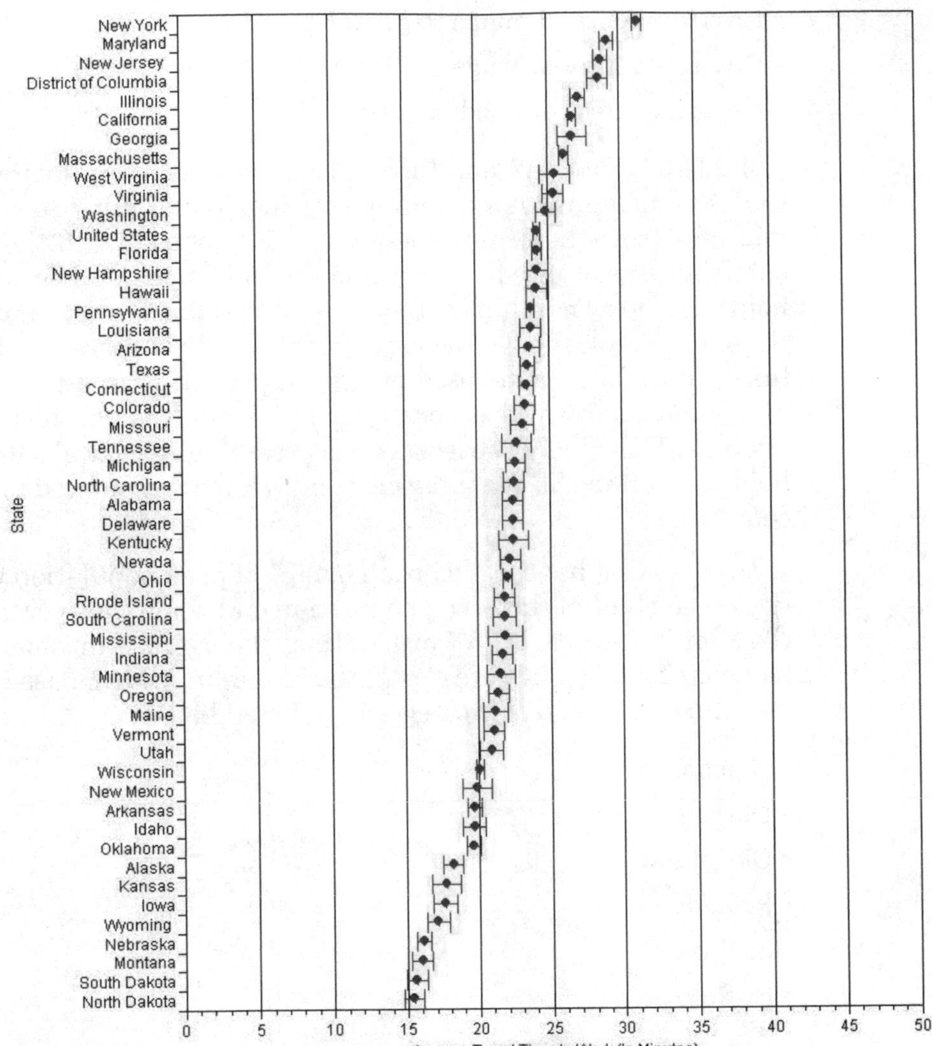

FIGURE 1.2 Average Travel Time to Work (In Minutes) Workers 16 years and over. *All results of the 1997 Economic Census are available on the Census Bureau Internet site (www.census.gov) and on compact discs (CD-ROM) for sale by the Census Bureau.*

Why Does Urban Sprawl Lead to Decay?

There are many effects of sprawl:

- Economic polarization
- Land consumption
- Environmental damage to wetlands

- Environmental damage to green spaces
- Environmental damage to farms
- Negative effect on biodiversity

Table 1.1, Table 1.2, and Table 1.3 demonstrate the economic polarization that accompanies the expanding housing "doughnut." As the population migrates from the center, the best paying jobs go with them. Generally, suburbia is marketed toward middle and upper-middle income households. Home ownership is predominant in suburban communities. When these households leave the city, property values there fall and erode the tax base. Information-based businesses, wanting to attract a ready supply of educated workers, locate near the suburbs and further erode the tax base. Effectively, the least educated and least capital-intensive households are left in the declining city, and wealth is displaced to surrounding counties.

In cities that have lost more than 20% of peak population when minorities exceed 30% of the urban population and when the average income per resident in the city is 70% or less than the average income of the suburban counterpart, the core city in the region may have passed the point of no return. Cities in this category are listed below:

- Baltimore
- Detroit
- Cleveland
- Philadelphia
- St. Louis
- Buffalo

When cities meet these criteria, regional intervention, in the form of revenue sharing and planning incentives to reverse the flight of capital, may be the last resort. ("Thinking Regionally: Stretching Cities" by David Rusk for *The State of the American Community*, ed. Robert McNulty, Washington D.C.: *Partners for Livable Communities*, 1994, p. 45-46 as cited in *Changing Places, Rebuilding Community in the Age of Sprawl*, Richard Moe and Carter Wilkie, Henry Holt and Co., 1997, p. 101.)

Excessive land consumption can result in environmental damage to wetlands, green spaces, farms, and even biodiversity. Table 1.4 and Table 1.5 indicates the pattern of reduced density in housing. This doesn't take into account increased lot sizes, the additional lengths of paving, and the infrastructure that must stretch between them. Similar patterns have occurred in commercial development of malls, office parks, and big box retail. These

TABLE 1.1 Characteristics of United States labor force (*Continued*)

Subject	Number
LABOR FORCE STATUS	
Persons 16 years and over	**191,829,271**
In labor force	125,182,378
Civilian labor force	123,473,450
Employed	115,681,202
Unemployed	7,792,248
Armed Forces	1,708,928
Not in labor force	66,646,893
Males 16 years and over	**92,025,913**
In labor force	68,509,429
Civilian labor force	66,986,201
Employed	62,704,579
Unemployed	4,281,622
Armed Forces	1,523,228
Not in labor force	23,516,484
Females 16 years and over	**99,803,358**
In labor force	56,672,949
Civilian labor force	56,487,249
Employed	52,976,623
Unemployed	3,510,626
Armed Forces	185,700
Not in labor force	43,130,409

COMMUTING TO WORK	
Workers 16 years and over	**115,070,274**
Drove alone	84,215,298
In carpools	15,377,634
Using public transportation	6,069,589
Using other means	1,512,842
Walked or worked at home	7,894,911

(All results of the 1997 Economic Census are available on the Census Bureau Internet site (www.census.gov) and on compact discs (CD-ROM) for sale by the Census Bureau.)

structures are usually one or two stories in height and surrounded by a sea of parking.

The metropolises of Milwaukee, Chicago, Detroit, and Cleveland are shown on the map in Figure 1.3. Evidence of the housing "doughnuts" expansion can be seen in the vast shaded areas surrounding the center cities.

TABLE 1.1 *(Continued)* Characteristics of United States labor force

OCCUPATION	
Employed persons 16 years and over	**115,681,202**
Executive, administrative, and managerial occupations	14,227,916
Professional specialty occupations	16,305,666
Technicians and related support occupations	4,257,235
Sales occupations	13,634,686
Administrative support occupations, including clerical	18,826,477
Private household occupations	521,154
Protective service occupations	1,992,852
Service occupations, except protective and household	12,781,911
Farming, forestry, and fishing occupations	2,839,010
Precision production, craft, and repair occupations	13,097,963
Machine operators, assemblers, and inspectors	7,904,197
Transportation and material moving occupations	4,729,001
Handlers, equipment cleaners, helpers, and laborers	4,563,134

INDUSTRY	
Employed persons 16 years and over	**115,681,202**
Agriculture, forestry, and fisheries	3,115,372
Mining	723,423
Construction	7,214,763
Manufacturing, nondurable goods	8,053,234
Manufacturing, durable goods	12,408,844
Transportation	5,108,003
Communications and other public utilities	3,097,059
Wholesale trade	5,071,026
Retail trade	19,485,666
Finance, insurance, and real estate	7,984,870
Business and repair services	5,577,462
Personal services	3,668,696
Entertainment and recreation services	1,636,460
Health services	9,682,684
Educational services	9,633,503
Other professional and related services	7,682,060
Public administration	5,538,077

(All results of the 1997 Economic Census are available on the Census Bureau Internet site (www.census.gov) and on compact discs (CD-ROM) for sale by the Census Bureau.)

Low-density development caused environmental damage that now affects the watershed in many regions. Runoff areas that once filtered rain through the soil to natural aquifers now travels over parking lots and roofs where it picks up an increased level of contamination and must be industrially filtered before returning to the natural watershed. Since

TABLE 1.1 *(Continued)* Characteristics of United States labor force

CLASS OF WORKER	
Employed persons 16 years and over	**115,681,202**
Private wage and salary workers	89,541,393
Government workers	17,567,100
Local government workers	8,244,755
State government workers	5,381,445
Federal government workers	3,940,900
Self-employed workers	8,067,483
Unpaid family workers	505,226

NOTE. Data based on twelve monthly samples during 2000. For information on confidentiality protection, sampling error, nonsampling error, and definitions, see http://factfinder.census.gov/home/en/datanotes/exp_c2ss.html.

TABLE 1.2 Mortgage status and selected monthly owner costs

Housing units with a mortgage	36,688,336	36,444,809	36,931,863
Less than $300	262,175	246,399	277,951
$300 to $499	2,141,987	2,091,560	2,192,414
$500 to $699	4,765,721	4,695,396	4,836,046
$700 to $999	9,055,145	8,966,058	9,144,232
$1,000 to $1,499	10,946,765	10,832,405	11,061,125
$1,500 to $1,999	5,262,980	5,188,964	5,336,996
$2,000 or more	4,253,563	4,194,973	4,312,153
Median (dollars)	1,085	1,082	1,088

Housing units without a mortgage	18,859,574	18,697,734	19,021,414
Less than $100	382,200	355,508	408,892
$100 to $199	3,734,177	3,656,360	3,811,994
$200 to $299	6,074,711	5,997,466	6,151,956
$300 to $399	4,021,534	3,961,147	4,081,921
$400 or more	4,646,952	4,584,808	4,709,096
Median (dollars)	287	285	289

All results of the 1997 Economic Census are available on the Census Bureau Internet site (www.census.gov) and on compact discs (CD-ROM) for sale by the Census Bureau.

TABLE 1.3 Gross rent as a percentage Of household income

Less than 15 percent	5,738,417
15.0 to 19.9 percent	4,992,595
20.0 to 24.9 percent	4,581,976
25.0 to 29.9 percent	3,844,598
30.0 to 34.9 percent	2,743,932
35.0 percent or more	10,817,540
Not computed	2,221,743

All results of the 1997 Economic Census are available on the Census Bureau Internet site (www.census.gov) and on compact discs (CD-ROM) for sale by the Census Bureau.

TABLE 1.4 Population 1790-1990 *Source: US Census*

United States	Population			Housing units			Area measurements				Density			
		Change from preceding census			Change from preceding census		Total area		Land area		Population per—		Housing units per—	
	Total	Number	Percent	Total	Number	Percent	Square kilometers	Square miles	Square kilometers	Square miles	Square kilometer	Square mile	Square kilometer	Square mile
1990 (Apr. 1)	248 709 873	22 167 674	9.8	102 263 678	13 853 051	15.7	9 809 155	3 787 319	9 159 116	3 536 338	27.2	70.3	11.2	28.9
1980 (Apr. 1)	r226 542 199	23 240 168	11.4	r88 410 627	19 706 312	28.7	9 372 614	3 618 770	9 166 759	3 539 289	24.7	64.0	9.6	25.0
1970 (Apr. 1)	203 302 031	23 978 856	13.4	68 704 315	10 377 958	17.8	9 372 614	3 618 770	9 160 454	3 536 855	22.2	57.5	7.5	19.4
1960 (Apr. 1)	179 323 175	27 997 377	18.5	58 326 357	12 189 281	26.4	9 372 614	3 618 770	9 170 959	3 540 911	19.6	50.6	6.4	16.5
1950 (Apr. 1)	151 325 798	19 161 229	14.5	46 137 076	8 698 362	23.2	9 372 614	3 618 770	9 200 214	3 552 206	16.4	42.6	5.0	13.0
1940 (Apr. 1)	132 164 569	8 961 945	7.3	37 438 714	...	...	9 372 614	3 618 770	9 206 435	3 554 608	14.4	37.2	4.1	10.5
1930 (Apr. 1)	123 202 624	17 181 087	16.2	...	...	...	9 372 614	3 618 770	9 198 665	3 551 608	13.4	34.7	...	...
1920 (Jan. 1)	106 021 537	13 793 041	15.0	...	...	...	9 372 614	3 618 770	9 186 551	3 546 931	11.5	29.9	...	...
1910 (Apr. 15)	92 228 496	16 016 328	21.0	...	...	...	9 372 614	3 618 770	9 186 847	3 547 045	10.0	26.0	...	...
1900 (June 1)	76 212 168	13 232 402	21.0	...	...	...	9 372 614	3 618 770	9 187 543	3 547 314	8.3	21.5	...	...
1890 (June 1)	62 979 766	12 790 557	25.5	...	...	...	9 355 854	3 612 299	9 170 426	3 540 705	6.9	17.8	...	...
1880 (June 1)	50 189 209	11 630 838	30.2	...	...	...	9 355 854	3 612 299	9 170 426	3 540 705	5.5	14.2	...	...
1870 (June 1)	38 558 371	7 115 050	22.6	...	...	...	9 355 854	3 612 299	9 170 426	3 540 705	4.2	10.9	...	...
1860 (June 1)	31 443 321	8 251 445	35.6	...	...	...	7 825 154	3 021 295	7 691 368	2 969 640	4.1	10.6	...	...
1850 (June 1)	23 191 876	6 122 423	35.9	...	...	...	7 748 386	2 991 655	7 614 709	2 940 042	3.0	7.9	...	...
1840 (June 1)	17 069 453	4 203 433	32.7	...	...	...	4 642 710	1 792 552	4 531 107	1 749 462	3.8	9.8	...	...
1830 (June 1)	12 866 020	3 227 567	33.5	...	...	...	4 642 710	1 792 552	4 531 107	1 749 462	2.8	7.4	...	...
1820 (Aug. 7)	9 638 453	2 398 572	33.1	...	...	...	4 642 710	1 792 552	4 531 107	1 749 462	2.1	5.5	...	...
1810 (Aug. 6)	7 239 881	1 931 398	36.4	...	...	...	4 461 754	1 722 685	4 355 935	1 681 828	1.7	4.3	...	...
1800 (Aug. 4)	5 308 483	1 379 269	35.1	...	...	...	2 308 633	891 364	2 239 692	864 746	2.4	6.1	...	...
1790 (Aug. 2)	3 929 214	...	...	...	...	...	2 308 633	891 364	2 239 692	864 746	1.8	4.5	...	...

TABLE 1.5 Density per unit 1940-1990 *Source: US Census*

Year	Housing	Population	Population
1990	70.3	28.9	2.4
1980	64.0	25.0	2.6
1970	57.5	19.4	3.0
1960	50.6	16.5	3.1
1950	42.6	13.0	3.3
1940	37.2	10.5	3.5

While the number of people per household has decreased, the density of households has increased.

> Runoff areas that once filtered rain through the soil to natural aquifers now travel over parking lots and roofs where it picks up an increased level of contamination and must be industrially filtered before returning to the natural watershed.

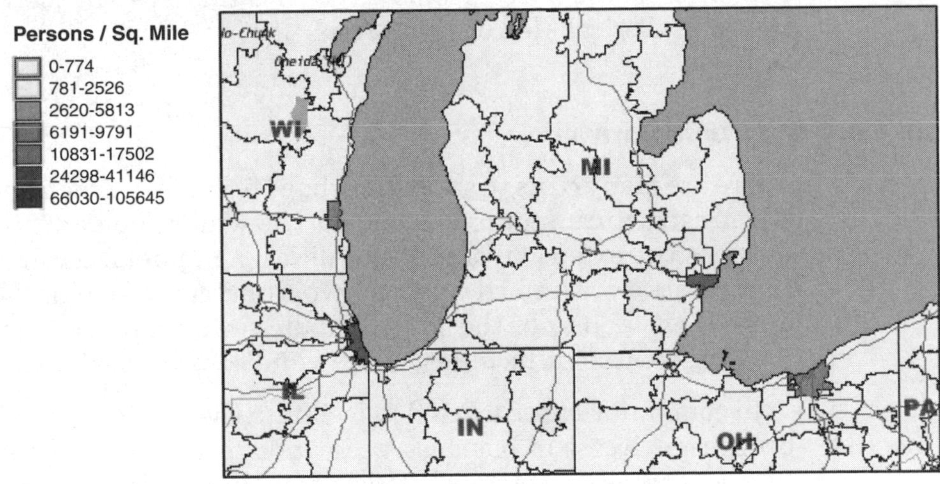

FIGURE 1.3 Michigan population density

the industrial filters are seldom designed for large storms, untreated runoff then flows unfiltered into rivers, streams and reservoirs. In urban areas and older incorporated towns, combined sewers regularly overflow gray water (run-off) and black water (sewage).

When pollutants affect a watershed, life within the watershed is endangered. The water pollution control facility in Muncie, Indiana is upstream of Anderson (a long time manufacturing city now promoting itself as an outer ring bedroom community) and Indianapolis. Like other large-scale waste treatment facilities, it employs biologists to collect, measure, preserve, catalog, and compare the species and size of botanical and biological specimens at set intervals along the watershed. In 2001 they were pleased to record the return of several species not seen for nearly 20 years. Downstream, in Anderson, a chemical "spill" still under investigation by the Department of Natural Resources was attributed to an industrial source and caused dead fish to litter the riverbank all the way to Indianapolis. Worse still, the toxins were dangerous for humans and animals exposed directly and through the food chain. It will take years for the ecosystem to recover.

Unchecked and unplanned growth in urban development seldom goes hand in hand with economic development and social health. The result is more likely to be economic blight and a breakdown of a healthy social environment. While some factions might consider adopting a "no growth policy" as a viable option, there are a number of practical approaches that can be taken. Developing an attitude of "cityship" where elected officials and policy makers have sufficient identification with the principle statistical metropolitan area promotes policies that sustain the whole Consolidated Statistical Metropolitan Area.

The Cost of Urban Sprawl

There are many costs to sprawl. Perhaps first among them is the high cost of infrastructure required to support new development. Infrastructure includes the extension of roads, utilities, and public services. It requires that rivers be dammed and reservoirs be constructed. Where density exceeds the ability of the soil to handle sewage and storm water contributions, treatment facilities, gutters and sewers must be provided.

In communities structured to facilitate the primacy of the car, reduced pedestrian access to business, recreation, social, and community opportunities erodes the sense of belonging and human interaction that has traditionally renewed people's sense of social responsibility. It promotes human isolation especially for invalids, children, and the elderly. This is especially true when taxpayers will not support the extension of public transportation to their communities.

Sprawl consumes undeveloped land and natural features such as wetland green spaces and farms. In some cases, the consumption of land endangers species.

Tax support of government subsidies becomes essential to encourage inner city and edge city redevelopment. Because outward growth leads to inward decay, subsidy for existing sites with abandoned, underutilized, or disintegrating structures is another hidden cost of expansion. The percentage of vacant housing is illustrated in Figure 1.4. Subsidy is needed to stimulate redevelopment or blight and decay will be exacerbated. Loss of the tax base, as the most viable businesses migrate to greener pastures, creates a local government less economically able to address redevelopment issues, snowballing the process.

About two-fifths of the estimated 34 million central-city housing units are at least 50 years old. This equates to more than 13 million units. Less than one-fifth (18 percent) of the 54.1 million suburban housing units are 50 years or older. Although suburban units tend to be newer, in all, some 23 million units are at an age where most building systems have exceeded their intended service life. The Stutz Motor Car building in Figure 1.5 is a good example of an older building. Some have already been renovated more than once.

Similar distribution of aged buildings runs across other building types concurrent with the initial and peak development periods for each area. The transformation of the economy from a manufacturing base to a service base has already left scores of industrial facilities abandoned or underutilized, such as the old Indianapolis bottling plant in Figure 1.6. Changes in national priorities, including military spending, closed hundreds of United States

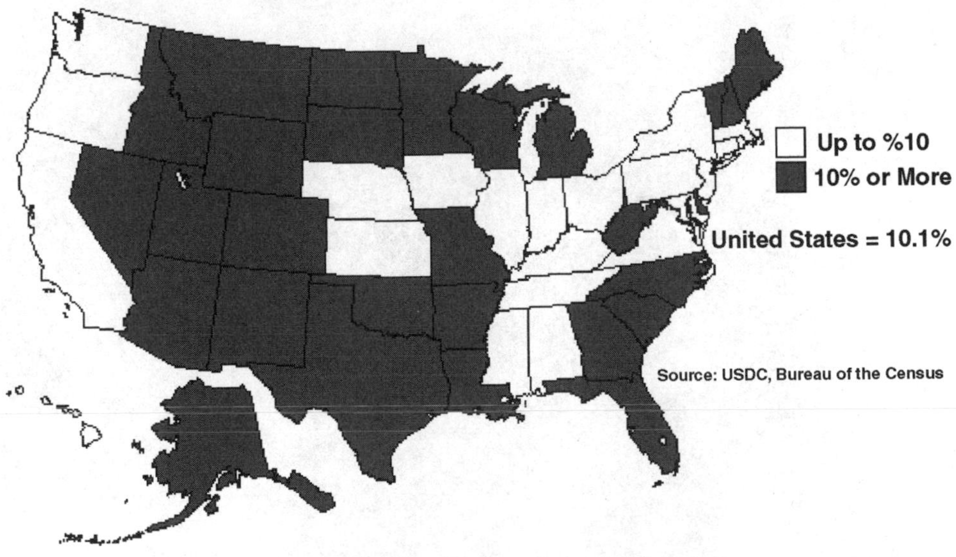

FIGURE 1.4 Percent vacant housing, US Census

FIGURE 1.5 Stutz Motor Car Building, Service Alley *Photo: Stephen Culbert*

FIGURE 1.6 Old Bottling Plant, New Rail Line, Indianapolis *Photo: Stephen Culbert*

fastfacts

About two-fifths of the estimated 34-million central-city housing units are at least 50 years old. This equates to more than 13 million units. Less than one-fifth (18 percent) of the 54.1 million suburban housing units are 50 years or older. Although suburban units tend to be newer, in all, some 23 million units are at an age where most building systems have exceeded their intended service life. Some have already been renovated more than once.

military bases worldwide. Strip commercial areas like the one-story retail malls with huge parking lots will become increasingly defunct over the coming decade. The supply of ready-to-rehab buildings is abundant.

OBSTACLES TO OVERCOMING URBAN SPRAWL

There are several obstacles to urban redevelopment, particularly in the urban core and downtown, but they primarily boil down to this: Development will not happen if investors, be they public or private, cannot see a timely return on investment.

Determining the appropriate level of redevelopment in relation to the existing building and site conditions, available funds, and market absorption is crucial. Rehabilitation is described in degrees as follows:

- Minor rehabilitation involves repairs and improvements of a primarily cosmetic nature or replacing fixed equipment. Painting, caulking, replacing or refinishing cabinets or fixtures are examples of minor rehabilitation.

fastfacts

Development will not happen if investors, be they public or private, cannot see a timely return on investment.

- Moderate rehabilitation is more extensive. It includes modernizing wiring, heating and cooling systems, and/or minor reconfiguring of the existing plan.
- Substantial rehabilitation generally means removing all interior walls and mechanical equipment (i.e., gutting) and redesigning the floor plan significantly. It may also include structural alterations or improvements.

The work required to salvage existing facilities from oblivion runs the gamut of the foregoing, and in some cases, re-facing and partial demolition will be needed to increase marketability. Sometimes, additions will be required to fulfill program requirements if, for example, high bay space or clear spans are required where there are none.

Higher land costs, disparate land ownership in the same area, and the cost of developed property acquisition each contribute to overall project costs to the degree that acquisition of undeveloped land cannot.

Land is valued and taxed on its market value. Land used for agriculture and woodland and other similar low-density uses is still valued for the potential it has for urban form development. If it's located adjacent to transportation arteries, water, or is particularly scenic, if it's near the perimeter of a CSMA (Consolidated Statistical Measuring Area i.e., large urban center) then its value is increased far beyond the actual use of the land. Guess which value is the basis of taxation? Potential value. No wonder farmers frequently oppose the bond issues for new schools.

In an environment of decline, whether prompted by national economic conditions or by localized blight, property-based taxes cut like a two-edged sword. Property values and their development potential plummet, and so do revenues available for TIF (Tax Increment Financing) redevelopment districts as well as the maintenance of other commonly held infrastructure and services.

In each case the property owners find themselves land rich and cash poor, with few options but to sell or develop their land. Every state has some form of property tax. Ask your political leaders how easily real estate based taxes can be shifted to another source that is more equitably distributed. This generally drives sales, user, and visitor taxes higher.

Rigid zoning ordinances, land-use restrictions, and permitting processes can cause delays and added project costs.

Rigid zoning ordinances, land-use restrictions, and permitting processes can cause delays and added project costs. It is not unusual for development planning, design, permitting, and construction to take half a decade. Economic uncertainty over such a long time frame increases risk to the developer.

Single-use zoning can make the acquisition of a large existing facility or campus unattractive. The effort in applying for rezoning or variance(s) required to make a mixed-use development work can affect its timeline. When purchases are contingent on re-zoning, mixed-use proposals can lose out to purchasers who would raze the structures and start over with single use or parceled development plans. The risk and cost associated with seeking variance(s) for as yet unpurchased property can be considerable depending on how well-developed the preliminary plans for the property must be.

Uncertain environmental standards and property status contribute to the pool of obstacles and unknowns that cause lenders to be wary. This is especially true in Brownfield development when the property is an orphaned site. An orphaned site was usually polluted and then abandoned, often by an enterprise that no longer exists. It may have liens, especially for federally mandated emergency environmental cleanup. It has become the problem of a local unit of government. Only when the government catalogs the hazards, remedies them, and indemnifies the new owner against exposure for the original contamination, can the new owner be sure that they have a site sufficiently clean for the new use, and that they cannot be sued for exposure to original contaminants by third parties.

Exclusionary land use controls keep the poor out of the suburbs by placing such prescriptive requirements on developments that low income buyers are priced out of the market without subsidy.

Another obstacle to redevelopment is the perception of higher risk when obtaining insurance and financing. This perception affects lending practices for proposed projects because it is difficult to quantify unknowns. Removing as many of the unknown costs as possible, prior to obtaining insurance and financing, will improve the possibility of favorable terms. On large projects especially, the cost of facility analysis, building type studies, schematic designs, and even selectively destructive probes can be well worth their cost. If key tenants have been secured and identified, the project will be more attractive to a financier. Lenders will feel much more comfortable with a nationally known tenant versus start-up businesses and non-profits.

During the construction, other barriers to rehabilitation can arise such as hiring qualified workers, complying with the myriad of codes for asbestos, construction, fire safety, accessibility, energy efficiency, lead-based paint, radon, and historic preservation. Rent control and back property taxes, liens, or high tax rates can also impede financing and occupancy of rehabilitated property, especially housing.

COMBATING THE NEGATIVE EFFECTS OF URBAN SPRAWL: THE ROLE OF REDEVELOPMENT IN EFFECTING POSITIVE CHANGE

States, cities, and even suburbs need to recognize that sprawl is fiscally irresponsible because it requires government expenditures for expansion and infrastructure to support it. Planning for "smart growth" can reduce the effects of sprawl. Communities can develop incentives for smart growth like identifying priority-funding areas for publicly funded infrastructure improvements. They can fund rural legacy programs in which property development rights transfer from farm owners to the state in order to preserve green space, and brownfield redevelopment programs that encourage the cleanup and redevelopment of contaminated sites with tax abatement or credits. (http://www.huduser.org/periodicals/rrr/rrr_12_2001/1201_3.html)

Redevelopment authorities or corporations are set up by municipal governments to invest money in areas targeted for revitalization. Usually they receive initial funding from the city with additional matching grants from state and federal sources. Where public/private partnerships exist on specific projects, there may also be matching funds from private corporations or endowments.

"State law allows a city council to create a redevelopment agency to administer one or more "project areas" within its boundaries. An area may be small, or it can encompass the entire city.... Unlike new counties, cities and school districts, it can be created without a vote of the citizens affected. Unlike other levels of government, it can incur bonded indebtedness without voter approval. Unlike other government entities, it may use the power of eminent domain to benefit private interests." These are fearsome words used by a critic describe the powers of redevelopment authorities in California ("Redevelopment, the Unknown Government / Unaccountable" By Mayor Chris Norby, City of Fullerton accessed at downeyeagle.com 2/18/2002).

Overcoming obstacles to redevelopment is usually the job of local governments and redevelopment authorities.

Administrative Assistance

At the administrative level of government, some jurisdictions make redevelopment a little easier by streamlining the redevelopment and permitting process. They reduce the number of reviews, applications, and fees. Some provide one-stop reviews with all stakeholders and oversight agencies to expedite the process. This can be especially useful to the developer when Planned Unit Development (PUD) is involved. The downside is that it won't prevent bad press if there has not been sufficient involvement with neighbors and stakeholders affected by the development. Neighbors may still remonstrate the attempt at rezoning property to PUD.

Notification rules are sometimes minimal. Ideally, rules regarding the proximity and length of notice should be respectful of the scale of the proposed change.

Regional land use planning oversight allows several local governments to co-ordinate their efforts to the benefit of the region at large. It may mitigate the rate of growth in outlying areas and increase the rate of tax base retention in blighted urban areas, preventing further decline in the region. Governments can negotiate urban growth boundaries for various types of districts.

Legislative Assistance

Local governments can adopt zoning ordinances in concert with comprehensive land use plans and consistently enforce them to prevent disparate site uses and values. They can use the following standards:

- Proscriptive or performance zoning standards that enable creative land use
- Construction and site development standards, in lieu of prescriptive standards and single use zoning areas only

State governments can also provide help:

- Enabling legislation for regional government authorities. Where states don't answer this call, local governments can create advisory bodies that assist local governments in coordinating local planning with regionally agreed goals.

- Tax burden balancing by government coalitions. An example of this is the Port Authority of New York and New Jersey.
- Restructuring of sales tax for revenue sharing

Strategic Assistance

Redevelopment authorities can prioritize and focus on specific areas of blight in the use of state development funds for existing developed areas. This allows the "renaissance" of an area to be perceivable and to anchor unfunded co-development. Usually this begins in the downtown and inner ring areas, and then spreads along transportation corridors into nodes at intersections to anchor image corridors that connect districts and neighborhoods.

Local governments can, within the comprehensive plan, purposefully locate scatter-site low-cost housing and mixed-use development so as to disperse/distribute the poor and working class populations. Many suburban communities are averse to doing so because it reduces the tax base and increases the tax burden by introducing a population that may require government services and assistance, and potentially reduce the aesthetic appeal to neighboring upscale development.

Housing Authorities can target publicly funded projects to sites and development areas identified in the comprehensive plan. Keeping projects at the smallest possible scale may make low income housing more palatable to middle and upper income neighbors. Scattered sites create administrative and maintenance hurdles for the housing authority, but the benefits to the inhabitants and the general community by creating neighborhood opportunity for the poor are profound. Where this can be achieved, it can yield several community benefits. Scattering low-taxable-value properties may help distribute the burden caused by concentration of such housing in the inner ring areas of older cities. In theory, adopting a scatter-site approach to low-income housing helps prevent blight because a mixed-income tax base has the ability to support development bonds, infrastructure, and services.

Within areas of mixed-use development, some moderate and low income people whose jobs are largely in services and retail can live close to work and may not have to support cost of employment and housing expenses. Permitting mixed-income residential zoning may encourage low income residents to "be good neighbors" and maintain their property to the extent their means permit. Middle and upper middle class neighbors will undoubtedly exert social pressure in this cause.

Some planners promote a more controlled approach to planning and managing growth. They adopt a regional view to land use planning and enforce requirements such as the mandatory public land set-asides and development of the set-aside land into something more than a lawn or parking lot. It may also discourage development except along existing road edges at limited scale with mandatory landscape requirements. This is a hard sell in some communities where this approach would be seen as government interference not government intervention.

INFRASTRUCTURE MAINTENANCE AND IMPROVEMENT

Local governments can initiate clean-up programs. Depending on the scale and complexity of the cleanup area, these programs can be executed by the combined forces of citizen groups, inmates, ordinance violators, contractors and/ or city staff.

State involvement in infrastructure maintenance and repair can take some of the burden off local governments. The state department of transportation should carefully plan the location and rate of growth of highways. This can be done in a way that affirms regional government agreements for managed growth. They can plan mass transit to connect areas for strategic uses, such as the reduction in traffic or the synergistic connection of business centers.

Opportunities for local governments to provide improvements are myriad, and include providing and maintaining public parking, parks, sanitation and lighting. These opportunities are limited only by the funds available and the requirement that they serve the public (i.e., they cannot extend onto private land).

States can also co-fund public infrastructure improvement projects with cities and business partners by use of loans or outright grants where it will foster new business growth, attract relocating business, or retain core businesses.

The federal government and states can bolster local governments with the extension of governmental borrowing capacity.

TAX ABATEMENT AGREEMENTS

The city may also enter a tax abatement agreement to provide additional incentive to attract a major business that may anchor an area or contribute significantly to the overall tax base or employment base.

Redevelopment authorities sometimes require contracts with businesses in exchange for project-specific tax abatement or infrastructure support. These contracts may promote social equity in gender, race, wages, workforce development, or other items on the political agenda that the city needs the business to support. There may be business retention clauses with penalties for early release from obligation. The incentives offered and the obligations required are negotiated and vary in strength depending on the relative attractiveness of the business to others seeking incentives, the availability of funds, and the depth of need for revitalization.

LAND FOR DEVELOPMENT

New land for development can be created within existing developed areas by reclaiming abandoned properties. This happens in several ways. Brownfields were usually industrial sites, although they could be military, transportation, or retail fuel sites. Sometimes cleanup of these sites are addressed by local redevelopment authorities in land consolidation programs and then sold to developers for new, "clean" uses. Grayfields, like brownfields, are abandoned sites that contribute acres of blight to a district. The difference is the cleanup required generally involves non-hazardous or minimally hazardous materials. While the vision of dying malls predominates, the image of grayfields, abandoned warehouses, factories, town centers, churches, and depots illustrate the extent of available grayfield sites ripe for development.

Land Assembly involves the purchase of adjacent properties by a redevelopment corporation for the assembly of the parcels into a larger parcel. Usually, owners will agree to a fair price for the real estate. Property can then be cleaned up, and provided with infrastructure like curb cuts, walks, lights, utility ties etc. It will then be sold to support a new enterprise that will benefit the community as a whole. Traditionally this has been for a public use such as a school, hospital, or utility. Courts have upheld the city's right to use land assembly and eminent domain for private busi-

Grayfields, like brownfields, are abandoned sites that contribute acres of blight to a district. The difference is the cleanup required generally involves non-hazardous or minimally hazardous materials.

ness where it can be demonstrated that the project, so located, can favorably affect taxes, employment, or revitalization.

In a classic example of the use of eminent domain, the politics and economics surrounding the [original] World Trade Center were intense. The twin towers were originally intended to reinforce New York's status as a world port. Opposition caused them to be moved from the Fulton Fish Market on the river, inland to "Radio Row," a strip of blighted electronics stores. "The Rockefellers used the Port Authority of New York and New Jersey, a powerful public agency, to condemn the 16-square-block area and finance the construction of the towers." (Column by William Fulton, "Governing", February 2002 Issue: Economic Development.)

BUSINESS LOCATION SERVICES

When new businesses emerge and existing businesses seek to relocate, they often contact the redevelopment authority. This is to their benefit because the redevelopment authority tries to balance a larger vision with implementation. In combining agency expertise and agency consultant's expertise, there may be other opportunities that businesses are not aware of or a different way they may fit into a larger picture.

Addressing the issue of strategic co-development, redevelopment director David Nieh in San Jose explained strategic co-development's simplest form of implementation.

"For example, one thing that happens a lot in blighted downtowns, and this is not just San Jose, you have some of the neighborhood services...you know drycleaners and hair cut places and all things that you need like that, and they may be spread out all over the place. Whereas, if we have a plan to kind of design and build another building, or to fix up and adaptive reuse other buildings, we may locate them into one area which may make more sense so they kind of symbiotically help each other generate commercial traffic. So there are certain groupings of businesses that make sense. Or we may be for example upgrading our transportation system and we know that area is going to be a mess for a few years to come. And a business is kind of flailing a little bit, says we are looking to potentially relocate, where do you think is the best place. So the Agency can help direct or offer guidance to facilitate them moving to a place that makes sense. Some incentives, or maybe has a better parking supply or better visibility maybe, so these are ways we can begin to offer assistance to both types of businesses."(David Nieh, Architecture and Urban Design Program Manager, City of San Jose in phone interview with Dorothy Henehan, Summer 2001.)

SUPPORTIVE ORDINANCES

Redevelopment authorities can work with planners to develop model ordinances that encourage redevelopment in several ways. For example, Urban Collage Inc., of Atlanta, Georgia developed a "Grayfields Redevelopment Tool Kit" for the ten-county Atlanta Regional Commission. The "tool kit" outlines case studies and planning techniques that can be employed in redeveloping aging commercial centers. Model ordinances listed in the published Community Choices tool kit cover such topics as:

- Establishing Overlay Districts that can be used in tandem with existing zoning to allow planned unit development to increase or reduce existing levels of zoning regulation to maximize the creative and integrated use of land in an existing zoned area.
- Encouraging Infill Development is a more traditional method of addressing blighted districts. Developing the vacant lots and abandoned properties between buildings permits the most economic and efficient use of existing infrastructure while curbing the momentum of sprawl.
- Developing Transit-Oriented Development (TOD) is desirable because of its links with all transportation options, including mass transit and the car.
- Reestablishing Traditional Neighborhood Development balances car and pedestrian traffic in comparatively compact development. Pedestrian-friendly amenities may include park facilities, greenways, and bike trails.
- Platting Conservation Subdivisions where about 40% the developed land is conserved in it's natural state. Recreational opportunities are encouraged to promote community cohesion.
- Implementing mixed income "Life-Cycle" Housing in communities incorporates a variety of rental and ownership modes as well as a range of unit styles. The mix includes starter housing, single-family housing, multi-family housing, efficiency living units, group homes, and assisted living. The mix enhances familial continuity within neighborhoods by promoting convenient proximity between mixed housing types for all family members irrespective of age or income. This also makes it easier for domestic service workers to live near their employers. Paired with mixed-use commercial or transportation districts, life cycle housing also promotes walk to work opportunities for at least some of the neighborhood's inhabitants.

Corridor Redevelopment creates a local identity by introducing decorative gateway features, coordinating landscape and hardscape elements, street lighting, and sign regulations within the right of way. Redevelopment can also include architectural restrictions that will promote an image corridor. Requisite elements in the right of way are not limited to vehicle lanes, turn areas, curbs and gutters, meters, transit stops, street/pedestrian lighting, storm drainage infrastructure, overhead or underground utilities, or traffic signal poles. Sidewalks, bicycle lanes, and other structures are not regarded as options in areas intended for pedestrian use. Methodist Hospital Depot, shown in Figure 1.7, is a strategic transit-oriented catalyst to connect life science research and providers. The renovations, such as those shown in Figure 1.8, will encourage suburbanites to return to urban neighborhoods and enhance a commuter's image corridor from the suburbs.

ANCHORING THE URBAN CORE AND DEFINING URBAN FORM

To counteract the centrifugal force of sprawl reeling out of control, planners can attempt to reinforce the central city by encouraging the growth

FIGURE 1.7 Methodist Hospital Depot *Photo: Stephen Culbert*

FIGURE 1.8 Street Renovation and Infill on N. Delaware St. *Photo: Stephen Culbert*

and development of the elements of a well-anchored urban core. Usually redevelopment efforts begin in the Central Business District or on its periphery.

The well-anchored urban core is simultaneously a neighborhood, civic center, cultural center, entertainment center, and commerce center. The center is an effective location for educational, medical, government, and cultural institutions because they serve the population drawn from the hinterland. Professions like law, finance, accounting, architecture etc. rely upon a critical mass and proximity to government, commerce, and institutions to prosper. The impact of communication technology has made this made somewhat less critical. There are times when email, faxes, and conference calls cannot replace face-to-face and serendipitous incidental contact. The words "I'll be right there" can be crucial.

In order to encourage more people to commute from the suburbs to the central business district, many cities established Image Corridors, through which commuters can travel all but unaware of the blighted conditions just beyond their vision. The intent is not malicious. Cities will often subsidize refurbishment and painting programs for residences and small businesses in blighted areas to create these corridors. Commuters need to feel safe getting to the central business district. Image Corridors create a perception that the city is in better condition, that crime is lower, and poverty is scarcer than it actually is. Sometimes there's a beneficial spillover effect from the Image Corridors that improves the aesthetics and commerce of adjacent areas. The spillover effect can be so strong it results in the gentrification of areas along and adjacent to the Image Corridors. Cities also create Image Corridors along interstates and other arterial roadways that improve the image of industrial warehousing and distribution businesses that require access to these highways.

Transportation that serves these institutions and centers, especially inter-modal public transportation, is drawn towards hubs and transfer points. Until we can beam ourselves from here to there, this is likely to remain so.

Some would argue that, the center should also contain industry. Some have suggested that casinos should be part of the entertainment district. Others might include churches in the mix to support the neighborhood vision of downtown.

The center should provide the defining urban form. Urban form is derived from an element or series of elements that collectively express the history, culture, and values of the community. The style and character and materials of the buildings, landscape elements, urban amenities, monuments, and open spaces are among the elements that define character. Leading architects and planners have met to discuss whether cities should be tall or broad, condensed or dispersed, resonate with the past or with imagined futures, be concerned with locality or the global economy. Here are some of their questions:

- Should city plans be formed of tight grids and spaces, defined edges, transition zones?
- Should its plan involve long blocks, squares, rings, and or rectangles?
- How does one incorporate climate, natural edges, intentional buffers, historic places, religious and cultural institutions, and political barriers?
- What form should the cross section of the city take? Is cross section as important as plan form?
- Who decides which streets should be quiet and narrow, or broad and swift; who decides how and where they terminate?
- Should a city's image look forward, backward, both, or elsewhere?
- What is unique to a given city in terms of history, culture, economy, resources, climate, and scenery that can be celebrated in its forms and the selection of structures for re-use?

Although these questions were discussed in a European forum, they are universal; seeking their answers can apply in any urban context, and should be understood by planners and managers, designers, developers, and corporate decision makers whose work affects the built environment.

PRIVATE INITIATIVES INTENDED TO CURB SPRAWL.

In The Geography of Nowhere, James Howard Kunstler describes tools used by private entities to stem the tide of suburban and rural sprawl and to preserve agricultural land for its current use. These include land trust purchases, stipulated land leasing conditions, and purchased development rights or restrictions. In some communities, this approach fails when agricultural lands are purchased, even with development restrictions, by wealthy landholders. Generally, the land then reverts to privately held woodland. In some cases it goes to industrialized farm operations that take some of the cherished scenic qualities from the agricultural landscape. Some states have adopted various forms of development rights purchases as well. (James Howard Kuntsler, The Geography of Nowhere, [New York: Simon and Schuster, 1993])

Generally people outside the planning and development industry simply do not have their attention focused on the same issues that concern planners, architects, and developers. And they don't base their purchase decisions on altruistic visions or values that include "a better environment for everyone".

Unfortunately most people who buy homes in the suburbs do so, not with malice toward the environment and their neighbors, but with the hope of living their version of the American dream. In some cases, they want to escape the perceived dated visual images or crime or deterioration of edge cites and outer ring suburbs. So many of today's homebuyers were born in suburbia and edge cities that few have experienced the pleasures of the walkable and provincial urban neighborhoods of the first part of the 20th century. In the last census, the median age in the U.S. was 35, the oldest ever.

Sometimes these neighborhoods can be overly idealized, and now suburban developers cashing in on the TND (traditional neighborhood development) trend create simulacra towns in the suburbs. An example of simulacra is shown in Figure 1.9. These neighborhoods have the forms, shapes and layouts of traditionally planned towns, but have sprung full-grown from the loins of Zeus. In other words, they have no real past or even connection to the type of architecture they tend to evoke. Creating

FIGURE 1.9 Unabashed simulacra of Disney
Photo: Stephen Culbert

FIGURE 1.10 New historic light fixtures and New Georgian architecture in suburbia.
Photo: Stephen Culbert

better suburbs with walkable neighborhoods and some lifestyle amenities, and creating them based on the best historical models this country has to offer, as in Figure 1.10, may not be the worst sin development has seen.

Perhaps some residents don't care for the inconvenience of the long commutes, the congestion and smog generated by heavy traffic, and the environmental destruction like fish kills and reduced biodiversity or even the homogeneity of the population distribution in their home environment. But when was the last time you heard someone outside the industry complain because they had to drive a mile to buy a loaf of bread? Doesn't driving a mile to buy a loaf of bread seem unquestioningly normal to someone who's done this for a lifetime?

Speaking of the renewed popularity of downtown living, planner Cynthia Bowen commented on some of the reasons for its appeal. "From a planning perspective, how can you disagree with new urbanism. You are looking at open space, preserving open space. You are looking at trying to conserve resources. ...in a city you have all your services there, you know, every day common services like a grocery store, video rental, dry cleaning, coffee store, bookstore, things that you would utilize on a day-to-day basis, are right there outside your door. The cost of living downtown is typically higher than it would be to live out in the suburbs. In the suburbs you would also have a heck of a lot more land. But it's more about a convenience factor in being in essence where it is happening. The fact that you can immediately get to entertainment and recreation is very important. That you can immediately get to your place of work and yet still get home to do things, to be with your family, things like that... New urbanism is also getting into this idea from a planning perspective of providing a unique array of choices in terms of housing, supposedly going from affordable housing all the way up to the higher end."

There is a side effect of the new urbanism that is rarely discussed: the reverse of white flight. "People then move from the suburbs back in and then cause displacement or dispersion of the people around them because then they can't afford to stay in the market because it affects all the properties around it." Increasing the valuation of the property does improve the tax base, but the people who are already there can't afford to stay there and it drives them back out to other areas of the city. One might achieve more parity and social equity in a mixed-use area, if there was a different basis for local taxing. This, however, would require significant legislative action. In choosing to renew the city, planners and policy makers should be cognizant that there is always a downside to any vision, and prepare to mitigate it.

Where communities invoke zero growth policies, development and sprawl tends to leapfrog past the community and pull the necessary infrastructure extensions with it. Generally well intended, no growth policies are often encouraged by strict environmentalists and preservationists, the NIMBY (Not In My Back Yard) opponents, and those folks I'll affectionately refer to as the a' ginners. No growth policies are shortsighted. Where leapfrog development efforts to pull infrastructure are stymied by unwilling neighbors, traffic and congestion and sprawl will be exacerbated.

MITIGATING ADMINISTRATIVE AND COMMUNITY OBSTACLES TO SPECIFIC REDEVELOPMENT PROJECTS

For the developer and design team, following these steps can prevent remonstrance or at least mitigate the administrative conditions encumbering a project:

- Contact the redevelopment authority to help you find a suitable property to develop where the benefits of existing infrastructure, public investment and desirable location can be maximized.
- Carefully evaluate the context of the site. If it's right for the project, is it also right for the neighbors? Understand the downside for the neighbors and take steps to mitigate it.
- Address issues such as traffic and impact on infrastructure in advance.

Obtain covenants, easements, and agreements where possible.

- Address as many issues on site as possible, such as parking, storm drainage etc.
- Select use or mixed-uses compatible with and sensitive to the existing context. Usually these are uses no more than one or two steps up or down from the existing and grand fathered zoning of the adjacent properties.
- Provide edges and buffers between dissimilar uses and undesirable features. These are actual physical elements added to the project such as berms, plantings walls, fences, and setbacks as well as the thoughtful positioning of constructed program features to create minimal inconvenience for neighbors.
- Providing cut off lights in commercial spaces. Screening trash and delivery areas are examples.
- Early in the process, identify neighbors and other stakeholders. Begin a dialogue with them, preferably prior to an administrative review with the local plan commission staff. (An exception to this might be where the local government is assisting in the redevelopment process with land assembly through the use of eminent domain.)
- Provide adequate notice, and schedule adequate time for dialogue into the design development process. If remonstrance is anticipated, the use of design-build project delivery may not be viable.
- Offer amenities to compensate for variances. Administrators or neighbors have suggestions. For example, providing a new walk where on street parking is to be added. Provide a public amenity such as a bus shelter, water feature, or public art that's not required. Connect to existing pedestrian paths and public transportation (if it's available.)
- Schedule an administrative review. Some jurisdictions require one. Others permit them. Some jurisdictions invite (or require) each agency with jurisdiction over a site to send a representative. At the very least, contact the state or local construction plan review authority and the local fire department.
- Contact the zoning and redevelopment authorities if variance is sought, or if public assistance such as infrastructure improvements are needed to make the project viable.
- Be prepared to demonstrate the enhanced tax impact the project will contribute. State it in time to payback if possible.
- Demonstrate any other public good contributed by the existence or location of the project or its tenants. This includes impact on tax base,

but be honest, show it net of added tax burden for infrastructure and support.

The costs of urban sprawl and poor land development practices are well-documented. The first indication of the problem with unchecked urban sprawl was noted after World War II. The solutions to these problems eluded city officials for many years although well-intentioned initiatives tried to address the need for positive change. Progressive planners are developing new solutions using many tools such as business and government participation. Another tool is an understanding of land development patterns and the factors that influence them.

CHAPTER 2

INFLUENCING FACTORS IN LAND DEVELOPMENT PATTERNS

The forces of change in our built environment can involve complicated factors. Strategic land use and development planning processes are just two of them. Understanding these forces will give designers, owners, and developers better insight in the site selection process for specific projects. This understanding can aid owners and designers in understanding the potential for existing sites and structures.

WHAT ARE THE FORCES OF CHANGE IN OUR CITIES?

The many forces affecting change in our cities include the following:

- Economic change
- Globalization
- Market trends
- Finance opportunities
- Trade
- Foreign trade zones
- Regionalism
- Environmental change
- Pollution
- Waste management

- Water purity
- Acid rain
- Climatic change
- Technological change — the Internet has drawn us closer until physical separation all but disappears
- Transportation change
- Inter-modal transportation
- Suburban air service
- Just in time delivery
- World tourism
- Social change
- Housing patterns
- Education
- Crime
- Political change
- Real and perceived security issues in the face of acts of terrorism
- Changes in resources
- Under funded mandates
- Demographic change
- Race
- Language
- Age
- Handicaps

To make the most of change, city governments, business owners, and developers each need to understand the forces that create change. To create and implement a strategic vision for the city and region, they must work together to make the most of these forces for change.

ECONOMIC CHANGE

Economic development requires at least a fundamental conceptual understanding of the nature of economy. Jane Jacobs' book, *The Nature of Economies*, draws parallels between natural sciences and economics (Jane Jacobs, *The Nature Of Economies*, [New York: Vintage Books, 2001]).

The words "economy" and "ecosystem" share common roots. Economy literally translates from the Greek to "house management". Ecology translates as "this logic" or "knowledge". Ecology can be thought of as the economy of nature. Economy can be thought of as the ecology of wealth. Biomimicry is a process of developing products and production methods learned from natural principles. In sustainable design we can apply these concepts to economic development and ultimately to urban form.

The notion of a sustainable physical environment is directly related to the notion of a sustainable economy. Since "life is ruled by processes and principles we didn't invent and can't transcend, whether we like it better not, and that the more we learn of these processes and the better respect them the better our economies will get along." and "Limits are part of it… an… awareness of them can prevent futility" (Jacobs, p. 11).

Development, whether economic or physical, is significant qualitative change, usually built up in increments. Likewise, expansion is growth measured as quantitative change. Isolated instances of qualitative change can be significant in stimulating additional changes. For example, infusing an anchor business into a local economy can spawn related businesses and act as a magnet to attract new and relocating businesses.

Sticking close to home, when Anthem Insurance moved their corporate headquarters to Indianapolis, the city saw the move as sufficiently important to co-anchor the technology corridor south of downtown. They exercised eminent domain to remove an existing thriving produce distribution business in order to consolidate enough land for the Anthem campus. Had Anthem elected to locate in the beltway or, worse, in another city, a significant opportunity would have been lost. Many of the employees drawn in to serve that business would have been located outside the county.

During the Hudnut Administration, the Indianapolis Sports Corporation was created. It was part of the mayor's strategic vision for the city to become the amateur sports capital of the nation. The Indianapolis Sports Corporation existed to attract key businesses and associations from the sports industry.

In the mid 1970's Indianapolis had built Market Square Arena, but it was the construction of a football stadium about 10 years later that changed downtown. Indianapolis built the stadium and then lured the Baltimore Colts. With Market Square Arena housing the Pacers and various minor league hockey and soccer teams and with the Colts in the Hoosier Dome at the other end, the sports corridor was created.

The corridor was expanded under the Goldsmith administration to relocate minor league baseball to a new downtown stadium. Eventually, Market Square Arena was replaced with a new field house, as shown in Figure 2.1, to the south and in direct alignment with the football stadium. As these developments occurred, Indianapolis successfully won the bids to relocate national associations governing basketball, swimming, and ice skating to the canal area of the White River State Park, west of the terminus of the "sports district". Focused academic programs in sports physiology at Indiana University-Purdue University at Indianapolis were developed along with the growth of some of the premier practices in sports medicine at Methodist and Indiana University hospitals.

Development might be described as, "differentiation emerging from generality."(Jacobs, p. 16) The businesses and associations mentioned in the amateur sports capital illustration above are examples of differentiations emerging from the generality of sports.

FIGURE 2.1 Conseco Fieldhouse now anchors the sports corridor in Indianapolis, north of the tracks. *Photo: Stephen Culbert*

Differentiations become the generalities from which further differentiations emerge. Practical application of this theory expanded to the realm of urban form and architecture can be found in the use of Pattern Language (Christopher Alexander, Sara Ishikawa, and Murray Silverstein, *A Pattern Language: Towns, Buildings, Construction*, [New York: Oxford University Press, 1977]). Alexander's team identifies successful patterns that progress from the most general to the most specific. The designer or planner can identify and select from patterns for their sphere of influence. Pattern Language is intended to involve the users in the process of designing. It is also intended to equip designers and planners to identify patterns in human behavior and movement. Using these observations, they create design responses based on observed patterns.

In *A Timeless Way of Building* (Christopher Alexander, *A Timeless Way of Building*, [New York: Oxford University Press, 1979]), a theory of architecture, building, and planning is created which is centered in ancient cultural processes. Societies have always pulled the order of their world from their own beings. From these processes, the observed patterns of the language evolved. In traditional society, design and construction patterns are understood subconsciously, in the same way Westerners understand languages and how they evolve. In either case there is a known structure. Like words in a sentence or paragraph, the mind seldom replicates the same idea with precisely the same words, except as an imperative. Cultural understanding of form and language is dependent on the generative sequence of steps. Just as the words in a sentence or a paragraph will either make no sense or an entirely new sense when rearranged, patterns need to be applied in a logical sequence to make sense when constructed as form. (http://www.patternlanguage.com/leveltwo/recipesframe.htm?/leveltwo/../sequencetheory/sequenceopener.htm)

"Development depends on co-developments." (Jacobs, page 19) In other words, the successful outcome of an economic effort depends in part on the success of the other economic efforts occurring independently but alongside it. Co-developments of one business are differentiated into multiple units of smaller businesses. The pattern repeats as mathematical fractals of the original. These practical fractal businesses increase the diversity of the local economy. Such growth can only occur in its ultimate form where there's the critical mass of the city to support the many permutations of this diversification.

Consider an economy such as Detroit in the 1980's, steeped in automotive manufacturing and related businesses. Without a great deal of diversity, that metropolitan area took a severe hit both economically and demographically as manufacturing infrastructure aged and competition from foreign manufacturers emerged.

Today's Detroit strives to develop industry and services based outside, and not exclusive to, the automotive industry, and is experiencing a slow renaissance. With a ready supply of technically skilled manufacturing workers, it continues to be attractive to some manufacturers. The ready supply of re-educated workers became the basis of a ripe workforce for the technology revolution of the 1990's.

Diversification in an economy is as essential as diversification in a stock portfolio. Nature loathes monopoly. To the extent that the economic developers support a monopoly, it should be understood as only temporary. Although monopoly can be in an efficient mechanism for dispersing initial capital, it eventually stifles diversification and market development in favor of the status quo and bureaucracy. When small amounts of capital are distributed to many competitors, some will be under capitalized and will fail. The most innovative and market-sensitive companies will survive.

Without trade and competition, an economy will stifle. Competition requires continuous innovation. Trade encourages exchange of progressive ideas. Even recycling is a form of trade, when castoff products become imports to stimulate new businesses. Trade cannot survive without transportation. Whether by road, train, ship, wire or the Internet, there must be a conduit for exchange.

So whether the exported products are agricultural with minimal value-added, manufactured with medium value-added, or primarily informational with nearly all added value, some form of transportation conduit is required to convey them to their exporters. Export is the root of economic expansion and the basis for trade. The layers of value added to exports before they are exported determines overall economic success in a community. For example, a resource is mined, combined, milled, formed, and assembled before it leaves the community. The result is generation of more jobs and ultimately more profits than a resource that is simply mined then shipped. The richest economies in the world are the most diverse.

The dynamic proximity and the frontier spirit exhibited by the owners of start-up entrepreneurships in Silicon Valley are two factors that enabled and encouraged symbiotic co-developments in the silicon industry in the 1980's and 1990's. This is particularly evident when contrasted with the Interstate 95 (Route 128) corridor in New England where the culture was more established and the arrangement of dynamic proximities was more linear than matrixal (Anna Lee Saxenian, *Regional Advantage: Culture and Competition in Silicon Valley and Route 128* , [Cambridge, MA: Harvard University Press, 1994]).

Newly occupied existing buildings are increasingly valuable assets to cities because they raise the tax base and allow cities to improve and extend infrastructure that serves the whole community. On a larger scale, they help to mitigate urban and suburban sprawl.

Post 9-11, technologies in general have taken a harder hit than blue chip industries. Even though there is a great deal of symbiotic co-development, Silicon Valley may find itself in a Detroit-like quagmire. Because there is a strong supply of educated innovators with cutting edge skills and an existing network with dynamic proximity, they have the tools in place to innovate their way out of the current economic set-back before most other industries and regions.

Obsolescence can be a source of economic growth in the face of new generalities and the preservation of knowledge about to be lost. Typewriter repair is going the way of the buggy whip in the face of generations of computers that themselves are made obsolete in ever-shortening intervals. Economic survival requires continuous modification and expansion of the current knowledge base and physical and economic tools. Contractors engaged in salvaging small quantities of gold from obsolete computer equipment made a discovery that the unassembled part, especially the chips, had inherent value far greater than the gold on the secondary market. In this way, preserving the best examples of period form and planning can add dimension to our communities as sources of reclaimed knowledge and cultural continuum. What about the utilitarian and the ordinary? Should communities cleave to it just because it's old fabric? Figure 2.2 shows the City Market in Indianapolis. Completed over 20 years ago, architects preserved the main structure and an historic marker; they added two wings and created plazas. The city leased booths to food vendors and kiosks for small shops.

There's an engine plant in this region that builds new engine lines continuously under an existing newer high bay located in long span spaces in its plant. By perpetually re-tooling, they keep the plant from obsolescing the way the steel industry in Pennsylvania did. Retooling and automating production and distribution areas helps them maintain a technological advantage. This advantage even extends to their own company in bidding for contracts. It takes is a bit of surplus space under the roof and a revolving program of commitment to improve the process of making engines.

It is essential to economic survival to continuously modify and expand the current knowledge base and physical and economic tools.

FIGURE 2.2 City Market Interior *Photo: Stephen Culbert*

Translating this commitment to reality requires process engineers who hone the process for more efficiency. This commitment requires the support of "on call" architects, engineers, and contractors capable of responding rapidly to key shifts in process or corporate strategic vision. The co-ordination of facilities managers can control diverse physical assets and schedules.

Other parts of the same facility, with lower bays and closer column spacing, were built at the turn of the 20th century. They house servant functions like maintenance shops and storage areas. In contrast to the state-of-the-art production areas, they have been given the minimum maintenance required to keep them safe and habitable. By prioritizing the use of the firm's assets to focus on the core functions (making money by making engines), they make the most economic progress and maximize return on the investment in their physical assets.

Economically small and mid-sized communities use the following models:

- Larger or more successful communities of similar size
- Common denominators of success
- Their own existing set of resources and attempts to exploit or market them

Communities sometimes also seek to cannibalize the enterprises of a competing community by offering them incentives to relocate. This is as economically shortsighted a move as city dwellers fleeing to the suburbs. The region will show no net growth or expansion. To stem such destabilizing activity, some state redevelopment authorities are prohibited from using incentives and abatements for enterprises relocating within the state. It is better, in terms of regional growth and sustainability, to entice new enterprises and enterprise expansions than to encourage existing ones to relocate. There's very little a community can do but knuckle under when that same enterprise extorts from them incentives not to relocate in the future.

The key common denominator of economic success is an educated or skilled population permitted to be creative and resourceful. Without this form of human capital, the infrastructure of a successful economy cannot be made to work. An educated population can be imported like any other natural resource or it can be nurtured. The net out migration of college graduates from the Midwest and a net immigration in economically successful areas like Silicon Valley and the research corridor are examples of this.

To be very specific, economically stressed communities should invest their limited resources in their schools and adult education, even before such essentials as sewers, roads, and policing. Schools should work in concert with economic development initiatives to offer the skill sets that targeted industries are seeking. Figure 2.3 and Figure 2.4 illustrate the educational level of a percentage of the population of the United States. Educated workforces are more capable of adding value to whatever exports they produce.

In most communities, school systems are controlled and funded through property taxes exclusively by school boards. They are regulated minimally by the state. In some communities, especially where schools have

Percent of Persons Age 25 and Over With Less Than a High School Diploma, 1990

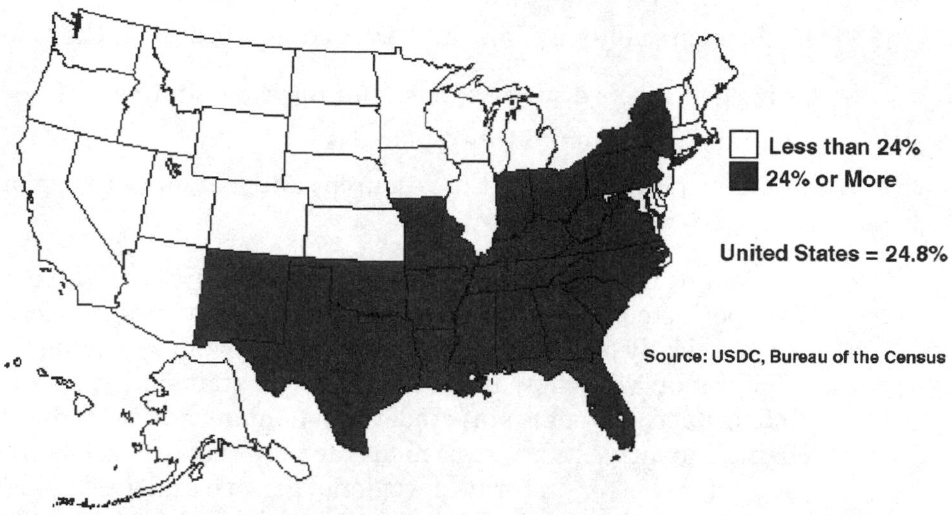

Produced by: University Extension—Office of Social and Economic Data Analysis

FIGURE 2.3 Percent of population with less than a high school diploma, US Census

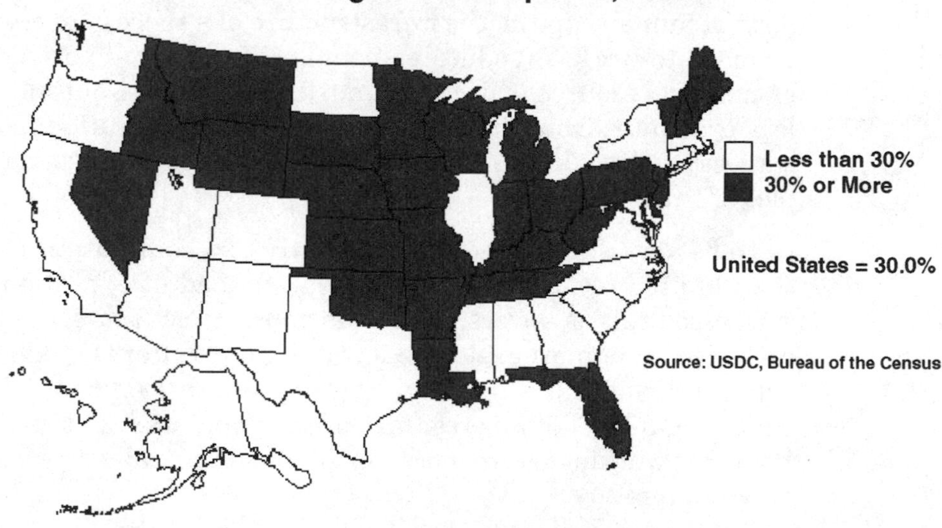

Produced by: University Extension—Office of Social and Economic Data Analysis

FIGURE 2.4 States with over 30 percent of adult population with a high school diploma, US Census

experienced decline, the executive branch has taken over. When the mayor (or equivalent) has control of the schools, it is easier to influence the perceived and actual quality of the public school system. It is also easier for the public to identify with one public official in a board of officials. In most jurisdictions there is little campaigning for such important posts, yet the school board is an entity with broad taxing powers and it makes important policy decisions. Some may prefer a strong executive branch in local government where the board is appointed by and responsible to the executive. When the mayor (or equivalent) has control of the schools, it is easier to directly influence their performance. The executive may prioritize the funding and focus of education to assure that schools perform as a marketable community asset. Some school systems allow charter schools as magnets for special purposes. An example of a public school that can anchor downtown neighborhood development is shown in Figure 2.5.

When Steve Goldsmith, former Indianapolis mayor, proposed the appointment of the superintendent and school board, it was initially perceived as a power grab. Then the same thing happened in Chicago. If improved rates of attendance, graduation, and better scores on standardized tests are reliable indicators, there has been a marked qualitative change in those

FIGURE 2.5 Pacer Academy in Union Station with preserved headhouse, beyond.
Photo: Stephen Culbert

school systems. It's a strategy worth considering, especially where education has fallen into default. Control of the school system still remains with the voters. Changes such as these need to be empowered at the level of the state legislature. Power is not ceded directly to the state by the federal government or to municipalities and counties by the state. All are left local and independent.

Idleness and need co-exist in many economies. Governmental devices such as make-work projects and protectionism, like those developed under the New Deal of the 1930's and the 1940's, can rarely be sustained. If they don't spawn competitive enterprise or yield workers with transferable skills, profit will never come and government resources will be depleted. Witness the fall of the USSR, where government controlled the means and profits of all production. The unsubtle Soviet joke, "We pretend to work; they pretend to pay us," might be voiced in many such subsidized economies. The best hope for trade is globalization of the free market economy. As the global economy continues to emerge, it has the potential to introduce an element of economic and political accountability, transparency, and democracy.

It's a mistake, however, to assume that an economy that rejects mining, fishing, agriculture, and manufacturing will long survive on the basis of exported but intangible information, services, and technological developments alone. The window of time in which developing economies have doubled their production has been decreasing exponentially in the last decade. This is largely due to reverse engineering of high-tech products and the decreased cost of imports. Canada, Japan, and parts of Europe are already peer markets for the United States. It won't be long before most of Asia and large parts of South and Central America are as well.

Communities must actively resist economic stagnation. The tools for resisting stagnation include the following:

- Radical departure (bifurcation) positive feedback loops
- Negative feedback controls
- Emergency adaptations (Jacobs, p. 86)

Radical departures generally begin locally and almost by accident, but succeed because they enable by advantage. In business, the equivalent might be the development of a sideline market that eventually replaces the core business which has become technologically or socially obsolete or uncompetitive. When development of sidelines fail, the assets of failed enterprises can be the fuel that feeds start-up enterprises, provided they can be purchased at discounts.

Radical departures can have unintended consequences, consequences that can create self-regulation and stability in one realm, and simultaneously create stress and instability in another. An example of such a radical departure affecting the quality of the built environment, the perception of social justice, and employment practices and employment costs is the enactment of the Americans with Disabilities Act. Its effects are far reaching. Some saw it as a politically popular make-work law at a time when the economy was beginning to rebound. Politically unpopular due to the costs of implementation, its requirements were viewed as economic burdens by employers, developers, property owners, transportation providers, and governments.

Of the suits filed seeking remedy under the bill, the majority have been under the employment provisions. The majority of these cases have been resolved with the legal finding in favor of the employer.

It is discouraging, but understandable, that clients seek to avoid implementing the requirements of this federal law. Building departments are empowered to enforce the requirements of the law as they apply to the structures on the property, if the building code has adopted Americans with Disabilities Act Accessibility Guidelines or a chapter that is the legal equivalent. The building department is rarely empowered to address site conditions, such as the continuity of accessible paths, public transportation connections, grades and parking that are also requirements under the law. Site issues can be some of the most common infractions in new construction.

The rudder of sustainability is feedback. In positive feedback loops, market information is collected and interpreted. Responses are formed and disseminated while outcomes are measured against models. At the scale of a single business unit, the equivalent might be test marketing an idea for a new product or service. On a regional economic planning scale, it might be the self-selection pursuit and encouragement of targeted areas of business growth and the de-selection of others.

For redevelopment authorities, feedback is used in an effort to assess community potential for growth and development. The Joint Venture Silicon Valley benchmarks the different statistics associated with livability in San Jose and the Silicon Valley. They benchmark, for example, how much capital is going into the area from venture capitalists. It is compared against San Jose and the Silicon Valley itself for future years to come, as well as against other competing cities such as Seattle, Austin, Boston, etc. Reviewing the comparisons allows San Jose to assess how they can remain competitive. It promotes dialog and forums as well as discussion and links between the decision makers of Silicon Valley and San Jose [(David Nieh, Architecture and Urban Design Program Manager, City of San Jose, Interview, 2001)].

Negative feedback controls are necessary in any ecological or economic system loop for the health of the system. The usefulness of negative feedback is that economic engineers and social planners can identify it, verify it, interpret its meaning, and implement responses to limit its negative impact on the benchmarks that measure development. Hubris, vanity, or greed can blind us to negative feedback or its correct interpretation. Monocular viewing of information can stymie appropriate responses and development of the needed solutions because some options will go unexplored.

Nature gives us chaos. Emergency adaptations are the human way to respond to chaos. Nature gives us that too. In the widely known Butterfly Effect (a variant on the chaos theory), multiple variables of cause and effect are not reductive when one exceeds about a half dozen variables. "The Lorenz butterfly is significant because it illustrates the concept of sensitive dependence upon initial conditions" ("Edward N. Lorenz," The Exploratorium, 1996 http://www.exploratorium.edu/complexity/CompLexicon/lorenz.html on 8/21/2002 7:16 PM; Deterministic Nonperiodic Flow Journal of Atmospheric Sciences1963, Edward Lorenz, 1963 cited by Jacobs, in *Nature*).

Small events, both good and bad, become amplified as they affect multiple variables. Society and culture may determine what our collective needs and priorities are; it cannot dictate the methods of response and certainly not the specifics of form. Similarly well-written zoning elucidates community priorities, but does not conscribe a method of response.

A recent headline reads "Downtown Vacancy Highest Since '97" (ULI's Commercial Real Estate News Roundup: August 2002) and, in the wake of the Sept. 11th events, vacancy rates in downtown areas reflect tenant's concerns over occupying target buildings. During the same period, overall office building demand rose. This may be some of the first evidence of market change that reflects change in the national psyche. Figure 2.6 shows the blighted conditions above street level that plague many CBD's (Central Business District).

Maintaining fiscal fitness depends on a community's ability to support economic diversity and to seek and implement the refueling of development. Market failures occur when parties outside the primary contract are affected adversely. An example of such is when city property values dropped after white flight commenced. Generally, retaining existing businesses and residents is in a community's self interest.

FIGURE 2.6 The blight above street level. *Photo: Stephen Culbert*

ECONOMIC DEVELOPMENT AND SELF-REFUELING

In nature, competitive success for animals is dependent on successful feeding, breeding, and habitat maintenance (such as not over-grazing a grassland). Drawing an economic analogy from nature, "feeding and breeding" are equivalent to creating businesses and keeping them healthy; "habitat maintenance" means preserving a business environment that is diverse, complex, competitive and proactive. Such an environment fosters co-development, creates new markets, and encourages innovations that give a competitive edge. Competition is essential because it prevents the stifling disincentives to innovation and efficiency that monopoly encourages. Preserving the arena for competition maintains and grows a competitive market. "Nobody commands an economy that has vitality and potential...it springs surprise upon surprise instead of knuckling down and doing what is expected of it, or wished for." (Jacobs, *Nature*, p. 138)

The gifts of consciousness, for most humans, include a sense of morality, the recognition of dissonance and error, a sense of awe, aesthetic sensibilities and the urge to revise. Nature also gives us improvisation, the ability to change a known paradigm incrementally through applied creativity. The honing process of a sculptor is analogous to the scope and program exercises of an owner or the design definition process of an architectural team.

REGIONALISM

Cities can no longer afford to view themselves as cities and suburbs. The city is the regional center, but the suburbs are the economic engines that sustain it. Neal Pierce and Curtis Johnson coined the term "citistate" to describe this shift. In light of the fact that suburbs are now replacing many functions traditionally found in central business districts, cities must reexamine what it is that they have to offer the region and reframe their arguments for regional coalitions. There's a school of thought emerging:

- The suburbs no longer need the cities.
- The suburbs are based essentially in communications technology.
- The suburbs replace density, diversity, and face-to-face contact.

Edge cities, especially along beltways and other transportation intersections, have developed their own employment hubs that serve as lower-density central business districts. This is especially true in terms of the relocation of centers of wealth. Higher income residents in surrounding suburbs are notably tax averse. To bring the city and the suburbs together, the value of sustaining a center must be clear to the taxpayers that will support it. Regional co-operation, whether legislated or voluntary, is a trend that will sustain cities and suburbs in a global economy. Can suburbanites safely ignore the deteriorating conditions in the inner cities?

If edge cities are predominately economically independent of the central city, why should they foster any relationship with the central city? Correlations exist between the conditions in central cities and various measures of suburban well being. Urban redevelopment is in the economic interest of the suburbanites (Todd Swanstrom, *Ideas Matter: Reflections On The New Regionalism*, [Albany, NY: State University of New York Press]).

Are the disparate conditions that persist only a product of free will and a market economy or are they subtly driven by such unattractive values as racism and economic escapism? There are arguments and observations to indicate some truth in each view. Community trends currently support the observation that separation between cities, edge cities and suburbs is increasing. Should public policy support such trends? Support reinforces social, political, and economic alienation between races, classes, and ethnicities. In some cases, this polarization has had the effect of substantially eroding the legitimacy and faith in elected government and the rule of law. A case in point is the 1992 L.A. riot (Saurezopf, 1993). There are political trade-offs that must be made to consolidate the resources and political energy of a region. These can be emotionally charged and socially driven NIMBY (Not In My Backyard) issues like race, poverty, policing, schools and taxes.

An example is UNIGOV which consolidated the government of Marion County, Indiana under former mayor, now U.S. senator, Richard Lugar in 1972. A half dozen small governments and the city of Indianapolis were merged into a single entity. Only the incorporated cities of Lawrence, Speedway, Southport, and Castleton declined to be consolidated. Castleton was later absorbed. Consolidation under UNIGOV greatly strengthened the mayor's position in eliciting business from outside the region. It facilitated a relationship with suburban Marion county residents that caused them to participate in government and invest in the revitalization of downtown. This included building two stadiums, a government center, and a downtown mall over the next two decades. Trade-offs, which were required to make UNIGOV happen, kept existing township school districts, police, and fire departments separate from city-county control. The trade-offs, especially where schools are concerned, have prevented mayors from using city funds and influence to turn around the struggling public school system. Presently, there is a trend toward smaller and more decentralized government. This contrasts with the trends in economically competing countries like Japan and Germany where regionalism is increasing. Consider the European Union as a regionalized economic unit that covers most of a continent. Referenda on regionalism show a high degree of opposition to another layer of government, especially if it has authority over local governments or the ability to move funds from the suburbs to downtown or, worse yet, blighted urban neighborhoods.

Critical density and diversity are attributed to cities and particularly to central business districts. Traditionally, specialization has been possible in the CBD (Central Business District) because it draws clientele from all the surrounding hinterlands. Dynamic proximity permits a level of sophistication to develop in the CBD that is more difficult to achieve in the suburbs.

Suburbs are now replacing many functions traditionally found in central business districts. For example:

- Central business districts
- Clean industries
- Tourist bureaus
- Symphonies
- Museums
- Nature centers

Density and dynamic proximity may not be the keys to survival and growth in the CBD. The keys may be diversity, specialization, innovation, and early adoption of new ideas that begin in the CBD and bleed out into the region. Critics of regionalism, such as Jane Jacobs, describe regional solutions as being merely "an area safely larger than the last one to whose problems we found no solution." (Jacobs as quoted in Notes from "Can You Be an Urbanist and Still Like Cities?" From Governing's, May 2001 issue, by Alan Ehrenhalt, http://governing.com/5assess.htm

The debate over the value of regional government and planning agreements are largely framed and limited by economic interests, social values, and political perceptions. Some consider regional planning to have socialist overtones and prefer that market forces entirely control regional, economic, and physical development.

Compassion for the poor and disenfranchised is no longer sufficient to fuel an interest in bolstering the economies of cities. Economic subsidy is harder to procure due to the anti-welfare wars waged chiefly by Republicans in the 1990's. There are now more Americans living in suburbs and edge cities than in major cities or rural areas. The force of the political will and self-interest (popular will) has shifted to the suburbs. It requires demonstrations of enlightened self-interest to motivate suburbanites to invest in regional government coalitions.

In studies of correlations, the gap between the per capita tax base in the city and the suburbs as a proportion has been used to measure economic health. The closer this ratio is then there is less disparity between city and suburb and there is greater potential for economic growth. (Ledebur & Barnes, 1992 Larry Ledebur and William Barnes, *Local Economies: the U.S. Common Market of Economic Regions*. Washington D.C., National League of Cities, 1994) In some areas, the contrast between suburban and urban living is slight. Refer to Figures 2.7 and 2.8.

Instead of a social, economic, and ethnic melting pot with demographic distributions, the concept of integrated diversity promotes ethnic communities that can thrive and grow separately in a spatial and social sense. There does not have to be political or economic exclusion. (Thomas Angotti, *Metropolis 2000: Planning, Poverty and Politics*, [New York: Routledge, 1993]). In one model, each government unit and each private government partner has a veto over corporate regional policy. Such vetoes assure protection to smaller and weaker members and promote good faith and trust in reaching agreements. Holding such a veto wields enormous political power. In essence the veto also has the possibility of being used capriciously. If one has doubts, consider the geo-political structure of the United

FIGURE 2.7 Suburban living *Photo: Stephen Culbert*

FIGURE 2.8 Urban living *Photo: Stephen Culbert*

Nations. Veto of a pending resolution can be exercised by any of several nations on the UN Security council for cause or no cause.

To quote Swanstrom, " Regional development strategy that included facilitating the relationship of work and residence to a higher density, mixed use developments surrounded by greenbelts, and infill development in cities could help people become less dependent on both (private) automobiles and (public) mass-transit. This strategy might also give people more free time to devote to the institutions of civil society. A vision of regional planning that made people less dependent on markets and government and helped buttress the institutions of civil society so that people could control their own communities would, inspire action." (Swanstrom, p. 12) Achieving such a vision will require inspired leadership with a strong grass roots political base and years of building trust. Spreading such a vision will require more successful regional governmental models like Portland, Minneapolis-St. Paul, and Pittsburgh.

ENVIRONMENTAL CHANGE

Environmental changes can come from many sources. Each factor generates imbalances and disruptions in earth's ecosystem. Measurable negative feedback takes the form of species decline, health effects, deforestation, erosion, and other reductions in the quality of life. Nature has instruments such as microbes, soil filtration, reforestation, and pressure changes to deal with these disruptions and restore equilibrium. Consider environmental changes from these manmade sources:

- Air pollution
- Acid rain
- Toxic run-off
- Ground contaminants
- Global warming
- Chemical spills

Next, consider natural sources of environmental change. Natural destructive processes do not always move at the same pace as man-made processes:

- Disease
- Earthquakes

- Storms
- Floods
- Droughts
- Fire
- Volcanic eruptions

Collectively, industrial hygiene, pre- and post-consumer recycling, wastewater, water purity management, traffic management and reduction, alternative fuel development, alternative technologies, diagnostic techniques, and medical practices are corrective responses generated by the negative feedback to environmental punishment. Responses in the built environment include passive technologies:

- Insulation
- Thermal massing
- Natural ventilation
- Sustainable materials

These can generally be incorporated in construction with the use of thoughtful and conscious design effort with minimal cost to the owner. Active technologies used to respond to the environment are exemplified by the following methods:

- Environmental controls
- Water management
- Waste streaming
- Permaculture

These technologies add costs that have to be justified by increased market appeal, payback calculations, or subsidies. Because the owner's or developer's primary profit goal eclipses their need for social capital, most owners and developers are unlikely to be spurred to development as an act of environmental consciousness. It is likely to require continuously reinforced public education to accomplish the change of heart, deeper understanding, and sense of responsibility needed to stimulate compliance with its provisions. For others it will take the force of law and threat of personal penalties to enforce it. In some cases, the required actions such as soil remediation may be so cost prohibitive as to create a disincentive to development without subsidy. Today's subsidy and the cost of enforcing environmental laws are a form of penance that the public must pay for the greed and ignorance of past public policies toward the environment.

TECHNOLOGICAL CHANGE AND THE USE OF APPROPRIATE TECHNOLOGY

Smart buildings that automatically sense and adjust environmental systems technology are becoming increasingly commonplace, especially with an increasingly digital workforce occupying them. See Table 2.1 which shows efficiency data for technology in the residential sector. Programmed multilevel security interfaces have replaced or augmented existing mechanical security systems in sensitive business areas. Multi-modal communications hubs are springing up, sometimes hidden in church spires and office penthouses across the country. The demand has been driven by pressure to maintain high profit levels, the real or perceived increases in the level of corporate espionage technology, and competition to provide the timeliest service possible.

Runoff that was once filtered through the soil to natural aquifers now travels over parking lots and roofs where it picks up an increased level of contamination and must be industrially filtered before returning to the natural watershed.

Communications devices such as wireless phones and computers and common technologies such electronic filing, web links and call forwarding, have reduced office space needs because many information brokers can now work from anywhere. Hotelling, where an employee alternates the use of office space with others or keeps a mobile workstation, is common for employees who spend most of their time away from the office. Figure 2.9 shows energy costs for lighting which are a factor in this business model. For employees with more portable work, dial-up and plug-n-go setups are also space savers for the parent company. Small business consortiums have arrangements to share overhead spaces such as conference rooms, reception areas, mail rooms, copy rooms, and even overhead staff. Business practices such as "Just in time delivery" are facilitated with automated materials-handling systems that have reduced the spatial needs for warehouse and distribution. Automated CAD CAM (Computer Assisted Design and Computer Assisted Manufacturing) and visualization technology have reduced the spatial need for assembly and quality control in manufacturing businesses. The need for unskilled and semi-skilled production workers has also decreased. The economy has shifted to a service base with traded information as the primary commodity.

TABLE 2.1 Selected residential-sector technology cost and performance characteristics

Equipment Type	Relative Performance[a]	1995		2005		Approximate Discount Rate (Percent)[d]
		Installed Cost (1996 Dollars)[b]	Efficiency[c]	Installed Cost (1996 Dollars)[b]	Efficiency[c]	
Electric Heat Pump	Minimum	3,295	10.0	3,295	10.0	20
	Best	5,648	14.5	5,648	16.9	
Natural Gas Furnace	Minimum	1,530	0.78	1,530	0.78	15
	Best	3,530	0.95	2,941	0.96	
Room Air Conditioner	Minimum	706	8.7	706	9.7	100
	Best	1,000	12.0	1,000	12.5	
Central Air Conditioner	Minimum	2,471	10.0	2,471	10.0	50
	Best	3,530	14.5	3,588	16.9	
Refrigerator (18 cubic ft)	Minimum	588	690	588	483	19
	Best	765	550	823	400	
Electric Water Heater	Minimum	412	0.88	412	0.88	111
	Best	1,765	2.60	1,246	2.80	

[a]Minimum performance refers to the lowest efficiency equipment available. Best refers to the highest efficiency equipment available. [b]Installed costs, shown in 1996 dollars, include retail equipment costs plus installation costs for average unit sizes. Actual sizes and equipment costs can vary.

[c]Efficiency measurements vary by equipment type. Electric heat pumps and central air conditioners are rated above for cooling performance using the Seasonal Energy Efficiency Ratio (SEER). Heating performance of heat pumps is measured by the Heating Season Performance Factor (HSPF). For the heat pumps shown, the HSPF ratings are 6.8 and 10.2 for 1995 and 6.8 and 11.0 for 2005. Natural gas furnace efficiency ratings are based on annual fuel utilization efficiency. Room air conditioner ratings are based on seasonal energy efficiency ratio (SEER). Refrigerators ratings are based on kilowatthours per year. Water heater ratings are based on energy factor (delivered Btu divided by input Btu).

[d]Although the RDM does not use discount rates directly in evaluating efficiency purchase decisions, approximate discount rates can be derived from the parameters of the equipment choice model.

Source: Arthur D. Little, EIA Technology Forecast Updates, Reference Number 41615 (June 1995).

Modeling Technological Change and Diffusion in the Buildings Sector by Andy S. Kydes and Steven H. Wade for the National Energy Information Centerfound Table 1 provides data for several types of equipment. http://www.eia.doe.gov/oiaf/archive/issues98/modtech.html

Relocation of manufacturing sites for consumer disposables and later consumer durables are likely to be followed by changes in the construction industry. It will happen first with components assembled off-site and

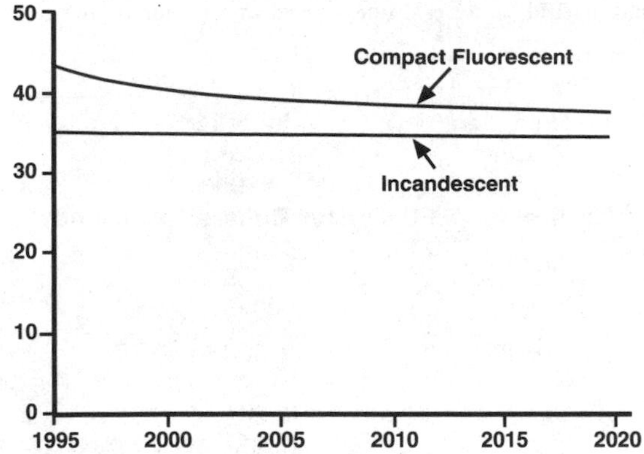

FIGURE 2.9 1996 dollars per thousand lumens

later with whole buildings. In rural areas, pre-manufactured homes outpace conventional construction. In healthcare and manufacturing, building modules such as MRI units or drug manufacturing pods are already constructed off site and simply interfaced with existing structures and specially-placed infrastructure. It is not likely that on-site construction will ever be entirely replaced, but it has the potential for growth. This has left a lot of vacant high bay space. In certain industries, the vacated space is likely to be contaminated.

Americans have been pampered with the best and most widely available technological developments of any country in the world. While it is a matter of national pride, it may also be a disguised weakness because we have grown accustomed to the conveniences and comforts of our lifestyles. Even the poor in this country live better than the middle class in many of the world's poorer nations. The 19th and 20th centuries gave the middle class these innovations:

- Telephones
- Radios
- Televisions
- Computers
- Copiers
- Dittoes
- Fax machines
- Stock tickers
- Holographic billboards
- Plasma screens.

Computers gave us the ability to manage, sort, store, compile, analyze, and rapidly retrieve huge quantities of data. It is rare that households don't have ready access to machines like washers, dryers, microwaves, hair dryers, and vacuums to make domestic life easier. Research has developed strong, lightweight, durable materials like nylon, plastics, vinyl, and fiberglass. Many people even enjoy the convenience of coffee makers that grind the beans and start the coffee before the alarm goes off in the morning. We have the convenience of ready-made clothing, packaged foods, and drive-through restaurants and banks. Transportation evolved from sweat-powered bipedals and wagons to high-speed vehicles for land, air, and sea using an assortment of fuel sources. Transportation meant someone had to build roads and bridges. Heating and refrigeration technology and antibiotics have advanced medicine, curbed diseases, and extended the "life" of many types of food as well as human beings. It has also changed shopping patterns, and made us generally much more comfortable as we live and work. Modern household conveniences and contraception have even created an environment where an increasingly large share of women have "elected" to work and "elected" to bear fewer children, resulting in changed economic dynamics and social/ family structures. With each technological change, there have also been negative consequences; it is human nature. Negative consequences may come in the perceived widening of the gulf between the "haves" and the "have-nots" within small communities and on a global scale. Another consequence is the rate at which technology can be appropriated by other cultures. The computer revolution and the migration of manufacturing have made reverse engineering more swift. In any case, the development and sharing of technology is crucially intertwined with the other factors that influence changes in our environment.

> **Transportation evolved from sweat-powered bipedal and wagons to high-speed vehicles for land, air, and sea using an assortment of fuel sources. Transportation meant someone had to build roads and bridges.**

SOCIAL CHANGE

Financial capital and physical rebuilding will not restore a community whose social life has been depleted. "It is fashionable," Jacobs wrote, "to suppose that certain touchstones of the good life will create good neighborhoods — schools, parks, clean housing and the like. How easy life would be if this were so!... There is no direct, simple relationship between good housing and good behavior..." and "important as good schools are, they prove totally undependable at rescuing bad neighborhoods." (Alan Ehrenhalt, *The Lost City: The Forgotten Virtues of Community in America*, [New York: Basic Books, 1996]) Social equity is at issue in the inner city and core city redevelopment as well. When gentrification begins, as evidenced in Figure 2.10, in the blighted neighborhood, taxes increase not only for the properties where value has been added, but also for adjacent properties as potential value rises. This forces a lot of homeowners and small business owners to relocate. In some cases, the opportunity for affordable homeownership is displaced forever with the owner.

Exclusionary land use controls keep the poor out of the suburbs by placing such prescriptive requirements on developments that low income buyers are priced out of the market without subsidy. The poor in the city are predominantly minorities and they are concentrated in the urban core or the inner ring neighborhoods. White poor are predominantly dispersed throughout edge cities and suburbs, well integrated with middle class neighbors. "What this country lacks is not the capacity to end the isolation of

FIGURE 2.10 Gentrification *Photo: Stephen Culbert*

the minority poor, it lacks the will. (Regionalism, the New Geography of Opportunity, — A Collection of Essays Henry G. Cisneros Secretary of Housing and Urban Development for Cityscape, Special Issue December 1996 http://www.huduser.org/periodicals/cityscpe/spissue/current.html.

Exclusionary land use controls keep the poor out of the suburbs by placing such prescriptive requirements on developments that low income buyers are priced out of the market without subsidy.

Test scores in racially and economically integrated school settings have been compared against those in isolated settings. They demonstrate that the average score for all students is pulled up in the integrated settings. This is attributed to the most able minority students being challenged by their white peers. While the scores for the white students did drift lower in the integrated setting, the average for all students was higher. (Cisneros)

Using the schools as a model for an analogy, economic opportunity tends to pull the region upwards economically. Integrating "fair share" housing policies through regional agreements will create an atmosphere of racial opportunity in the suburban areas of economic regions. Montgomery County, Maryland has a "fair share" plan that uses a set of mandates, incentives, and partial subsidy to provide a minimum of 15% affordable housing units. Even DHUD (Department of Housing and Urban Development) now supports scatter-site public housing by refusing funding to projects solely inhabited by the poor.

"Morning and evening rush hours now begin earlier and end later than they did 20 years ago. This leaves little time for other activities, such as grocery shopping or even visiting with local family members. In addition, women who used to be home during the week to take care of family business are now in the work force, and have to take care of errands "after hours" (Metropolitan Report Changing Land Use and Lifestyles Alter Commuting Habits, Copyright © 2000 Baltimore Metropolitan Council. April 26, 2000 at http://www.baltometro.org/NL/NLv1n2c.htm). The change in workforce demographics has driven the popularity for transportation-based development and access-driven development all over the country.

Another effect of social change on the built environment is captured in the musings of a conservative. Women joined the workforce in increasing numbers since World War II and the economy expanded. It did not expand, however, at the rate the federal government did. In a middle class two-income family, suppose she makes 42% and he makes 58% of the family's gross earnings. Add together 17% federal income tax, 16% FICA, 6% sales tax, and 3% state income tax and you will see that you've already consumed the 42% she contributes. The tax bite, as a percentage, can be even stiffer on single-income households. See Table 2.2. and Table 2.3. While there are deductions to offset the bite, they are minimal in view of other taxes such as property, excise, gasoline, etc.

According to the Heritage Foundation, often quoted US Census data suggests the top quintile of society in 1997 had $13.86 of income for every $1.00 received by the bottom quintile. After adjusting for a number of factors including the number of people in the quintiles, the average number of hours worked, the number of working age individuals, the effect of taxes, losses and benefits, the real rate of disparity in income per man hour is $3.18 to $1.00. They conclude, "Differences in income in the United States are the natural result of vast differences in ability and behavior between individuals. In general, those persons at high income levels tend to be married, to work large numbers of hours per year, to have high levels of skill and productivity, and to provide higher levels of savings and investment necessary to sustain the overall prosperity of the economy. By contrast, individuals in the lowest income quintile tend generally to be non-married, to work little, and to have lower levels of skill and productivity." Such and analysis demonstrates the differences in conclusions one might draw when scrutinizing the data set with different sets of values. (Data are from "Income Inequality: How Census Data Misrepresent Income Distribution" by Robert E. Rector and Rea S. Hederman, Jr., Center for Data Analysis Report #99-07 dated September 29, 1999, http://www.heritage.org/Research/Labor/CDA99-07.cfm)

Divorce has changed family demographics as well. Children, described as "yours, mine, and ours," must be supported by married couples. This arrangement usually causes financial strain on the consolidated family, especially when former partners can't or won't support their offspring. Other stresses, such as the needs of aging relatives, can add additional financial and physical stresses to the family lifestyle. In the recession of the late 1980's and early 1990's, some families became disenchanted with materialism and the maintenance of the consumer lifestyle of ever-increasing consumption. They began to experiment with "voluntary simplicity." Since it's anti-consumptive by its very nature, the movement has received relatively little press coverage. Basically voluntary simplicity means that well educated and/or formerly high earning adults retreat into

TABLE 2.2 Share of individual income tax in percent. *Source: Congressional Budget Office, "Preliminary Estimates of Effective Tax Rates" (September 7, 1999). http://www.cbo.gov/showdoc.cfm?index=1545&from=4&sequence=0)*

Raw Data: Share of Individual Income Tax (in %)

Income Category	1977	1979	1981	1983	1985	1987	1989	1991	1993	1995	1999 (Projected)
Highest 20%	68	67	66	68	68	72	72	72	75	77	79
Fourth 20%	20	20	20	20	19	18	17	18	17	16	16
Middle 20%	10	10	10	10	9	8	9	9	8	8	7
Second 20%	3	4	4	3	3	3	3	2	2	1	1
Lowest 20%	0	0	0	0	0	0	-1	-1	-1	-2	-2
All Families	100	100	100	100	100	100	100	100	100	100	100
Top 1%	20	19	17	20	21	24	24	23	27	29	29
Top 5%	38	37	36	38	39	43	44	42	46	49	50
Top 10%	50	50	49	51	52	56	56	55	59	61	63

Share of Total Family Income (in %)

Income Category	1977	1979	1981	1983	1985	1987	1989	1991	1993	1995	1999 (Projected)
Highest 20%	47	48	49	50	51	51	52	51	52	53	54
Fourth 20%	22	22	22	22	22	22	21	22	22	21	21
Middle 20%	16	15	15	15	15	15	14	15	15	14	14
Second 20%	10	10	10	9	9	9	9	9	9	9	9
Lowest 20%	5	5	4	4	4	4	4	4	3	3	3
All Families	100	100	100	100	100	100	100	100	100	100	100
Top 1%	9	10	10	11	12	12	13	12	13	14	15
Top 5%	22	22	22	24	25	25	27	25	26	27	28
Top 10%	32	32	33	35	35	35	37	36	37	38	39

TABLE 2.3 Mean Taxes, 1981, 1990, 1999 *Data excerpted from Table 665, Stastical Abstract of the United States, US Census Bureau*

	1980	1990	1999
Federal Income Tax	15.3	12.4	15.9
State Income Tax	3.3	3.8	4.8
FICA	5.3	6.2	6.1
Property Taxes on Own Home	2.3	2.5	2.4
	26.2	24.9	29.2

much simpler and generally less lucrative lifestyles. Emphasis is placed on increased family interaction, family cohesion, spiritual, intellectual, and recreational pursuits. Usually this means that someone has already set aside the financial resources required to supplement life's comforts while they pursue less stressful and time consuming work. Sometimes individual health issues mandate this lifestyle shift. Usually, savings generated by investments in high growth businesses facilitates it. As we enter another down economic cycle, many of these boomers may seek to return to their former professions.

The following factors contribute to changing social demands in the arrangement of residential space:

- Internet access
- High-speed wiring
- Telecommuting
- Aging parents
- The delay in age of giving birth
- Re-marriages
- Smaller families
- Teenage pregnancy
- Gay coupling
- Mainstreaming of handicapped adults
- Other forms of domestic partnerships

Proximity preference in housing is also important. For example, it is a financial and psychological plus to locate families close to the following:

- Transportation
- Routine shopping
- Schools
- Daycare
- Adult day care
- Social services
- Doctors
- Churches
- Long time friends
- Public and cultural institutions.

Conversely, its absence is a penalty. Life education is another social factor in play. Driven by economics, it starts with daycare. It progresses to K-12 education and then to trade schools and universities. With the high rate of college attendance, a bachelor's degree has become the entry-level document of an increasing percentage of middle-class occupations. Advanced degrees will proliferate as working adults seek to maintain their economic advantages. To remain competitive, many businesses require continuing education for their staff. Businesses have realized savings by placing the burden of training onto the individual employee. While some companies provide in-service training or company matching funds for out-sourced courses, others have moved it off the company's expense rolls by requiring employees to train on their own time and, sometimes, with their own resources as a condition of continued advancement, if not employment.

These changes provide a ready market for learning institutions with locations convenient to centers of employment and travel. The market is also for distance learning and institutions where the instructors, not the students, commute. In small communities, university extensions and trade schools might operate out of high school facilities nights and weekends. Indiana University-Purdue University at Indianapolis offers extension courses out of an underutilized basement mezzanine in Glendale Mall and at several local high schools in addition to its downtown campus. The Wharton School of Business now offers Master of Business Administration degrees in its traditional Philadelphia location and at facilities in San Francisco at a nominally higher cost. The University of Phoenix exists only in cyberspace.

National health consciousness began with the anti-smoking and anti-smog campaigns of the 1960's and 1970's and blossomed under the Clinton administration's failed attempt to provide universal health coverage. The insurance and medical industry responded to the potential loss of revenue by creating a government plan that increased the number of Health Maintenance Organizations (HMO's), complimentary medicine centers, and related therapies. They promoted wellness education and offered incentives to exercise as never before. Consciousness of the flaws in the health insurance system may be remedied somewhat with enactment of the Health Insurance Portability & Accountability Act (HIPAA).

Places for families to work out and recreate were planned to be near home, work, school, and transit. Transit-Oriented Development (TOD) planning focuses high density mixed-use for a half-mile area around a planned station. (A plan by Calthorpe and Associates, focuses on a light rail transit (LRT) station at Hiawatha / Lake St. in Minneapolis and can be seen at http://www.ci.minneapolis.mn.us/citywork/light-rail/index.html.)

POLITICAL CHANGE

In 1997, The Maryland General Assembly passed the Smart Growth and Neighborhood Conservation Act. It was one of the first acts by states designed to encourage revitalization of established communities. The state's commitment to direct funds is beneficial to older urban neighborhoods and industrial centers.

In Baltimore, studies by the Transportation Steering Committee showed that re-investment in existing city and suburban neighborhoods reduces sprawl and make better use of past infrastructure investments in highways and transit facilities. Applying new-urbanist mixed-use zoning policies and development strategies in existing neighborhoods can stabilize and revitalize them (Ibid.)

Regional governments and quasi-governmental districts are taking shape all over the country in recognition of economic and social interdependence between adjacent communities and neighborhoods. For example, regional government agreements can make more efficient use of contracting for public services by implementing mutual assistance agreements, pooling funds, and negotiating contracts for services. Legislative bodies set the agenda for taxation, subsidies, and deductions. Political influence shifts from "left" to "right" and seems to seek a popularly supported equilibrium.

For example, while welfare reform advocates insist on "back to work" policies, many parents cannot afford to send their children to licensed daycare without subsidy. At an average rate of $130 per week per child, the parents of 2 children need to earn over $23,000 to pay the cost of childcare. Add travel and wardrobe costs and soon one needs to earn a median household income just to cover the cost of going to work, not including living expenses or personal savings. ("Runzheimer Analyzes Historic Day Care Costs Day Care Costs In U.S. More Than Double Since 1985; Monthly Costs Over $500", at http://www.runzheimer.com/corpc/news/scripts/112601.asp and Day-Care Costs Send Parents Home, By Ethan Forman for Eagle-Tribune Publishing http://www.eagletribune.com/news/stories/20010112/FP_001.html.)

Because of this, daycare is heavily subsidized. The subsidy rate that maximizes net government revenue by including second wage earners in the workforce is likely to be between 15% and 30% (U.S. Census Bureau). Another form of social subsidy is in a Federal tax code that supports single-family and vacation home ownership. Tax breaks for homeowners amount to a de facto subsidy of this residential form.

DEMOGRAPHIC CHANGE

Demographic change takes many forms. Lewis Mumford described four great migrations since Europeans first settled on the American continent. First the pioneers out-placed Native Americans with settlements and camps. Next agriculture replaced wilderness. With the dawn of the industrial age, migration moved farmers and foreigners to the cities. Lastly, with affordable transportation, those who could escape the squalor and density of the city did so, creating the first suburbs.

The turn of the 21st century may initiate a fifth migration, the return of empty nesters, gays, minorities, and gen-Xers to the urban core as a residential area. Why come back? To take advantage of the convenience of a truly walkable lifestyle, car-free, and close to culture, sport, entertainment, and high-end employment. Home-based businesses, consultancies, and artists' studios benefit by locating close to the critical business mass and research institutions. Pioneering investors can target real estate with the history, aesthetic character, and location potential that is ripe for renovation and development.

As shown in Figure 2.11, for example, a grandmother in her 90's has chosen downtown Santa Barbara as a location to retire although it is far from her grown children's homes. She chose it because she can walk to the ocean, the park, museum, or shopping district and still enjoy the convenience and security of assisted living, peers enjoying a similar lifestyle, and the southern California climate.

FIGURE 2.11 A child talks with her grandmother in an assisted living courtyard in Santa Barbara. *Photo: Stephen Culbert*

To support the fifth migration and the evolution of these demographic groups pioneering the return to downtown living, the urban core will eventually need to provide housing and lifestyle support for the growing families of the Gen-Xers and the age-related needs of retired Boomers. Downtown will need to provide affordable housing, public transportation, and parking that will allow working class residents to reside in or commute to downtown for work in the service industries required to sustain it. Examples are shown in Figure 2.12 and 2.13. Downtown areas will need to incorporate businesses like grocery stores, healthcare, life learning, and childcare.

LATIN CULTURE IN AMERICA

Latinos are the fastest-growing population group in the United States. Even traditionally non-Latino and non-Hispanic areas such as the Deep South and Midwest have encountered exponential growth of the Latino population in the 1990's. Las Vegas, the nation's fastest-growing metropolitan area in the 1990's, has also shown significant growth of the Latino population. This growth is largely attributed to domestic migration from defunct industrial areas in metropolitan Los Angeles and to natural increase rates exceeding that of other racial and ethnic groups. In 1997 the top Latino states in America were located in the following states:

FIGURE 2.12 Glove Factory apartments, early conversion to provide downtown housing. *Photo: Stephen Culbert.*

FIGURE 2.13 Renaissance Place, The 1st suburban condo's built downtown in the 1980's. *Photo: Stephen Culbert.*

- California
- Texas
- New York
- Florida
- Illinois

The top Latino counties in 1997 were:

- Los Angeles County
- Dade County, Florida
- Cook County, Illinois
- Harris County, Texas
- Orange County, California.

The top Latino cities in 1992 were:

- New York
- Los Angeles
- Chicago
- San Antonio
- Houston

The U.S. Census Bureau treats New York's five boroughs as separate counties (Source: US Census Bureau.)

In describing demographics in 1995, the United States was 74% Anglo, 12% Black, less than 1% Native Americans, 3% Asians and 10% Latino. By 2025 Anglos are projected to have dropped to 62% of the population. Blacks and Native Americans will have increased marginally to 13% and 0.8% of the population respectively. There will be dramatic increases in the population of Asians to 6.2% and Latinos to 17.6%. Latinos cannot be grouped singularly by any factor of race, language, national origin, culture, religion, or ethnicity. Rather, it is a combination of these factors and a sense of contrast to other groups that defines Latinos as a group. Blacks and Asians have been grouped in similar ways. (Profile Of General Demographic Characteristics Census 2000 http://www2.census.gov/census_2000/datasets/demographic_profile/0_United_States/2kh00.pdf Gives national breakdown by race, age, gender.)

Overwhelmingly, Asians and Latinos tend to live in urban areas. In 2025, Latinos are projected to outnumber Blacks in this country by 16 million. If Puerto Rico's population is included with U.S. Census numbers, Latinos already outnumber all groups except Anglos. If the population of Latinos in the United States were ranked among Latin American countries, they would be the fifth largest. For these reasons, the geopolitics of metropolitan areas in the US will change dramatically as these demographic shifts occur. Population data is shown in Figure 2.14 and Table 2.4.

Some metropolitan areas stretch across national borders. With the North Atlantic Free Trade Agreement (NAFTA) as an economic force, trans-

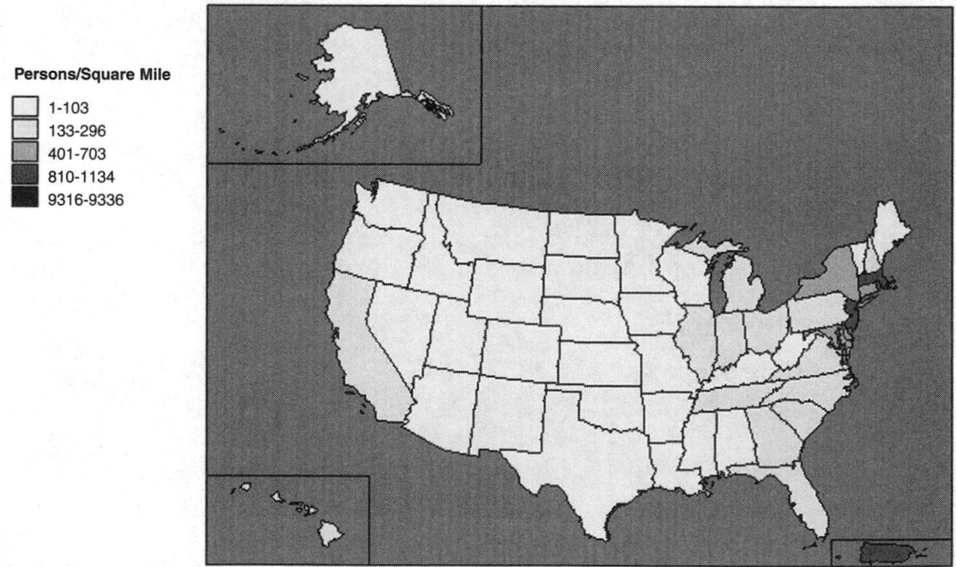

FIGURE 2.14 Total persons United States by state-map

TABLE 2.4 Population, housing units, area, and density: 2000 *(Continued)*

Geographic area	Population	Housing units	Area in square miles			Density per square mile of land area	
			Total area	Water area	Land area	Population	Housing units
United States	281,421,906	115,904,641	3,794,083.06	256,644.62	3,537,438.44	79.6	32.8
Alabama	4,447,100	1,963,711	52,419.02	1,675.01	50,744.00	87.6	38.7
Alaska	626,932	260,978	663,267.26	91,316.00	571,951.26	1.1	0.5
Arizona	5,130,632	2,189,189	113,998.30	363.73	113,634.57	45.2	19.3
Arkansas	2,673,400	1,173,043	53,178.62	1,110.45	52,068.17	51.3	22.5
California	33,871,648	12,214,549	163,695.57	7,736.23	155,959.34	217.2	78.3
Colorado	4,301,261	1,808,037	104,093.57	376.04	103,717.53	41.5	17.4
Connecticut	3,405,565	1,385,975	5,543.33	698.53	4,844.80	702.9	286.1
Delaware	783,600	343,072	2,489.27	535.71	1,953.56	401.1	175.6
District of Columbia	572,059	274,845	68.34	6.94	61.40	9,316.4	4,476.1
Florida	15,982,378	7,302,947	65,754.59	11,827.77	53,926.82	296.4	135.4
Georgia	8,186,453	3,281,737	59,424.77	1,518.63	57,906.14	141.4	56.7
Hawaii	1,211,537	460,542	10,930.98	4,508.36	6,422.62	188.6	71.7
Idaho	1,293,953	527,824	83,570.08	822.87	82,747.21	15.6	6.4
Illinois	12,419,293	4,885,615	57,914.38	2,330.79	55,583.58	223.4	87.9
Indiana	6,080,485	2,532,319	36,417.73	550.83	35,866.90	169.5	70.6
Iowa	2,926,324	1,232,511	56,271.55	402.20	55,869.36	52.4	22.1
Kansas	2,688,418	1,131,200	82,276.84	461.96	81,814.88	32.9	13.8
Kentucky	4,041,769	1,750,927	40,409.02	680.85	39,728.18	101.7	44.1
Louisiana	4,468,976	1,847,181	51,839.70	8,277.85	43,561.85	102.6	42.4
Maine	1,274,923	651,901	35,384.65	4,523.10	30,861.55	41.3	21.1
Maryland	5,296,486	2,145,283	12,406.68	2,632.86	9,773.82	541.9	219.5
Massachusetts	6,349,097	2,621,989	10,554.57	2,714.55	7,840.02	809.8	334.4
Michigan	9,938,444	4,234,279	96,716.11	39,912.28	56,803.82	175.0	74.5
Minnesota	4,919,479	2,065,946	86,938.87	7,328.79	79,610.08	61.8	26.0
Mississippi	2,844,658	1,161,953	48,430.19	1,523.24	46,906.96	60.6	24.8
Missouri	5,595,211	2,442,017	69,704.31	818.39	68,885.93	81.2	35.5
Montana	902,195	412,633	147,042.40	1,489.96	145,552.43	6.2	2.8
Nebraska	1,711,263	722,668	77,353.73	481.31	76,872.41	22.3	9.4
Nevada	1,998,257	827,457	110,560.71	734.71	109,825.99	18.2	7.5
New Hampshire	1,235,786	547,024	9,349.94	381.84	8,968.10	137.8	61.0
New Jersey	8,414,350	3,310,275	8,721.30	1,303.96	7,417.34	1,134.4	446.3
New Mexico	1,819,046	780,579	121,589.48	233.96	121,355.53	15.0	6.4

migration is more common than ever before. Skilled laborers from the United States commute to industrial areas across national borders. Unskilled

TABLE 2.4 *(Continued)* Population, housing units, area, and density: 2000

Geographic area	Population	Housing units	Area in square miles			Density per square mile of land area	
			Total area	Water area	Land area	Population	Housing units
New York	18,976,457	7,679,307	54,556.00	7,342.22	47,213.79	401.9	162.6
North Carolina	8,049,313	3,523,944	53,818.51	5,107.63	48,710.88	165.2	72.3
North Dakota	642,200	289,677	70,699.79	1,723.86	68,975.93	9.3	4.2
Ohio	11,353,140	4,783,051	44,824.90	3,876.53	40,948.38	277.3	116.8
Oklahoma	3,450,654	1,514,400	69,898.19	1,231.13	68,667.06	50.3	22.1
Oregon	3,421,399	1,452,709	98,380.64	2,383.85	95,996.79	35.6	15.1
Pennsylvania	12,281,054	5,249,750	46,055.24	1,238.63	44,816.61	274.0	117.1
Rhode Island	1,048,319	439,837	1,545.05	500.12	1,044.93	1,003.2	420.9
South Carolina	4,012,012	1,753,670	32,020.20	1,910.73	30,109.47	133.2	58.2
South Dakota	754,844	323,208	77,116.49	1,231.85	75,884.64	9.9	4.3
Tennessee	5,689,283	2,439,443	42,143.27	926.15	41,217.12	138.0	59.2
Texas	20,851,820	8,157,575	268,580.82	6,783.70	261,797.12	79.6	31.2
Utah	2,233,169	768,594	84,898.83	2,755.18	82,143.65	27.2	9.4
Vermont	608,827	294,382	9,614.26	364.70	9,249.56	65.8	31.8
Virginia	7,078,515	2,904,192	42,774.20	3,180.13	39,594.07	178.8	73.3
Washington	5,894,121	2,451,075	71,299.64	4,755.58	66,544.06	88.6	36.8
West Virginia	1,808,344	844,623	24,229.76	152.03	24,077.73	75.1	35.1
Wisconsin	5,363,675	2,321,144	65,497.82	11,187.72	54,310.10	98.8	42.7
Wyoming	493,782	223,854	97,813.56	713.16	97,100.40	5.1	2.3

GCT-PH1. **Population, Housing Units, Area, and Density: 2000**
Data Set: Census 2000 Summary File 1 (SF 1) 100-Percent Data
Geographic Area: **United States -- State: and Puerto Rico**

NOTE: For information on confidentiality protection, nonsampling error, and definitions, see http://factfinder.census.gov/home/en/datanotes/expsf1u.htm.

and semiskilled workers are imported to United States urban areas to support industries like tourism, construction, and other services. (Mike Davis, *Magical Urbanism, Latinos and Reinvent the U.S. Big City*, [New York: Verso, 2000]) The disparity in wages and the “spoiler effect” that Latinos have had in recent mayoral elections in metropolises such as New York, Los Angeles, and Chicago have tended to pit Latinos against blacks and Asians as they compete for local power, jobs, and education.

Yet most of the literature on “globalization” has paradoxically ignored its most spectacular U.S. expression. This neglect, moreover, is not for want of a richness of data and ideas. Unfortunately, many of us still view the world chiefly in terms of black and white. By 2050, there may be no majority race or ethnicity in the urban areas of this country. This is already true in some metropolises. Perhaps it is time to consider regionalism as an economic fact that traverses international borders.

SECURITY IMPLICATIONS OF DEMOGRAPHIC TRENDS

Demographic trends have three kinds of security implications. First, they can lead to changes in the nature of conflict. Second, they can affect the nature of national power. Third, they may influence the sources of future conflict. (Demographics and the Changing National Security Environment, a Policy Brief by Rand "Population Matters" RB-5035, 2000)

"World population growth continues at a significant, albeit slowing, rate. Recent middle-range estimates indicate that global population could increase from 6 billion now to 7.3 billion in 2025 and 9.4 billion in 2050. Nearly all this growth will take place in the developing world." (Rand)

YOUNGER POPULATIONS IN DEVELOPING COUNTRIES

While urbanization continues throughout the world, its security implications are probably greatest in developing states. High population growth in agricultural areas, subsequent soil depletion and deforestation, declining agricultural commodity prices, and perceptions that cities offer better economic opportunities, have convinced more and more persons in rural areas to migrate to urban ones as shown in Figure 2.15. One-half of the world population is now urban, compared to only 17 percent in 1950. By 2015, the developing world will contain 23 "megacities" with populations of at least 10 million residents. (Rand)

Recent advances in transportation and communication have made intercontinental migration easier. This has increased the size, visibility, and impact of ethnic diasporas or dispersion of a once cohesive people. Historically this has usually been after a precipitating or catalyzing event. Biblically, the Diaspora occurred after the Babylonian exile. In more recent times, people from African nations were dispersed throughout Europe and the Americas through slavery. More families of Irish descent live outside Ireland than in it, thanks to the potato famine. After WWII the Jews of

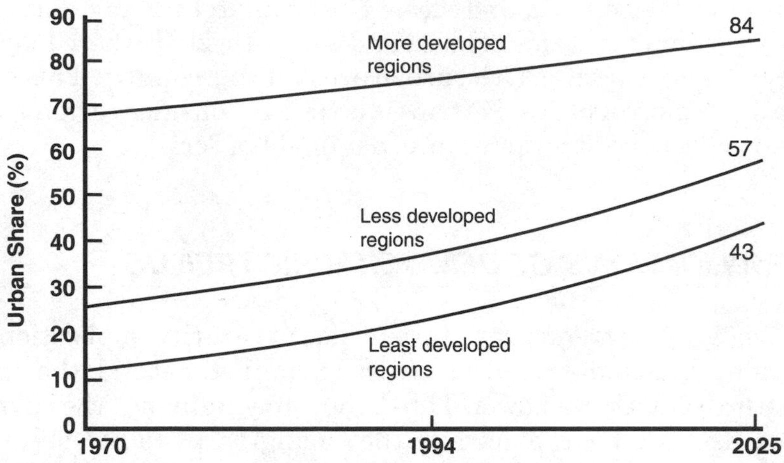

FIGURE 2.15 Urban population growth 1970–2025

Europe were left without homelands. The Palestinians were displaced by the British-supported Zionist intervention in Palestine in 1949. In the 1990's Hutus and Tutsi had civil wars that exiled tribes to neighboring nations in Africa. Within ethnic diasporas, activist groups can become a strategic asset for their home nations and territories. In extreme cases, rival diasporas might engage in violent conflict with their host countries to advance the causes of their home states.

Population pressures increase the likelihood that water rights will be a source of future conflict. Control of freshwater may be a more powerful instrument of coercion. This is particularly true in arid regions where many developing countries are experiencing high population growth. Such nations are vulnerable to threats to their water supply during conflict, especially if much of their water comes from external sources.

The increased urbanization of the world will require new action:

- New tactics
- Training
- Technologies for warfare
- Experience through modeling, practice, and simulation

Over the long term, the United States will need new technologies so that its ground troops can operate more effectively in urban areas. Today one U.S. resident in ten is foreign-born, a proportion similar to that recorded over 150 years ago. Although the share of the foreign-born population is considerably above the record low of 4.8% in 1970, it is also off the record high of 14.8% in 1890. ("In 90's, Immigrant Population Grew Faster Than Native-Born," Friday, September 17, 1999, by Randolph E. Schmid, Washington, The Associated Press)

According to the Census Bureau, during the 1990's, the nation's foreign-born population increased about four times faster than that of the native-born population. The rate was 27.5%. That figure represents a real growth of nearly 5.5 million residents. Immigrant groups are chiefly from Hispanic countries, Asia, and the Pacific.

INTERPRETING DEMOGRAPHIC DATA

Interpreting demographic data can be a challenge. For example, with the release of earnings statistics from the 2000 Census, it appears that Midwestern cities like Detroit, with longstanding demographic problems including out-migration, segregation, and far-reaching poverty, have something to celebrate. Personal income was up, overall poverty was down, and home prices had increased dramatically. But is it really good news? Is the news really true? Here are some facts to consider:

- Economies in Midwestern cities were at a particularly low economic ebb in 1989, especially relative to other regions of the country.
- The 1990 Census missed many people due to its polling methods. Nowhere was this more evident than in the major cities where transience and homelessness are commonplace.
- During the 1990s, many downtown areas gained population. Developers and realtors sought out middle and upper-income empty nesters and singles as the market focus for downtown housing developments. See Table 2.5.
- Due to the strength of the economy and low unemployment rates during the last half of the 1990s, previously unemployed people found permanent jobs. Welfare reform created new jobs. Many of these were low-income service jobs that edged people just over the threshold of poverty. The effect of increased foreign immigration during the same period was to keep wages in these jobs at a minimum.

In the west, some cities like San Antonio are able to annex land outside their boundaries. This usually includes adjacent affluent suburbs. Annexation raises the average household income while incomes in the original political boundaries stagnate or even recede. It creates a politically-induced regionalism that has sustained some cities as organisms, even as

TABLE 2.5 Housing characteristics by unit type, year built, occupancy duration, and value. *Source: United States Census Bureau* *(Continued)*

	Estimate	Lower Bound	Upper Bound
Total housing units	**115,904,650**	*****	*****
UNITS IN STRUCTURE			
1-unit, detached	69,696,206	69,450,315	69,942,097
1-unit, attached	6,463,097	6,382,480	6,543,714
2 units	5,348,994	5,256,163	5,441,825
3 or 4 units	5,618,388	5,525,346	5,711,430
5 to 9 units	5,966,119	5,878,915	6,053,323
10 to 19 units	5,042,714	4,953,013	5,132,415
20 or more units	9,071,115	8,969,511	9,172,719
Mobile home	8,604,733	8,392,132	8,817,334
Boat, RV, van, etc.	93,284	81,571	104,997
YEAR STRUCTURE BUILT			
2000	2,074,556	2,030,395	2,118,717
1995 to 1999	8,536,191	8,432,970	8,639,412
1990 to 1994	8,480,468	8,362,102	8,598,834
1980 to 1989	18,274,758	18,134,228	18,415,289
1970 to 1979	21,154,043	20,980,381	21,327,706
1960 to 1969	15,376,686	15,247,927	15,505,445
1950 to 1959	14,721,485	14,593,493	14,849,477
1940 to 1949	8,405,886	8,292,348	8,519,424
1939 or earlier	18,880,577	18,631,211	19,129,943
ROOMS			
1 room	1,798,631	1,756,515	1,840,747
2 rooms	4,447,750	4,372,482	4,523,018
3 rooms	11,528,397	11,410,346	11,646,448
4 rooms	20,631,307	20,481,071	20,781,543
5 rooms	25,422,932	25,261,839	25,584,025
6 rooms	21,462,475	21,330,193	21,594,757
7 rooms	13,630,089	13,513,959	13,746,219
8 rooms	8,719,724	8,634,964	8,804,485
9 rooms or more	8,263,345	8,163,309	8,363,381
Median (rooms)	5.8	5.6	6.0

the population or the economy has otherwise declined. State-sanctioned special district bonding authorities have commonly been formed to cross municipal boundaries in the delivery of utilities, policing, transportation, educational services, and infrastructure. They may also address regional

TABLE 2.5 (*Continued*) Housing characteristics by unit type, year built, occupancy duration, and value *Source: United States Census Bureau*

	Estimate	Lower Bound	Upper Bound
Occupied housing units	**104,733,569**	**104,508,735**	**104,958,403**
YEAR HOUSEHOLDER MOVED INTO UNIT			
2000	9,624,395	9,491,643	9,757,147
1995 to 1999	42,642,501	42,454,617	42,830,385
1990 to 1994	16,243,358	16,109,078	16,377,638
1980 to 1989	16,242,768	16,111,763	16,373,773
1970 to 1979	10,016,233	9,914,672	10,117,794
1969 or earlier	9,964,314	9,859,169	10,069,459
HOUSE HEATING FUEL			
Utility gas	52,767,270	52,293,055	53,241,485
Bottled, tank, or LP gas	6,664,447	6,446,670	6,882,224
Electricity	32,207,553	31,875,217	32,539,889
Fuel oil, kerosene, etc.	9,822,057	9,572,689	10,071,425
Coal or coke	173,700	146,998	200,402
Wood	1,790,047	1,689,572	1,890,522
Solar energy	42,371	35,928	48,814
Other fuel	467,719	442,581	492,857
No fuel used	798,405	768,888	827,922
SELECTED CHARACTERISTICS			
Lacking complete plumbing facilities	529,339	505,478	553,200
Lacking complete kitchen facilities	624,524	596,071	652,977
No telephone service available	3,189,411	3,103,370	3,275,452
OCCUPANTS PER ROOM			
1.00 or less	100,349,105	100,124,961	100,573,249
1.01 to 1.50	2,878,076	2,820,880	2,935,272
1.51 or more	1,506,388	1,468,486	1,544,290
Specified owner-occupied units	**55,547,910**	**55,231,468**	**55,864,352**
VALUE			
Less than $50,000	5,313,804	5,173,156	5,454,452
$50,000 to $99,999	16,715,393	16,574,041	16,856,745
$100,000 to $149,999	13,224,565	13,066,172	13,382,958
$150,000 to $199,999	8,143,929	8,053,356	8,234,502
$200,000 to $299,999	6,461,012	6,386,673	6,535,351
$300,000 to $499,999	3,996,600	3,939,312	4,053,888
$500,000 to $999,999	1,394,729	1,360,140	1,429,318
$1,000,000 or more	297,878	282,469	313,287
Median (dollars)	120,496	120,014	120,978

environmental issues such as watershed protection, flood control, and air pollution control.

Less commonly, city-county governments have been formed. City-county governments have worked in Indianapolis, Jacksonville and Nashville. There is a proposed plan for Charlotte. But what happens when the substantial outflow to suburbia extends beyond the county boundary as in Cleveland and Detroit? Only legislative acts by state government can address this. Usually it's in the form of imposed geographic growth limits on communities and complex per capita-based revenue sharing formulas. Such forced equalization may enable cities to access the bonding power required to rebuild their tax base and subsequent infrastructure and economic refueling.

A new form of regional government, the Regional Asset District, has been created with bonding authority for the development and management of publicly owned cultural, historical, and scientific assets like zoos, museums, arts centers, and sports facilities. While the subject assets may primarily be centered in the district, outlying facilities need simply to benefit the entire region.

So the question of whether a city's income increase is a result of wealthier people moving back to the city or is due to growing earning power by those who never left must be deciphered using more focused tract data for comparison. Even in this case, census tracts don't necessarily replicate neighborhood, development areas, or other existing sets of political boundaries.

How one measures real improvements in the quality of life in urban neighborhoods, especially beyond downtown, may not be accomplished by relying only on the census and empirical data that make headlines. In terms of boundary-constrained cities on the East Coast and in the Midwest, some argue that poverty has actually gone up. Perhaps tax revenue per capita, measured at the same interval and within the same boundary and adjusted for incremental tax increases, would provide more meaningful measures. (Source: Rust Belt Cities May Be Seeing A Rebirth by Mike Swift — 06/05/02 — (11 & 9) http://research.uli.org/DK/SpPer/re_SpPer_Commercial_fst.html

PSYCHIC/SPIRITUAL CHANGE

In our increasingly secular and consumer-oriented culture, purchased entertainment, free media, and recreation have replaced the role that religion, schools, community groups, cultural institutions and books have held for earlier generations. These institutions still hold a significant role in many lives regardless of age. However, for the laziest and busiest segments of our society, information sources, worldview, lifestyle, and political choices are often the product of the most easily accessible and least thought-provoking sources. Tabloids, radio, networks, dumbed-down reporting, low cost call-in programming, and whatever the next guy at the water cooler is spouting can be compelling influences.

In Europe and Canada, a similar trend toward secularism has been observed, although the pull of consumerism on individuals may not be quite as strong. In some places there is a strong movement to preserve local and regional culture. This is especially observable in areas where Anglo-American involvement is most visible through media, entertainment, and name branding. Due current events such as political scandals, church debacles, domestic terrorism, war, and accounting violations at major institutions, public trust is at a low point. It is unclear whether rock bottom has been reached.

Culture, lifestyles, political, and economic ideas move wherever commerce is open. Is it too late to fight the flow of money? Should we? The answers to these questions will become evident over time. Education of the masses such as the no smoking campaigns of the 1970's, the AIDS prevention campaigns of the 1980's or the personal investment campaigns of the 1990's will incrementally engineer public attitudes in favor of those core ideas. Professionals with expertise in construction, design, environmental engineering, transportation, law, and infrastructure will shape the messages that the media will send. Professional organizations find many ways to promote ideas. Their leaders are the expert voices within the profession or industry they represent. The Urban Land Institute promotes various strategies on responsible yet profitable development and markets. Construction Market Data and Engineering News Record analyze emerging and traditional construction market sectors. The Construction Specifications Institute promotes cross-professional communication and mutual understanding among the key players of the built environment. Also, The American Institute of Architects (AIA) promotes peer review of best practices, continuing education, enlightened design, and political action for legislation affecting the profession. Professional groups are excellent sources for training and making contacts for future leaders.

Active participation in professional institutes is of great value to the community. It's a place to begin self-education and the critical examination of ideas. Political appointment, community groups, or elected positions are other ways to shape how other citizens view the world and effect positive change. Entry-level community influence can begin with merchants, neighborhoods, and historic associations. Depending on community size and level of activism, involvement may be as easy as volunteering and participating. Appointed office and commissioner status is relatively simple to attain. Not withstanding political debts, one need only demonstrate consistent excellence, expertise, and the ability to negotiate in difficult circumstances. It is significant just how few individuals are needed to place a candidate on a ballot for local elections. Count up the precincts and wards, add the nominating committee members and a few endorsing officeholders, and one is practically there, as long as the party can deliver the vote.

A move for better communication between government units and citizens is one of the blessings that have come out of the 9-11 attacks. It has reawakened a spirit of cooperation and awareness between groups that had previously been aloof. With this move toward greater interface, opportunities will abound to influnce or participate in decisions that shape the future of land development.

CHAPTER 3
COMPREHENSIVE LAND USE PLANNING AND ZONING

ACHIEVING LIVABLE COMMUNITIES

The lack of a development plan hinders progress in any city. Owners, builders, and developers want to know what the administrative requirements and ordinances will be before they begin a project. If a community's executive branch wants to stay ahead of the ill effects of recession, then it should publish a development plan. To receive certain state and federal benefits, it is a must. While planning is subject to change, it provides a blueprint for success in the redevelopment of a city. The results of good planning are shown in Figure 3.1. A plan that builds on prior plans demonstrates continuity and foresight for the city. While it is politically advantageous to adorn a city with unique development plans, it is immature and unwise for a city of significant size to start over every time there is a new administration.

PLANNING

The most essential role of the planning department is in identifying and solving a community's problems. Through comprehensive district plans and the zoning ordinances drafted, it will also protect important community features and guide how the community grows. Public and business participation in this process are crucial, because the primary challenge of the execution of these plans is the preservation and protection of property rights. While planning is a political, economic, and aesthetic process, planning

FIGURE 3.1 Upscale rowhouses create housing where there was once an arena. Less costly exterior finishes are used for semi-private exposures. *Photo: Stephen Culbert*

efforts may not always serve the existing residents and voters if they do not own property and tend to remain silent.

Planning Department Structure and Processes

Neighborhood groups negotiate with developers to reach agreements about existing zoning requirements, how they might be modified to allow a new use for an existing site. While this can be a benefit because it creates a process to find compromises and to arrive at an agreement, continued over-regulation can raise the costs of development. If the cost is too great, developers may select opportunities outside the jurisdiction. It may be time to re-zone the area.

Planning staff must be exacting and coordinated about what commitments get adopted. Aesthetically-focused and vaguely-worded commitments can be difficult to enforce. Some commitments are violated by the design requirements from another authority, rendering them unenforceable.

Planning Department Organizational Structure

In all but regional matters, such as transportation planning or watershed protection, the state cedes power to local government for the purpose of land use planning. "Simply stated, without the consent of the Legislature, localities do not have the power to act on a statewide level or in a way that will affect statewide policies and objectives." (Carrigan, Christian, "Ballot Box Planning And Zoning – Limits To Referenda Do Courts Limit Initiative and Referendum Power?", http://www.msandr.com/ballot.htm, February 15, 2002) Powers of a local government include enacting a zoning ordinance, re-zoning an area, adopting a plan, or amending any of these. They are Legislative acts because they form rules or policy that can be applied to all future cases.

Adjudicative powers are interpretive and rely on a specific set of facts or circumstances unique to a case in question. Adjudicative powers are ceded to the planning commission, which is usually appointed by the elected governor. The commission executes the legislated mandates including granting variances and conditional use permits, permitting exceptions to existing rules, and approving a planned unit development, subdivision or tentative subdivision map. Individual members of the commission might be characterized as accommodationists or reformists, depending on whether they appear to favor expedited development or some specific goal. They are primarily selected to represent the interests of the voting public as a check on the plans of the professionals who work for them. In essence they become a jury to review plans and variances to plans. Regular commission meetings create a forum for these representatives to gather feedback from the public. The commission will usually rely on the planning department staff's review and recommendations as a part of this process, and staff support can be significant to a variance petitioner's success. Applications for variance and staff files are "public information" and may be requested for review by interested parties and the press. The planning director and planning staff will execute the directives of the Planning Commission. Their primary duties include these actions:

- Maintaining and updating the Master Plan and coordinating city-planning efforts
- Providing planning recommendations to the Planning Commission
- Furnishing information to the Planning Commission, City Council, and the public regarding plans and petitions
- Preparing the capital improvements budget
- Recommending priorities for spending

• Facilitating interdepartmental cooperation

(Planning Department Organizational Structure http://www.emich.edu/public/geo/557book/b320.plngchart.html, February 15, 2002)

Interdepartmental cooperation comes into play at two levels when multiple agencies must review a project or when multiple units of government are stakeholders in the proposed plan. These stakeholders may represent environmental, transportation, economic development, construction, infrastructure, sanitation, or public safety interests. This might include participation in regional government coalitions and regional service or asset districts.

Key Roles and Responsibilities

The local governing body, such as the city council or its equivalent, should adopt a Comprehensive Plan. These bodies require public hearings and extensive public involvement in the plan drafting process. Some locations allow plans to be adopted by appointed planning commissioners. However, when the state requires plans to be adopted by local government bodies, the adoption creates a legislative act that gives the plan more strength. In such a case, plan commissions must make decisions based on the goals and guidelines set forth in the plan, or the petitioner may have recourse with the legislative body.

The Comprehensive Plan (also called the Master Plan or General Plan) will include plans for the future physical development of a community that are geographically and functionally comprehensive. At minimum it will address land use, public facilities, and circulation elements. The Comprehensive Plan has been established through court cases as dominant over zoning ordinances. The plan is established as the basis for zoning regulation. This relationship is critical to avoid the reality of spot zoning or favoritism.

fastfacts

The Comprehensive Plan (also called the Master Plan or General Plan) will include plans for the future physical development of a community that are geographically and functionally comprehensive.

Planning should consider the broad implications of social issues and ills, and attempt to accommodate the essential concerns of all segments of society. It should also look toward a proactive vision for the community that makes the most of its inherent advantages to create a framework for a sustainable future. The 3 C's of master planning are as follows:

- Comprehensiveness
- Co-ordination
- Continuity for the long range

Long range planning usually means 10-20 years. (Planning Department Organizational Structure, http://www.emich.edu/public/geo/557book/b320.plngchart.html, February 15, 2002)

Comprehensive plans, and supporting neighborhood plans, require periodic re-evaluation. With reevaluation come revisions, edits, and deletions to existing plans. An excellent tool is a zoning map as in Figure 3.2. If the incremental changes have become sweeping, whole new adoptions may be initiated.

Establishing zoning ordinances after the comprehensive plan may seem logical, but in many communities, zoning actually came first. As suburbia developed in the early 20th century, those who had escaped the squalor and decaying infrastructure of the city wanted to preserve their investment in new pristine environments. Zoning became that protection. Zoning was, unfortunately, used to create exclusionary rules that prevented many types of businesses and people from creating the same environment that the suburbanites had just "escaped."

Just as there are futurists who make the news every January and, especially at the turn of every decade, planning is perceived as being long on theory and short on practical application. The zoning ordinance is the tool that a community ultimately relies on to protect its property interests. The comprehensive plan establishes the direction for a political unit and its broad concepts of land use. The district (or neighborhood) plan assigns uses to specific properties. In some smaller locations, these plans may be combined.

The zoning ordinance is the tool that a community ultimately relies on to protect its property interests.

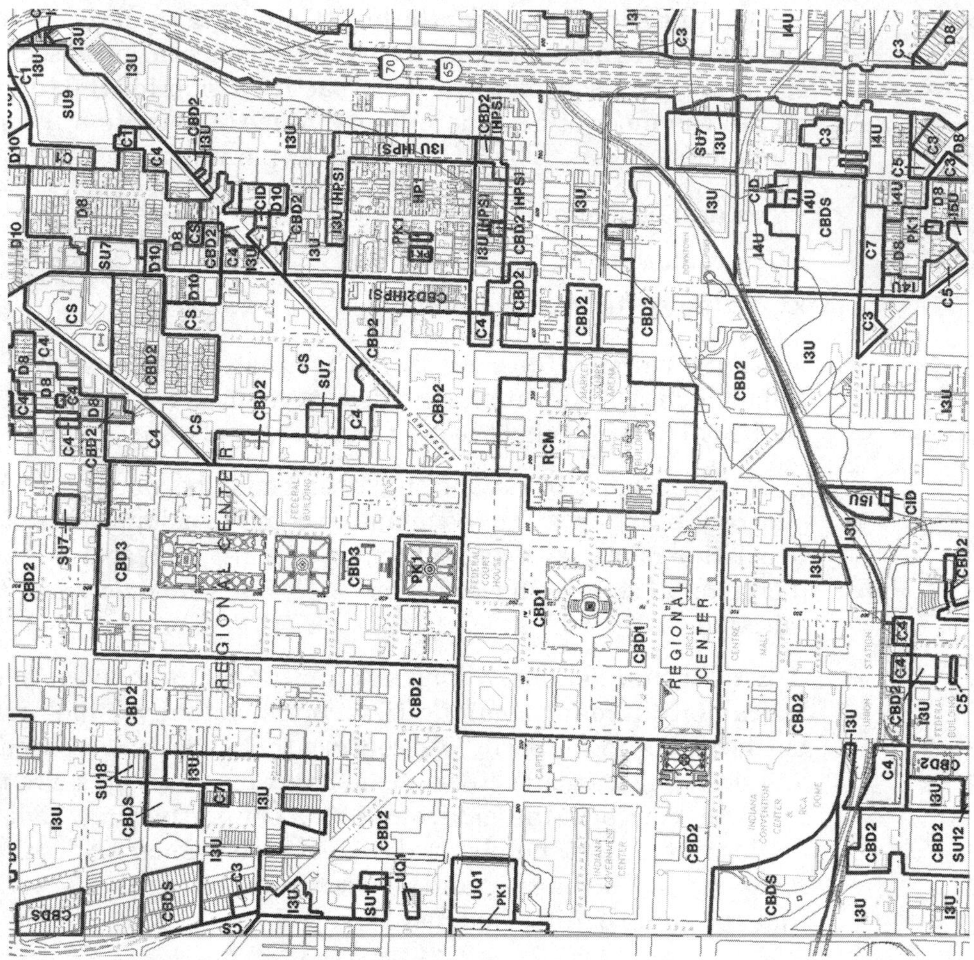

FIGURE 3.2 Marion County zoning base map

A comprehensive plan results from analysis of data and plans for incremental land use modifications to fit a developed and recorded vision. Planners derive the comprehensive plan after analysis of demographic, ecological, economic, infrastructure, transportation, crime, health, and geographic data. GIS (Graphic Information Systems) may be used to record any of the quantifiable or physical data in a graphic database in layers that can be used for modeling, quantifying, and comparing variables.

A widely-used method of plan analysis is SWOT. SWOT is an acronym for strengths, weaknesses, opportunities, and threats.

Benchmarking is a method of analysis that compares the essential qualities of similar communities or enterprises. For example, on a regional

Zoning Ordinances, or land use controls, are the primary tools by which elements of the comprehensive plan are applied to specific existing parcels of land and property.

basis, Indianapolis is often compared with other second tier metropolises like:

- Lexington and Louisville, Kentucky
- Kansas City, Missouri
- Columbus and Cincinnati, Ohio
- Nashville, Tennessee
- Milwaukee, Wisconsin

The cities are similar because they are more or less central to the US population. They have similar populations, each has manufacturing as a key component in its economy, and each has agricultural hinterlands. Each is located close to an interstate highway.

Nationally, Indianapolis is often compared to markets that are similar in size such as:

- Baltimore
- Phoenix
- New Orleans

Because of a difference in the scale and complexity of the economy, inappropriate benchmarks would be:

- Chicago
- St. Louis
- Detroit
- Minneapolis

Competing with one another at a slightly smaller scale are:

- Springfield-Peoria, Illinois
- Ft. Wayne, Indiana
- Lafayette, Indiana

- Toledo and Dayton, Ohio
- Lansing and Grand Rapids, Michigan

SWOT analysis should be performed on several of the benchmarked communities, so that the strengths of other communities can be considered and possibly adopted.

As plans are being developed, planners seek input from several external sources including political leaders and appointees, business leaders, neighborhood representatives, and the general public.

Plan Analysis Tools

SWOT analysis is a framework for analyzing strengths and weaknesses, and the opportunities and threats. It can help planners and developers focus on plan and project strengths, and take the greatest possible advantage of opportunities available. SWOT will help identify weaknesses and threats so they can be minimized. A concept known as the "Five Forces Model" was first articulated by Michael Porter. Although the model described relationships between competitors within an industry, it can be tailored to development, project issues, or even personal decisions. A lot of lip service has been given to SWOT, however, only a few governments and business enterprises have a formal method for performing such an analysis. Applying SWOT analysis to Project Specific Analysis may require answering many questions. One of the issues regards the strengths of the project:

- How many modes of transportation are available?
- What is the image of the community to outsiders?
- What industries are strong performers?
- How large is the market within a given distance?
- How visually attractive is the community? Are there well-developed areas for public recreation?
- Is there a downtown housing supply?

Analysis of the weaknesses addresses the following questions:

- How congested are the transportation modes?
- Is there sufficient diversity in the economic base that the community can weather a downturn in a specific industry?
- Are the established industries long-term growth industries?

Opportunities are a very important part of the process:

- Would building infrastructure for another mode of transportation improve the supply of available workers in another part of the community?
- Are there natural or manmade features that might be attractions outside the community? Would improving schools attract new businesses?
- Are there bifurcations of existing industries that can be encouraged?

Finally, there is the identification of the threats:

- Is there enough density to support the development of mass transit without public subsidy?
- Are there too few types of industry to sustain the downturn in one of the major industries?

Applying SWOT analysis to Project Specific Analysis may require answering questions such as:

- Strengths: Does the investor/developer have strong and favorable ties to the community? Have the developer and the design team worked together successfully before? Is the image for the new project an improvement that will enhance the environment? How is the project perceived and received in the community? Is there an economic advantage for the community in locating an enterprise here?
- Weaknesses: How many un-quantifiable items of work are in the project? How many can be reduced? Has discovery been sufficient? Are there liens? Will the time cost of money overcome the advantages of starting with a viable shell when time to rezone or develop in phases is required?
- Opportunities: Is the neighborhood fabric or history a potential source of inspiration? Are there architectural elements that exist that are worthy of preservation and perhaps highlight in the design? Can the project use matching funds available for redevelopment? Are there infrastructure improvements the community is willing to make to attract the project?
- Threats: Will the neighbors remonstrate against a proposed new use or a request to rezone? Will someone buy the property before the investor is ready to commit? Are there potentially costly abatement issues yet to be resolved? How closely located are competing enterprises? Which building element hasn't yet failed, but is at the end of its

service life? Can replacing it be deferred? Can an existing competitive advantage be sustained?

A SWOT analysis is a function of time, resources, and scale. Even an informal or cursory analysis can be beneficial at the project level for site selection or tenant market identification. Governments, planners, and developers use GIS to overlay database information to locate jobs, housing, economic development districts, social services, etc. GIS databases can overlay broad information sources addressing tax and school districts, locations of utilities and other infrastructures, police, fire, sanitary districts, political districts, geographic, and demographic information. It can contain information as specific as manhole elevations, street lamp replacement schedules, property ownership, and permit information. Cities can contract for database maintenance with corporations who also sell layers of information

FIGURE 3.3 City incentives to redevelop include improving and ceding a right-of-way.

to the public and provide maps to public entities. An example is the topographic map shown in Figure 3.4. Architecture, planning, engineering, and survey firms have entered the arena offering these services to cities, towns, utilities, and governments to catalog specific information sets. Some will even offer continuing service to keep the set updated on a contract basis. Some cities have created GIS-based toolkits that overlay indexed information pertaining to redevelopment resources including city agencies, community development corporations, neighborhood associations, and other adopted plans for the area.

Planners use external input as an essential feedback check that validates or suggests adjustment to the comprehensive plan. It is otherwise possible to steer a plan to serve an unsupported agenda or to devise one in support of an erroneous belief. In generating plans for themed districts, Calthorpe and Associates also use a gaming technique with public representatives in workshops that focus on the plans of specific areas. Each team is given icon chips to allocate among the targeted uses for an area. Results of the plans are compared and discussed. In some communities, planners host camps or seminars to educate policy makers and the public about essential concepts in planning. Sometimes the seminars are followed by a charette, an intense brainstorming session, where members of the community and planning department facilitators address specific needs or problems. Others hold public town hall meetings to address specific planning

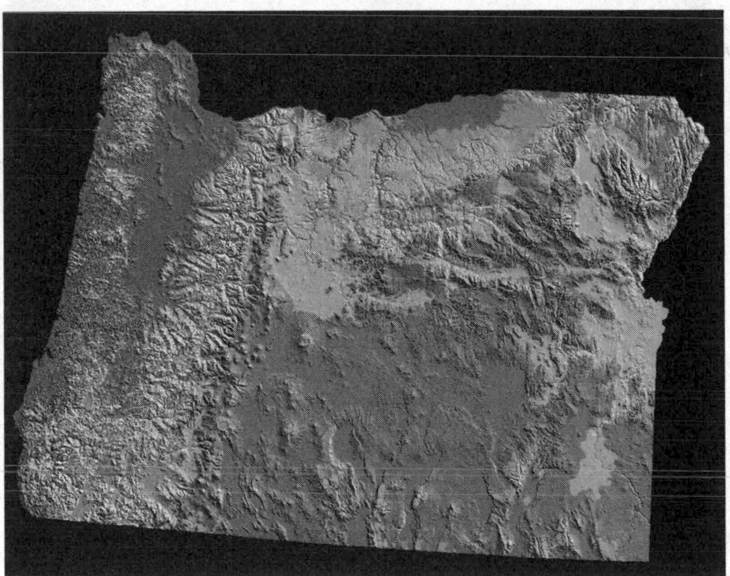

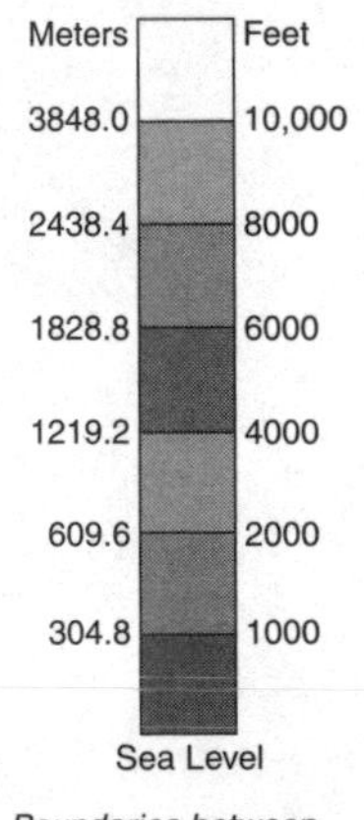

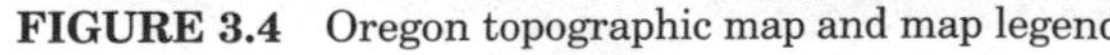

FIGURE 3.4 Oregon topographic map and map legend

initiatives or district plans. Often questionnaires are used to gather and quantify feedback on issues that planners have deemed relevant. Planners may then develop an "order of magnitude" list that identifies proposed projects by size, required resources, available funds, priority, and projected time for execution.

Citizens Affecting The Planning Process

Public input is critical to maintaining the community trust and adding validity to any plan presented to the legislative body for adoption. Public meetings are common to most land use planning departments.

In some states citizens can promote by initiative or referendum to change land use plans. "Initiative or referendum petitions aimed at curbing 'sprawl' address a wide range of local government actions anywhere from approval of a Planned Unit Development, to amendment of a local zoning ordinance or general plan." (Carrigan) Referenda are usually intended as reforms to Legislative acts. The elected officials of state and

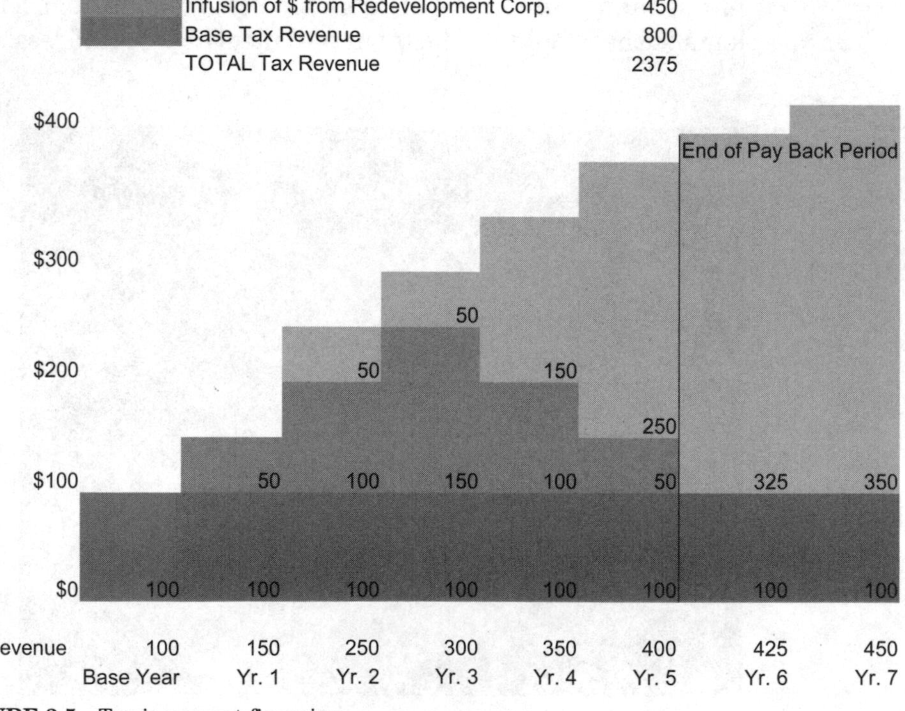

FIGURE 3.5 Tax increment financing

local government control these. They set public policy and laws for general application in all jurisdictions of state. In the land use context, rezonings, modification, enactment of zoning ordinances, and adoption or alteration of land use plans are all legislative acts. Administrative acts are delegated by governments and implemented by commissions and departments. They include case-specific interpretation of the laws such as variances, conditional use permits, exceptions, planned unit developments, and subdivision approvals. In some areas the approval of a subdivision requires a vote, which then makes it subject to referenda.

Citizens also have the right to remonstrate, Figure 3.6, against proposed (site specific) alterations in adopted land-use plans. Exercising this option allows concerned citizens to voice their concerns regarding the applicability and effects of proposed land-use changes before the administrative body. This can be effective especially when citizens are well organized and backed by neighborhood associations, merchant associations, and other groups that represent blocks of voters and tax payers.

"The recent proliferation of ballot box planning and zoning presents new challenges for the developer and land use practitioner." (Carrigan, p.

FIGURE 3.6 Citizen demonstrators

2) It's not enough to involve merchant and business groups. With involvement of neighborhood groups at the earliest stages of planning, it's the local residents who can make the most political noise.

ZONING

In their description of the inception of the City Beautiful Movement with an urban cleanup program in Harrisburg Pennsylvania, and the subsequent movement that followed it, Moe & Wilkie (Page 37) describe the awe of visitors to the World's Columbian Exposition. An historian says, "Throughout the nation people began to wonder why cities couldn't be as orderly and beautiful as the Columbian exposition." Zoning ordinances, or land use controls, are the primary tools by which elements of the comprehensive plan are applied to specific existing parcels of land and property. They have enforceable police power behind them because they are intended to enact legislation.

> **Zoning Ordinances, or land use controls, are the primary tools by which elements of the comprehensive plan are applied to specific existing parcels of land and property.**

A Brief History of Zoning

The City Beautiful Movement continued for about 30 years during the latter portion of the 19th and the first portion of the 20th century. Exposition-inspired Public building programs, including landscape and architecture derived from Greek, Roman and other classical architecture.

Quotations from Daniel Burnham, master architect of the Columbian Exposition of 1893, "Make no little plans they have no magic to stir men's blood and probably will not be realized. Make big plans; aim high in hope and work, remembering that nobler, logical diagram once recorded will never die, but long after we are gone will be a living thing, asserting itself with ever growing insistency. Remember that your sons and grandsons are going to do things that would stagger us. Let your watchword be order and your beacon award or run."

What follows is a brief history of the zoning in America (Moe & Wilkie, Page 40).

> Laissez-faire urbanization lead to conflicts between neighbors, and ultimately to the establishment of the zoning laws. Conflicts included incompatible neighboring property uses, racial tension, an encroachment on a potential expansion, and even blocked sunlight. The growth of the automobile and roads, and the subsequent decline in other forms of mass transportation had a disbursing affect on urban area populations. It also had a crowding affect on streets and infrastructure designed for another era.

In 1932 Frank Lloyd Wright published *The Disappearing City* where he first introduced the centripetal forces of modernization that pooled the city from its center. Later, Wright developed utopian plans to bring about a Broad Acre City that was never actually constructed. His were the first plans for demassifying the city. And he considered this ideal. His was a placeless low-density environment with concentrations of people in towers surrounded by broad acres of greenery and connected by avenues and highways. And in a way, modern-day suburbs developed after cars became the chief source of transportation. Los Angeles and Phoenix resemble the development he described. As a futurist, Wright was on target about many of the forces decentralizing our cities now. These forces are described in James Howard Kunstler's book *The Geography of Nowhere*.

Urban planners entered the picture with the formation of the Regional Planning Association of America as a response to the decentralization of the city and the dawn of suburbia. They hoped to plan cities where they could control urban sprawl and the chaotic environment that would lead to what amounted to low-density slums exported from the more dense inner city slums. They hoped to create order and regional control of the growth cities.

Under the New Deal's Federal Resettlement Administration, urban slum dwellers and disenfranchised former farm workers were actually relocated into three "Green" cities with the purpose of tearing down urban slums and replacing them with parks. The plan cities raised the ire of contractors, developers, and local politicians and some accused the government of acts of socialism. Home ownership increased after the FHA was formed in 1934. The G.I. Bill in 1944 made owning a house and even more affordable.

The FHA's ranking practices for neighborhoods contributed greatly to the sub-urbanization of America. This is because of its preference for new homes and infrastructure in white neighborhoods over older homes and neighborhoods in terms of securing and insuring loans. All these criteria give almost exclusive attention to market values or the stability of property values and placed virtually no value on the social stability of a community.

Standardized suburban design was promoted by the FHA's bulletin "Planning Profitable Neighborhoods" which offered suburbanites more density, increased privacy, and more accessibility to the automobile. However these designs neglected to incorporate some of the humanizing aspects of older neighborhoods with narrower streets, less predictability, mixed uses, and more intimacy. The FHA discouraged neighborhoods comprised of rentals and privately owned homes. Flight to the new suburbs increased the decline and blight in urban neighborhoods, due to a declining tax base.

The Housing Act of 1937 permitted and encouraged the wholesale destruction of slum neighborhoods because they were deemed to be detrimental to safety health or morals. Although well-intentioned, it further concentrated poverty in the urban core because it replaced slums housing with "Project" type housing on a one-for-one basis and left a vast tracts of land empty. Once again it was money that talked as business leaders realized it was expensive to raze block after block. Oddly, it was bankers, the Federal Home Loan Bank Board, who attempted the rescue. They examined lending criteria and maps that showed all areas written off based on so-called security reasons. The marketplace, left to its own devices, could not maintain or revitalize most of these areas.

The government's housing program was insufficient, and according to a national survey, it favored "new construction at the expense of repairing what existed." As the board reported, "it has left the preservation of existing standard housing virtually untouched." The board urged neighborhood conservation and "the development of maximum benefits from what we already possess."

The FHA favored the predictability of traditional styles and uniform lot sizes. This policy helped spread colonial revival architecture across the suburbias of America, when loans were measured for conformance with these standards. When local zoning ordinances later bought into single use the zoning and prescriptives, this further helped to obliterate any sense of regional or vernacular housing styles that incorporated indigenous materials and reflected the local climate and culture. The mixed uses of the traditional community were not present to sustain the new suburban development. As the population out-migrated from urban neighborhoods to suburbia, single-use shopping districts evolved to support the needs of relocated residents with expendable income. A commensurate loss of urban shopping opportunity resulted.

For some politicians, neighborhood conservation and stabilization programs have been and continue to be unattractive because they involve relatively slow processes and the results to not have the visual impact or instant gratification of sweeping programs and new construction. In similar ways, infrastructure programs, like improved sewers, are often deferred because more visual improvements like repaved roads and are more observable by a wider range of voters.

Relatively cheap land and low taxes in outlying areas further eroded the population, retail, and even the industrial base of cities. The development of the automobile as the primary mode of transportation, the razing of neighborhoods for highway construction within cities, followed by the creation of interstate highways to connect regions, exacerbated the demassification of cities.

Development of the automobile-oriented infrastructure also changed marketing practices and the look of retail architecture forever. What ever was being sold had to be understood at 30, 40, 50, 60 miles an hour from a car. Retail could take place anywhere a car could go. So retail sought out the

FIGURE 3.7 Goodman Jewelers resisted eminent domain.

least expensive land accessible to the greatest number of vehicles. Usually this was at the intersection of principal highways. Interior suburban malls developed because the experience of shopping could be separated from the experience of living and working.

In the rush to raze neighborhoods to make room for new development and roads, infill development lagged greatly and left a gaping holes in existing neighborhoods and actually created blight where there had been none or little. Disenfranchised residents resisted relocation to the unfamiliar and detail-sparse housing projects that replaced them. As evidenced in events like the 1964 Watts riot in Los Angeles, sometimes housing conditions were an element that led to revolt.

To the extent that measurable variables could be defined, logistical regression studies of the effect of the development of transportation routes on land use and urbanization in general have supported the empirical findings that land development follows the development of new or enhanced transportation routes (Sanchez). Further, this finding is exacerbated when applied to previously non-urban areas, and where routes are new as opposed to enhanced existing routes. While road construction appears to be the catalyst to development, the "chicken and egg" question occurs to many since the development along the new routes tends to be a self-reinforcing loop. (Guilano) Differentiation among the land uses triggered by route development is also affected strongly by the ease of access to the developed site. Access is an independent variable from distance to an interchange or the mere existence of a new route. Property value, or rather the change in property value, is a variable that is indicative of type of land use. (Ryan) (G. Guliano; "Land Use Impacts of Transportation Investments: Highway and transit". (Hanson, 1995 pp. 305-341. T. Sanchez, K. Dueker, A. Rufolo, T. Moore, And B. Parker; "Indirect Land Use And Growth Impacts: Phase I Report (Draft) Oregon Department Of Transportation", 1999. S. Ryan; "Property Values And Transportation Facilities: Finding Transportation-Land Use Connection" Journal Of Planning Literature, 13 (4):412-427)

With the evolution of technology, the economy of the United States shifted during the 20th century from agrarian to industrial to a service-based economy. Most of the service dollars are earned in information-based businesses. In the '70s and '80s a substantial number of industrial jobs were lost and new service industry jobs were created. Service sector jobs were often lower paying than the industrial jobs they replaced. The change and the economic base changed where people worked. Suburban communities pursued the clean industries and service sector jobs. Jobs could now be located in the economical and undeveloped land in an adjacent suburb. And hence, edge cities developed.

The continually expanding circles of development have led to continually expanding circles of the deterioration as a pattern in urban areas across the country. It is no longer simply the core city at stake, but edge cities and inner suburbs as well. As sprawl continues into exurbia, consuming farms, woods, and mountains, what will be the fate of these areas?

The decentralization process and its implications were aptly described by Indiana's First Lady, Judy O'Bannon, at the Joseph Taylor Symposium on Building Community in America conducted March 8, 2001 at Indiana University Purdue University at Indianapolis: "We all went north of 38 St. after we had used, abused, and discarded everything south of 38th Street." And she continued, to describe the disposable nature of property and the havoc it wreaks, "We treat people like paper plates."

People fail to recognize that as metropolitan regions sprawl, taxpayers pay for the new infrastructure of roads, sewers, bridges, law enforcement, hospitals, libraries, and schools required to support the out migrated population of the city. The new communities buy into 30-year bond issues that they may or may not have the population and tax base to support at the end of the issue because residents will have moved on. So the problems of the city have followed those fleeing the city into the suburbs.

Even the planned communities of today, with their invented histories and supporting functions of retail, child-care centers, and workout gyms located in newly built neighborhoods with sidewalks on a least one side of the street, suffer from Simulacrum.

Instruments of Zoning and Planning

Zoning breaks comprehensive plans down into broad land use groups. Most of these groups are single-use by definition. Planned unit development (PUD or DP, development plan) zoning differs from single use and is widely interpretive at the administrative level. It generally permits a mix of uses, without specifying which uses are included in that mix. Hypothetically, Ray's Disco Roller-Fishing, Big Deal Manufacturing, Tent City Tower, and the All Night House of Prayer could occupy adjacent space in a PUD if a staff administrator were crazy enough to recommend them and the legislative body cavalier enough to approve it. Table 3.1, Undesirable Neighboring Uses, shows adjacencies that are incompatible and lists and quantifies the likely objections to the use as a neighbor.

TABLE 3.1 Undesirable neighboring uses

What makes these uses undesireable or incompatible neighbors?

	OBJECTION													
USE	commuity mores/ bias	excessive density/ over development	pedestrian traffic undesireable/ vagrant	low(er) property value	noise	refuse	aesthetics	odor	real or percieved physical danger	scale of enterprize	crime or percieved crime attraction	excessive or insufficient light	vehicular traffic attraction/ generation	Total Objections
funeral parlors					1					1		1	1	4
churches		1				1	1					1	1	5
police and fire stations*	1				1				1			1	1	5
advertising structures	1						1	1	1	1			1	6
animal agriculture					1	1	1	1		1			1	6
schools		1				1	1				1	1	1	6
animal processing					1	1	1	1		1		1	1	7
businesses office, service		1				1			1	1	1	1	1	7
clinics	1		1			1		1			1	1	1	7
graveyards			1	1				1		1	1	1	1	7
non-public utility structures*				1	1		1	1	1	1			1	7
parkland			1	1		1			1		1	1	1	7
public utility structures and radio towers*				1	1		1	1	1	1			1	7
used car sales		1						1	1	1	1	1	1	7
vehicle and machine service stations							1	1	1	1	1	1	1	7
hospitals		1	1		1	1				1	1	1	1	8
retail		1				1	1		1	1	1	1	1	8
sex businesses	1		1				1	1	1	1	1	1		8
threaters / cinemas			1			1	1		1	1	1	1	1	8
airport			1	1	1		1	1	1		1	1	1	9
light industry		1			1	1	1	1	1		1	1	1	9
parking lots			1	1		1		1	1	1	1	1	1	9
restaraunts			1		1	1	1		1	1	1	1	1	9
social and government service offices		1	1		1	1		1		1	1	1	1	9
wagering establishment	1	1	1					1	1	1	1	1	1	9
warehouse,storage		1		1	1	1		1	1	1	1	1		9
distribution				1	1	1	1	1	1	1	1	1	1	10
incarceration and inmate facilities	1	1		1		1	1		1	1	1	1	1	10
parking structures		1	1	1	1		1		1	1	1	1	1	10
pools (swimming)				1	1	1	1	1	1	1	1	1	1	10
depots			1	1	1	1	1	1	1	1	1	1	1	11
gas stations			1	1	1	1	1	1	1	1	1	1	1	11
junk yards	1			1	1	1	1	1	1	1	1	1	1	11
waste management	1			1	1	1	1	1	1	1	1	1	1	11
heavy (smoke stack) industry	1	1		1	1	1	1	1	1	1	1	1	1	12
liquor businesses	1		1	1	1	1	1	1	1	1	1	1	1	12
public housing		1	1	1	1	1	1	1	1	1	1	1	1	12
bars	1	1	1	1	1	1	1	1	1	1	1	1	1	13

*Typically, these are exempt from mandated zoning.

Most governments serious about permitting PUD development have established statements of purpose and enforceable guidelines that may include development standards. These standards stipulate criteria critical to the design development that may include:

- Lot area

- Floor area
- Ratios of floor space to land area
- Area in which structure may be built ("buildable area")
- Open space
- Setback lines and minimum yards
- Building separations
- Height of structures

The developer may also be required to prove he has the means to execute and enforce the conditions of the rezoning commitment. He may have to show proof of financial ability in the form of a bond or other similar assurance. He may also have to demonstrate that he has an economic mechanism in place that can maintain any permitted common uses such as internal streets, lighting, sewerage etc. He must provide for the "operation and maintenance of all common facilities, including private streets jointly shared by such property owners." (Marion County Dwelling District Zoning Ordinance, http://www.indygov.org/dmd/zoning/keymap.htm)

Developers who fail to execute the agreed elements of the plan commitment in a timely way may lose their rezoning. In such a case, " the Commission may initiate an amendment to the zoning ordinance so that the land will be zoned into a category or categories which most nearly approximate its then existing use or such other zoning category or categories which its deems appropriate."(Ibid)

fastfacts

Zoning breaks comprehensive plans down into broad land use groups. Most of these groups are single-use by definition. Planned unit development (PUD) or development plan (DP) zoning differs from single use and is widely interpretive at the administrative level.

It makes some sense then to define compatible groups or single uses that can be mixed and provide for DP zoning by defined divisions. This allows flexibility, but also assures the public that incompatible new uses will not be inserted or that the density of the proposed development will be consistent with the comprehensive plan. The Denver Land Use and

TABLE 3.2 Land use categories and characteristics, based on the land uses assigned in Marion County, suggests some potentially compatible mixed uses in terms of adjacency within a neighborhood and / or sharing a common structure. They reflect the opinion of the author. (*Continued*)

The following is a list of land use categories and characteristics that apply to both developed and undeveloped parcels of property in Marion County. Next to the land use categories are the abbreviations, colors, and index numbers that identify them on the Comprehensive land Use Plan Map.

On black-and-white maps, a land use is identified by its abbreviation only. For example, the map abbreviation for Very Low Density Residential use is "VLD." The map abbreviation for Community Park is "CP." In addition to their land use category abbreviations, parks are also identified on the map by the abbreviation "E" for existing or "P" for proposed park.

Residential

Very Low Density (VLD) Color: Yellow Index No.: l

This land use is appropriate for areas that have extreme topography, that are conducive to estate development, or that are environmentally limited to very low densities. These areas may be unserved by sanitary sewers, or service may be infeasible. A Very Low Density land use designation includes a recommendation of 0-2 dwelling units per gross acre. Very Low Density use is often recommended adjacent to Urban Conservation areas as a means of protecting these sensitive areas.

Low Density (LD) Color: Orange Index No.: 2

The Low Density land use designation is appropriate for areas that do not have the physical constraints present in Very Low Density areas. The residential density level recommended for this category is 2-5 dwelling units per acre.

Medium Density (MD) Color: Brown Index No.: 3

Medium Density is the land use category with the highest density normally serviceable in suburban areas. The density level recommended for this category is 5-15 dwelling units per acre.

High Density (HD) Color: Dark Brown Index No.: 4

This residential land use designation is assigned to areas suited for development of more than 15 dwelling units per acre. The High Density land use category is appropriate only within relatively intense urban areas.

Commercial

Office Buffer (OB) Color: Pink IndexNo.: 5

This land use category is for low-intensity office uses, usually outside an integrated center. The following uses are representative of this category: medical services, insurance, real estate, financial and credit institutions, architectural and engineering firms, legal services, and other related professional services. Office Buffer recommends physical development that reflects residential characteristics and scale.

Office Center (OC) Color: Pink Index No.: 6

This category is appropriate for integrated office development that generally includes three or more buildings, approximately 100,000 square feet or more of total leasable office space, and an internal street and parking network. Office Centers are typically significant employment centers, and their activity is usually more intense than Office Buffer areas.

Commercial Cluster (CC) Color: Red Index No.: 7

The Commercial Cluster category is assigned to retail and service businesses that have historically developed independently of one another along roadways. This category recognizes some existing commercial strips, but additional "strip-type" non-"center" development is not encouraged.

TABLE 3.2 *(Continued)* Land use categories

Note on commercial retail centers (below): All of these shopping centers provide for integrated development of primarily retail businesses. Advantages of retail center development over cluster development include shared parking, fewer curb cuts along arterial roadways, fewer signs, and more uniform landscaping and design. This plan distinguishes among Neighborhood, Community, and Regional shopping centers.

Neighborhood Shopping Center (NSC) Color: Red Index No.: 8

Gross floor area	Up to 125,000 sq. ft.
Site acreage	5 to 15 acres
Service area radius	2 miles
Anchor	Grocery store, drug store
Location	Located on a collector near an arterial
Outlots	1 to 3

Note: These centers are usually developed to function as a unit on one parcel. Tenant mix usually includes several types of specialty stores. These centers should not include any establishment that would tend to regularly draw customers from outside the immediate neighborhood.

Community Shopping Center (CSC) Color: Red Index No.: 9

Gross floor area	From 125,000 sq. ft. up to 700,000 sq. ft.
Site acreage	15 to 40 acres
Service area radius	5 miles
Anchor	Large supermarket, discount store or department store
Location	Located on an arterial, usually close to another arterial
Outlots	4 to 6

Note: These centers are usually planned as single projects, although they may be subdivided with outlots for free-standing stores.

Regional Shopping Center (RSC) Color: Red Index No.: 10

Gross floor area	700,000 sq. ft. and up
Site acreage	40 to 120 acres
Service area radius	15 miles or more
Anchor	Three to five department or discount stores
Location	Located on a primary arterial close to or intersecting another primary arterial
Outlots	7 or more

Note: A Regional Shopping Center is a major enclosed shopping center with outlots and often includes a number of smaller specialty retail centers clustered around the central mall. All the centers together are considered the Regional Shopping Center.

Heavy Commercial (HC) Color: Red Index No.: 11

This land use category is designed for commercial uses characterized by extensive outdoor storage and display, such as mobile home sales or sales of heavy construction equipment. Heavy Commercial uses should not be located near residential areas.

Downtown Mixed Use (DMU) Color: Red Index No.: 12

This category includes a wide variety of uses at very high density or high intensity levels. It provides for hotels, apartments, retail trade, professional, governmental, sports, and personal services. It also includes significant public and semi-public uses. These uses are located in the Regional Center area, or central business district. Individual buildings that contain a mix of different land uses are not uncommon.

TABLE 3.2 *(Continued)* Land use categories

Industrial
Light Industrial (LI) Color: Light Purple Index No.: 13
This land use category is designed for those industries which conduct their entire operations within completely enclosed buildings. One purpose of this category is to buffer Heavy Industrial uses from less intensive uses. Light Industrial uses should create minimal impact upon adjacent properties.
Heavy Industrial (HI) Color: Dark Purple Index No.: 14
This land use category is designed for intensive industries characterized by smoke, noise, and outdoor storage. Such categories can be difficult, expensive, or impossible to eliminate or buffer, and may be a nuisance to adjacent nonindustrial properties.
Airport Related (AR) Color: Salmon
This category is for businesses and industries that require a location adjacent to or near the airport, that are beneficial to airport activity, and that depend on airport facilities for all or part of their business activities.
Parks
Neighborhood Park (NP) Color: Dark Green
This land use is designed to provide open space and facilities to satisfy the everyday recreation needs of the immediate neighborhood. These parks serve people within walking or bicycling distance. Typically, Neighborhood Parks are between 5 and 25 acres, although a site of at least 10 acres is preferable. Neighborhood Parks typically contain basketball and tennis courts, playground equipment, and sitting or picnicking areas.
Community Park (CP) Color: Dark Green
This category is designed to provide a major recreation area with organized programs oriented toward family and all-age-group recreation. The size should range between 25 and 100 acres, the park should serve between 10,000 and 50,000 people, and it should be no more than 15 minutes driving time from its intended users. Typical facilities include recreation centers, swimming pools, and picnic areas. Community Parks often combine intensive recreation facilities and natural areas for more passive activities. These parks should be centrally located with good access to several neighborhoods and junior or senior high schools.
Regional Park (RP) Color: Dark Green
This category provides for large parks ranging in size from 100 acres to several thousand acres. They are intended to serve a population within one hour's driving time. Typical facilities and activities include play areas, picnic areas, shelters, nature centers, and trails. Most Regional Parks contain rivers, lakes, or other natural features to provide the park users a natural retreat from the urban environment.
Linear Park (LP) Color: Dark Green
These are public park trails that can be located on or parallel to floodways, streams, parkways, wooded areas, and abandoned railroad rights-of-way or other public easements.
Special Uses Color: Grey
The main uses included in this category are colleges, universities, cemeteries, airports, military installations, hospitals, waste disposal plants, schools (except elementary schools), fire stations, and other public or semi-public facilities that serve the entire community rather than just the local neighborhood. These uses will be identified on the land use plan map by the following abbreviations and/or names:

TABLE 3.2 (*Continued*) Land use categories

Land Use	Map Notation
Hospital	H
Schools	
Senior High School	SH
Junior High/Middle School	JH
Private High School	PS
College or University	By name
Cemetery	C or by name
Significant Public Facility	By name
Fire Station	FS
Other	Public use or by name

Urban Conservation (UC) Color: Light Green

This category identifies and thus helps preserve the character of land possessing special environmental or valuable natural characteristics that requires careful attention with regard to development proposals. Steeply sloped areas, woodland areas, wetland areas, and areas with significant aquifer or other waterbody resources are all examples of this designation.

Source: Marion County Land Use Categories and Characteristics, Indianapolis — Marion County Comprehensive Plan (http://www.indygov.org/dmdplan/documents/adopted_lu_plans/comp_plan_91/appb/appb.html February 10, 2002)

Transportation Plan (by Calthorpe Associates with Fregonese Calthorpe Associates) implements a new type of zoning strategy. Instead of the traditional single use zoning, the plan recommends zones that group compatible uses into areas. These can be themed to create further identity for a neighborhood such as an UED (Urban Entertainment District) which would encourage a mix of cultural and entertainment uses with housing, service, parking and transit options. Sometimes these areas are even more specifically defined such as a "museum district" or a "sports corridor".

Overlay districts can be used to emphasize an area's historic character as in "wholesale district" or to encourage specific types of business development and retention such as "technology center" or "medical mile." Overlay districts may come with taxation incentives, and in the case of redevelopment, may be called enterprise zones or redevelopment districts.

Targeted capital improvements supported by the power to spend public funds may be used to catalyze or anchor complimentary development or redevelopment in an area.

The planning unit that manages capital assets for the city may also target certain areas for land acquisition if there is the need for land assembly for specific public projects or to create larger parcels attractive to developers. Property may be obtained through tax default agreements, negotiated, purchase, or where the public benefit can be demonstrated through eminent domain proceedings. Generally eminent domain is a last resort that drives up the cost of land and the expense of the sale. The proceeding itself can encumber timelines for redevelopment projects.

Targeted capital improvements supported by the power to spend public funds may be used to stimulate or anchor complimentary development or redevelopment in an area.

These may be infrastructure, or they may be actual buildings that house public uses. For example, a library, police station, and a firehouse were used to stem the blight at 42nd and College Avenue near my home. A struggling church occupies the fourth corner of the intersection. A youth center has developed facing the other façade of the library. The presence of these entities has reduced crime in a mixed income racially integrated neighborhood.

For example, Marion County (Indiana) lists the major zoning districts shown in Table 3.3.

These use groups are further articulated into divisions which define nuances of use and gradations from light to intense, clean to dirty, and simple to sophisticated development. Special cases are addressed under special use. Again referring to Marion County's ordinance, Table 3.4 shows the zoning divisions.

The land uses listed in the following table are examples of related uses to illustrate increasingly intense use. "Intensity" in this case is subjectively defined by the author, and is based on the extent to which the listed use generates or carries traffic, puts a burden on the land or infrastructure, increases constructed volume (Floor Area Ratio), and supports the living and economic activities of lesser or greater numbers of people, and the frequency (or constancy) with which the site is occupied. Lastly, the degree of objection to the use by residential neighbors was considered.

For example: Local streets are less intense than highway interchanges. A cemetery is used far less intensely than a landfill, because of the burden on the land and the objectionable nature of the traffic and use, relative to

TABLE 3.3 Index of major zoning districts - Marion County, Indiana

A	Airport
C	Commercial
CBD	Central Business
D	Dwelling
FW, FP	Flood Controls
HD	Hospital
HP	Historic Preservation
I	Industrial
SU	Special Use
PK	Park
UQ	University Quarter

TABLE 3.4 Zoning divisions - Marion County (*Continued*)

D-A	Dwelling Agriculture
D-S	Dwelling Suburban
D-1, D-2	Suburban areas with moderate topography
D-3, D-4	Medium and medium-high density single-family areas
D-5	Urban developed area
D-5II	Located in urban areas in which redevelopment efforts are ongoing or where infill housing is needed
D-6	Located in suburban areas. Low-density multifamily use
D-6II	Low-density multifamily use to be used as a transition between high-density and low-intensity uses
D-7	Medium-density multifamily located throughout the metropolitan areas and associated with primary traffic generators
D-9	Suburban high-rise apartments
D-10	Central and inner-city locations for high-density multifamily use
D-11	Mobile dwelling project district for high-density single-family use
D-12	Medium-high density two-family subdivisions with the intensity of single-family development
D-P	A planned unit development
	COMMERCIAL DISTRICTS
C-1	Office Buffer District
C-2	High Intensity Office-Apartment District
C-3	Neighborhood Commercial District
C-3C	Corridor Commercial
C-4	Community-Regional Commercial District
C-5	General Commercial District

TABLE 3.4 *(Continued)* Zoning Divisions - Marion County

	COMMERCIAL DISTRICTS
C-6	Thoroughfare Service District
C-7	High Intensity Commercial District
C-ID	Commercial-Industrial District
C-S	Special Commercial District
	CENTRAL BUSINESS DISTRICTS
CBD-1	Core activities of all types with a side variety of related land uses
CBD-2	Support uses for CBD-1 - less land use intensity than CBD-1
CBD-3	Exclusive off-apartment district around Memorial Plaza
CBD-S	A special primary district requiring Metropolitan Development Commission approval of all uses, site and development plans
	INDUSTRIAL DISTRICTS
I-1-S	Restricted Industrial Suburban District
I-2-S	Light Industrial Suburban District
I-3-S	Medium Industrial Suburban District
I-4-S	Heavy Industrial Suburban District
I-5-S	Heavy Industrial Suburban (Outside Storage) District
I-1-U	Restricted Industrial Urban District
I-2-U	Light Industrial Urban District
I-3-U	Medium Industrial Urban District
I-4-U	Heavy Industrial Urban District
I-5-U	Heavy Industrial Urban (Outside Storage) District
	SPECIAL USE DISTRICTS
SU-1	Churches
SU-2	Schools
SU-3	Golf Courses, Golf Driving Ranges
SU-5	Radio Receiving or Broadcasting Towers and Accessory Buildings
SU-6	Hospitals and Sanitariums
SU-7	Charitable and Philanthropic Institutions
SU-8	Correctional and Penal Institutions
SU-9	Buildings and Grounds Used by Any Department of Town, City, Township, County, State or Federal Government
SU-10	Cemeteries
SU-13	Sanitary Landfill
SU-16	Amusement parks and Swimming Pools Privately Owned and Open to Public Patronage
SU-18	Light and Power Substations

TABLE 3.4 (*Continued*) Zoning divisions - Marion County

	SPECIAL USE DISTRICTS
SU-20	Telephone Exchange Offices
SU-28	Petroleum Refineries and Petroleum Products
SU-34	a. Club Rooms b. Fraternal Rooms - Fraternity and Lodge c. Ballrooms - Public
SU-35	Telecommunication Receiving or Broadcasting Towers and Associated Accessory Buildings
SU-37	Library
SU-38	Community Center
SU-39	Water Tanks, Water Pumping Stations and Similar Structures Not Located on Buildings
SU-41	Sewage Disposal Plant
SU-42	Gas Utilities
SU-43	Power Transmission Lines
SU-44	Off-track Mutual Wagering Facilities, Licensed as Satellite Facilities under IC 4-31-5.5 (Off-Track Betting Facilities)
	AIRPORT DISTRICTS
"A"	Airport Special Use District - Permits Public municipal airports Airspace District (Secondary) - A secondary district which consists of Instrument and Non-Instrument Approach Surface Areas
	HISTORIC PRESERVATION DISTRICTS
HP-1	Historic Preservation District One
HP-2, HP-S	Historic Preservation District - Secondary
HOSPITAL DISTRICTS	
HD-1	Hospital District One
HD-2	Hospital District Two
	PARK DISTRICTS
PK-1	Park District One - Permits all sizes and ranges of public park land and facilities
PK-2	Park Perimeter - Special District Two - Assures that the area peripheral to public parks will be compatible and harmonious with park uses
	UNIVERSITY QUARTER DISTRICTS
UQ-1	University Quarter District One - Permits and facilitates the development, expansion, etc., of a major university complex or campus
UQ-2(B)	University Quarter District Two (Butler University) - Permits and facilitates the development, expansion, etc., of University-related group dwelling uses
	FLOOD CONTROL DISTRICTS
FW	Floodway - A secondary district designed to regulate development with floodway areas
FP	Floodway Fringe (Flood Plain) - A secondary district designed to regulate development within flood plain areas as above

the cemetery. A church is less intensely used than a school, because of the constancy with which the school is occupied relative to the church which may be occupied at peak capacity just a few hours per week and a school may be occupied at or near capacity at least 5 days each week. Different schools, generally defined by the age group served, may use up more or less land and generate the demand for greater or lesser parking and built volume per student. Hotel/motel use might be objectionable to most residential uses, but is compatible with many commercial and some industrial uses. These are not intended to be absolutes that fit each circumstance, but more a rule of thumb. Such groupings might still preserve incompatible uses from co-developing in the same area, but allow diverse uses within it. See Table 3.5. Larger communities might wish to further differentiate between areas based on the scale of operations or percent of nonresidential mix in neighborhoods.

There are several approaches to comprehensive planning. The first is the traditional model that primarily emphasizes single-use zoning and the segregation of living, working and other uses. The next is Smart Growth planning which is aimed at controlling growth and urban sprawl and reducing blight, with the essential beneficial outcomes being sustainable economy and environment. New Urbanism is an approach which divides land into districts no more than ½ to 1 mile in diameter, and promotes high density buildings, maximizes walk-ability, and encourages mixed uses and district (neighborhood) identity through defined urban forms and public spaces. New Urbanism is challenging to incorporate in existing urban and suburban areas. It can be complimentary toward Smart Growth Planning.

The Plan

"Today's designers of residential areas are increasingly influenced by the grid plans, narrow streets, intimate scale, and convenient shopping of nineteenth-century American towns"(Philip Langdon "A Good Place to Live", The Atlantic Monthly, March 1988)

New urbanism is based in large part on planning principles derived early in the development of planning as a profession. Frederick Law Olmsted, Jr. was arguably the father, or at least the intellectual leader of the American city planning movement at the turn of the twentieth century. Several of the key observations that were cornerstones of his philosophy are uncannily accurate, even today, and have been adopted to varying degree by planners, new-urbanists, and transportation planners.

TABLE 3.5 Land uses grouped by activity and arranged by intensity (*Continued*)

		INTENSITY SCALE	< Least Intense Most Intense>			< Least Intense Most Intense>		
			SUBSTANTIALLY PRESERVED LAND			MINIMAL DEVELOPMENT		
USE GROUP	Living / Learning Land Use	Cultural						
		Educational						
		Single Family Residential				Single Family Residential- ultra-low density, estate, exclusive	Single Family Residential- ultra-low density, ranch or farm	
		Multiple Family Residential						Multi- Family Residential- land conservation development
	Earning Land Use	Rural/ Agricultural	Land Preserve, Reserves	Scenic Land		Cultivated Crops, Orchards, Vineyards	Woodland, No Hunting	
		Industrial						
		Entertainment & Recreation	Tracks and trails- no motorized vehicles					
		Commercial						
	Communal or Public Land Use	Water	Wetlands, Swamps, Glades, Bogs and Reefs	Springs, Fountains and Water Features	Coastline, unimproved	Lakes, Bays & Harbors, Gulfs	Non-navigable Rivers, Streams, Creeks and Swales	Falls, Shoals, Tidal Pools, and other scenic features
		Transportation and Parking	Paths, walks and trails- no motorized vehicles			Surface Open, Short term, bicycle parking, horse hitching		
		Public Land	Protected Land and Preserved Properties			Gardens	Reservations	

TABLE 3.5 *(Continued)* Land uses grouped by activity and arranged by intensity

USE GROUP		INTENSITY SCALE	< Least Intense		Most Intense>		
			NEIGHBORHOOD DEVELOPMENT				
USE GROUP	Living / Learning Land Use	Cultural	Churches, mosques, temples etc.			Observatories	Galleries, Reading Rooms
		Educational	Daycare, Pre-School	Adult Learing Centers,Adult Day centers	Elementary School		
		Single Family Residential	Single Family Residential- low density, 1-2 story	Single Family Residential- medium density 1-2-1/2 story, narrow lots	Vacation Cottages		
		Multiple Family Residential	Duplexes, Quads,	Bed and Breakfast	Communes, Cloisters, Monestaries, Convents	Spa, Retreat Centers	Assisted Living
	Earning Land Use	Rural/ Agricultural	Livesotck Grazing	Greenhouses			
		Industrial	Zone Utiliites- clean				
		Entertainment & Recreation	Golf Courses,				
		Commercial	In-home service businesses				Small Scale Personal Service and Consulting Businesses
	Communal or Public Land Use	Water	Bridges, pedestrian	Docks& Piers- Rereational			
		Transportation and Parking	Redidential surface parking lot	Surface Open, Short term, small scale	Right-of-way- local		
		Public Land	Parks, Playlots, Pools, Commons etc.	Reservations	Libraries, Parks Buildings	Police, Fire and Paramamedic Stations	Arboritums, Aviaries, Greenhouses, Nature Centers

TABLE 3.5 *(Continued)* Land uses grouped by activity and arranged by intensity

		INTENSITY SCALE	< Least Intense Most Intense>							
			HIGH DENSITY LIVABLE-COMMERCIAL DEVELOPMENT							
USE GROUP	Living / Learning Land Use	Cultural	Cemetaries, Mausoleums, Funeral Homes	Embassies	Private Clubs, Reception Facilities	Ampitheaters	Outdoor Museums			
		Educational	Colleges and Universities, and Graduate Programs	Middle School	Residential Schools- boarding, military, handicapped	Training Centers	High School	Trade and Vocational Schools		
		Single Family Residential	Single Family Residential- high density Condominiums, Rowhouses, Zero Lot-line							
		Multiple Family Residential	Skilled Nursing Facilities, Hospices, Treatment Centers	Multifamily Apartments and Condominiums, lowrise	Apartments/ Condos	Multifamily Apartments and Condominiums, highrise	Halfway Houses, Supervised Residences, Orphanages	Dormitories, Fraternities, Sororities		
	Earning Land Use	Rural/ Agricultural	Grain Storage							
		Industrial	In-home retail or assembly shop	Light, clean, manufacturing, assembly, or shipping	Laboratories, testing, R & D, non-hazardous materials					
		Entertainment & Recreation	Dance and Martial Arts Studios	Gymns and sports cneters	Driving Ranges	Zoos				
		Commercial	Café, Coffee or Sandwhich shop- local draw	Retail, Convenience- Local	Office- low density, lowrise	Financial and Personal Services	Pubs and Bars, Local Draw	Immediate Care Clinics, Medical Offices	Consumer Fuel Stations, Service Stations, Carwashes	
	Communal or Public Land Use	Water	Coastline, Improved	Beaches, Riverwalks, Boardwalks, Piers	Docks& Piers and Walks-Commercial	Docks& Piers- Fishing				
		Transportation and Parking	Off-street Surface, Long Term, Park-n-Ride	Parking Structure, Long Term	Off-street Surface, Short Term, Shared Commercial Parking	Passenger Trolley and Rail Lines and sidings	Mass Transportation Stop	Right-of-way- collector, commercial	Right-of-way- intersection with light	Right-of-way- conduit, boulevard or parkway
		Public Land	Cemetaries, Crematories, and Mausoleums	Clinics, Medical Offices	Local or State Gov't Offices, Courts, and Legislative spaces	Military- administration and training				

TABLE 3.5 (*Continued*) Land uses grouped by activity and arranged by intensity

USE GROUP		INTENSITY SCALE	< Least Intense		Most Intense>		< Least Intense		Most Intense>	
			MEDIUM INDUSTRIAL, MARGINALLY HABITABLE				HEAVY INDUSTRIAL, MINIMALLY HABITABLE AREAS			
USE GROUP	Living / Learning Land Use	Cultural								
		Educational	Alternative Schools	Residential Schools-reform						
		Single Family Residential	Mobile Homes, Migrant Housing	Tent Cities, Squatters Areas			Tent Cities, Squatters Areas			
		Multiple Family Residential			Shelters		Hotel/ Motel lowrise, midrise			
	Earning Land Use	Rural/ Agricultural	Woodland, Hunting	Hatcheries & Fish Farming	Fur Farms, Furriers		Feedlots and Animal Processing	Logging, Milling	Livestock Feedlots and Animal Processing Structures	
		Industrial	Recycling Collection Center, Light Commercial Salvage	Medium, assembly manufacturing,or shipping. No smoke stacks.	Warehousing, Distribution	Laboratories, testing, R & D, hazardous materials	Utilities- smoke or heat generation	Heavy, raw materials, manufacturing, smoke stacks	Water and Waste Water Treatment Facilites	Waste management operations, Dumps, Landfills,
		Entertainment & Recreation	Tracks and Trails-off-road vehicles, horses, etc	Fairgrounds	Amusement Parks	Sex Businesses, Srtip Clubs				
		Commercial	Automotive and Machine Service and Rental	Personal and Small Business Storage	Automotive and Machine Sales and Leasing	Industrial Re-Fueling Stations, Consumer Fuel Stations, Service Stations, Carwashes				
	Communal or Public Land Use	Water	Bridges, vehicular	Navigable Rivers, and Creeks	Bridges, rail		Locks, straits	Docks & Piers-Industiral		
		Transportation and Parking	Vehicle Marshalling lots	Right-of-way-highway, limited access			Right-of-way-highway, interstate or toll	Right-of-way-highway, interchange	Airports, Mass-Transportation Depots	
		Public Land	Military-operations and martialling	Jails, Prisons, Asylums					Water and Waste Water Treatment Facilites	Dumps, Landfills,

TABLE 3.5 (*Continued*) Land uses grouped by activity and arranged by intensity

		INTENSITY SCALE	< Least Intense				Most Intense>
			CENTRAL BUSINESS DISTRICT OR ENTERTAINMENT DISTRICT				
USE GROUP	Living / Learning Land Use	Cultural	Museums	Theaters, Opera Houses, Concert Halls	Cinemas		
		Educational					
		Single Family Residential					
		Multiple Family Residential	Hotel/ Motel highrise				
	Earning Land Use	Rural/ Agricultural					
		Industrial					
		Entertainment & Recreation	Off-track Wagering	Stadiums, Arenas, Ball Parks			
		Commercial	Retail, - Regional Draw	Office- high density, High rise	Restaurants- Regional Draw	Convetion and Exhibition Centers, Visitor's Centers	Pubs and Bars, Night Clubs Regional Draw
	Communal or Public Land Use	Water					
		Transportation and Parking	Parking Structure, Short Term				
		Public Land	Hospitals, Clinics				

FIGURE 3.8 Gingerbread is used here to promote high-density housing. *Photo: Stephen Culbert*

Olmstead advocated a well thought-out master plan as the central tool in engineering the city towards a bright future, managed growth, and especially regional transportation. He stated, "The main framework of any city plan is the transportation system, including in that term the public ways, both of local and of general importance, the street railways, the rapid transit railways, where such exist, the long-distance railways with their terminals, and the facilities for water-borne traffic." He expressed the critical need for public adherence to the plan as the guiding document in permitting land use. "This laying out of main transportation lines is not a thing to be done quickly and once for all, but a matter for painstaking and patient study and unremitting attention, beginning with the preparation of a general tentative plan and then proceeding gradually but persistently to execution, modifying the general plan from time to time, whenever it can be shown that a change, in view of all facts, really makes the plan as a whole better for the interests of the community, but never permitting the plan to be disregarded or set aside in execution."

Olmstead held that government planners should not micromanage neighborhood development. This was the province of the residents and taxpayers. Olmstead felt planners should address the arteries, collectors and

FIGURE 3.9 Custom streetlights, paving, and furniture tie the redeveloped warehouse district to an expanding corporate campus. *Photo: Stephen Culbert*

feeders that provided access to mass transit hubs, but that local streets should be developed and maintained by the property owners at minimal standards that would permit their use. Logically, he maintained, the funding of rapid or mass transportation for the suburbs couldn't precede the development that will pay for it. The eventual existence of transportation lines would depend mainly upon whether provision had been made in advance for such lines in the lay-out of the city. The actual cost of providing service would ultimately prove whether mass transit was efficient enough compete with private transportation options and change the urban landscape forever.

Within neighborhoods, Olmstead did not believe that residents should be routinely expected to travel distances of more than ¼ mile, ½ mile at the outside, to conduct the routine business of living.

Perhaps somewhat patronizingly, Olmstead didn't believe women and children were capable of more. In Jane Jacob's classic of urban and social thought, *The Death And Life Of Great American Cities*, she discusses the effects wrought of the implementation of such attitudes in a chapter in that segregation of genders and ages was scheduled daily when all the men left the neighborhood, and created matriarchal culture because men's places of livelihood were largely removed from the neighborhood. Although this may be one area where Olmstead erred, it is certainly still indicative of many, largely suburban and edge city areas.

Discussing land use within urbanized areas, he saw local streets serving primarily utilitarian purposes and as essential to providing light and air in heavily urbanized areas. In allocating land for streets he suggested "about 30 percent." It was in allocating land for the arteries, collectors, feeders, and streets with tracks that his views differed most radically from the new urbanists and their "quiet streets." Olmstead was about efficiency, and the wider the street, the more volume, speed and types of traffic it could accommodate. The faster the traffic moved, the less dense residential areas could be. In his time, this was seen as a positive alternative to the squalor of narrow streets, high-density housing, and a lack of sanitation and utility alternatives.

Although electric communications were in their infancy in 1911, Olmstead saw transportation arteries as opportunities for fostering lines of communication. He said, "It is nobody's business at present, and it ought to be made somebody's business to provide for the main channels of intercommunication."

Olmstead regarded land set aside for public recreation as vital to any urban plan because it improved health and most especially aided in rearing and developing the next generation. His concerns in acquisition of public open space and parkland were quite pragmatic: "equitable distribution and cheapness". He demonstrated remarkable savvy in his understanding of real estate values and land acquisition. "Most pressing is the acquisition of such parks in regions that are rapidly being built up, for the obvious reason that the enormous jump in the value of property which takes place through the erection of buildings upon previously vacant land is generally followed by a period of comparatively slow rise or even of decline in value as the buildings depreciate. Delay is apt to add but little to the cost in a region where buildings must be torn down in any case to make a park, whereas it adds enormously to the cost in regions at the growing margin"

Olmstead's ideas on how much space to devote to recreational land began with areas for small children in well distributed plots, "but 100 ft. square may be of value for such use." They escalated towards set aside land for a fully integrated park with multiple activities at "20 acres if possible, ...for a "full-fledged recreation center." In describing the efficient use of recreational land recommended in all, "about 5 percent of the total area devoted to local parks, play grounds, and squares is a reasonable minimum standard at which to aim, and that more than 10 percent may be uneconomical."

Olmstead defined specific amenities in increasing order of elaborateness and cost. Consistent with his view that a master plan should evolve incrementally, he intended for parks to be developed and maintained as community esteem for healthy recreation and concomitant public resources permitted:

- Areas for the "playing of little children" in wading pools and sand piles
- "A few pleasant shaded walks and benches"
- "A branch public library with rooms for public uses such as lectures"
- "Areas for 'active games' including big field games and a running track"
- Game areas "both outdoors and under cover"
- Bathing facilities, some with swimming pools

In conceptual terms defined by Olmstead nearly a century ago, our future may be our past but for minor modifications.

(Frederick Law Olmsted, Jr., "The City Beautiful", The Builder 101, (July 7, 1911):15-17.; John W. Reps, Professor Emeritus, http://www.library.cornell.edu/Reps/DOCS/olmst_11.htm, June 10, 2002)

Urban Core

"One key component with the downtown core is the ability to have activity in it is that we need more people down there more of the time. And that's where housing is a very large co-initiative. We believe that without housing, the rest of this cannot succeed. You basically get an empty downtown at night." (David Nieh)

The Downtown Master Plan

District plans are common in most jurisdictions. The most frequently cited district plan is the CBD (Central Business District). Because the CBD is nearly always the most intensively cultivated real estate in the jurisdiction, and a common use area for citizens and businesses from other districts, careful planning is essential.

Compassion for the poor and disenfranchised is no longer sufficient to fuel an interest in bolstering the economies of cities with economic subsidy, due to the anti-welfare wars waged (chiefly by Republicans) in the 1990's. There are now more Americans living in suburbs and edge cities than in major cities or rural areas. The force of the political will and self-interest (popular will) has shifted to the suburbs. It requires demonstrations of enlightened self-interest to motivate suburbanites to invest in regional government coalitions. In studies of correlations, the gap between the per capita tax base in the city and the suburbs as a proportion has been used to measure economic health. The closer this ratio is to one, the less disparity there is between city and suburb and the greater potential for economic growth. (Larry Ledebur and William Barnes, Metropolitan Disparities and Economic Growth. Washington D.C: National League of Cities, 1992)

Critical density and diversity are attributed to cities and particularly to central business districts. Traditionally, specialization has been possible in the CBD because it draws clientele from all the surrounding hinterlands. Dynamic proximity permits a level of sophistication to develop in the CBD which is more difficult in the suburbs.

Suburbs are now replacing many functions traditionally found in central business districts. For example suburban cities often promote their

FIGURE 3.10 New old houses create a traditional walkable street. *Photo: Stephen Culbert*

own central business districts, clean industries, and even sponsor tourist bureaus, symphonies, museums, and nature centers.

Density and dynamic proximity may not be the keys to survival and growth in the CBD. The keys may be diversity, specialization, innovation, and early adoption of new ideas that begin in the CBD and bleed out into the region.

Changes after 9-11-2001

Psychic changes will surely affect the way planning is approached in this country after our national loss of innocence regarding terrorism in America. In reference to this subject, Kathryn Schultz has stated, "Our sanitation systems, our street patterns, the materials we build with, and the codes we build by have all been shaped by health threats: cholera, yellow fever, industrial waste, fire, earthquakes. But some of the most pressing contemporary health concerns in the United States — heart disease, cancer, diabetes, obesity, asthma, depression — are all too often dismissed by planners as irrelevant."

"We need to capitalize on all of those forces as we try to imagine how America will rebuild in the aftermath of the attacks. We need to remember that problems are not more grave because they are more novel; that crises we inflict on ourselves are not more threatening than those that originate outside our borders; that needless sickness and death are not any less heartbreaking when they are less newsworthy; that public works are not less appropriate when they are directed towards long-term planning than immediate emergencies." ("America after 9-11-01" by Kathryn Schulz for Gristmagazine.com. A version of this article was published in the Detroit Free Press on August 1, 2000.)

Surely, such planning efforts will place a greater burden on public infrastructure and cause owners of other soft targets to assert some added physical measure of safety in planning and design. It may mean site hardening or it may mean surveillance or restricted access on new and existing sites.

Transit Oriented Plans

Peter Calthorpe, who practices chiefly in California, has promoted a pattern of development based on transportation hubs acting as nodes about which industries develop. Within these communities are places to work and live for people at all strata within that industry, and the basic life services such as groceries, healthcare, parks and gyms. The intent is to make the bulk of life's activities walkable.

It's difficult to impose such a structure within existing communities. And such communities may lack the critical mass to allow sufficient differentiation for the community to thrive long term without co-development. The very fact that this experiment is being applied to existing communities, like Palo Alto, may allow the communities to succeed because of existing differentiation and co-development that resists being displaced. Calthorpe's concept allows for a string-of-pearls, different industries at each node, all the pearls making up the necklace of the community. Perhaps this will also be a factor in the ultimate success of his planning concepts. Calthorpe's approach is being adopted in other megalopolises. Supporting feedback was provided by the American Public Transportation Association when it reported national transit use in the past five years has grown by 21%, while driving has increased only 11%. (APTA figures were released April 16, 2001 and quoted by 10000 friends of Pennsylvania on their site at http://www.10000friends.org/Web_Pages/News/News_Archives2001.htm, September 13, 2002)

Smart Growth Plans

Communities adopting Smart Growth comprehensive plans in Wisconsin, for example, are eligible for incentives from the state. Plans are evaluated by the state on the basis of nine elements:

- Issues & opportunities
- Housing
- Transportation
- Utilities & community facilities
- Agricultural, natural & cultural resources
- Economic development
- Intergovernmental cooperation
- Land use
- Implementation

(Smart Growth For Wisconsin http://www.mlui.org/projects/growthmanagement/sprawl/wisconson2.html, February 15, 2002)

They are expected to establish goals including:

- Promoting redevelopment
- Providing transportation choices

- Protecting natural areas and resources
- Encouraging the retention of farmland and forest
- Maximizing the efficiency of infrastructure and public services
- Preserving cultural, historic and archeological places
- Cooperating with units of government
- Forming or reinforcing community identity
- Providing variety of housing types, ownership, and price levels
- Assuring sufficient supply of land of the right types to meet market demand
- Promoting local economic development or stabilization
- Determining the balance between property rights and community needs
- Providing multi-modal, efficient and economical transportation system (ibid)

In a move that goes beyond mere incentives, cities with populations over 12,500 will soon be required to adopt traditional neighborhood ordinances.

New Urbanism, an Approach to Planning and Zoning

In an article "The Same Old Salad," planner Eric Cotton of Tampa, Florida wrote, "New Urbanism is another name for subdivision with different dressing on the same salad mix of homes with some commercial and office space mixed in." New Urbanism is already being misused and misrepresented by those who don't understand it, and by those who think of it as a style. An example is shown in Figure 3.11. It is also being used by the greedy to sell an inappropriate scale of site development where it could not otherwise exist. It's therefore important for community planners to play a key role in educating their communities as to what is and isn't part of the new urbanism, and how it fits into the long range comprehensive plan for development.

Not surprisingly, a great deal of the so-called New Urbanist development is neither. Physically, the new urbanism draws upon the patterns and traditional forms, and organizational hierarchies. Public spaces are planned with understandable shapes and defined edges. Often each open space is set aside for a specific public purpose: commerce, government, education, recreation etc. There are axial relationships between public spaces and open land. Housing may have a greater density, but most likely this

FIGURE 3.11 Marketed as New Urbanism, these residences were built on a farm field. *Photo: Stephen Culbert*

is achieved by surrounding or infilling the surrounding neighborhoods with relatively low density single family residences, using multifamily housing as a transition or buffer between the single-family areas and the public space. What makes Planned Unit Developments different than suburbia is that mixed uses are permitted in commercial environments, including housing and offices above retail spaces. Light commercial uses near industrial areas serve working populations and act as buffers to other areas.

The best-planned developments also take into account natural features, views and landforms, and existing transportation opportunities. These are not unique to the movement, but common to good public land use planning. The optimal mix can occur in a green field or in an existing neighborhood.

My friend, Bruce Anderson, and his family chose to live in Indianapolis' Meridian-Kessler neighborhood and describes his experience this way:

"I live in a new urban environment in an old urban neighborhood. I question whether new urbanism is an issue of how land is developed as much as it is a revitalization of the ideas and the integration of multiple uses into a tight circle that defines neighborhood, defines community. ...Indianapolis'

fastfacts

What makes Planned Unit Developments different than suburbia is that mixed uses are permitted in commercial environments, including housing and offices above retail spaces. Light commercial uses near industrial areas serve working populations and act as buffers to other areas.

greatest challenge is its educational system, not necessarily true of all major cities. I think all major cities suffer with the taxing issue, not necessarily an issue of how those communities are developed. I don't spend $8,000 a year to send my child to private school. I could, but I don't. I chose to live in the neighborhood I do because I can walk to a grocery store, I can walk to an ice cream shop, I can walk to Café Patachou which is certainly a defining community focus area of the Butler-Tarkington, Meridian-Kessler neighborhood. I am four blocks from a university. I am five minutes from the church, and there are three churches to pick from on one intersection. Four actually; two in one building.

There is a credible mix of poverty and wealth in Butler Tarkington and power and lack of power. My first weekend I was out and running around in the neighborhood, I had the pleasure of passing [former] Governor Orr walking his dog down the sidewalk, going down to an area where people probably ride the buses up into work and probably don't make more than three bucks an hour. I think new urbanism recognizes the value of smaller definition of what a city is. And the concept of busting up zoning is absolutely what is necessary to make our cities work. Suburban communities really do struggle to work. And I grew up in a ring development. And it's because you have to travel. You are absolutely dependent on a vehicle to do anything and I put up with a lot of crap fixing up an older home to have the advantage of not having to drive everywhere I want to go. I think it's very powerful. I think if the community works and respects each other – it's a wonderful place to live, but what make Butler Tarkington and Meridian Kessler work are the five private educational institutional institutions."

New urbanism largely deals with the quality of life in edge cities and suburbs. These new urban developments are more utopian than urban in nature and construct. As a result, developers seek greenfields where they can be established to avoid the messy mechanisms of existing political structure, infrastructure, industries and distribution.

fastfacts

New urbanism largely deals with the quality of life in edge cities and suburbs. These new urban developments are more utopian than urban in nature. As a result, developers seek greenfields where they can be established to avoid the messy mechanisms of existing political structure, infrastructure, industries, and distribution.

When a community abandons industry and distribution, urban form will seek a new shape that reflects the nature of the economy that drives it, and the results is low-density convenience-driven suburbia. To exclude industry and distribution from the economic development of a community is to undermine its longevity, diversification, and access to markets.

The form of the house, or rather, housing, will dictate the look of a community. Carl Feiss wrote, "Minor buildings, in the aggregate, create the urban scene. They are the body of any city." (Moe and Wilkie) The house is the construction industry's most essential unit, just as the family is the basic social unit within most cultures. Residential construction comprises two-thirds to three-quarters of all construction area and construction dollars. Whether the homes are look-alikes, or reprise the Stone Age, the Jetsons, traditional Colonial America or something else is more a fashion statement, and market driven. New commercial buildings serving the community tend follow the tone set by residential construction, either for better marketing or because the community requires it.

The new urbanism tends to emulate traditional architectural styles, however this is intrinsically a matter of marketing. What the new urbanists market of essential difference is a mix of compatible uses, and such a mix is independent of style so long as the scale and rhythm of the mix of styles and uses is maintained in a consistent way.

To quote architect Bruce Anderson again, "I think the reason it's traditional has nothing to do with the fact that it's new urbanism. I think the fact that it's traditional, or, if you will classical, which is really what it is, lies in the fact of marketing, marketability. They are simply copying that which they wanted to reflect. There are very few modern design communities in the United States that are successful from a business venture, from an economic standpoint. They exist all over the place in Europe, but they don't necessarily exist here. So when you are looking at something you want to emulate, you'll emulate that which is successful, not that which is not ...I do think that the marketing decision has very little to do with architecture... new urbanism is just simply urbanism rediscovering itself. You can't stop growth."

This is not to say that new greenfield communities should not draw upon successful models whether past or present. Indeed they should. One should

> The new urbanism tends to emulate traditional architectural styles, however this is intrinsically a matter of marketing. What the new urbanists market of essential difference is a mix of compatible uses, and such a mix is independent of style so long as the scale and rhythm is maintained in a consistent way.

FIGURE 3.12 These mid-20th Century homes are just two blocks from a thriving commercial/residential district. New Urbanism emulates such neighborhoods. *Photo: Stephen Culbert*

not forget, however, that many of these so called successful models are derived from civilizations that were the most segregated, most hierarchical in the history of humanity. Often the best inventions are actually innovations, developments of or refinements of existing patterns and processes. Architects and planners should not stop thinking and analyzing the built environment because successful patterns exist.

Speaking of the contrast between new urbanism, preservationist colleague Troy Thompson stated, "…One of the things that is happening in preservation in general right now is the experts have been pushed out. It is being run by neighborhood groups, and I think, to the detriment of preservation. I think there is a role for the expert. And that again is very much a part of the American attitude, being very much anti-expert, anti-idealism, anti anything except the mass opinion, and I think the mass opinion just because it is mass does not make it right. And that's something that is starting to be addressed in preservation in unique ways even in the United States… going back to [this] point, [are] preservation and traditional architecture, friend or foe? I would argue that they are foes. That they do not serve one another. That they actually compete with one another in a very American market-driven way."

The developer of the McNamara Train Shed property, Figure 3.13 and Figure 3.14, wished to tear down the historic train shed that sits along the rails to trails greenway on a lot wooded with mature trees. The property had been grandfathered in light commercial use. The existing building was adjacent to medium density apartments to the north and south (15-20 units per acre.) One-story single-family residences (about 6-8 units

FIGURE 3.13 McNamara Train Shed looking from the East. *Photo: Stephen Culbert*

FIGURE 3.14 McNamara Train Shed looking from the Northwest.
Photo: Stephen Culbert

per acre) were buffered from the shed building by the wooded area of the lot on the west and a wide manicured lawn on the east. Using "new urbanism" as a vehicle to push for rezoning as a PUD on roughly a 4-acre site, the developer intended to build a mixed-use development with a density equivalent to roughly 60 housing units per acre. It also inserted a higher level of commercial use, including facilities that would attract traffic from outside the neighborhood. The new development would have severely eroded existing buffers and edge to the commercial development. The neighbors, citing the district plan, were successful in persuading the plan commission to reject the petition, but not without first engaging in considerable political fireworks. After observing the process of this particular case, it was evident to me that the developer's proposal for the site generated such a clamor because it was out of scale and character with the existing adjacent development.

Kunstler

Kunstler is an advocate of slow planned growth into walkable orderly communities. He speaks with admiration of communities like Seaside whose planning forms and materials evoke the planning that occurred during the City Beautiful Period. He is a strong advocate for relinquishing dependence on the automobile, in particular. Best known for his widely read *Geography of Nowhere* (New York: Touchstone Books, Reprint edition, July 1994) which outlines the history of blight and simulacra in America, his latest work, *Home From Nowhere: Remaking Our Everyday World For The 21st Century* (New York: Touchstone Books, March 1998) offers a neo-traditionalist prescription for how to rebuild our cities to make them places worth coming home to.

Katz

Peter Katz is director of the Congress for the New Urbanism which outlines the principles of the New Urbanist Movement. The New Urbanist Movement is catching on in midsize communities. Katz's work has particularly influenced planning in the Midwest.

Katz's home state, Michigan, has recently called for the adoption of Hannover Principles. Residents in Grand Rapids now recognize that their daily lives are interconnected with nature. In statements to a committee that is rewriting the city's outdated master plan, citizens insisted that their community grow in a way that simultaneously improves the environment and strengthens the local economy. The committee's vice-chairman responded by recommending that Grand Rapids adopt the Hannover Principles as the foundation of its work. (Guy, Andrew, "Better By Design, Grand Rapids Embraces New Planning Principles", Michigan Land Use Institute, July 11, 2001 http://www.mlui.org/projects/growthmanagement/sprawl/guy-bydesign.asp)

William McDonough and Michael Braungart

William McDonough (former dean of the University of Virginia School of Architecture) and Michael Braungart wrote the Hannover Principles in 1992. The principles served as the design mission statement for the 2000 World's Fair in Hannover, Germany. The principles became one of the best-known and earliest "manifestos" of sustainable design principles. They particularly emphasize the interrelationship of human with the natural and built environment as ecology. They challenge people to seek ways to tread lightly and humbly on the earth.

Given their concise arrangement, they have since been adopted or referenced by a range of government units, agencies, organizations, designers, and planners. They affect the mission and ethics of governments in areas that extend beyond design and recycling. The Environmental Protection Agency's "7 Principles" stem from the Hannover Principles. An abbreviated version of The Hannover Principles is printed below:

- Insist on rights of humanity and nature to co-exist
- Recognize interdependence
- Respect relationships between spirit and matter
- Accept responsibility for the consequences of design
- Create safe objects of long-term value
- Eliminate the concept of waste (waste = food)
- Rely on natural energy flows

- Understand the limitations of design
- Seek constant improvement by the sharing of knowledge

(McDonough, William, "Hannover Principles Design for Sustainability for the City of Hannover, Germany", New York: 1992, http://www.mcdonoughpartners.com/projects/p_hannover.html

Calthorpe

The Charter of The New Urbanism was formed by the agreement of 266 design and planning professionals in 1966 at the Congress of the New Urbanism. It articulates the essential articles of faith and understanding required for the edification of adherents to the New Urbanism. Implementing planning and design decisions rooted in the articles will foster humanist social re-engineering of the built environment at essentially three scales: 1) region 2) neighborhood, district corridor, 3) block, street, and building. (*Charter of The New Urbanism, Congress of the New Urbanism*, essays by Randall Arendt et al., edited by Michael Leccese and Kathleen McCormick, for McGraw-Hill Companies, 2000)

There are 27 articles of the charter. While most articles of the charter can be applied in renovation and rehabilitation projects, only those that particularly address rebuilding issues are cited below:

At the Regional and Metropolitan scale the charter states:

- Article 4: "Development patterns should not blur or eradicate the edges of the metropolis. Infill development within existing areas conserves environmental resources, economic investment, and social fabric while reclaiming marginal and abandoned areas. Metropolitan regions should develop strategies to encourage such infill development over peripheral expansion.
- Article 6: "Development and redevelopment of towns and cities should respect historical patterns, precedents and boundaries.

In discussing the rebuilding issues at the Neighborhood and neighborhood connections scale the charter asserts:

- Article 10: "The neighborhood, district and corridor are the essential elements of development and redevelopment in the metropolis. They form identifiable areas that encourage citizens to take responsibility for their maintenance and evolution."
- Article 17: "The economic health and harmonious evolution of neighborhoods, districts and corridors can be improved through graphic urban design codes that serve as predictable guides for change."

At the most Intimate scale addressed, the charter lists these:

- Article 20: "Individual architectural projects should be seamlessly linked to their surroundings. This issue transcends style."
- Article 21: "Revitalization of urban spaces depends on safety and security. The design of streets and buildings should reinforce safe environments, but not at the expense of accessibility and openness."
- Article 27: "Preservation and renewal of historic buildings, districts, and landscape affirm the continuity and evolution of urban society."

(Ibid.)

"Perhaps a lasting contribution of New Urbanism will be to rekindle interest in the purpose of that exists already. Today the American preservation movement has enjoyed far more success in reclaiming Historic environments-traditional neighborhoods, small-town main streets, at large historic downtown districts-than others have had in building facsimiles of them."(Richard Moe and Carter Wilkie, *Changing Places The Building Community In The Age Of Sprawl* published by Henry Holt and Company 115 West 18th Street N.Y., N.Y. 10011, 1997)

A theory in regional development identified as the Pedestrian Pocket scheme has been developed and popularized by Peter Calthorpe, a planner in San Francisco. Under the scheme, a series of pedestrian nodes are strung together by hubs of inter-modal public transportation. Economically, each pedestrian node serves the needs of a "sponsoring" business or industry sector by providing for the work environment and basic domestic and daily recreational needs of the population that serves the sector. Under this scenario, the population is grouped, not by race or economic status, but by common professional, industrial, or institutional interest. It's sort of a modern day company town concept, except that workers will be employed by a consortium of related businesses in the major industry or in basic support services. Reinforcing Calthorpe's approach, Alex Marshall states, "Bringing back the street, is not possible unless we bring back the forms of transportation that made it essential." Reversing the public ardor for the automobile may be all but impossible. And if it is, the new urbanism is fated to be nothing but an exercise in nostalgia.

Duany, Plater-Zybek

Seaside is an exercise in deliberate nostalgia, like the set from "The Truman Show" come to life. Co-developer Duany opined that, "The newest idea in planning is the nineteenth-century town... If learning from the past has been valuable at the scale of the individual house, why not try it at the scale of a small town? " (speaking to Florida developers)

FIGURE 3.15 Pacer Academy occupies a portion the former Union Station train shed. It is a public school magnet.

FIGURE 3.16 Pacer Academy street icon

"For at least two decades there has been a growing interest in "vernacular architecture"—commonplace buildings of the past, embodying folk wisdom about design and construction"

"There are many traditions for the designers of neo-traditional towns to draw on, and the choice of which heritage to use is influenced heavily by geography, climate, and other characteristics of the location."

"Duany and Plater-Zybek seek, and often get, the job of writing the codes; they are well aware that the person who draws up the codes usually wields more power than the architect who actually designs the buildings." (Philip Langdon "A Good Place to Live", The Atlantic Monthly, March 1988)

To that end Duany and Plater-Zyberk have worked with Doris Goldstein, a Jacksonville attorney, to develop town charters that encourage popular decision-making after the developer's work is mostly completed. Instead of lawyerly homeowners'-association documents, which usually make it hard for a suburban or resort development to do anything other than maintain the status quo, the documents drawn up by Goldstein allow people to face one another in town meetings and vote on whether to alter the community.

Dover, Correa, Kohl, Cockshutt, Valle

In 1991 in Palm Beach County Florida, the firm Mark Schimmenti and Dover, Correa, Kohl, Cockshutt, Valle developed a Master plan and zoning code for the town of Riviera Beach. Although their plan incorporated several aspects of the tenets of the New Urbanist plans and forms, it did something masterfully. They consolidated the urban code into performance criteria that could be summarized graphically on a one page chart that referenced a small shaded map. Streets were first classified by use (traffic volume) or as waterfront. Then each street type was assigned allowable, required, and prohibited uses, such as lot coverage, building and use placement, height, area and volumetric parameters. The town was subdivided into several neighborhoods, each allowed to emphasize qualities desirable for that area—a condominium district, a hotel district, etc. Each neighborhood was allowed certain exceptions to the rules or had additional rules applied which would enhance its ability to develop in the desired direction.

While such a performance code might not be achievable in lower Manhattan, it might be just what's needed in many small towns and edge cities that lack the resources for a full time planning and development department, or in planned unit developments and New Urbanist towns.

Pattern Language

Patterns can be adapted into zoning requirements, however performance-based requirements yield greater differentiation than prescriptive requirements. Within his domain, the property owner can apply patterns in site design and layout. At the building scale, patterns can be applied to specific building details, plan relationships and construction methods. Most of the patterns are derived from historic cultures and the best of California mission architecture, but are written broadly enough that they have been applied in many cultures and on other continents.

In a most surprising context, I had occasion to actually apply a Pattern Language principle professionally. The Southern Division of the Navy (NAVFAC) actually required the use of a minimum of 10 client-selected patterns. The client awarded points in the selection process for identifying and applying additional patterns to a design-build proposal for a joint military facility. Although the project entailed a campus of facilities with diverse military uses, the effect of the patterns applied at the site and building scale introduced a network or connected interior and exterior spaces, discreetly zoned parking areas; hierarchical building forms and spatial arrangements; passive use of natural light, shade and ventilation; and introduced human scale at the building edges. After participating in a Pattern Language studio as an undergraduate, it was gratifying when our firm won the commission, based on our successful interpretation of the patterns with program requirements.

Critics of Pattern Language claim that use of the process yields look-alike structures. Used as performance requirements, nothing could be further from the truth! Study projects where the design is pleasing and human. Reverse engineer the designs with an eye toward seeking patterns, and you will find that many of the most talented designers understand patterns, if only subconsciously, and apply them frequently. Pattern seekers may identify other working patterns by closely observing what works in their cultural and regional environment.

It seems conceivable that land use and urban form might be might governed in a creative fashion that lists mandatory patterns and optional complimentary patterns that physically express qualities that are desired in land use. These could be taken from the pattern books or could be developed locally based on regional models. This is not far from the Planned Unit Development, or Development Plan zoning concept, but gives a little more control to the designer and developer's outcome to inhabitants, neighbors and governors of property being developed. It helps assure that PUD's will be good neighbors. This is especially important when the PUD is planned as urban infill where there are existing residential and business neighbors.

Legal Aspects of Zoning

Zoning exhibits legal aspects:

- Use districts
- Agricultural zones
- Residential zones
- Commercial and commercial/residential zones
- Factory/industrial zones
- General provisions
- Special regulations
- Sign regulations
- Nonconforming structures and uses
- Conditional uses
- Planned unit development

Transportation factors heavily into understanding compatible land use. Types of roads and streets are as follows in descending level of intensity of use:

- Freeway (interstate, toll roads)
- Expressway (limited access highway)
- Primary arterial street.
- Secondary arterial street
- Collector street
- Minor (local residential) street

While the climate of fear spun by the tragedies of September 11th, 2001 has not yet proved whether it will be a passing phase or deeply rooted in emotion in the American psyche, its implications on urban form should be observed. Already there are those who would abandon downtowns and certainly skyscrapers. Prior to the tragedy there were trends toward hotelling in office space planning and even more widely towards telecommuting and teleconferencing. These trends will likely to be exacerbated by the event, if only in the short term. Despite the unlikelihood of a repeat of the tragedy, such events cause people to contemplate the advantages of low-density development when considering the appropriate locations for and dispersal of assets, personnel, and housing with regard for their personal safety.

CHAPTER 4
DEVELOPMENT AND SUSTAINABILITY

NATURE OF DEVELOPMENT

Previously, development was defined as qualitative and expansion was defined as quantitative. Development and expansion each exist in both the physical environment and economic environment. Rarely does qualitative development occur without quantitative expansion to support it. To support and sustain developmental growth in a community, development must be multilateral and multi-modal as in Figure 4.1 and Figure 4.2. The most effective development is also proactive. Gifts or subsidies may be required to initiate or stimulate re-development, but they generally should not be maintained lest they create an entitlement trap. This means that communities must be attractive to residents and businesses seeking a location and they must be sufficiently diverse and complex to retain them and support their growth. Communities must actively seek a variety of development and redevelopment opportunities, for monoculture is its own trap.

How Do Communities And Neighborhoods Market Themselves?

Planners and redevelopers need to seek out a diverse mixture of businesses and other entities that will provide economic stability to the community. It is important for strategists to understand the kinds of questions the prospective businesses will be asking. These will vary in importance and applicability with the type of business and the scale of operation.

FIGURE 4.1 The first catalyst project on College Avenue at 42nd Street

FIGURE 4.2 The catalyzing projects on College Avenue sparked development of the Kaleidoscope Youth Center on 42nd which reclaimed an old school.

Here are a few of the key questions asked by prospective new businesses:

Transportation and Access

- What elements to support the business and its market are available within a 500-600 mile radius?
- Where are the sources or delivery points for raw materials and value-added materials?
- Are there multiple sources?
- Can they be delivered in multiple modes of transportation?
- What are transportation costs?
- What modes of transportation are readily available?
- Is the city a delivery hub for an air freight carrier?
- Is it a passenger transportation hub? Are there private airports available?
- Is it on a waterway?
- Is it on a rail line?
- Is it on an interstate interchange or principal highway?
- How often will weather delay deliveries or work progress?
- Is there an available site along the commuter rail line?*
- If you don't have an empty site along the rail line, is there a building we can rehabilitate?*
- Is there a shuttle bus running from the rail station to my prospective front door?*
- How is the commuter bus service in that area? *
- Do you have express lanes on your interstate to make sure buses bring employees to my building on time?" *

(*These questions quoted from Plants Sites & Parks Magazine Reed Business Information — Clint Johnson - 01/16/03 cited in ULI's Commercial Real Estate News Roundup: February 2003)

Real Estate

- What is the absorption rate of industrial space?
- What is the absorption rate of office space?
- What is the absorption rate of warehouse and distribution space?

- Is there existing space available?
- How close are these elements to one another?
- What is the cost of land or a building?
- How much of the workforce needs to be at one location on a regular basis?

Workforce & Education

- Is there an existing workforce trained or trainable for the new business?
- How hungry are they?
- Are they unionized?
- What will the costs of wages, benefits, and unemployment taxes be?
- What opportunity is there for useful and critical incidental interaction between competitors' employees?
- How are the schools perceived?
- "What are the local SAT scores?" is one of the first questions asked to benchmark a community.

Business Climate

- What opportunity is there to form symbiotic business coalitions and alliances?
- Are there available start-ups and small businesses that can be relied on to outsource portions of the work, allowing focus on the core business?
- How well does the region support these businesses?
- How much of the work force can telecommute or travel?
- Is public transportation available for the workforce?

Quality of Life

- What quality of life does the city offer the workforce, especially the portion that will be transferring to the new location?
- What are the crime statistics?
- What is the cost of living?
- What social and entertainment amenities are available?
- How stable are the neighborhoods?
- How good are inter-ethnic relations?

In the process of benchmarking, business owners ask, "How do the answers to these questions compare to our current business location?

How do these compare with other prospective locations?" They seek to quantify the answers so that qualities can be compared and analyzed. Sometimes they seek the assistance of a relocation consultant. Given the answers to these questions, is it any wonder that the Silicon Valley in California has enjoyed such tremendous growth in business in the last two decades?

David Nieh states, "The [redevelopment] Agency woos and courts with public outreach. The public outreach is local as well as more regional or national. For example, working with Palladium, obviously they are a national developer. And then on the other side of the spectrum, we have small business owners for example that will come to us and say that we want to improve our façade, or that we have masonry, brick or block that in California, because it is in the earthquake zone, their buildings are falling apart and they are not reinforced. So we work with them and there are grants on both things to kind of help them physically fix up their businesses. San Jose seeks to optimize these factors…For example, we have the greatest maximum tax base, it may not be the optimum tax base in terms of its sustainability... you can live in a place that has great manufacturing and does all these types of things, but you can't go get a haircut or get something dry cleaned, then that's a big problem if you can have basic services to serve the population. So that's the balance that needs to be gained so that cities are sustainable and will continue to flourish so that we don't get blight back. These are some of the lessons learned from redevelopment especially from the 60's and 70's where they just wiped out whole blocks because that kind of the planning philosophy and theories back then."

Courting Development

Here are other ways that cities court development. Cities can develop globalization plans to make the city user-friendly to foreign visitors:

- Infrastructure improvements including multilingual signs
- Maps
- International symbols
- Metrication
- Currency exchange sites
- Hiring multilingual staff to provide city services, law enforcement, and education and encouraging business to do likewise
- Courting information-based businesses

Focusing on workforce development is done largely through public schools, libraries, and state worker education programs. Improving and altering the business climate occurs through several vehicles:

- Coalitions
- Incentives
- Public/private partnerships used to spur urban reinvestment
- Anchor projects that draw in related businesses and restore health to a district
- Related businesses and industries that locate people near each other

Eighty percent of business growth comes from retaining and expanding existing businesses rather than attracting new ones. Cities need to foster quid pro quo relationships with major businesses, while still maintaining public safety and security. Governments can streamline regulatory processes and oversight.

Incentives are a part of the City of Austin's SMART Growth program. Projects are evaluated against criteria that include pedestrian-friendly design, street-level commerce, landscaping, and access for people with disabilities. Bonus points are available to owners if they incorporate local businesses into their development plans. (ULI's Commercial Real Estate News Roundup: August 2002) An example of catalytic anchor development sponsored though public/private partnership is The Navy Yard near the southeast neighborhood of Washington D.C. Initially slated to absorb only Navy operations and 5,000 federal workers moving in from Virginia, the project has expanded. Noting the location just a mile from the seat of the U.S. Congress, with significant frontage on the Anacostia River, District of Columbia Mayor Anthony Williams saw this site as an opportunity to provide additional benefit to Washington, D.C.'s economy.

In a workshop led by The Center for Urban Development, a planning agreement between the district and the GSA(General Services Administration) defined a vision of the river edge as an appealing public space connected to the city with walkable streets, squares, and public waterfront access. Through collaboration with the GSA, this move is attracting defense contractors and a mix of urban scale-residential, light commercial, and incidental services in adjacent development.

By fostering Sister-City relationships, it is amazing what development concepts can be learned from each other. Indianapolis has a sister city in Scarborough, Ontario, an edge city near Toronto. Scarborough's UED's (Urban Entertainment Districts), Figure 4.3, draw people to the center

FIGURE 4.3 Spaghetti factory was one of the first tenants in the Urban Entertainment District established in the old wholesale district during the mid-80's revival of the CBD.

of town and reinforce the doughnut. Sports, shopping, culture, food, bars, and other entertainment venues keep people connected to the center of the city.

Market Forecasting in Retail Development

The half-life of any retail format is only about 10 years. In the late 1990's the trend shifted away from expansion by large discounters (big box) development to mid-size centers with entertainment complexes. Specialty retailers are in a consolidation mode.

The absorption rate for speculative retail space is cyclical and generally runs in decade-long intervals between oversupply and undersupply. It appears that currently there is an oversupply of available space and consequently many spaces are not leased. Despite this, many mid-size and super-size malls are still making money and spending money on development.

The differences between the successful malls and the under-subscribed malls continue to polarize. See Figure 4.4. Much of a mall's success depends on whether the mall is focused on a market of haves, have-nots, or wannabes.

Market indicators used to measure the potential sales per square foot correlate well with the average rate of personal debt, the rate of personal bankruptcy, the ratio and actual value of per capita disposable income, and the rate of consumer spending. Sources such as Construction Market Data, Engineering News Record, and the Census Bureau and the Bureau of Economic Statistics can provide customized statistics for evaluation. ("Outlook for Stores and Shopping Centers, Retail Construction Gets Back on Track" by Ralph Gentile for Engineering News Record http://www.enr.com/magstore/Download/cmfsus9r.pdf 3/25/2002 1:15 PM)

The absorption rate for speculative retail space is cyclical and generally runs in decade-long intervals between oversupply and undersupply.

FIGURE 4.4 One by one mall tenants are turning a second face toward the parking lot. This improves business for the stores because they can extend their hours of operation if they choose. It also allows the mall to compete more effectively with many nearby strip centers.

FIGURE 4.5 Icons mark a secondary entrance at the re-tooled Glendale mall. Malls that increase the number of entrances and exits benefit by increased traffic.

It is important to understand the target market. Re-use of existing space, even retail space, can be shaped to a new paradigm. Since retail is so transitory, recovering the shell and infrastructure costs can be significant in meeting the re-imaging challenge essential to the business. At the low end, new upgrades for malls start with an exterior facelift, a few new finishes, and interior icons. More progressive conversions involve re-skinning the exterior and incorporating diverse mixed uses. Creating two-faced malls, integrating mass transit options and other non-retail (but regularly used) enterprises shifts the mall toward the paradigm of New Urbanism.

Traditional mall mixes include merchandise like clothing, books, music, jewelry, shoes and gifts. Offering higher education, public libraries, and service businesses such as medical offices, banks, brokers, shipping, and a hair salon diversifies the mix. Mixing in hardware stores, drug stores, and grocery stores may also generate advantages for the mall by offering convenient choices for the shopper. See Figure 4.6.

American culture is known for its adeptness at multi-tasking and passion for convenience, Figure 4.7. Since shopping often pairs well with entertainment and recreation, co-locating a variety of restaurants and bars,

FIGURE 4.6 Converted space in a mall's only grocery store

theaters, and cinemas are pretty much a given. Not all shoppers are looking for fast food. Some diners are looking for quick shopping options.

Incorporating other forms of recreation that don't require significant structural alterations for the developer can result in moderate-sized tenancies like dance schools, karate, gymnastics studios, and fitness centers drawing shoppers to the adjacent retail. Providing other conveniences that support the shopper, like child-care, laundry, and vehicle services on site enhances the local traffic drawn to the mall and the length of time the shopper will spend in the vicinity.

"The use of the name 'lifestyle center' is critical in all of this, because it gets to the point of people using where they shop to define who they are," said Geoffrey Booth, director of retail development at the Urban Land Institute in Washington, D.C. "The real estate industry has to provide a product that is in tune with what the demographic is demanding." Many Americans, after traveling abroad and seeing urban retail developments elsewhere, grew dissatisfied with conventional U.S. shopping centers. "Some call the trend toward lifestyle centers the 'Europe-ization' of the shopping experience," he said. "This started as an innovation, but it's now clearly a trend." ("Developers, Architects Design Projects to Provide

FIGURE 4.7 The mall's interior renovation included the addition of an upper concourse with access via a grand staircase, a glazed elevator (far left), and a 2nd set of elevators. The library is visible on the upper concourse.

Urban Comforts". KRTBN Knight-Ridder Tribune Business News: Tampa Tribune — Dave Simanoff -07/18/02 as reported in ULI's Commercial Real Estate News Roundup: August 2002).

One has to evaluate the potential rent generated by each of the various tenants to determine the allowable build-out cost that will make leasing a particular space profitable. This may require more detailed analysis and tracking than is typically required in a more homogenous setting.

Malls can be vertical, and not just in very high land value locations such as Trump Tower and Water Tower Place. Multi-level malls can be built at grade (and just above or below) in converted CBD high-rise and mid-rise structures. An example is shown in Figure 4.8. Depending on the size of the proposed enterprise, connectivity to other buildings at multiple levels may enhance traffic. This is more true in cold, rainy or otherwise severe climates.

FIGURE 4.8 A converted department store with upper level offices now houses the central business district's only full service grocery store.

For the elite customer, semi-private fashion-oriented mini-malls located near high-end office space can be tailored to suit shoppers' needs with by-appointment personal shopping. These may co-locate with related cosmetology, home fashion, and design service businesses.

Since Middle America enjoys the widespread use of machines like automobiles and cell phones, we're not likely to part with them for something less convenient. Walkable communities are increasingly an option and a choice, but by no means are they a panacea that will meet the needs of everyone.

fastfacts

Malls can be vertical, and not just in very high land value locations such as Trump Tower and Water Tower Place. Multi-level malls can be built at grade (and just above or below) in office and or residential space in converted CBD high-rise and mid-rise structures. Depending on the size of the proposed enterprise, connectivity to other buildings at multiple levels may enhance traffic. This is truer in cold, rainy or otherwise severe climates.

Re-development must plan for the continued use of automobiles in a way that allows drivers to feel safe. Parking must be affordable. Walking distances must be kept reasonable to the climate and the driver's physical abilities. When designing, consider what it's like to pull up in a handicapped van, unload, and then wheel the chair a quarter mile to shopping destinations, then have to trek back the same distance while towing your merchandise. Picture a parent with young children and baggage to carry. Envision the design architect who takes home large rolls of drawings, books of specifications, a laptop, gym bag, and an umbrella.

Parking facilities should be well distributed in a commercial (retail) district. Limiting their scale and buffering their presence will reduce the visual blight caused by too many half-full lots fronting the access streets. Where density and high land value generate the need for parking structures, providing retail and other commercial uses on the front of the structure will preserve the continuity of the street form and rhythm. Where parking lots are in the rear, a second façade should be established for entry directly from the lot. Allowing windows overlooking the lot, supplemented by entry and site lighting, will make lots perceptually, if not actually, safer.

Observations about mass transit are empirical. Very few people will opt for mass transportation given the affordable alternatives of an automobile commute or a reasonable walk. While some people on the train in Chicago or Philadelphia may be able to work, read, and even make calls during their commute, people on commuter trains from Brooklyn to Manhattan and from Georgetown to Catholic University during rush hour may not. There, wearing a Walkman might cause overcrowding in

fastfacts

Parking facilities should be well distributed in a commercial (retail) district. Limiting their scale and buffering their presence will reduce the visual blight caused by too many half-full lots fronting the access streets. Where density and high land value generate the need for parking structures, providing retail and other commercial uses on the front of the structure will preserve the continuity of the street form and rhythm. Where parking lots are in the rear, a second façade should be established for entry directly from the lot.

My observations about mass transit are empirical. Very few people will opt for mass transportation given the affordable alternatives of an auto commute or a reasonable walk.

the standing-room only cars. This is not intended to bash those cities. Now, picture yourself boarding the same train with the aforementioned items belonging to the design architect or a young parent.

Dorothy lived in Muncie, Indiana during the coldest winter on local record and worked on the campus two and a half miles from home. During the day she could catch a bus. After 6:00 P.M. she had to walk. The nearest grocery store was about a mile in the opposite direction from home. The trip was so inconvenient it took two canvas sacks, a backpack, and a paper grocery bag to make the trip as infrequently as possible. You don't want to get splashed from head to toe with icy water while lugging a load like this. It's very hard on the paper sack.

Moving to the desert, she lived in Tempe and worked in Phoenix. Getting less than ten miles from home to work took about two hours each way and included walking about two miles to and from stops. Going to a major mall in Phoenix required leaving very early in the day and making my trip as brief as possible in order not to miss the bus home. Now, picture the person in the wheelchair doing this through the desert. Working at the periphery of downtown Indianapolis when it still had trolleys (decorated busses) available at midday, a late lunch or appointment could leave you with a hearty unplanned walk back to the office. With only two trolleys on the route, so could an irregular interval or breakdown. Soon you stop planning errands downtown at lunchtime.

Visiting Montreal, some friends found themselves stranded at the wrong end of the line when they chose to visit a reggae club that was not downtown. The transit had stopped running. That night they accepted a ride from a stranger.

Mass transit options need to be convenient, connective, and swift. Transit should run seven days a week. Hours of operation for most lines need to extend sufficiently before and after regular hours of retail business operation to allow people to accomplish life basics like going to work, shopping, and returning home. On Fridays and Saturdays it should extend from UED's to the hinterlands at extended hours.

If a local mass transit system cannot provide that level of service at an agreeable price, it is destined to fail. Lacking collapse, it will become, through subsidy, a parasite on the community. Economic development must precede the transit development to assure sufficient patronage. See Figure 4.9. Compact neighborhoods will provide the opportunity to create the critical mass of riders per mile (or stop) to maintain a fiscally viable system. It can be risky not to provide adequate parking to support the re-development while the demand for transit builds.

Brownfield Redevelopment

Obsolete and abandoned industrial and military property with existing infrastructure, distribution facilities, access to transportation, land area, and high bay space can be returned to economic vitality by attracting businesses. There are community advantages to retaining and attracting heavy industry, despite the negative attention generated by potential pollution and traffic. Although finding new users with businesses similar to the ones they are replacing is challenging, doing so will maximize the advantage the business realizes in reuse of the existing facility and reemployment of the skilled workforce.

*Counties with 40 percent or more of workers working outside county of residence, 1990.
Source: Rural Economy Division, Economic Research Service, USDA, using data from the Bureau of the Census.

FIGURE 4.9 Commuter dependence (United States Census)

There are approximately 450,000 brownfield sites across the United States that are contaminated, unused, and often abandoned. In the last 10 years, state programs have successfully facilitated reuse of more than 40,000 sites. (Proceedings of Brownfields 2001, a meeting of the National Governors Association on September 24-26, 2001 in Chicago, Illinois accessed www.nga.org/center/topics/1,1188,D_374,00.html

The increased property tax base from the anchor businesses and from co-development of related industries and services is a great advantage. Also the rate of personal income growth increases due to manufacturing versus service jobs and the increased rate of (inner city) employment. Aesthetic and psychic benefits from brownfield revitalization and blight reduction will yield a decrease in crime because of the perception of habitation and decreased community need. This is particularly true with respect to property crimes.

fastfacts

Obsolete and abandoned industrial and military property can be returned to economic vitality by attracting businesses to industrial property with existing infrastructure, distribution facilities, access to transportation, land area, and high bay space. There are community advantages to retaining and attracting heavy industry, despite the negative attention generated by potential pollution and traffic. Although finding new users with businesses similar to the ones they are replacing is challenging, doing so will maximize the advantage the business realizes in reuse of the existing facility and reemployment of the skilled workforce.

Indemnification of the new owner for the ecological sins of the prior owner is more crucial than government-funded cleanup re-certification of the site in encouraging the sale of such properties. Usually with redevelopment of industrial properties, not all of the structure can reasonably be converted to fit the new set of program needs, but generally, significant areas and equipment can. Refer to Table 4.1. This is especially helpful to start-ups that need cheap space, albeit imperfect. They may phase out existing facility infrastructure incrementally as business (Governing and Congressional Quarterly, http://www.governing.com/, has articles on brownfield development.)

TABLE 4.1 Project comparison of brownfield redevelopment projects winning EPA awards, Years 2000-2001 (*Continued*)

Project Comparison of Brownfield Redevelopment Projects Winning EPA Awards, Years 2000-2001

Project length (years)	1.0	2.6	5.0	3.0	4.5	2.3	5.0	11.0	2.9
Year of Award	2000	2000	2000	2000	2000	2000	2000	2000	2000
TOTAL PROJECT COSTS (millions)	$1.00	$3.10	$4.20	$7.99	$15.10	$55.45	$61.50	$309.10	$310.00
TOTAL REMEDIATION COSTS (millions)	$0.65	$1.38	DND	$0.29	$1.30	$3.55	$11.50	$74.80	$2.00
REMEDIATION % of Total Cost	65.0%	44.5%	DND	3.6%	8.6%	6.4%	18.7%	24.2%	0.6%
Major Cost Elements	$650,000 - Environmental cleanup	Assessment $99,800	$4.2 million	$7.7 million	Armory $8.8 million	Housing - 49.7 million	Environmental - $10 million	Site remediation: $74.8 million	Total project cost - $310 million
	Total cost - $1.5 million	Remediation $824,000		$285,000 - Environmental costs (Study and consent order)	Open space land acquisition $2.9 million	Infrastructure - 0.7 million	Due diligence - $1.5 million	Breakdown of the remediation costs:	Due diligence/remediation cost - $2 million
		Demolition $460,000			Plant demolition $1.3 million	Pedestrian Bridge - 2.4 million	Refurbish Exterior - $10 million	Preliminary design investigations: $3.3 million	
		Infrastructure $1,740,000			Park $2.1 million	Environmental Investigation - 0.65 million	Refurbish Interior - $40 million	Remedial design studies and results: $3.3 million	
		New Facility $2,500,000			Roads $1.75 million	Environmental Remediation - 2.0 million	New Buildings & Infrastructure - $130 million	Remedial action: $50.0 million	
		Total Project Cost $5,623,800			River restoration $3.5 million includes Remediation $1.2 million			Site certification: $2.2 million	
								Operations & Maintenance: $2.1 million Groundwater/surface water investigations and studies: $11.4 million Federal and state regulatory oversight costs: $3 million Infrastructure costs: $47.1 million Costs of sale: $4.9 million Private sector development costs: $166.1 million Private sector land costs: $16.2 million	

TABLE 4.1 (*Continued*) Project comparison of brownfield redevelopment projects winning EPA awards, Years 2000-2001

	Average, Year 2000										
Project length (years)	**5.8**	8	8.5	12	6	2	9	6	8	9	4
Year of Award	**2000.0**	2001	2001	2001	2001	2001	2001	2001	2001	2001	2001
TOTAL PROJECT COSTS (millions)	**$85.27**	$2.19	$5.05	$19.25	$27.90	$32.00	$51.44	$104.80	$106.45	$133.70	$2,414.00
TOTAL REMEDIATION COSTS (millions)	**$11.93**	$0.89	$0.30	$1.25	$5.24	$5.00	$9.77	$4.80	$5.80	$23.50	$12.30
REMEDIATION % of Total Cost	**14.0%**	40.5%	5.9%	6.5%	18.8%	15.6%	19.0%	4.6%	5.4%	17.6%	0.5%
Major Cost Elements											
		Legal fees/staff costs (City of Astoria) - $60,000 Remediation/predevelopment (City of Astoria) - $225,000 Infrastructure/remediation (developer) - $600,000 Project costs (State of Oregon) - $1,300,000	Site investigation - $71,034 Asphalt cap construction - $40,000 Groundwater remediation - $12,235 Subsurface remediation - $176,000 Infrastructure - $4,750,000	Environmental due diligence/remediation - $1,250,000 Redevelopment/infrastructure - $18,000,000 (estimated)	Site remediation - $2,861,000 Demolition - $2,380,000 Development - $22,657,000	Demolition/site preparation - $5,000,000 Remediation – $6,000,000 New construction - $16,500,000 New equipment - $4,554,000	Site preparation - $3,770,000 Site acquisition - $3,000,000 Construction - $44,440,000 Remediation - $6,000,000 Infrastructure/public improvements - $4,000,000	Cleanup and demolition - $15,000,000 Environmental investigation - $1,200,000 Remediation - $3,600,000 Infrastructure/redevelopment - $100,000,000	Demolition and cleanup - $5,800,000 Total project costs - $106,450,000	Due diligence/predevelopment - $3,000,000 Landfill acquisition - $10,000,000 Remediation – $20,500,000 Taxes - $200,000/year Infrastructure - $100,000,000	Environmental due diligence - $300,000 Remediation - $12,000,000 Total project cost - $415,000,000 Future development - $2,000,000,000

State and local programs

Programs in five states (Maryland, Massachusetts, Michigan, New Jersey, and Pennsylvania) were cited as exemplary in a report by the National Governors Association (NGA) Center for Best Practices because of the extent to which they level the playing field, making brownfield projects competitive with greenfield projects. States recognize that for every dollar reinvested in economic redevelopment, at least $10 and sometimes at much as $100 in economic benefits to the community are generated. (Hirshorn, Joel, New Mission for Brownfields, National Governors Association, Natural Resources Policies Studies, 2000 www.nga.org/center/divisions/1,1188,C_ISSUE_BRIEF^D_306,00.html

Common denominators of success in these programs include:

- Public support for the program by the governors
- A regional view of brownfield project planning and selection in contrast to a project specific view of planning
- A paradigm shift at the highest levels of government. Sites are not viewed as liabilities so much as an economic development opportunities and a resource to be exploited in attracting new businesses. Michigan's legislation ties public funding of cleanup to redevelopment of the sites, and further supports redevelopment efforts through grants and loans to local agencies that hold the same standards.
- Interagency support for brownfield redevelopment. Although the state EPA may be the lead agency, support from the Departments of Commerce, Economic Development, Transportation, Health, and Building Services are often required. Massachusetts has created an Office For Brownfields Revitalization that offers assistance:
  - To sellers and communities to market sites, fund site assessments, find companies seeking new locations, and find aggressive state support for priority projects. Also to provide indemnification for parties that did not originate the contamination
  - To owners and buyers in the form of tax credits for cleanups in target areas
  - To developers to obtain financing, insurance, and consultant services. Also to develop public/private partnerships, facilitate work with local authorities and take advantage of municipal tax abatement.
  - To financiers in the form of loan support and insurance to limit loss on clean-up financing and even legal defense against third party claims when there is also a contemporaneous construction loan

- Incentives for developers and business to choose brownfield sites. States and localities may develop brownfield redevelopment zones, which, like enterprise zones, offer tax incentives to locate and develop within them. States may also target funds toward mitigation of contamination and protection of the watershed. For this reason, many have targeted funds for waterfront areas contaminated by shipping, shipbuilding or other heavy industry. New Jersey offers an Urban Tool Kit, a catalog of resources for cities, agencies and developers interested in pursuing brownfield redevelopment. New Jersey will also provide grants to local governments to acquire and dispose of orphaned sites.
- Reduced or limited liability for site redevelopers. Under old polluter-pay policies which sought deep pockets to cover the costs of remediation, any prior owner of the site could be held responsible for clean-up even if they had not created or exacerbated the harm. This policy resulted in many abandoned and orphaned sites and the spread of blight. States now have options where owners can establish themselves as "innocent parties" and get a level of indemnification. This allows sites to be cleared and reused.
- Reducing or eliminating barriers to redevelopment, so that the federal biases of the Superfund program and the protection of public health are the only ones that create challenges. Some states have entered into an unenforceable gentleman's agreement with the EPA that the agency will not enforce cleanup and penalties on target sites that have voluntarily engaged in clean-up efforts through the state programs.
- Programs to conduct site assessments at the state agency level when requested by property owners or community groups to protect public health. Agencies offer public education programs about the health effects of exposure to listed site materials. In Michigan, Baseline Environmental Assessments (BEA's) conducted on over 3,000 sites have been used to establish covenants with neighbors. The state will take on cleanup if BEA's have determined that health threats are imminent.

Clean-up requirements are tailored to the proposed new use(s) of the site and the protection of adjacent property and watersheds from further contamination. This is key to the redevelopment issue. Michigan has legislated "due care" provisions that prohibit the exacerbation of existing contamination, and mitigate undesirable exposures to property users and third parties. It contains reporting provisions to notify the state if contamination is migrating from the site.

Residential redevelopment carries a higher burden for cleanup than commercial use because of the likelihood that residents will have contact with the soil after redevelopment has occurred. Cleanup required for most commercial purposes will be less extensive and some states approach these on a risk-benefit basis, with the final risk analysis left to the developer. The land value of a site developed for commercial purposes will generally exceed the value if developed for housing. Given these facts, proposing commercial uses for redevelopment is economically more attractive to most site redevelopers, although some may add housing to the mix. Full cleanup of the site will free it from use restrictions.

To be sustainable, redevelopment must not only create wealth and jobs during the project development process, but also after the site is occupied. States like Maryland have tied brownfield redevelopment funds to a wide range of economic development incentives. Because the types of businesses attracted to such sites tend to be start-ups, they may need additional seed support to help them become well established. This support must necessarily be temporary, or it will instead become a subsidy that drains the economy rather than enhancing it. Economic developers can solicit businesses that create a strategic mix of related business to occupy these developments, and hopefully germinate proximity advantages for these businesses and co-development of other related businesses.

Pennsylvania's redevelopment initiative emphasizes incentives for government-sponsored land conservation planning and the development of greenways. Tracking new development to previously developed land is an offshoot of these priorities. The program offers cash incentives to municipalities and redevelopment agencies for posting brownfield sites available for development in a brownfield directory. The project is underpinned with various grants, loans, and tax abatements, but to further the goal of encouraging development in existing developed areas, the state offers infrastructure improvement grants to cities and redevelopment agencies that may be used in conjunction with other incentives. The state permits third party enforcement of buyer–seller agreements that address cleanup issues.

Methods

"The level of public scrutiny associated with redeveloping brownfield properties far exceeds the normal standard for development." (Property Purchase & Finance, Decision Tree and Decision Modeling, Brownfield Redevelopment International, http://www.brnfldsred.com/decision.html, February 22,2002)

The investor/ developer, especially if public funds are used, must be prepared to make the investment of time and money to woo the public's support. "The first step in the Brownfield Redevelopment Process is determining a fair valuation of the property. BRI can provide a realistic valuation of the property by reviewing available real estate data including demographics, absorption rates, community comprehensive plans, zoning maps and property appraisals. Once a valuation of the property has been determined for the property "as clean", appropriate deductions are made for anticipated environmental costs and any other development complications." (Ibid)

The developer must factor in the full extent of his likely financial exposure. It must be fully understood prior to starting the redevelopment process, or it most certainly will spell disaster. Consultants can assist clients in negotiating with agencies for Prospective Purchaser and Voluntary Cleanup Agreements, which offer some measure of developer protection. They can help developers find loans and grants, usually from redevelopment agencies to assist in cleanup, project planning, potential tenant identification, and public interface. Developers need to carefully analyze potential lease arrangements and project timing. Several likely models should be compared. Data analysis of the "Internal Rate of Return," "Return on Investment", and "Depreciation" should be evaluated for each option. Project cost estimates need to be computed in a brownfield project just the way they would in any other redevelopment project. Factors such as professional environmental evaluation, clean-up, demolition, environmental insurance, and waste streaming need to be added to the budget's line items. Items that address the value of incentives need to also be quantified.

Overwhelmingly, mixed uses are the most common path for brownfield redevelopment, since many of the albatross facilities are too large to suit a single new use. Developers need to target their efforts at multiple tenant development. Rarely will the cost advantages of redevelopment be enough to stimulate corporate powerhouses to pursue it, though they may have other reasons to do so. While not always the case, tenants in redeveloped brownfield sites will be units of government, agencies with green agendas, and young or fringe businesses that need large amounts of affordable and flexibly sized space. Given this riskier mix, brownfield site projects will usually need redevelopment agency assistance in securing loans.

After purchasing a site, developers must attend to the cleaning and redeveloping of the brownfield. Remediation of brownfield sites happens in several ways and the following list is by no means exhaustive:

- Tanks, drums and pipes that may leak must be removed cleaned and recycled. Removing these items may require excavation or demolition.

- Soil may be removed and treated off site with micro-organisms that chemically change the contaminated soil through the by-products of their digestion and life cycle. In other cases, soil may be stockpiled on the site and treated or contained. Suitable fill materials will need to replace soil to meet the existing grade.
- For tanks and pipes that will remain in service, secondary containment may be required to reduce the hazards should there be a spill.
- Construction that has been contaminated with chemicals by contact can be demolished and waste streamed to separate contaminated from non-contaminated waste, and recyclable or salvageable materials from those that will go directly to a landfill.
- Selective abatement of materials such as lead paint can be effected using various types of chemical peels that produce land-fill acceptable byproducts. Lead paint can also be encapsulated with other materials.
- Friable materials can be selectively abated using wet or misting processes and bagged removal. Alternately, friable materials may be encapsulated if new building systems or anchors will not penetrate them. Encapsulation is frequently used to isolate floor materials.

Trained professionals must execute this type of demolition due to the hazards present in the removal process. Although architects and engineers involved in the design of the new uses may recognize many potentially hazardous materials, they are rarely legally qualified to specify removal methods or to evaluate site materials for the presence of such substances. Abatement and abatement design are regulated professions in most states.

Green Design

In the 1980's a keen design interest in "green design" first emerged as a reaction to the 1978 Arab oil embargo. About this time an economic recession rooted in the declining infrastructure of the steel and automotive industries took hold, especially in the northeast and central United States. The recession caused a mass migration to warmer and drier areas of the country that were not prepared to handle the demand for water and other services required by the burgeoning growth.

Initially, green design meant incorporating passive and active solar design, day-lighting, and natural ventilation. Construction materials such as wood, wood products, rubber (EPDM) linoleum, and natural stone were preferred to more durable but more energy consumptive materials like concrete, masonry, asphalt, and metals. Xeriscaping, the use of indigenous plants in landscaping, was enforced in some areas where water was expensive or difficult to obtain.

At first, green design methods were stipulated as requirements by environmentally motivated individuals for residential design and by select commercial clients with a "green agenda." Occasionally, energy saving design was mandated for government projects, primarily as a method of reducing operating costs.

As awareness of environmental issues grew, communities required water rationing, sprinkler schedules, mandatory recycling, waste separation, separated sewers (Figure 4.10), and co-generation. Standards for lighting, ventilation, and water flow were reduced. Low flow fixtures were mandated. Sealants and insulation were widely promoted and retrofitted into existing cavities. For new construction, minimum R-values were mandated in some jurisdictions where energy codes were adopted. To get to the minimum R-values economically, insulation products were used that generated annoying and harmful off-gasses or in the case of fire, potentially lethal gasses. Buildings became tight, and even moldy. The air was filled with indoor pollutants. In these "dark times", some office workers referred to themselves as "mushrooms" because of the dark and humid environment where they worked. As people became aware of "sick building syndrome", Legionnaire's Disease, and indoor pollutants, they sought

FIGURE 4.10 Industrial wastewater is processed to better than storm water quality and landfill acceptable materials at this reclaimed refinery site.

IAQ (Indoor Air Quality) standards. Ventilation requirements were established. The most zealous clients of progressive designers demanded active energy management systems such as photocell operations and programmable controls for interior lights and HVAC (Heating, Ventilation, and Air Conditioning) systems. Other options were off-peak thermal or cooling storage using mass or ice and to conserve water they employed gray water recovery. To reduce energy demand they installed earth berms, roof ponds, and permaculture (xeriscaped roof gardens). There were a few tax incentives, primarily aimed at homeowners.

Manufacturers responded to the increased market demand for energy efficiency with high output efficient furnaces, HID (High Intensity Discharge) and high efficiency fluorescent lamps, as alternatives to traditional incandescent lamps, and water-saving valves. Some energy providers had credit programs for energy reduction. These programs usually stipulated minimum payback periods that had to be calculated. Even for large institutional clients, payback periods needed to be brief enough to realize operations benefits for offsetting first costs for design and materials. For example, one school department didn't want to bother with any system that had a payback less than 3 years, regardless of the size of the investment. It was the result of administrative decisions and budget cycles.

Payback periods, perhaps more than any other factor, affect the viability of any of these applied technologies to design. In "throw-away" architecture where the owner or developer builds on speculation or for fickle hospitality and retail markets, these materials and methods will not even be considered if the payback is anything short of immediate. The solar market lost its tax incentives when the Reagan administration came to power. Many of the technologies couldn't exist without subsidy. With the increased public awareness of energy savings, water conservation, air quality control, and desire for sustainable materials and reduced waste, an increasing number of alternatives have become available at prices competitive with the elements they replace.

LEED Program/Energy Star

When the economy slows, businesses may refocus their capital expenditures from new construction to renovation and reconstruction in order to direct capital more efficiently. This is the economic incentive many owners need.

To promote the ultimate in recycling, the U.S. Green Building Council's Leadership in Energy and Environmental Design (LEED) program has recently established guidelines for documenting sustainable design practices for existing buildings. Depending on a the number of points obtained during project review, buildings submitted for LEED certification may receive one of four ratings: general certification, silver, gold, or platinum. A building receives no certification rating if it has not achieved basic criteria.

On federal government projects and increasingly on state and local government projects, developers are required to achieve minimum certification under the program. Green initiatives in local communities such as Seattle now require construction of city buildings over 5,000 square feet to meet a specific LEED ratings. In Seattle silver is the minimum rating allowed.

> With the increased public awareness of energy savings, water conservation, air quality control, and desire for sustainable materials and reduced waste, an increasing number of alternatives have become available at prices competitive with the elements they replace.

Documenting LEED certification criteria for such owners has become a separately saleable service specialty. Firms specializing in re-construction designs would do well to have at least one key staff member become LEEDs certified. When a design team member is familiar with the techniques required to achieve higher ratings, he can provide input at the conceptual and design development stages. Project costs for a certified consultant to review the project and the potentially costly design documents modifications required to achieve ratings can all but be eliminated if LEEDs is not an afterthought in the design process.

LEEDS will likely become a benchmark and selling point on commercial projects in the future because it rates the success of conservation measures in construction. Perhaps commercial interest will begin with government contractors, ISO 9000 series manufacturers, and multifamily residential developers with an eye for "green-seeking" tenants. Unlike the solar programs of the 1970's and 1980's, tax abatement may not be the primary incentive to developers. For those without government connections, payback will be the strongest incentive for green design. Implementing visible green business practices will garner the fringe benefit of public goodwill, employee approval, and political cache. There are several broad areas from which LEEDs projects can gain points in the certification process. These include:

- Sustainable sites

- Water efficiency-implementing water conservation techniques (use reduction, active systems such as on-site treatment, filtration, erosion control, re-use of gray-water, and pavement and footprint minimization)
- Energy and atmosphere- energy conservation can be achieved through energy use reduction, natural lighting, co-generation, active or off-peak systems, passive systems, use of renewable and/ or efficient energy sources
- Materials and resources- use of renewable construction materials like boulders and rammed earth that require minimal energy consumption to manufacture, transport, place, and maintain
- Re-use of materials (recycling) including site & building salvage
- Reuse of the existing structure in whole, part or as a shell, with or without addition(s)
- Use of renewable resources, chiefly managed and harvested lumber
- Use of "local" construction materials is generally defined as materials produced and transported no more than 500 miles or one day's drive. To a limited degree, this may have the effect of reintroducing regionalism in indigenous forms inspired by indigenous materials in the built environment.
- Reuse of an existing structure can be a project's single greatest sustainable feature. Finding the right structure for re-use that also meets the clients' location and program requirements is the challenge.
- Innovation and design process involve creative techniques in construction such as waste management and demonstration projects, and even the act of project certification itself.

Jean Vollum Natural Capital Center, Portland, Oregon
Bronze rating, or basic certification, under the LEEDs program in new construction is readily achievable using conventional building techniques, lightly modified. The hidden costs are in seeking the certification itself, for example, "commissioning" systems is a prerequisite for certification. It may help the owner identify maintenance and warranty issues proactively; it also costs considerably more than the customary testing and start-up measures of conventional construction. In January 2002, the 106 year-old Vollum Center, formerly a two-story warehouse, became the first historic building renovation in the United States to receive a LEED gold rating. (http://www.ecotrust.org/programs/.html July 5, 2002)

To create a prototype project representing the best in building reclamation, developers sought out a unique mix of tenants — all companies and organizations with existing "green" business practices. Located in the Pearl District, the project fills a 70,000 square foot brick and timber warehouse built in 1895, and expanded with a 10,000 square foot roof top addition. The cost of renovation was $12.5 million. Pearl District redevelopment is focused on a mix of commercial and residential uses incorporated into abandoned warehouse businesses.

Key areas addressed in the project include reuse of materials, use of sustainable resources, energy conservation, and water conservation:

Re-use of Materials

- Salvaged timber from demolished on-site construction was used to construct portions of a 3rd floor addition.
- Recycled carpet, tires, and paint
- On-site sorting meant 98 percent of construction debris was recycled in some fashion.

Use of Sustainable Materials

- Only certified sustainably harvested wood products were used for general construction.

Energy Conservation

- Energy conservation was addressed in the electrical systems chiefly by implementing initially low lighting levels, providing additional day lighting from skylights and enlarged windows, and responsive controls connected to photocells and occupancy indicators.
- Energy efficient mechanical systems could be downsized and cooling loads reduced by including operable windows and more liberal tolerances.

Water Conservation

- Storm water runoff was cut by 95 percent using techniques such as an eco roof, bioswales, and capture of the runoff from paved and construction covered surfaces.
- Low flow plumbing fixtures contributed to clean water savings.

Sports Entities in the Urban Environment

Sports entities, especially major league franchises, are a status symbol and a benchmark in the comparison of cities as potential markets for development. See Table 4.2. This is especially true in 2nd and 3rd tier metropolises that may lack some of the other historic, cultural, institutional,

TABLE 4.2 Population (in thousands) per major league franchise

Franchise Market	POPULATION (Thousands)
New York, East Rutherford, New Jersey	2650
St. Louis	2604
St. Louis	2604
Pittsburgh	2359
Los Angeles, Anaheim	2047
Cincinnati	1979
Chicago	1832
San Antonio	1592
Philadelphia	1547
Columbus	1540
Washington, D.C., Baltimore	1522
San Diego	1407
Houston	1393
Dallas	1306
Tampa Bay	1198
Raleigh-Durham, (North) Carolina	1188
San Francisco, Oakland	1173
Memphis	1136
Boston	1136
Jascksonville	1100
Detroit	1091
Atlanta	1028
Sacremento	899
Seattle	889
Kansas City	888
Milwaukee	845
Tucson, Arizona	844
Orlando	823
Phoenix-(Glendale), Arizona	813
Miami	775
Portland, Vancouver	755
Charlotte	750
Cleveland	737
New Orleans	669
Salt Lake City, Utah	667
Denver, Colorado	646
Nashville, Tennessee	616
Minneapolis, Minnesota	594
Buffalo	585
Indianapolis	536
Green Bay	227
Calgary	Canadian cities not calculated
Ottawa	
Toronto	
Edmonton	
Montreal	

proximal, and scenic assets of older, larger, coastal cites. It is usually tax money that builds the stadium and much of the supporting infrastructure for each sport. Generally much of the wealth generated by the franchise is exported to the home locale of the franchise owners and players. Jobs directly generated by the facility and the franchise rarely equal the investment, however the value of a stadium to a community as an intangible asset cannot be denied. Professional sports have certain value in attracting and retaining other businesses to the metropolitan region. A stadium can elevate adjacent land values, especially if it's located in a CBD. Building a stadium can place a heavy burden on the central city, especially if the franchise is not regionally supported. However, it is facilities such as these that give the center to the CBD. Detroit has just spent more than $360 million, including $80 million in public money, to relocate the Tiger's baseball stadium from an outer suburb to the CBD for this reason. Such an asset can anchor a redevelopment district. Thirty major real-estate development projects representing $2.2 billion in mostly private investment have been initiated downtown near the new stadium. ("Take me out to the (whole new) ballgame", David Barkholz, April 3, 2000 at http://www-personal.umich.edu/~bowmanc/crain.html 9/3/2002 3:27 PM)

fastfacts

Sports entities, especially major league franchises, are a status symbol and a benchmark in the comparison of cities as potential markets for development. This is especially true in 2nd and 3rd tier metropolises that may lack some of the other historic, cultural, institutional, and scenic assets of older, larger, coastal cites.

The immediate commercial boost a stadium gives an area is largely in restaurants and souvenir shops. The success of these ventures depends in large part on increased attendance, distance to parking and residual disposable funds for the outing. If ticket prices are too high, if parking is too near, if it's too difficult to get downtown for the game, the growth won't flourish. The fact that Compuware and General Motors are investing in major corporate facilities downtown will give these businesses the through-the-week business they need for long term survival. Compuware is building a new world headquarters campus. General Motors is relocating some of its existing facilities from within the metropolitan area. Loft apartments and condos have been built into surrounding warehouses, introducing a downtown population to Detroit for the first time.

The money spent by Detroit on Comerica Park is small change compared to $240 million spent for the Baltimore Ravens, the San Francisco 49ers' $525 million sports complex, and team owner George Steinbrenner's request for $1 billion in public funds to build a new Yankee Stadium in Manhattan. ("Stadium Welfare Around the U.S.", AFSCME Publications, September/October 1997, http://www.afscme.org/publications/public_employee/1997/peso9728.htm, September 1, 2002)

Due to the depth of commitment required for such an effort, it may be time to create mechanisms whereby sports entities cannot hold a city up to "extortion" (threats to relocate) at intervals of 10, 15, or 20 years. Might it not be more efficient to buy the team, or its relocation rights, than continuously rebuild the stadium with taxpayer funds? Consider for the moment that about 2,000 principal shareholders and more than 100,000 others own the Green Bay Packers. Shareholders bought team stock in the 1990's to make it difficult for the team to pick up and leave town. A similar move is afoot by a group of Montreal Expos fans to change the form of ownership from a private to a publicly held and traded corporation, like the Boston Celtics.

This move still allows the league its share of control. Since revenue sharing in the NFL(National Football League) includes television rights, but not stadium rights, market size is less of a locational factor for privately owned franchises than the structure of the stadium deal. Teams keep the profits generated from the facilities. As a portion of the team's assets, stadium revenue has grown from 14-22% on average. If a city can own other structures and franchise their management, broadcast public information television, and operate bus lines, it is not a great leap to create a form of ownership that permits the city to own a team and facilities and take bids or proposals for management contracts. They already sell the name rights to corporations for money used to maintain the facility. In cites like Indianapolis and Houston, Conseco Stadium and Enron Field may be faced soon with bankrupt namesakes. Some of the "obsolete" facilities are 15-25 years old and not exactly falling down. In the Detroit Free Press on September 26, 1999, architect Alex Pollack wrote, "...no historic ballpark in America has ever been saved after its team abandoned it." The demolition of older venues is another thorny issue. They have become functionally obsolete for their primary tenants who require more complex staging areas, more extensive suites, increased seating capacity, higher parking, and inflated ticket prices. "By 2003, when the Green Bay Packers want to move into a renovated Lambeau Field, nearly half of the teams in the

National Football League will be playing in stadiums built since 1995...Nine of eleven referendums on NFL stadiums have won approval since the mid-1990s." (Content, Thomas, "Stadium Surge Prods Packers, Taxpayers Nationwide Ante $10B", Press-Gazette, Sunday, September 03, 2000, http://www.packersnews.com/archives/0009/0903pack.shtml September 3, 2002)

Demolition is costly and often requires the expertise of implosion experts. Demolition may not be necessary based on the condition of the facility itself. There may be a sufficient number of road shows, concerts, minor league sports, and convention events to keep it filled and marketable without the primary tenant. But here is where government can choose to create a favorable monopoly, if it seals the deal. If the old venue is destroyed, the previously mentioned events and sports need to negotiate with the franchise that controls the use of the new venue. The higher rents charged in the newer venue can be used to subsidize the cost of the new facility. Unless there's so much ancillary trade to go around that it can support two stadiums, the old one will inevitably be torn down, or worse, mothballed.

Demolition is costly and often requires the expertise of implosion experts.

Some cities explore renovating their stadium for continued use, but rarely does renovation win out. Of the 84 most recent major league stadium projects only 15% were renovations. In a recession, some cites may wish to lock-in favorable prices with design build agreements. Others, failing to sell the required bonds, may look more seriously at renovation. Albatross stadiums cost about one million dollars a year just to maintain. As pieces of real estate, they may be valued at about a quarter of a billion dollars.

Here are but a few of the proposed new uses for Tiger Stadium as the team moved to its new digs in Comerica Park:

- Themed retail and restaurants in conjunction with sports franchises that might expect a lesser draw. These could include soccer, women's basketball, equestrian sports, and even bullfighting.
- Combined venue for sports, military, and police training facilities
- Condos
- Mixed use, undefined

- Mixed use, housing and business
- The Campus Martius, a central park surrounded by office buildings

The Minnesota Vikings' Metrodome is less than 20 years old, but is now considered obsolete by all three teams that play there. This creates a greater political challenge than Detroit faced because the burden per capita is greater. The Vikings had not decided between a renovation and a new structure as this was written. Paul Moberg of Minneapolis watches the posturing and politicking closely in his role as founder of the anti-stadium group GAGME, or Grassroots Against Government-Mandated Entertainment.

Markets rich with private cash have made competition difficult for smaller, "poorer" teams. Markets can sell a lot of seats to the masses at reasonable prices if capita per franchise is favorable, as in New York. Markets can generate the same return per team if the capital per seat is high, as in San Francisco. Markets such as these may find themselves able to negotiate retention agreements. "Teams are going to have to ante up significantly more for new stadiums," says Aaron Barman of Prudential Securities, after the San Francisco Giants built a new $345 million stadium, putting most of the cost burden on the team and the fans and a $155 loan through Chase Securities. The Giants share of the revenue was largely generated by selling 30,000 season tickets, half of those with a licensing surcharge. (Peter Waldman, "If You Build It Without Public Cash, They'll Still Come," Wall Street Journal, March 31, 2000)

In contrast to the San Francisco capital market, New York has historically been a capita market with shared stadiums. As mentioned above, the Yankees and the Mets had requested a new $1 billion complex, with heavy public subsidy for the construction, prior to the disaster of 9-11 and its estimated $100 billion effect on Lower Manhattan. Given that hit to the community, the team's best hope is a $500 million renovation of the existing Yankee Stadium and rehabilitation of the surrounding area. The Yankees/Mets cable channel should help the team recoup some of the revenue lost in the stadium deal. (Fitzgibbon, Jorge "Yankees' hopes for new stadium on hold", The Journal News, Oct. 30, 2001, http://www.thejournalnews.com/newsroom/103001/30stadium.html)

The Gaming Industry

The gaming industry is an economic trap for most of the communities where it is located, perhaps with the exception of gaming destination cities like

Las Vegas, Reno, and Atlantic City. These cities are centers of tourism and have an aggregation of gaming choices. Detroit is an example, but similar flaws exist in the relationship of the gaming industry to small and mid-size cities that try to rescue a failing economy by attracting gaming with economic development funds. Job creation was the biggest selling point in persuading Michigan voters to permit three casinos to establish themselves in Detroit, however the turnover rate in the casinos has exceeded 50% per year for an estimated 15,000 jobs. When one casino laid off 400 workers just months after opening, the extent of the overstatement became real. Building a prison would have been a better bet for economic stability.

fastfacts

The Gaming Industry is an economic trap for most of the communities where they are located, perhaps with the exception of gaming destination cities like Las Vegas, Reno, and Atlantic City, which are centers of tourism and have an aggregation of gaming choices.

Casinos love a down market. In an up market, such miscalculation might be over-looked. In a recession, with the city economy still centered in just two industries (high tech and automotives), widespread layoffs can amount to taxpayers gambling away their severance pay and public benefits in hopes of a pay-off. The majority of the casino ownership is out-of-state, so profits are not necessarily retained and reinvested in the community. Tax revenue is another point used to sell the public on the idea of permitting casinos in the community. Casinos may as add as little as 1% of their adjusted gross revenue to the public coffers. In Detroit, this amounted to half of the predicted contribution, or an over-estimate of nearly $75 million in 2000. "There was seventy three million dollars in taxes paid to the city for last year on reported revenue of $743 million." (Everett, Todd ,"How Do The Casinos Measure Up?" Detropolis, March 5, 2001 http://www.detropolis.com/business/default.php, September 6, 2002)

The city of Detroit has attempted to exercise eminent domain in land assembly for three proposed casinos to operate in downtown Detroit. A judge prohibited them from doing so. Perhaps he saw that the "public good" was not so well served by an industry with a 35 % profit margin that is largely exported local earnings. (Waldmeir, Pete, "MGM Take Weakens

Detroit's Hand", The Detroit News http://www.webarchives.net/october_1999/mgm_take_weakens_detroit.htm, September 6, 2002) Since land assembly has taken longer than expected, temporary gaming facilities have opened and local citizens have asked, "Would the permanent casinos provide more profits or drain revenue?" (Everett) If the city gives away land and infrastructure to support the casinos that export the wealth of the city in exchange for a paltry payoff to the tax base, the answer may be no.

fastfacts

Casinos love a down market. In an up market, such miscalculation might be overlooked. In a recession, with Detroit's economy still centered in just two industries (high tech and automotives), widespread layoffs can amount to taxpayers gambling away their severance pay and public benefits in hopes of a pay-off. The majority of the casino ownership is out-of-state, so profits are not necessarily retained and reinvested in the community.

Detroit has emerged as the busiest commercial border crossing in the country. Few people are prepared to come into the city, pay the taxes, pay for community policing, and pay to send their children to private school. "It's too much of a sacrifice," said Kurt Metzger, director of the Michigan Metropolitan Information Center at Wayne State University. "Downtown is going to be for affluent folks and white folks only," said Center director Paul Taylor. "They're building a Tigers stadium, a Lions stadium, a Hard Rock Cafe. They're not building for black folks and poor folks, but for affluent folks and white folks."

("Motown Rebound", Detroit Free Press, April 15, 1997, Metro http://www.freep.com/news/econ/qecon15.2.htm, September 6, 2002)

Funding Development Initiatives

Local funds for redevelopment are usually established using a taxing mechanism called TIF (Tax Increment Financing, Figure 4.11). Redevelopment authorities use it to sustain their activities. Taxes in the target area are first measured. Then seed money is used to complete the

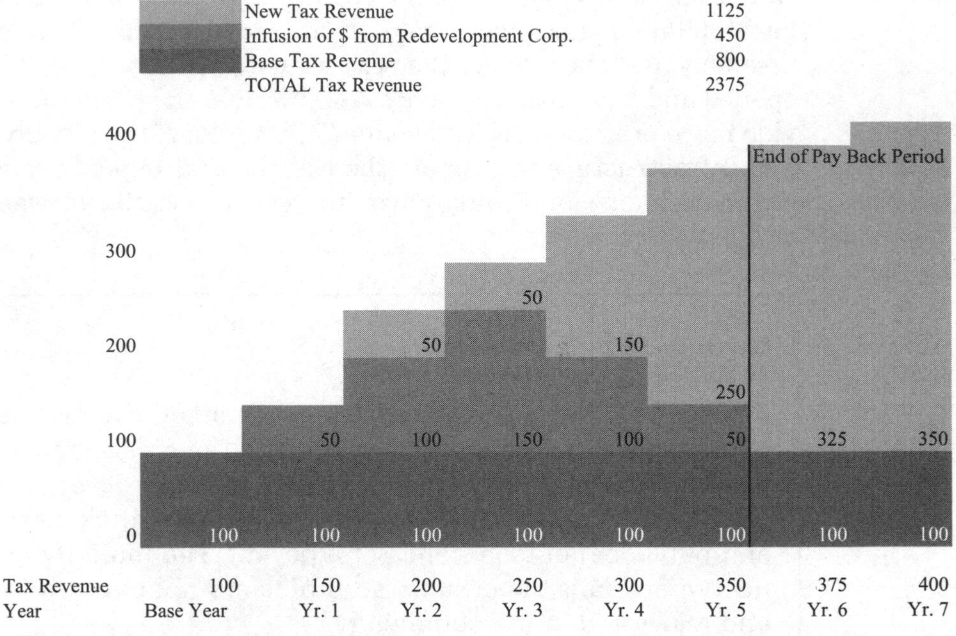

FIGURE 4.11 Tax increment financing

infrastructure projects, land assembly, and cleanup required to attract new business and or housing to an area. As new business and housing in an area grows, less incentive is required to attract new business. The target area has become more desirable. Eventually, the tax value of the new businesses far exceeds the investment required to spur the revitalization. The difference between the original tax revenue for an area and the eventual tax revenue after revitalization is called the tax increment. The difference between the tax increment less the investment and base can be used in whole or in part to invest in the redevelopment of other areas.

David Nieh described TIF this way, "So let's say there is a piece of land and it is worth $100 in taxes, and let's say that, after we declare it a redevelopment area, redevelopment maybe improved the properties around it, maybe pulled the utilities to it, the tax now on that piece of land has an accessed value and the generating tax is now $300. Well, that difference, the $300 minus $100 is the tax increment. The difference [in value accrues] between the date when it was declared a redevelopment area and when the current value [is reassessed]. In this example, the $200 goes straight into the agency's coffers. And then what the agency typically does is it bonds this money so it essentially takes a loan against this money planning to repay it maybe in 50 years. So all of a sudden this $200 at today's current prices is all of a sudden worth about $4,000. About 20 times. And then we can take this $4,000 and put it into projects, usually capital projects. So for example the Saturday Redevelopment Agency...We've built public facilities, museums, libraries and such, as well as the different public facilities and museums....so those are some of the typical public facilities that we build. In terms of the private facilities a lot of times for example, there is a need for more parking in the downtown area. We can ante into a developers project and ask them to build more parking and we will pay for it, but it then becomes public parking. So that's another way that in a private public partnership, how we get things done."

Private Funds/ Matching Funds

The state department of commerce or your local redevelopment authority can provide lists of resources for private redevelopment funds. Most states publish directories that list public and private fund sources unique to the state. Both private and public funds generally require some level of match to obtain grant money. Government programs will often permit private grants or in-kind contributions to make up the match amount.

Ecotrust is an organization committed to the development and conservation of a regional economy in a bio-economic zone that extends from coastal Northern California to Alaska. There are fourteen principles to a Conservation Economy as outlined by Ecotrust with its partners Ecotrust Canada, Shorebank Pacific, and Shorebank Enterprise Pacific. Although the funds of its Natural Capital Fund go primarily toward its own development projects, Ecotrust sometimes funds the work of others if it passes a litmus test for consistency with the trust's values.

Funds for the Jean Vollum project were drawn from Natural Capital Fund which invests in projects with capacity for appropriate development and conservation in the coastal temperate rain forest region. The Fund is intended to serve as a catalyst, leveraging other investments through partnerships, joint ventures, and other collaborations. As the ventures mature and are able to access other sources of funds, such as bank financing, the Fund investment will be recovered and redeployed.

Ecotrust, the fund's parent agency, invested primarily in the initiatives to create capacity for economic development, understanding, policy reform, and conservation. Eligible project must meet certain criteria:

- Strongly catalytic
- Capital recovery

- Early entry
- Early exit
- Income earning

Each project must generate a modest return of 2-3% to grow the fund and cover administrative costs. The fourteen principles to a Conservation Economy espoused by Ecotrust are grouped as:

Environmental

- Maintain and restore ecosystem health
- Preserve biological diversity
- Promote compact cities and towns

Economic:

- Increase resource efficiency
- Reduce dependence on non-renewable resources
- Reduce dependence on synthetic substances that accumulate in nature
- Choose products and suppliers consistent with the other principles
- Turn waste into a resource
- Support policy changes that assign actual social and ecological costs benefits to goods and services

Social Equity:

- Meet fundamental human needs and provide diverse economic opportunities for all
- Improve the resilience of individuals, businesses, and communities in responding to economic transitions
- Provide broad access to knowledge, particularly of place and natural systems, while preserving cultural diversity
- Diversify local economies
- Promote the accountability of businesses and government agencies to local communities

These elements align quite nicely with the LEED criteria now required on projects involving federal money and adopted widely on state and local government projects.

Federal Programs and Resources:
A catalog of sources for federal government funds can be found at The United States Nonprofit Gateway. It identifies a wide variety of funding sources —from government agency programs to private grants. The site also has links to government agencies.

The General Services Administration(GSA) serves federal agencies as clients, helping them to locate and purchase or lease property for federal workers. They aim to invest in properties that will increase in value so as to reduce the burden of maintaining and purchasing real estate on federal taxes. Because of this, they have a vested interest in acting as a partner in community redevelopment. Http://governing.com/3gsa.htm and Governing Magazine's home page are two sites offered by the General Services Administration. "We look for ways we can leverage our investments to stimulate other investment in neighborhoods and communities," says Bob Peck. ("Federal Spaces Community Places" a Sponsored Section Produced By The U.S. General Services Administration accessed at Http://Governing.Com/3gsa.Htm, February 18, 2002):

- The Rails to Trails Conservancy at http://www.railtrails.org/rtc_active_pages/home/main.asp offers information resources for those who would develop parks and other public uses from abandoned railroad property and rights-of-way.
- For funds and design guidelines regarding parking issues, try www.parking.org.
- The National Assembly for State Arts Agencies offers information resources and representation for state and regional arts programs. Contact the assembly at: http://www.nasaa-arts.org/.
- The American Association Of Museums provides information on what's involved in starting a museum, and provides reference titles relating to museum management.
- The U.S. Department of Energy (DOE) offers programs to assist industry in reaching sustainable goals.
- The Industries of the Future is a program of the Office of Industrial Technology (OIT) and focuses on waste and energy consumption reduction in industry.

Since these industries are some of the most consumptive, they have been targeted for attention: Steel, Metal Casting, Aluminum, Chemicals, Petroleum, Mining, Agriculture, Forest Products and Glass. The Industries of the Future program employs energy assessments to assist companies in identifying energy issues such as inefficient motors, high loss compressed air systems, and high loss steam systems. For more information, refer to www.INIoF.org. National Industrial Competitiveness through Energy, Environment and Economics (NICE3) awards grants to assist with testing, demonstrating, and implementing innovative technologies that will significantly conserve energy or reduce industrial waste. Contact the Department of Energy (DOE) at www.doe.gov. or your state DOE for program information. (http://www.in.gov/doc/businesses/EP_industrial.html February 28, 2003}

As this is written, pending legislation to fund other national programs includes the Urban Park Recreation and Recovery Program (UPARR), a $30 million annual program that provides grants for the rehabilitation and enhancement of existing parks and recreation in areas with population over 50,000 people. Also the Community Character Act (CCA) is a bill authorizing grants to states for land use planning. Reauthorization is pending of the Transportation Equity Act of the 21st Century (TEA-21), a $217 billion statute that funds numerous programs that promote planning and livable community initiatives, in addition to funding almost all state transportation projects.

Preservation Funds and Assistance

Using the National Register of Historic Places registration form, you can download articles. It gives you tools for evaluating and nominating sites for national register designation. You can learn how to research a historic property and complete the NRHP registration forms, National Register Forms (http://www.cr.nps.gov/nr/). You may wish to begin by examining NPS Form 10-90, the basic National Register registration form to determine if national registration is appropriate for your project. Properties registered as state or federal historic places may be eligible for tax relief (20%) and, in some cases, project grants in exchange for maintaining a preservation covenant. If preservation is a principal aim in reclaiming a property, Figure 4.12 and Figure 4.13, these opportunities are certainly worth investigating.

National Park Service's Preservation Briefs, Preservation Briefs Online is available at http://www2.cr.nps.gov/tps/briefs/presbhom.htm. Under the Secretary of the Interior, the National Park Service administers federal historic preservation programs and develops standards referenced in the Secretary of the Interior's Guidelines for Historic Preservation. Contact these offices when projects are related to the listed agency and may have opportunities for the use of historic preservation subsidies.

FIGURE 4.12 The first catalyst project on College Avenue at 42nd St. was a police station, renovated from an old bank about 1989.

FIGURE 4.13 The most recent College Avenue catalyst project is a Branch library, designed by Walter Blackburn and Associates. *Photo: Stephen Culbert*

CHAPTER 5
COMPATIBLE NEW USES

PROJECT SEEKING, IDENTIFICATION, INITIATION AND DEVELOPMENT

An array of redevelopment projects illustrates the process of bringing a change-of-use property from the initial stages until the finished product. This section will clarify the basic steps in the project development process. The team players need to have their roles and relationships defined. Also, it is important to note how different project delivery methods affect the process.

AN OVERVIEW OF NEW USE PROJECTS

Before seeking a building to develop, investor/developers need to have an idea of what kind of use they want to fit into an existing building. Conversely, building owners who have land or property that would benefit from being returned to profitable use, need to understand some of the possible uses for their existing facility. This is true whether they intend to keep the property or offer it for sale.

Savvy design professionals and realtors on the owner's team can sometimes offer suggestions for new use or complimentary mixed uses that will fill the owner's operational needs and lease the parts of the building he can't use.

Almost any mix of clean uses can co-exist. The integration of office and industrial parks will continue. Supporting commercial and even residential uses will be incorporated where zoning or unit development plans permit. Business centers can take advantage of strategic proximity and specialized aggregation by combining interrelated but different business uses into sections of large office parks. Developers will hedge their interests by serving multiple specialized tenant markets in sections. Uses that are targeted for re-development groupings include:

- Warehouse/distribution
- Research/ high tech
- Incubator parks
- Medical parks

Such parks can be developed from existing urban fabric by creating transportation links or even land assembly in targeted areas. For example, Indianapolis is using a limited access People Mover located in the public right of way to connect a chain of hospitals and medical education facilities. A second phase will connect drug, medical research, and health insurance businesses.

Flex space, capable of supporting high tech businesses, is a reliable use that is often suitable for speculative development. Based on the absorption rate and location, laddered re-development of existing structures for such uses will leave the developer prepared to respond to market demands on short notice. Re-use of prepared structures, like gutted shell spaces or high-bay clean spaces for conversions, can further shorten construction time and potentially reduce construction costs. Having enclosed space ready to go may allow the developer to take advantage of off-season contractor pricing, further reducing costs.

Design deliverables for laddered re-development might be phased similar to this outline as applicable:

- Identify districts with suitable development rules for proposed use(s)
- Selection from available properties
- Site and building analysis for proposed use(s)
- Identification of site remediation and abatement issues.
- Identification of zoning and code issues to be addressed
- Obtain zoning variance if required
- Identifications of features to be preserved or restored
- Gross site preparation, access, connections to utilities
- Remediation and abatement

- Selective demolition
- Envelope upgrades and restoration such as replacement of windows, doors, roof
- Basic infrastructure
  - plumbing systems
  - basic building electrical service
  - vertical chases
  - exit paths
  - sizing central HVAC equipment
- Wayfinding and security
- Tenant specific development would be a late package and might include items to address specialized needs for communications, images, signs, frontage, security, localized climate control, additional plumbing, and loading docks

Records of an empirical field survey of periodical literature revealed a myriad of compatible new use combinations that have been used in successful projects. They have been arranged below in this manner:

<u>IBC Occupancy Category</u>

- Principal Original Occupancy or Use
- Adaptive Occupancy(s) or Use(s)

<u>Assembly</u>

- Churches
- Office
- Theater
- Cinema
- Single family
- Multi-family, condo
- Clubhouse
- Retail
- Recording Studio
- Mixed Use-Cultural Arts Facility
- Courthouses
- Office

- Library
- Museum
- Theater/Cinema
- Farmer's Market/ retail/ supermarket
- Rail/Trolley Passenger Depot
- Concession Stands
- Shops
- Linear Parks
- Outdoor Drinking Area
- Retail, Design Offices
- Museum (Black Heritage Center)
- Mixed Use: Library/Office/Police

<u>Business (Commercial, Office)</u>

- Office
- Office/ retail/ dining

<u>Educational</u>

- Schools
- Assisted living
- Condominiums
- Luxury multi-family residential (condominiums, apartments)
- Multi-family residential (apartments, 1- 2 bedroom, and affordable 1-bedroom & efficiency units)
- Hotel (boutique, luxury, limited service, full service)
- Retail
- Roof gardens
- Gyms/ health clubs

<u>Factory (Industrial)</u>

- Quarry
- Strip mall

- Big box retail
- Industrial buildings and sites
- Recommissioning
- Light manufacturing
- Multi-tenant industrial park
- Office
- Outdoor Recreation
- Storage
- Mixed use: storage and offices
- Mixed use: wholesale/retail complex with out-lot restaurants
- Hotel
- Museum
- Center for advanced technology
- Diesel engine company/railroad station
- Ammunition plant to military-owned leased commercial industrial setting with all infrastructure in place
- Major league baseball stadium
- Mixed use: residences, school, and a large-scale industrial laundry facility
- Mixed use: townhouses, a scenic public park, tennis courts, a jogging and bike trail encircling the island, a fitness and rowing center, a 150-slip marina with dry dock, three office buildings and a light industrial manufacturer.
- Business incubation
- Headquarters and R&D facilities
- Factory outlet mall
- Military production facility
- Partial demolition, dumping ground cleanup
- Mixed use: manufacturing, office, warehouse
- Mixed use: retail, hotel office
- Regional sports and entertainment complex
- Refrigerated storage and distribution
- Research and development and administrative facilities with a public plaza, cascading waterfalls and a sculpture garden

- Mixed use: downsized original industrial occupant, high tech manufacturing, multi-story hotel, big-box and strip scale retail- commercial parcels, luxury apartments and condominiums.
- Mixed use: themed social service center (The Family Center) addressing emergency needs services (food, clothing & assistance), senior services, employment services, day care services, GED classes, youth after-school & summer programs, day camps, counseling services and various recreational activities. Complex includes a three-acre park on the river's edge, in an urban core industrial area
- Mill
- Mixed use: office/retail/ entertainment
- Military Base
- Local airport
- Public park
- Private golf course
- Prison site
- Military museums
- Water treatment plant
- Planned Unit Development (PUD) with multifamily housing, daycare office
- Mixed Use: United States Army medical depot, health clinic, drug detoxification center, homeless shelter, public school classrooms, storage and administrative offices
- Mixed Use: light manufacturing business park with daycare center

<u>Hazardous</u>

- Wastewater treatment plant
- Plant redevelopment
- Armory with facilities available to the community
- River restoration and industrial park
- Scrap (metal) yard
- NFL practice fields
- Recycling drop-off center
- Municipal landfill
- Mixed-use: major hotel, office and retail
- Garbage transfer facility

- Six restaurants, gas station, hotel, office building, cinema, Target store, and medical center
- Service stations/fuel dispensing stations
- Retail
- Fast food
- Convenience retail
- Bakery
- Firehouse
- Museum of Modern Art with addition
- Photography and printing business
- Office
- Rail and truck freight depot and adjacent industrial land
- Housing and retail establishments to serve a variety of households and income levels
- Railroad switching and repair yard
- Roe University Football Stadium with meeting rooms
- Low and moderate income apartments and below grade parking, planted courtyards,
- Sculptured rocks, landscaped open spaces, private gardens, central public open space
- Pedestrian bridge access to downtown and the transit mall.

<u>Institutional</u>

- Skilled nursing care facilities
- Assisted living
- Hospitals
- Performing arts (with additions)
- Mixed use: office and light industrial zone, hotel with conference and banquet facilities, civic uses such as a new mental health educational center, child and elder care, and a diverse range of residential types

<u>Mercantile</u>

- Auto dealers
- Design office
- Convention center
- Branch banks

- Police station
- Daycare center
- Training center
- Entertainment/retail
- Museum of science and industry
- Malls
- Transit facility
- Higher education
- Adult education
- Community meeting rooms
- Library
- Power center
- Retail/mid-high rise
- Higher ed/ education administrative offices
- Restaurant, office, communications switching center, storage
- Retail low-rise
- Plasma center
- Offices-government services
- Small service companies
- Clubs and restaurants
- Children's museum

Residential

- One- and two- family residences
- Assisted living
- Group homes
- Bed & breakfast
- Small retail
- Small office
- Historic tourist site
- Salons
- Cafés
- Dormitories
- Office

- Apartments
- Classroom
- Fraternity House
- Mixed Use: classrooms, offices, technology laboratories
- Hotels
- Assisted living
- Housing

Storage

- Warehouse
- Multi-family residential (apartments,1-2 bedroom)
- High-tech office
- Information technology center

Utility

- Industrial land assembly
- Electric power generating plant
- Grain elevator

FIGURE 5.1 Minimally renovated and preserved, the Phoenix Theater provides professional premiere and experimental theater in what was once a church. *Photo: Stephen Culbert*

FIGURE 5.2 This historic school and addition have been converted into affordable professional office suites on the periphery of the CBD (Commercial Business District). An architectural practice on the lowest level has an attractive contemporary office interior.

FIGURE 5.3 The Indiana Oxygen Building was moved to preserve it from demolition by a large corporation that needed the land for expansion. The new owners set it on a new foundation and converted it to an upscale eatery, near the corporate neighbor that allowed it to be saved.

FIGURE 5.4 The old loading dock is one of the few clues that this is a converted factory building that is now a small hospital.

FIGURE 5.5 Two houses were joined and converted to this pub with on-site brewing.

FIGURE 5.6 Sheil Sexton, a general contractor, converted a warehouse for its corporate office. The design celebrates the construction process and technology with a symbolic icon and integrated interior art forms. *Photo: Stephen Culbert*

- Railyard maintenance and switching yard
- Meat packing plant
- Paper recycling facility
- Ballpark, municipal area
- Professional sports arena
- Planned urban community
- Utility structures
- Power plant
- Retail/ entertainment/ office
- Museum
- First-class tourist and community cultural center complex.

SELECTING A SUITABLE CONVERSION PROJECT

The process of selecting a suitable conversion project shouldn't be done in haste. Proper selection is the cornerstone of a successful conversion project. It doesn't matter if the intent is to sell or rent the building after the conversion project. The choices you make at this stage can make the difference between a highly profitable conversion and one that ends in bankruptcy.

> The process of selecting a suitable conversion project shouldn't be done in haste. Proper selection is the cornerstone of a successful outcome. It doesn't matter if the intent is to sell or rent the building after the conversion project.

What makes a sound decision? Many factors play important roles. One of the first considerations is determining the profit potential of the project. In addition, the durability of the building is important, especially if the property will be owned and operated by the investor/developer. If the building will be rented, one must consider the difficulty in managing the property. Indeed, property management should be carefully considered in any project, even one converted for resale.

> If the building will be rented, one must consider the difficulty in managing the property. Indeed, property management should be carefully considered in any project, even one converted for resale.

Commercial Buildings

Commercial multifamily rental buildings are very popular with first-time investors, especially buildings with 6-10 units. Buildings larger than 10 units will attract fewer buyers. This is a key consideration when buying larger properties for use as rental apartments.

One disadvantage to commercial buildings is the need for large down payments. Buyers may be required to put 20-30% down which can be a considerable front-end investment. On the other hand, since buildings can be financed with conventional commercial loans, borrowers and lenders can get quite creative their methods of financing. It's possible to purchase a building with no cash required for the down payment. There have even been deals where purchasers of a large property not only didn't put any money down, they left the closing meeting with more cash than when they walked in the door.

The creative use of second mortgages and other financing maneuvers can get an investor into a building without the long-term use of any of his own money. Here's a warning though, leveraging the maximum amount can be very risky business. If anything major goes wrong, the investor risks losing not just the property but also his good credit.

fastfacts

One disadvantage to commercial buildings is the need for large down payments. Buyers may be required to put 20%-30% down which can be a considerable front-end investment.

Nonresidential Properties

Nonresidential properties offer excellent opportunities for profit to conversion investors. At the small investment scale, these properties can start out as residential structures and end up as doctor's offices or real estate offices. Find residences located in commercial districts, (check the zoning) and the investment to convert to a nonresidential use can generate lucrative return.

Commercial projects are not for every investor, but they can produce the biggest bang for the buck. Converting an abandoned gas station into a fast food restaurant can surely increase the value of the property. The market value of an old house is likely to grow considerably if it's converted to offices for medical professionals. The profit potential will be greatest in this scenario if the offices are in a commercial district in close proximity to a hospital, clinic, nursing home, or pharmacy. Consider the increased value of the property and the profit to be made in these cases.

Find residences located in commercial districts and be sure to check the zoning. The investment to convert to a nonresidential use can generate lucrative return.

TABLE 5.1 Zoning uses compatible with IBC Occupancy Groups. Zoning groups are based on Marion County designations and descriptions. (*Continued*)

Zoning Uses Compatible with IBC Occupancy Groups			
IBC Occupancy Group-Division	**Building or Structure Use Examples**	**Potentially Compatible Zoning Districts**	**Compatible Zoning Use Description**
A-1	motion picutre theater, live theater, TV & radio studio audience	C-4	Community-Regional Commercial District
		C-5	General Commercial District
		C-7	High Intensity Commercial District
		C-ID	Special Commercial District (UED)
		CBD-1	Core activities of all types with a side variety of related land uses
		CBD-2	Support uses for CBD-1 - less land use intensity than CBD-1
		PK-1	Park District One - Permits all sizes and ranges of public park land and facilities
		UQ-1	University Quarter District One - Permits and facilitates the development, expansion, etc., of a major university complex or campus
A-2	banquet halls	C-3	Neighborhood Commercial District
		C-3C	Corridor Commercial
		C-4	Community-Regional Commercial District
		C-5	General Commercial District
		C-7	High Intensity Commercial District
		CBD-1	Core activities of all types with a side variety of related land uses
		CBD-2	Support uses for CBD-1 - less land use intensity than CBD-1
		SU-7	Charitable and Philanthropic Institutions
		SU-34	Club Rooms b. Fraternal Rooms - Fraternity and Lodge c. Ballrooms - Public
		SU-38	Community Center
		UQ-1	University Quarter District One - Permits and facilitates the development, expansion, etc., of a major university complex or campus
A-2	night clubs,	C-7	High Intensity Commercial District
		CBD-1	Core activities of all types with a side variety of related land uses
		CBD-2	Support uses for CBD-1 - less land use intensity than CBD-1
		CBD-S	A special primary district requiring Metropolitan Development Commission approval of all uses, site and development plans
A-2	resaurants	C-3	Neighborhood Commercial District
		C-3C	Corridor Commercial
		C-4	Community-Regional Commercial District
		C-5	General Commercial District
		C-6	Thoroughfare Service District
		C-7	High Intensity Commercial District
		C-ID	Commercial-Industrial District
		CBD-1	Core activities of all types with a side variety of related land uses
		CBD-2	Support uses for CBD-1 - less land use intensity than CBD-1
		CBD-S	A special primary district requiring Metropolitan Development Commission approval of all uses, site and development plans
		all I	INDUSTRIAL
		UQ-1	University Quarter District One - Permits and facilitates the development, expansion, etc., of a major university complex or campus

TABLE 5.1 (*Continued*) Zoning uses compatible with IBC Occupancy Groups. Zoning groups are based on Marion County designations and descriptions.

Zoning Uses Compatible with IBC Occupancy Groups			
IBC Occupancy Group-Division	**Building or Structure Use Examples**	**Potentially Compatible Zoning Districts**	**Compatible Zoning Use Description**
A-2	taverns and bars	C-3	Neighborhood Commercial District
		C-4	Community-Regional Commercial District
		C-5	General Commercial District
		C-7	High Intensity Commercial District
		C-ID	Commercial-Industrial District
		CBD-1	Core activities of all types with a side variety of related land uses
		CBD-2	Support uses for CBD-1 - less land use intensity than CBD-1
		CBD-S	A special primary district requiring Metropolitan Development Commission approval of all uses, site and development plans
		all I	INDUSTRIAL
A-3	amusement arcade, billiards	C-3	Neighborhood Commercial District
		C-4	Community-Regional Commercial District
		C-5	General Commercial District
		C-7	High Intensity Commercial District
		C-ID	Commercial-Industrial District
		CBD-1	Core activities of all types with a side variety of related land uses
		CBD-2	Support uses for CBD-1 - less land use intensity than CBD-1
A-3	art galleries, exhibit halls	C-3C	Corridor Commercial
		C-4	Community-Regional Commercial District
		C-5	General Commercial District
		C-S	Special Commercial District**
		CBD-1	Core activities of all types with a side variety of related land uses
		CBD-2	Support uses for CBD-1 - less land use intensity than CBD-1
		SU-7	Charitable and Philanthropic Institutions
		PK-2	Park Perimeter - Special District Two - Assures that the area peripheral to public parks will be compatible and harmonious with park uses
		UQ-1	University Quarter District One - Permits and facilitates the development, expansion, etc., of a major university complex or campus
A-3	auditoriums, courtrooms, lecture halls	C-5	General Commercial District
		C-7	High Intensity Commercial District
		C-S	Special Commercial District**
		CBD-1	Core activities of all types with a side variety of related land uses
		CBD-2	Support uses for CBD-1 - less land use intensity than CBD-1
		UQ-1	University Quarter District One - Permits and facilitates the development, expansion, etc., of a major university complex or campus
		SU-7	Charitable and Philanthropic Institutions
		SU-9	Buildings and Grounds Used by Any Department of Town, City, Township, County, State or Federal Government
		SU-37	Library
		HD-2	Hospital District Two
		PK-1	Park District One - Permits all sizes and ranges of public park land and facilities
		UQ-1	University Quarter District One - Permits and facilitates the development, expansion, etc., of a major university complex or campus

TABLE 5.1 *(Continued)* Zoning uses compatible with IBC Occupancy Groups. Zoning groups are based on Marion County designations and descriptions.

Zoning Uses Compatible with IBC Occupancy Groups			
IBC Occupancy Group-Division	Building or Structure Use Examples	Potentially Compatible Zoning Districts	Compatible Zoning Use Description
A-3	bowling alleys, indoor swimming & tennis,	C-3	Neighborhood Commercial District
		C-3C	Corridor Commercial
		C-4	Community-Regional Commercial District
		C-5	General Commercial District
		CBD-2	Support uses for CBD-1 - less land use intensity than CBD-1
		SU-16	Amusement parks and Swimming Pools Privately Owned and Open to Public Patronage
		SU-38	Community Center
		UQ-1	University Quarter District One - Permits and facilitates the development, expansion, etc., of a major university complex or campus
A-3	churches and funeral parlors	D-5	Urban developed area
		C-3	Neighborhood Commercial District
		C-3C	Corridor Commercial
		C-5	General Commercial District
		CBD-1	Core activities of all types with a side variety of related land uses
		CBD-2	Support uses for CBD-1 - less land use intensity than CBD-1
		SU-1	Churches
		SU-10	Cemeteries
		PK-2	Park Perimeter - Special District Two - Assures that the area peripheral to public parks will be compatible and harmonious with park uses
A-3	community halls, dance halls,	C-3	Neighborhood Commercial District
		C-3C	Corridor Commercial
		C-5	General Commercial District
		CBD-2	Support uses for CBD-1 - less land use intensity than CBD-1
		SU-7	Charitable and Philanthropic Institutions
		SU-34	Club Rooms b. Fraternal Rooms - Fraternity and Lodge c. Ballrooms - Public
		SU-38	Community Center
		UQ-1	University Quarter District One - Permits and facilitates the development, expansion, etc., of a major university complex or campus
A-3	libraries	SU-37	Library
		C-3	Neighborhood Commercial District
		C-3C	Corridor Commercial
		C-4	Community-Regional Commercial District
		SU-2	Schools
		SU-9	Buildings and Grounds Used by Any Department of Town, City, Township, County, State or Federal Government
		SU-38	Community Center
		PK-1	Park District One - Permits all sizes and ranges of public park land and facilities
		PK-2	Park Perimeter - Special District Two - Assures that the area peripheral to public parks will be compatible and harmonious with park uses
		UQ-1	University Quarter District One - Permits and facilitates the development, expansion, etc., of a major university complex or campus

TABLE 5.1 (*Continued*) Zoning uses compatible with IBC Occupancy Groups. Zoning groups are based on Marion County designations and descriptions.

Zoning Uses Compatible with IBC Occupancy Groups		Potentially Compatible Zoning Districts	Compatible Zoning Use Description
IBC Occupancy Group-Division	Building or Structure Use Examples		
A-3	museums	SU-7	Charitable and Philanthropic Institutions
		C-4	Community-Regional Commercial District
		CBD-2	Support uses for CBD-1 - less land use intensity than CBD-1
		CBD-3	Exclusive office-apartment district around a memorial plaza
		PK-2	Park Perimeter - Special District Two - Assures that the area peripheral to public parks will be compatible and harmonious with park uses
		UQ-1	University Quarter District One - Permits and facilitates the development, expansion, etc., of a major university complex or campus
A-3	passenger stations (waiting area)	Any D's except D-6II,D-9	DWELLING
		Any C's except C-I	COMMERCIAL
		CBD-2	Support uses for CBD-1 - less land use intensity than CBD-1
		CBD-3	Exclusive office-apartment district around a memorial plaza
		CBD-S	A special primary district requiring Metropolitan Development Commission approval of all uses, site and development plans
		All I's	INDUSTRIAL
		SU-8	Correctional and Penal Institutions
		SU-9	Buildings and Grounds Used by Any Department of Town, City, Township, County, State or Federal Government
		A-secondary	A secondary district which consists of Instrument and Non-Instrument Approach Surface Areas
		HD-1	Hospital District One
		PK-1	Park District One - Permits all sizes and ranges of public park land and facilities
		UQ-1	University Quarter District One - Permits and facilitates the development, expansion, etc., of a major university complex or campus
A-4	arenas	C-4	Community-Regional Commercial District
		C-7	High Intensity Commercial District
		CBD-1	Core activities of all types with a side variety of related land uses
		CBD-2	Support uses for CBD-1 - less land use intensity than CBD-1
		CBD-S	A special primary district requiring Metropolitan Development Commission approval of all uses, site and development plans
		UQ-1	University Quarter District One - Permits and facilitates the development, expansion, etc., of a major university complex or campus
A-4	skating rinks, tennis courts with spectator seating	C-4	Community-Regional Commercial District
		C-5	General Commercial District
		CBD-2	Support uses for CBD-1 - less land use intensity than CBD-1
		SU-2	Schools
		PK-1	Park District One - Permits all sizes and ranges of public park land and facilities
		UQ-1	University Quarter District One - Permits and facilitates the development, expansion, etc., of a major university complex or campus

TABLE 5.1 (*Continued*) Zoning uses compatible with IBC Occupancy Groups. Zoning groups are based on Marion County designations and descriptions.

Zoning Uses Compatible with IBC Occupancy Groups			
IBC Occupancy Group-Division	Building or Structure Use Examples	Potentially Compatible Zoning Districts	Compatible Zoning Use Description
		C-5	General Commercial District
		CBD-2	Support uses for CBD-1 - less land use intensity than CBD-1
		SU-44	Off-track Mutual Wagering Facilities, Licensed as Satellite Facilities under IC 4-31-5.5 (Off-Track Betting Facilities)
A-5	bleachers, grand stands	SU-2	Schools
		PK-1	Park District One - Permits all sizes and ranges of public park land and facilities
		UQ-1	University Quarter District One - Permits and facilitates the development, expansion, etc., of a major university complex or campus
A-5	stadiums	C-4	Community-Regional Commercial District
		C-7	High Intensity Commercial District
		CBD-1	Core activities of all types with a side variety of related land uses
		CBD-2	Support uses for CBD-1 - less land use intensity than CBD-1
		CBD-S	A special primary district requiring Metropolitan Development Commission approval of all uses, site and development plans
		SU-2	Schools
		UQ-1	University Quarter District One - Permits and facilitates the development, expansion, etc., of a major university complex or campus
B	airport traffic control tower	A	Airport Special Use District - Permits Public municipal airports Airspace District
B	animal hospitals, kennels and pounds	C-3	Neighborhood Commercial District
		CBD-2	Support uses for CBD-1 - less land use intensity than CBD-1
B	barber and beauty shops, dry cleaning and laundries, print shops, post offices	C-3	Neighborhood Commercial District
		C-5	General Commercial District
		C-3C	Corridor Commercial
		CBD-2	Support uses for CBD-1 - less land use intensity than CBD-1
B	car wash	C-3	Neighborhood Commercial District
		C-5	General Commercial District
		C-7	High Intensity Commercial District
		C-ID	Commercial-Industrial District
		CBD-2	Support uses for CBD-1 - less land use intensity than CBD-1
		I-2-S	Light Industrial Suburban District
		I-2-U	Light Industrial Urban District
B	civic administration, post offices	SU-9	Buildings and Grounds Used by Any Department of Town, City, Township, County, State or Federal Government
		CBD-1	Core activities of all types with a side variety of related land uses
		CBD-2	Support uses for CBD-1 - less land use intensity than CBD-1
		CBD-S	A special primary district requiring Metropolitan Development Commission approval of all uses, site and development plans
		CBD-S	A special primary district requiring Metropolitan Development Commission approval of all uses, site and development plans

TABLE 5.1 *(Continued)* Zoning uses compatible with IBC Occupancy Groups. Zoning groups are based on Marion County designations and descriptions.

Zoning Uses Compatible with IBC Occupancy Groups		Potentially Compatible Zoning Districts	Compatible Zoning Use Description
IBC Occupancy Group-Division	Building or Structure Use Examples		
		HD-1	Hospital District One
		HD-2	Hospital District Two
		UQ-1	University Quarter District One - Permits and facilitates the development, expansion, etc., of a major university complex or campus
		I-2-S	Light Industrial Suburban District
		I-2-U	Light Industrial Urban District
B	educational occupancies above 12th grade	C-2	High Intensity Office-Apartment District
		C-3C	Corridor Commercial
		C-4	Community-Regional Commercial District
		C-5	General Commercial District
		C-7	High Intensity Commercial District
		C-ID	Commercial-Industrial District
		CBD-1	Core activities of all types with a side variety of related land uses
		CBD-2	Support uses for CBD-1 - less land use intensity than CBD-1
		UQ-1	University Quarter District One - Permits and facilitates the development, expansion, etc., of a major university complex or campus
B	electronic data processing	C-1	Office Buffer District
		C-2	High Intensity Office-Apartment District
		C-3	Neighborhood Commercial District
		C-5	General Commercial District
		C-7	High Intensity Commercial District
		C-ID	Commercial-Industrial District
B	fire and police stations	SU-8	Correctional and Penal Institutions
		SU-9	Buildings and Grounds Used by Any Department of Town, City, Township, County, State or Federal Government
		D-6	(Dwelllings) Located in urban areas in which redevelopment efforts are ongoing or where infill housing is needed
B	laboratories, testing and research	Any I	INDUSTRIAL
		SU-9	Buildings and Grounds Used by Any Department of Town, City, Township, County, State or Federal Government
		SU-29	Petroleum Refineries and Petroleum Products
		HD-1	Hospital District One
		HD-2	Hospital District Two
		UQ-1	University Quarter District One - Permits and facilitates the development, expansion, etc., of a major university complex or campus
B	motor vehicle showrooms	C-3C	Corridor Commercial
		C-4	Community-Regional Commercial District
		C-6	Thoroughfare Service District
		C-7	High Intensity Commercial District
		C-ID	Commercial-Industrial District
		CBD-2	Support uses for CBD-1 - less land use intensity than CBD-1
B	professional service offices	Any C	COMMERCIAL
		Any CBD	COMMERCIAL
B	radio and television stations	SU-5	Radio Receiving or Broadcasting Towers and Accessory Buildings
		SU-35	Telecommunication Receiving or Broadcasting Towers and Associated Accessory Buildings
B	telephone exchanges	SU-35	Telecommunication Receiving or Broadcasting Towers and Associated Accessory Buildings
E	schools trhough 12th grade, more than 6 occupants	SU-2	Schools
E	daycare for children 2 1/2 years and older, more than 5 occupants	C-3	Neighborhood Commercial District

TABLE 5.1 (*Continued*) Zoning uses compatible with IBC Occupancy Groups. Zoning groups are based on Marion County designations and descriptions.

Zoning Uses Compatible with IBC Occupancy Groups			
IBC Occupancy Group-Division	Building or Structure Use Examples	Potentially Compatible Zoning Districts	Compatible Zoning Use Description
		I-3-S	Medium Industrial Suburban District
F-1		I-2-U	Light Industrial Urban District
		I-3-U	Medium Industrial Urban District
F-1	manufacturing, heavy: aircraft, automobiles, boats, recreational and other vehicles; metals, engines, machinery, construction, mills, paper products, wood products, wood distillation, leather products, photo & film products, disinfectantsmaufacturing services: laundries, incinerators, carpet cleaning, engine and machine repair & rebuilding, dry cleaning & dyeing,	I-4-S	Heavy Industrial Suburban District
		I-5-S	Heavy Industrial Suburban (Outside Storage) District
		I-4-U	Heavy Industrial Urban District
		I-5-U	Heavy Industrial Urban (Outside Storage) District
F-1	military base	SU-9	Buildings and Grounds Used by Any Department of Town, City, Township, County, State or Federal Government
F-2	factory industiral, low fire hazard	C-ID	Commercial-Industrial District
		CBD-2	Support uses for CBD-1 - less land use intensity than CBD-1
		I-1-S	Restricted Industrial Suburban District
		I-2-S	Light Industrial Suburbān District
		I-3-S	Medium Industrial Suburban District
		I-2-U	Light Industrial Urban District
H-1	high explosion hazard	I-3-U	Medium Industrial Urban District
H-2	fire or explosion hazard, closed system		
H-3	fire or explosion hazard, open system		
H-4	health hazards, toxic or corrosive substances		
H-5	hazardous production materials, semiconductor fabrication, research facilities		
I-1	hospitals and skilled care facilities, rehab facilities serving more than 16		
I-2	hospitals and skilled care facilities, rehab facilities serving 5-16		
I-3	incarceration and detention facilities		
I-4	adult and child daycare serving more than 5		
M	department stores		
	drug stores		
	markets		
	motor vehicle service stations		
	retail or wholesale stores		
	sales rooms		
R-1	boarding houses, transient		
	hotels and motels		
R-2			
R-3			
R-4			
S-1	Petroleum warehouse, flashpoints below 200 deg. F. (93 deg. C)		
S-1	Motor vehicle repair garages, exempt quantities of hazardous materials		
S-1	Storage, moderate hazard: aerosols, aircraft hangers, bags, baskets, belts, books, burlap, boots, buttons, cardboard, cloth, clothing, cordage, furniture, furs, glues, grains, horns & combs (non-celluloid), leather, linoleum, lumber, mattresses, mucilage, paper, pastes, photo engravings, resilient flooring, silks, soaps, sugar, shoes, sizing, tires, tobacco & tobacco products, upholstery, wax candles, wool.		
S-2	Parking garages, open or closed		
S-2	oil-filled and other types of transformers		
U	agricultural buildings, barns, greenhouses, grain silos (accessory), livestock shelters, stables	D-A	Dwelling Agriculture
U	carports, private garages	Accessory to any D use	DWELLING
U	fences (over 6'), retaining walls, sheds,	Accessory to any use	
U	tanks	SU-41	Sewage Disposal Plant
U	towers	SU-5	Radio Receiving or Broadcasting Towers and Accessory Buildings
		SU-35	Telecommunication Receiving or Broadcasting Towers and Associated Accessory Buildings

FIGURE 5.7 This photo shows the dramatic conversion of a modest frame house into attorneys' offices. The elevations that are not visible from the parking area and street still indicate the history of the structure as a home.

Flipping for Profit

A conversion project can be quick-flipped when it is sold as soon as possible for quick liquid capital. Playing the conversion game for quick profits can change the rules a bit. Developers understand that potential purchase options broaden because every building selected for conversion does not have to be a keeper. Design professionals engaged in property evaluation for the investor/developer need to understand the intentions to keep or flip the property. When a quick sale is planned as soon as the conversion is completed, the only major requirement is to establish that there is a market for the property. That means the investor/developer will need to do some market research, but it is time well spent before engaging design consultants.

Here's a word to the wise. When Dorothy was just out of school and on her first job, some eager young people approached her employer with the proposal to convert an abandoned restaurant and convert it into a discothèque geared for deaf clientele. It would have light shows and rhythmic music with palpable vibrations. Her boss asked her what she thought of the project. Eager to design something for such high-minded clients, she launched into a discussion of her design approach that would fit the program they had outlined.

As soon as the client left, her boss quickly explained that the project was obviously commercially unviable and that the clients had minimal resources of their own to risk on the project. It was a poignant moment of clarity. The point is that design professionals have to screen their client's ideas for their ability to pay, and if the success of the built project is a factor in getting paid, the investor/developer needs to sell the design professional on the viability of his idea.

fastfacts

Design professionals engaged in property evaluation for the investor/developer need to understand his point of view regarding his intentions to keep or flip the property. When a quick sale is planned as soon as the conversion is completed, the only major requirement is to establish that there is a market for the property. That means the investor/developer will need to do some market research, but it is time well spent before engaging design consultants.

In an up market all but the worst architects can afford to be selective in the projects they take. The best design professionals will be selective and conscious of the projects they undertake in any market conditions. The projects that are built will affect their reputation and reflect corporately on their skills for decades. Occasionally a moonlighting architect or someone with a start-up will be hungry enough to take on such work.

If the conversion is low-end and highly selective with minimal external image changes, few will take it on. It's low risk work, but it does little to build their design reputation. If the scope of the project can be classified as maintenance, repair, or is of limited scope that does not require the stamp of a design professional, the investor/developer should work directly with a knowledgeable contractor. The contractor should have the ability to generate sufficient documentation in order that both parties understand what will be demolished and what will be built. Before engaging a contractor or a design professional to execute designs, an investor has to work out his business plan first.

PROFIT POTENTIAL

The profit potential of a project is always a prime concern. It doesn't matter if the project is a quick flip or a keeper, the investor/developer must have a handle on the profit to be made or lost. General contractors, especially with small enterprises, will often take on conversion investments as quick-flip investments. This is an especially useful business practice for keeping their workers busy between contracted work assignments.

Experienced contractors or design professionals who specialize in renovation work should have sufficient database to estimate the cost of conversion work. R.S. Means publishes a series of books and software that includes the two most widely used estimating guides in the industry, *Means Building Construction Cost Data 2003 Book* (Phillip R. Waier, Editor, Publisher: Robert S. Means Co., October 2002) and *Means Square Foot Costs 2003 Book* (Barbara Balboni, Editor, Publisher: Robert S. Means Co., November 2002). Means offers about 39 guides in all including several tailored to the renovation market including *Means Repair & Remodeling Cost Data 2003 Book* (Howard M.Chandler, Editor, Publisher: Robert S. Means Co, November 2002).

Some editions are tailored for regional or foreign markets, others for merit-shop contractors. Most offer location-based factors in the appendices. When buying a property distressed by fire or some other natural disaster, insurance assessors and claims adjusters may use these guides as the basis for evaluating the cost of repairing the damage. Dorothy once worked with a client who contested the insurer's assessment of the damage to his multi-family property. A room-by-room inventory backed up by estimates generated chiefly with Means data resulted in the client increasing his settlement considerably. He was able to return the property to profitable use. These are useful resources used by many architects early in the design process to estimate the potential construction and demolition cost of the proposed work. The database maintained by experienced appraisers can be a great asset in determining the cost of conversion work. They can help determine the potential selling price for the completed project. Brokers may consult for free in hopes of getting the commission to sell the property. Generally, free advice is worth exactly what one pays for it. Appraisers will be able to determine the current market value of the property and the value with the proposed alterations and improvements. Prices for this service begin at a few hundred dollars. The more experienced the speculative investor/developer, the better able he will be to make his own estimate of market values. He may get to this point quickly by working on related building types in similar locations rather than customizing the program and location to suit a prospective tenant or purchaser. Taking time

fastfacts

The database maintained by experienced appraisers can be a great asset in determining the cost of conversion work. It can help determine the potential selling price for the completed project.

to check recent property transfers and current property prices in the area, one can estimate prices pretty closely. Don't confuse the asking price with the selling price or the costs to close the deal. It is not uncommon for properties to be sold for considerably more or less than the advertised asking price. To be safe, use the data for closed sales and proven sales prices. This will better target the profit potential of various buildings.

Keepers

The durable building is one that is not going to require any major repairs for at least 10 years. If the major mechanical, plumbing, and electrical systems are in good order and of recent vintage and there are no structural defects, the building is solid. A good roof is a really good idea if you don't want to see your investment damaged. A durable building is a keeper. If the building needs a new HVAC system within five years or the roof will need to be replaced in three, it may be suitable for quick flip conversion, but not for long term ownership as an owner-occupied or investment rental property. In some cases, if these are the only problems, the building might still be a keeper if these factors can be affordably addressed in the initial renovation. In assessing buildings, keep in mind that buyers will think differently than designers and owner/occupants. Designers should be aware that investors must consider this when formulating an

FIGURE 5.8 This obsolete service sink was scheduled for demolition to make room for new equipment. The condition of existing fixtures and equipment is not always the driving factor in re-using them.

offer to purchase and the potential profit picture. It is an unfortunate reality that the investor will almost always keep his true bottom line concealed from designers, unless they are on his staff exclusively. He will do this to keep from being oversold on improvements he doesn't need to make the profit picture work. So the design professional has to make an experienced guess of what the real construction budget is. Not knowing the true budget makes it difficult for designers to identify and propose repairs that are needed, but don't fit the stated budget, so some may hold back. Trust is important in giving and receiving the best service possible.

Managed Property

The rental management of a building may be the furthest thing from anyone's mind when inspecting potential conversion projects, but it shouldn't be. Management of a building can have an awful lot to do with the property's value. If the investor will be selling the property, he has no way of knowing if the new owner will manage the building personally or hire a management company. Either way, buyers want buildings that are not nightmares to manage. When you are checking out properties, think about management issues. For example, will existing building systems require many repair calls? How easy will it be to lease the units at the prevailing rent rate for the area? How many exterior and interior finish materials are there to be maintained? Are there many joints? Many systems?

Utilities

The availability and cost of utilities plays a part in selecting a building. For example, a property that is too far out of town to be served by cable television may have a high vacancy rate. Buildings served by a private septic system could be troublesome. Hard water can limit the life span of pipes and plumbing systems. Before buying any property, dig into the utility factors. Explore previous costs for heating, cooling, water, and other expenses. If the property is served by a private water well, confirm that the well produces enough water to satisfy the need of the number of tenants you expect to reside in the property. Do the same check on private

The rental management of a building may be the furthest thing from anyone's mind when inspecting potential conversion projects, but it shouldn't be. Management of a building can have an awful lot to do with the property's value.

sewage facilities. Determine if the area is served by public utilities or a private system. What works fine for a single-family house may make a mess when used by multiple families or commercial tenants.

Taxes

Real estate taxes are a fact of life in most communities. You should check the tax rate that will apply to your property. Keep in mind that the building will be reassessed once your work is done, and the value of the property is sure to go up, driving up the tax payments. This will become a factor when you sell the property, as well as if you hold it. Also check to see if there are immanent infrastructure improvements proposed for the area, either due to adjacent development or redevelopment or as a result of a deal made for the proposed project. There will be an added assessment to cover the cost of the project.

Condition

The physical condition of a building may not be very important, so long as you buy the property for a good price. If you are a contractor, you shouldn't be afraid of what it takes to bring a building back up to satisfactory standards. You should, however, spend enough time in the inspection process so that you are not faced with any surprises. As long as you are aware of what must be done and what the costs will be, almost any property can be a suitable purchase.

Location

Dare we repeat, the most tried and true rule of real estate is: location, location, and location. Location is everything in real estate. Once several potential investment properties have been identified, spend some time investigating the areas where potential buildings are located. Check the distances between the building and schools, shopping, and medical facilities. Be aware of the location of potential competitors. Be aware of their strategic advantages and their weaknesses, so your business can locate to out maneuver them. We can't stress enough how valuable location is to a real estate transaction, so please, don't skimp on this phase of the analysis.

FIELD OBSERVATION

Going into the field to look at potential properties can be very exciting. By the time you begin do site inspections, the investor should know the

> **fast**facts
>
> Location is everything in real estate. Once several potential investment properties have been identified, spend some time investigating the areas where potential buildings are located.

type of properties he wants to buy, where (generally) he wants them located, and how he will finance them.

Experienced investor/developers will have little trouble evaluating the structural and mechanical aspects of properties. Novice investors in the construction and remodeling business owe it to themselves to do some extra homework. Read books and learn what to look for when inspecting a potential property. The Urban Land Institute is an excellent source of this kind of information. If the investor will also occupy or manage the property, International Facility Managers Association (IFMA) and Building Owners and Managers Association (BOMA) may also be good resources in addition to books available at the local library.

Take scrupulous notes in the field. Sometimes it helps to have a checklist with space for comments, so that you don't leave out key observations important to making a comparison between properties. A small tape recorder comes in handy, but a pad of paper and a pencil will get the job done. The observer should write down everything possible about various properties. As the search continues, one may soon forget key issues pertaining to particular properties if you don't have some form of recorded notes. The information may prove invaluable when the time comes to decide which building to buy.

Field Observation Tools and Techniques

In the field, take the tools of the trade, minimally, a flashlight, tape measure, and a screwdriver. Ask the seller or listing agent to provide a ladder or extension ladder. The buyer has the right to observe the roof and areas above lay-in ceilings and inside accessible chases and shafts. A good light is the most important part of your tool kit as a building observer. A flat-bit screwdriver can be used to probe floor joists and sill plates for rot. However, never remove an electrical panel cover unless you're sure it's disconnected. Stephen carries a Leatherman tool and a pencil-size

fastfacts

Take scrupulous notes in the field. Sometimes it helps to have a checklist with space for comments, so that you don't leave out key observations important to making a comparison between properties. A small tape recorder comes in handy, but a pad of paper and a pencil will get the job done. The observer should write down everything about various properties. As the search continues, one may soon forget key issues pertaining to particular properties if you don't have some form of recorded notes. Recorded thoughts may prove invaluable when the time comes to decide which building to buy.

flashlight with him wherever he goes. These fit comfortably on a belt loop or in a pocket. Your tape measure will help to establish square footage in the building, as well as room sizes. If the owner has as-built drawings that he's willing to let you copy, this will save a lot of measuring time. For large spaces or tall spaces, sonic measuring devices can be used with accuracy to ¼ inch. This is a convenience especially when there's no companion to hold the "dumb end of the tape." In addition to your mechanical tools, don't forget your administrative needs, such as a tape recorder, pad of paper, pencil, and so forth.

It may sound silly, but it's a good idea not to go alone to a vacant property, especially in an unfamiliar part of town. At the very least, advise someone trusted of your plans. If you are searching in unfamiliar territory, a good street map may come in handy. You can get very precise information and driving directions off the Internet with just an address or intersection at Expedia.com (www.expedia.com) and Maps.com (www.maps.com) for this purpose. If it's out of town, you can make your travel arrangements while you're at it.

Ask plenty of questions when inspecting a building. Talk to the building owners whenever possible. If you must talk through a real estate broker, confirm the broker's comments with the property owner before moving too far ahead in the acquisition of the property. When looking at buildings that are already being used as rental property, talk to the tenants. They can tell you things that the owner might not. Dorothy moved a lot as a corporate brat growing up. Her mom always insisted on meeting the neighbors before making a home purchase. Like tenants, neighbors may have a lot to say about the manner in which the property has been maintained, its crime history, the aims they have for their own property, the hopes they have for the subject property. Unless you're serious about the property, don't start with the interviews. Chatty tenants and neighbors can take you on time-wasting tangents.

EVALUATION

The investor should go over the observed findings when he will be undisturbed. A minor mistake in evaluating a building can cost major money. Creating simple checklists to use may be helpful when comparing buildings under consideration. Dorothy likes using a checklist created in an Excel database and assigning values to criteria so it can be directly compared. Data can be sorted several ways without re-creating the sheet. Criteria are listed down the left in order of priority. Properties are listed across the top. Rating data or comments are inserted for each criterion. Data can be manipulated across all models. When considering specific repairs, refer to an appendix shared by Luther Mock in his seminar for making weighted evaluations for major systems selection in his envelope renovation business. It's called the Weighted Evaluation Master Form.

Red Flags

The investor should be judicious in the selection process. There are times when it pays to act quickly, but more often than not, a hasty decision will be a regrettable one. Experienced investor/developers will know a steal when they find it, but most should take enough time to make sure they are seeing all angles of a deal. It is better to lose a good deal than to buy a bad building.

Fire jobs can look like a wonderful opportunity, and they can be for people with the right experience, but they can turn into a disaster. Buildings damaged by fire can hold many secrets. These secrets and surprises can be quite costly, and they can bust your budget in the blink of an eye. Roger has a fair amount of experience in fire restoration, and is still leery of buying a fire-damaged building. While the prices may be very low, the value may be even lower with this type of building. This is one case where we suggest a painstaking assessment and the work of a professional appraiser, even for the experienced investor. This is generally not a good investment for a beginner.

FIGURE 5.9 Dutchmen, visible or concealed, are used to stabilize existing masonry walls. Here, a common star form Dutchman expresses where the wall construction is anchored to the deck construction.

> Experienced investor/developers will know a steal when they find it, but most should take enough time to make sure they are seeing all angles of a deal. It is better to lose a good deal than to buy a bad building.

There is nothing wrong with getting creative when purchasing real estate, but be careful not to get too creative. Usually, the more complicated something is, the easier it is for something to go wrong. If you run across a seller who is extremely anxious and who has an answer for your every objection, be very careful. This type of owner may just be looking for some sucker to unload a bad building on. If the deal seems too good to be true, it probably is.

Once the property has been selected, there is a lot of work to do, and much of it must be done prior to purchase. After finding what appears to be a suitable property, the investor must verify that the property is everything he plans. This is a complicated and time-consuming process. What follows are some tips on what may attract buyers and tenants and how design professionals may address the needs of renovation clients for their mutual profit.

CHANGING NATURE OF CLIENTS

Trends in businesses affect the services that clients want and how they want them delivered. So, who comprises this new breed of investor/developers that form the pool of redevelopment clients for the design professional? Designers should be aware of these trends in order to better understand clients when they come into the design office or email you an RFQ (request for qualifications.) Clients may be more or less the same indi-

FIGURE 5.10 Water behind a cement plaster canopy indicates water in the roof assembly and structural system above. Trapped moisture of this type can also be perilous for the overhead lights. It is important to note basic deficiencies that must be corrected as well as programmatic incompatibilities when assessing a building for a proposed alternate use. *Photo by Stephen Culbert*

> There is nothing wrong with getting creative when purchasing real estate, but be careful not to get too creative. Usually, the more complicated something is, the easier it is for something to go wrong.

viduals and enterprises that would have been attracted to redevelopment in the past, but they are ever more sophisticated. Do clients see architectural and related design services as commodities or valued services, a necessary evil or the combined skills of applied arts and sciences? If the designer looks at what else his client values, it will be easy to answer those questions without asking them.

Increased Client Sophistication

The larger the client's enterprise the more likely they will have trained facilities and operations programming staff or consultants. Retail, restaurant, and entertainment chains will have developed image models and franchise criteria which will be included in the design criteria. There may be little tolerance for locally available alternatives that may meet functional requirements but not image-driven or SOP (Standard Operations Platform) requirements.

Managing Complexity

Managing complexity is something that few design firms do really well. Sophisticated clients will often have complex needs. The following are several of the factors that can quickly complicate what appears on the surface to be a moderate cost project:

- Multiple users or uses, especially those requiring separation
- Multiple types of construction
- Multiple buildings with very different uses on a campus
- Multiple buildings with similar uses on scattered sites
- Large-scale projects
- Projects less than $1 million in construction cost.
- Renovating areas with more than one previous renovation

- Areas requiring extensive filed investigation or destructive discovery
- Areas requiring intensive space programming
- Multiple circulation paths or secure routes
- Multiple construction contracts
- Multiple owners or funding sources
- Multiple review authorities
- Multiple types of HVAC or other building systems
- Public interface and review
- Public funds
- Work restrictions
- Accommodating ongoing operations
- Phased work and construction sequencing
- Elective alternatives in program scope
- Permitted voluntary alternates
- Selective renovation and conservation
- Selective demolition
- Site reclamation
- Abatement
- Salvage equipment or construction

To keep complex design problems manageable, and profitable, designers should look for similarities and patterns in the program. It may help the designer to actually develop a language of responses to answer questions such as how to terminate a roof edge or connect skin to structure.

Streamlining how problems are viewed so that the same solution is applied to multiple circumstances is one way to conquer a building program with a great deal of complexity. Working with a firm that either specializes in renovation or in the major use type will offer advantages to the developer. Firms that specialize in building types often have a vocabulary of details from which they can draw and edit to suit a current project. Such a language allows them to offer their services affordably because they need not reinvent details at every step. It also gives them an experienced-based checklist of what problems a project is likely to present.

For example, a wastewater treatment facility had limited documentation of existing buildings and an overhaul of all facilities on the main industrial campus to address. The design team designed one structural approach for the renovation of existing masonry structures and a second for new non-tank structures. Briefly the team even looked at simplifying the number of bay sizes used. They looked for methods of construction that would reduce displacement time of ongoing operations. The owner needed durable low maintenance materials. The team limited the number of trades by using pre-cast concrete envelope and structural systems even where a lesser construction was allowed. Because there was an economy in scale since the work was bundled into just two phases, concrete ended up being more affordable than the combustible materials allowed by code for some of the structures.

From the designer's point of view, too much selectivity in demolition can become an unwieldy problem especially if this effort has not been properly included in the fee proposal. Many owners will want to use an historic percentage-based compensation approach and it is rare that a designer can win in this situation unless the percentage is bumped up considerably.

Flexibility

Corporate clients may weigh mobility against retaining or maximizing the re-sale potential of developed space. They will have an exit strategy that may include use of highly flexible easily re-leaseable space in preference to image building through architectural form and texture.

Start-ups and spin-offs will often be looking for leaseable space with high tech systems and connectivity, but priced just slightly higher than the garage across the street. Since start-ups have a high rate of failure, they want leases that they can sublease or release if things go sour. When a high tech startup takes off, its growth can be explosive and its ability to endure downtime as it grows may be fragile.

Flexibility of space is important in managing changing technology, changing processes, and flat or matrixal management structures.

fastfacts

Corporate clients may weigh mobility against retaining or maximizing the re-sale potential of developed space. They will have an exit strategy that may include use of highly flexible, easily re-leaseable space in preference to image building through architectural form and texture.

Downsizing and rightsizing create needs for diversification of potential uses of space without significant reinvestment. There is value to the property owner in building physical adaptability design. Space and aesthetics should be suitable for potential resale or reassignment. Table 5.2 indicates potential compatibility between uses defined in the Marion County zoning districts definitions.

TABLE 5.2 Potentially compatible adjacent uses or mixed uses (*Continued*)

Use Group		**Potentially Compatible* Zoning for Adjacent Use (or Mixed Use on the Same Site Development)** *Scale of proposed enterprise, planned site density and local ordinances should be carefully reviewed prior to commiting fund to any development plan. Market forces, such as disparate values may make some marked uses undesireable for the landowner with higher use. ** Compatiblity depends on local definition for this use.																																				
		Dwelling													Commercial										Business District				Industrial									
Use Description	Use	D-P	D-A	D-S	D-1, D-2	D-3, D-4	D-5	D-6	D-6II	D-7	D-9	D-10	D-11	D-12	C-1	C-2	C-3	C-3C	C-4	C-5	C-6	C-7	C-ID	C-S	CBD-1	CBD-2	CBD-3	CBD-S	I-1-S	I-2-S	I-3-S	I-4-S	I-5-S	I-1-U	I-2-U	I-3-U	I-4-U	I-5-U
DWELLING		X																																				
A planned unit development (housing presumed to be part of mix of uses*)	D-P (a.k.a. PUD)		X																																			
Dwelling Agriculture	D-A	X	X	X																																		
Dwelling Suburban	D-S	X	-	X	X																																	
Suburban areas with moderate topography	D-1, D-2	X	-	X	X	X																																
Medium and medium-high density single-family areas	D-3, D-4	X	-	-	-	X	X																															
Urban developed area	D-5	X	-	-	-	X	X	X																														
(Dwellings) Located in urban areas in which redevelopment efforts are ongoing or where infill housing is needed	D-6	X	X	X	X	X	X	X	X																													
Low-density multifamily use to be used as a transition between high-density and low-intensity uses	D-6II	X	-	X	-	X	X	X	X	X																												
Medium-density multifamily located throughout the metropolitan areas and associated with primary traffic generators	D-7	X	-	X	X	-	-	-	-	X	X																											
Suburban high-rise apartments	D-9	X	-	-	-	X	X	X	-	X	-	X																										
Central and inner-city locations for high-density multifamily use	D-10	X	-	-	-	X	X	-	-	X	-	X	X																									
Mobile dwelling project district for high-density single-family use	D-11	X	-	X	X	X	X	X	X	X	X	X	-	X																								
Medium-high density two-family subdivisions with the intensity of single-family development	D-12																																					

Profitability

Lets not forget why clients are in business. Revised corporate focus is on profit centers rather than service centers. Cost, competitive advantage, and productivity are the variables that determine the value of facilities expenditures. Image building may be out. Low cost flexible digs and leasing are in. In downtimes, some businesses stay lean and profitable by sticking to the core business and unloading extra services.

TABLE 5.2 *(Continued)* Potentially compatible adjacent uses or mixed uses

		Potentially Compatible* Zoning for Adjacent Use (or Mixed Use on the Same Site Development) *Scale of proposed enterprise, planned site density and local ordinances should be carefully reviewed prior to commiting fund to any development plan. Market forces, such as disparate values may make some marked uses undesireable for the landowner with higher use. ** Compatiblity depends on local definition for this use.																																		
		Special Use																							Airport		Historic		Hospital		Park		Universit y		Flood	
Use Group		SU-1	SU-2	SU-3	SU-5	SU-6	SU-7	SU-8	SU-9	SU-10	SU-13	SU-16	SU-20	SU-28	SU-29	SU-34	SU-35	SU-37	SU-38	SU-39	SU-41	SU-42	SU-43	SU-44	A	A-secondary	HP-1	S	HD-1	HD-2	PK-1	PK-2	UQ-1	UQ-2(B)	FW	FP
Use Description	Use																																			
DWELLING																																				
A planned unit development (housing presumed to be part of mix of uses*)	D-P (a.k.a. PUD)																																			
Dwelling Agriculture	D-A																																			
Dwelling Suburban	D-S																																			
Suburban areas with moderate topography	D-1, D-2																																			
Medium and medium-high density single-family areas	D-3, D-4																																			
Urban developed area	D-5																																			
(Dwelllings) Located in urban areas in which redevelopment efforts are ongoing or where infill housing is needed	D-6																																			
Low-density multifamily use to be used as a transition between high-density and low-intensity uses	D-6II																																			
Medium-density multifamily located throughout the metropolitan areas and associated with primary traffic generators	D-7																																			
Suburban high-rise apartments	D-9																																			
Central and inner-city locations for high-density multifamily use	D-10																																			
Mobile dwelling project district for high-density single-family use	D-11																																			
Medium-high density two-family subdivisions with the intensity of single-family development	D-12																																			

TABLE 5.2 *(Continued)* Potentially compatible adjacent uses or mixed uses

		Potentially Compatible* Zoning for Adjacent Use (or Mixed Use on the Same Site Development) *Scale of proposed enterprise, planned site density and local ordinances should be carefully reviewed prior to commiting fund to any development plan. Market forces, such as disparate values may make some marked uses undesireable for the landowner with higher use. ** Compatiblity depends on local definition for this use.																																				
		Dwelling													Commercial										Business District				Industrial									
Use Group		D-P	D-A	D-S	D-1, D-2	D-3, D-4	D-5	D-6	D-6II	D-7	D-9	D-10	D-11	D-12	C-1	C-2	C-3	C-3C	C-4	C-5	C-6	C-7	C-ID	C-S	CBD-1	CBD-2	CBD-3	CBD-S	I-1-S	I-2-S	I-3-S	I-4-S	I-5-S	I-1-U	I-2-U	I-3-U	I-4-U	I-5-U
Use Description	Use																																					
COMMERCIAL		X	-	X	X	X	X	X	X	X	X	X	-	X	X																							
Office Buffer District	C-1	X	-	-	-	-	X	X	-	X	X	X	-	-	X	X																						
High Intensity Office-Apartment District	C-2	X	-	X	X	X	X	X	X	-	X		-	X	X	-	X																					
Neighborhood Commercial District	C-3	-	-	-	-	-	-	-	-	X	-	X	-	-	X	X	X	X																				
Corridor Commercial	C-3C	-	-	-	-	-	-						-	-	X	X	-	X	X																			
Community-Regional Commercial District	C-4	X	-	-	-	-	-	X	X	X	X	X	X	-	X	X	-	X	X	X																		
General Commercial District	C-5	-	-	-	-	-	-	-	X	X	X	-	X	-	X	-	-	X	X	X	X																	
Thoroughfare Service District	C-6	-	-	-	-	-	-	-	X	X	-	X	-	-	X	X	-	X	X	X		X																
High Intensity Commercial District	C-7	-	-	-	-	-	-	-	X	X			X	-	X	-	-	-	X				X															
Commercial-Industrial District	C-ID	**	**	**	**	**	**	**	**	**	**	**	**	**	**	**	**	**	**	**	**	**	**	X														
Special Commercial District**	C-S	X	-	-	-	-	-	X	X	X	-	X	-	X	X	X	-	X	X	X	X	X	-	**	X													
Core activities of all types with a side variety of related land uses	CBD-1	X	-	-	-	X	X	X	X	X	X	X	-	X	X	X	X	X	X	X	-	X	X	**	X	X												
Support uses for CBD-1 - less land use intensity than CBD-1	CBD-2	X	-	-	-	X	-	-	-	-	-	-	-	-	X	-	X	-	-	-	-	-	-	**	X	X	X											
Exclusive off-apartment district around a memorial plaza	CBD-3	**	**	**	**	**	**	**	**	**	**	**	**	**	**	**	**	**	**	**	**	**	**	**	**	**	**	X										
A special primary district requiring Metropolitan Development Commission approval of all uses, site and development plans	CBD-S																																					

TABLE 5.2 (*Continued*) Potentially compatible adjacent uses or mixed uses

		Potentially Compatible* Zoning for Adjacent Use (or Mixed Use on the Same Site Development)																																		
		*Scale of proposed enterprise, planned site density and local ordinances should be carefully reviewed prior to commiting fund to any development plan. Market forces, such as disparate values may make some marked uses undesireable for the landowner with higher use.																																		
		** Compatiblity depends on local definition for this use.																																		
		Special Use																						Airport		Historic		Hospital		Park	Universit	y		Flood	
Use Group		SU-1	SU-2	SU-3	SU-5	SU-6	SU-7	SU-8	SU-9	SU-10	SU-13	SU-16	SU-20	SU-28	SU-29	SU-34	SU-35	SU-37	SU-38	SU-39	SU-41	SU-42	SU-43	SU-44	A	A-secondary	HP-1	S	HD-1	HD-2	PK-1	PK-2	UQ-1	UQ-2(B)	FW	FP
Use Description	Use																																			
COMMERCIAL																																				
Office Buffer District	C-1																																			
High Intensity Office-Apartment District	C-2																																			
Neighborhood Commercial District	C-3																																			
Corridor Commercial	C-3C																																			
Community-Regional Commercial District	C-4																																			
General Commercial District	C-5																																			
Thoroughfare Service District	C-6																																			
High Intensity Commercial District	C-7																																			
Commercial-Industrial District	C-ID																																			
Special Commercial District**	C-S																																			
Core activities of all types with a side variety of related land uses	CBD-1																																			
Support uses for CBD-1 - less land use intensity than CBD-1	CBD-2																																			
Exclusive off-apartment district around a memorial plaza	CBD-3																																			
A special primary district requiring Metropolitan Development Commission approval of all uses, site and development plans	CBD-S																																			

TABLE 5.2 *(Continued)* Potentially compatible adjacent uses or mixed uses

Use Group		Potentially Compatible* Zoning for Adjacent Use (or Mixed Use on the Same Site Development) *Scale of proposed enterprise, planned site density and local ordinances should be carefully reviewed prior to commiting fund to any development plan. Market forces, such as disparate values may make some marked uses undesireable for the landowner with higher use. ** Compatiblity depends on local definition for this use.																																				
		Dwelling													Commercial										Business District				Industrial									
Use Description	Use	D-P	D-A	D-S	D-1, D-2	D-3, D-4	D-5	D-6	D-6II	D-7	D-9	D-10	D-11	D-12	C-1	C-2	C-3	C-3C	C-4	C-5	C-6	C-7	C-ID	C-S	CBD-1	CBD-2	CBD-3	CBD-S	I-1-S	I-2-S	I-3-S	I-4-S	I-5-S	I-1-U	I-2-U	I-3-U	I-4-U	I-5-U
INDUSTRIAL		X	X	X	X	X	-	X	-	-	-	X	X	-	X	X	X	-	X	X	X	-	X	**	-	X	-	**	X									
Restricted Industrial Suburban District	I-1-S	X	-	-	X	-	-	-	X	X	-	X	X		X	X	X	-	X	X	X	-	X	**	-	X	-	**	X	X								
Light Industrial Suburban District	I-2-S	X	-	-	-	-	-	-	-	-	-	-	-	-	X	X	X	-	-	-	X	-	X	**	-	X	-	**	X	X	X							
Medium Industrial Suburban District	I-3-S	-	-	-	-	-	-	-	-	-	-	-	-	-	X	-	X	-	-	-	-	-	-	**	-	-	-	**	-	-	X	X						
Heavy Industrial Suburban District	I-4-S	-	-	-	-	-	-	-	-	-	-	-	-	-	X	-	X	-	-	-	-	-	-	**	-	-	-	**	-	-	X	X	X					
Heavy Industrial Suburban (Outside Storage) District	I-5-S	-	-	-	-	X	X	X	-	X	-	-	X	-	X	X	X	-	X	X	X	-	X	**	-	X	-	**	X	X	-	-	-	X				
Restricted Industrial Urban District	I-1-U	X	-	-	-	-	-	X	-	X	-	-	X	-	X	X	X	-	X	X	X	-	X	**	-	X	-	**	X	X	-	-		X	X			
Light Industrial Urban District	I-2-U	X	-	-	-	-	-	-	-	-	-	-	-	-	X	X	X	-	-	-	X	-	X	**	-	X	-	**	X	X	X	X	X	X	X	X		
Medium Industrial Urban District	I-3-U	-	-	-	-	-	-	-	-	-	-	-	-	-	X	-	X	-	-	-	-	-	-	**	-	-	-	**	-	-	X	X	X	-	-	X	X	
Heavy Industrial Urban District	I-4-U	-	-	-	-	-	-	-	-	-	-	-	-	-	X	-	X	-	-	-	-	-	-	**	-	-	-	**	-	-	X	X	X	-	-	X	X	X
Heavy Industrial Urban (Outside Storage) District	I-5-U																							**														

TABLE 5.2 (*Continued*) Potentially compatible adjacent uses or mixed uses

Potentially Compatible* Zoning for Adjacent Use (or Mixed Use on the Same Site Development)

*Scale of proposed enterprise, planned site density and local ordinances should be carefully reviewed prior to commiting fund to any development plan. Market forces, such as disparate values may make some marked uses undesireable for the landowner with higher use.

** Compatiblity depends on local definition for this use.

Use Group		Special Use																							Airport		Historic		Hospital		Park		Universit y		Flood	
Use Description	Use	SU-1	SU-2	SU-3	SU-5	SU-6	SU-7	SU-8	SU-9	SU-10	SU-13	SU-16	SU-20	SU-28	SU-29	SU-34	SU-35	SU-37	SU-38	SU-39	SU-41	SU-42	SU-43	SU-44	A	A-secondary	HP-1	S	HD-1	HD-2	PK-1	PK-2	UQ-1	UQ-2(B)	FW	FP
INDUSTRIAL																																				
Restricted Industrial Suburban District	I-1-S																																			
Light Industrial Suburban District	I-2-S																																			
Medium Industrial Suburban District	I-3-S																																			
Heavy Industrial Suburban District	I-4-S																																			
Heavy Industrial Suburban (Outside Storage) District	I-5-S																																			
Restricted Industrial Urban District	I-1-U																																			
Light Industrial Urban District	I-2-U																																			
Medium Industrial Urban District	I-3-U																																			
Heavy Industrial Urban District	I-4-U																																			
Heavy Industrial Urban (Outside Storage) District	I-5-U																																			

Maintaining attractive ratios of leverage (money from outside investors) to debt (expenditure of corporate capital) can result in the reluctance of companies, especially in down markets, to spend on anything that doesn't enhance profit. Sometimes this reluctance can include deferred maintenance and addressing life safety issues.

Cost, competitive advantage, and productivity are the variables that determine the value of facilities expenditures to the owners.

TABLE 5.2 (*Continued*) Potentially compatible adjacent uses or mixed uses

Potentially Compatible* Zoning for Adjacent Use (or Mixed Use on the Same Site Development)

*Scale of proposed enterprise, planned site density and local ordinances should be carefully reviewed prior to commiting fund to any development plan. Market forces, such as disparate values may make some marked uses undesireable for the landowner with higher use.

** Compatiblity depends on local definition for this use.

		Dwelling													Commercial										Business District				Industrial									
Use Group		D-P	D-A	D-S	D-1, D-2	D-3, D-4	D-5	D-6	D-6II	D-7	D-9	D-10	D-11	D-12	C-1	C-2	C-3	C-3C	C-4	C-5	C-6	C-7	C-ID	C-S	CBD-1	CBD-2	CBD-3	CBD-S	I-1-S	I-2-S	I-3-S	I-4-S	I-5-S	I-1-U	I-2-U	I-3-U	I-4-U	I-5-U
Use Description	Use																																					
SPECIAL USE DISTRICTS		X	X	X	X	X	X	X	X	X	X	X	X	X	-	X	X	X	-	-	-	-	-	**	X	X	X	**	X	X	-	-	-	X	X	-	-	-
Churches	SU-1	X	X	X	X	X	X	X	X	X	X	X	-	X	X	X	X	X	-	-	-	-	-	**				**	X	X	-	-	-	X	X	-	-	-
Schools	SU-2	X	X	X	X	X	X	X	X	X	X	-	-	X	X	-	X	-	-	-	-	-	-	**				**	X	X	-	-	-	X	X	-	-	-
Golf Courses, Golf Driving Ranges	SU-3	-	X	X	X	X	X	X	X	X	X	X	X	X	X	X								**				**	X	X	X	X	X	X	X	X	X	X
Radio Receiving or Broadcasting Towers and Accessory Buildings	SU-5	-	-	-	-	X	X	X	X	X	X	X	-	X	X	X								**				**	X	X	-	-	-	X	X	-	-	-
Hospitals and Sanitariums	SU-6	X	X	X	X	X	X	X	X	X	X	X		X	X	X								**				**	X	X	-	-	-	X	X	-	-	-
Charitable and Philanthropic Institutions	SU-7		X	-	-	-	X	-	-	-	-	-	X	-	-	-	-	-	-	-	-	-	X	**	-	X	-	**	X	X	X	-	-	X	X	X	-	-
Correctional and Penal Institutions	SU-8	X	-	-	-	-	-	X	-	X	-	X	X	-	X	X	X	X	X	X	X	X	X	**	X	X	X	**	X	X	X	-	-	X	X	X	-	-
Buildings and Grounds Used by Any Department of Town, City, Township, County, State or Federal Government	SU-9	X	X	X	X	-	X	-	X	-	X	-	-	X	-	-	X	-	-	-	-	-	-	**	-	-	-	**	X	X	-	-	-	X	X	-	-	-
Cemeteries	SU-10	-	-	-	-	-	-	-	-	-	-	-	-	-	-	-	-	-	-	-	-	-	-	**	-	-	-	**	-	-	-	X	X	-	-	-	X	X
Sanitary Landfill	SU-13	X	X	X	X	X	X	X	X	X	X	X	X	X	-	-	-	-	-	-	-	-	-	**	-	X	-	**	-	-	-	-	-	-	-	-	-	-
Amusement parks and Swimming Pools Privately Owned and Open to Public Patronage	SU-16	X	X	X	X	X	X	X	X	X	X	X	X	X	X	X	X	-	-	X	X	-	X	**	X	X	X	**	X	X	X	X	X	X	X	X	X	X
Light and Power Substations	SU-20	X	X	X	X	X	X	X	X	X	X	X	X	X	X	X	X	-	-	X	X	-	X	**	X	X	X	**	X	X	X	X	X	X	X	X	X	X
Telephone Exchange Offices	SU-28	-	-	-	-	-	-	-	-	-	-	-	-	-	-	-	-	-	-	-	-	-	X	**	-	-	-	**	-	-	-	X	X	-	-	-	X	X
Petroleum Refineries and Petroleum Products	SU-29	X	-	-	-	X	X	X	-	X	X	X	X	X	X	-	X	X	-	X	-	-	X	**	X	X	-	**	X	X	-	-	-	X	X	-	-	-
Club Rooms b. Fraternal Rooms - Fraternity and Lodge c. Ballrooms - Public	SU-34	X	X	-	-	X	X	X	-	X	X	X	X	X	X	X	X	-	-	X	X	-	X	**	-	X	-	**	X	X	X	X	X	X	X	X	X	X
Telecommunication Receiving or Broadcasting Towers and Associated Accessory Buildings	SU-35	X	-	X	X	X	X	X	-	X	X	X	X	X	X	X	X	X	-	X	-	-	X	**	X	X	X	**	X	X	-	-	-	X	X	-	-	-
Library	SU-37	X	X	X	X	X	X	X	-	X	X	X	X	X	X	X	X	X	-	X	-	-	X	**	-	X	X	**	X	X	-	-	-	X	X	-	-	-
Community Center	SU-38	X	X	X	X	X	X	X	-	X	X	X	X	X	X	-	X	-	-	-	-	-	X	**	-	X	-	**	X	X	X	X	X	X	X	X	X	X
Water Tanks, Water Pumping Stations and Similar Structures Not Located in Buildings	SU-39	-	-	-	-	-	-	-	-	-	-	-	-	-	-	-	-	-	-	-	-	-	X	**	-	X	-	**	-	-	X	X	X	-	-	X	X	X
Sewage Disposal Plant	SU-41	-	X	-	-	-	-	-	-	-	-	-	-	-	-	-	-	-	-	-	-	-	X	**	-	X	-	**	-	-	X	X	X	-	-	X	X	X
Gas Utilities	SU-42	-	X	-	-	-	-	-	-	-	-	-	-	-	-	-	-	-	-	-	-	-	X	**	-	X	-	**	-	-	X	X	X	-	-	X	X	X
Power Transmission Lines (High Voltage)	SU-43	-	-	-	-	-	-	-	-	-	-	X	-	-	X	-	-	-	X	-	-	X	-	**	X	X	-	**	-	-	-	-	-	-	-	-	-	-
Off-track Mutual Wagering Facilities, Licensed as Satellite Facilities under IC 4-31-5.5 (Off-Track Betting Facilities)	SU-44																																					

Productivity

Productivity enhancement through physical and environmental changes is in. Flexible ergonomic seating, better lighting, well-designed work stations, and enhanced connectivity can make the work flow in greater volume. Since the most recent recession began, one doesn't hear a great deal about corporate sleeping facilities, personal services, and recreational facilities designed to maximize employee time on task.

Managers see building systems as a tool for productivity enhancement:

- Interior Air Quality (IAQ)
- Illumination
- Day lighting

TABLE 5.2 (*Continued*) Potentially compatible adjacent uses or mixed uses

		Potentially Compatible* Zoning for Adjacent Use (or Mixed Use on the Same Site Development) *Scale of proposed enterprise, planned site density and local ordinances should be carefully reviewed prior to commiting fund to any development plan. Market forces, such as disparate values may make some marked uses undesireable for the landowner with higher use. ** Compatiblity depends on local definition for this use.																																		
		Special Use																							Airport		Historic		Hospital		Park		University		Flood	
Use Group		SU-1	SU-2	SU-3	SU-5	SU-6	SU-7	SU-8	SU-9	SU-10	SU-13	SU-16	SU-20	SU-28	SU-29	SU-34	SU-35	SU-37	SU-38	SU-39	SU-41	SU-42	SU-43	SU-44	A	A-secondary	HP-1	S	HD-1	HD-2	PK-1	PK-2	UQ-1	UQ-2(B)	FW	FP
Use Description	Use																																			
SPECIAL USE DISTRICTS		X																																		
Churches	SU-1	X	X																																	
Schools	SU-2	X	X	X																																
Golf Courses, Golf Driving Ranges	SU-3	X	X	X	X																															
Radio Receiving or Broadcasting Towers and Accessory Buildings	SU-5	X	X	X	-	X																														
Hospitals and Sanitariums	SU-6	X	X	X	X		X																													
Charitable and Philanthropic Institutions	SU-7	X	-	X	X	X	X	X																												
Correctional and Penal Institutions	SU-8								X																											
Buildings and Grounds Used by Any Department of Town, City, Township, County, State or Federal Government	SU-9									X																										
Cemeteries	SU-10										X																									
Sanitary Landfill	SU-13											X																								
Amusement parks and Swimming Pools Privately Owned and Open to Public Patronage	SU-16												X																							
Light and Power Substations	SU-20													X																						
Telephone Exchange Offices	SU-28														X																					
Petroleum Refineries and Petroleum Products	SU-29															X																				
Club Rooms b. Fraternal Rooms - Fraternity and Lodge c. Ballrooms - Public	SU-34																X																			
Telecommunication Receiving or Broadcasting Towers and Associated Accessory Buildings	SU-35																	X																		
Library	SU-37																		X																	
Community Center	SU-38																			X																
Water Tanks, Water Pumping Stations and Similar Structures Not Located in Buildings	SU-39																				X															
Sewage Disposal Plant	SU-41																					X														
Gas Utilities	SU-42																						X													
Power Transmission Lines (High Voltage)	SU-43																							X												
Off-track Mutual Wagering Facilities, Licensed as Satellite Facilities under IC 4-31-5.5 (Off-Track Betting Facilities)	SU-44																																			

- Wireless technology
- Personal mobility devices
- Effective product conveyance and delivery

These are investments that can reduce absenteeism, training costs, worker fatigue, and operations costs due to space devoted to storage. On-demand production and just-in-time delivery are two faces of the same coin. The purpose of both is to reduce the real estate investment required for storage.

Savings

Energy savings from energy storage and off peak energy use rates are attractive to most large enterprises. When sufficiently large, utilities may offer

TABLE 5.2 (*Continued*) Potentially compatible adjacent uses or mixed uses

Potentially Compatible* Zoning for Adjacent Use (or Mixed Use on the Same Site Development)
*Scale of proposed enterprise, planned site density and local ordinances should be carefully reviewed prior to commiting fund to any development plan. Market forces, such as disparate values may make some marked uses undesireable for the landowner with higher use.
** Compatiblity depends on local definition for this use.

		Dwelling													Commercial										Business District				Industrial									
Use Group		D-P	D-A	D-S	D-1, D-2	D-3, D-4	D-5	D-6	D-6II	D-7	D-9	D-10	D-11	D-12	C-1	C-2	C-3	C-3C	C-4	C-5	C-6	C-7	C-ID	C-S	CBD-1	CBD-2	CBD-3	CBD-S	I-1-S	I-2-S	I-3-S	I-4-S	I-5-S	I-1-U	I-2-U	I-3-U	I-4-U	I-5-U
Use Description	Use																																					
AIRPORT DISTRICTS		-	-	-	-	-	-	-	-	-	-	-	-	-	-	-	-	-	-	-	-	-	-	**	-	-	-	**	-	-	-	-	-	-	-	-	-	-
Airport Special Use District - Permits Public municipal airports Airspace District	A	-	X	X	-	-	-	-	-	-	-	-	-	-	X	-	X	-	-	X	X	-	X	**	-	-	-	**	X	X	X	X	X	X	X	X	X	X
A secondary district which consists of Instrument and Non-Instrument Approach Surface Areas	A-secondary																																					
HISTORIC PRESERVATION DISTRICTS			-	-	X	X	X	X	X	X	X	-	X	X	X	-	-	-	-	-	-	-	-	**	-	X	X	**	X	X	-	-	-	X	X	-	-	-
Historic Preservation District One	HP-1		X	X	X	X	X	X	X	X	X	-	X	X	X	-	X	X	X	X	-	-	-	**	-	X	X	**	X	X	-	-	-	X	X	-	-	-
Historic Preservation District - Secondary	HP-2, HP-S																																-					-
HOSPITAL DISTRICTS		-	-	-	-	-	-	-	-	-	-	-	-	-	X	X	-	X	-	X	X	-	-	**	-	X	-	**	X	X	-	-	-	X	X	-	-	-
Hospital District One	HD-1	X	-	-	-	X	X	X	-	X	X	-	-	X	X	X	X	X	-	X	X	-	-	**	-	X	-	**	X	X	-	-	-	X	X	-	-	-
Hospital District Two	HD-2																																					
PARK DISTRICTS		X	-	-	-	X	X	X	X	X	X	X	X	X	X	X	X	-	-	-	-	-	-	**	-	X	X	**	X	X	-	-	-	X	X	-	-	-
Park District One - Permits all sizes and ranges of public park land and facilities	PK-1	X	X	X	X	X	X	X	X	X	X	X	X	X	X	X	X	-	-	-	-	-	-	**	X	X	X	**	X	X	-	-	-	X	X	-	-	-
Park Perimeter - Special District Two - Assures that the area peripheral to public parks will be compatible and harmonious with park uses	PK-2																																					
UNIVERSITY QUARTER DISTRICTS		-	-	-	-	X	X	-	X	X	X	X	-	X	X	X	X	-	-	X	-	-	X	**	X	X	X	**	X	X	-	-	-	X	X	-	-	-
University Quarter District One - Permits and facilitates the development, expansion, etc., of a major university complex or campus	UQ-1	X	-	X	-	X	X	-	X	X	-	-	-	X	X	-	X	-	-	X	-	-	X	**	-	X	X	**	X	X	-	-	-	X	X	-	-	-
University Quarter District Two - Permits and facilitates the development, expansion, etc., of University-related group dwelling uses	UQ-2(B)																																					
FLOOD CONTROLS DISTRICTS		-	-	-	-	-	-	-	-	-	-	-	-	-	-	-	-	-	-	-	-	-	-	-	-	-	-	-	-	-	-	-	-	-	-	-	-	-
Floodway - A secondary district designed to regulate development with floodway areas	FW	-	X	-	-	-	-	-	-	-	-	-	-	-	-	-	-	-	-	-	-	-	-	-	-	-	-	-	-	-	-	-	-	-	-	-	-	-
FP Floodway Fringe (Flood Plain) - A secondary district designed to regulate development within flood plain areas as above.	FP																																					

incentives for incorporating such systems. Interest in efficient energy use is not particularly motivated by a desire for conservation of energy resources, but by a desire to maximize the efficient use of resources. Sustainability is a hot issue with government clients and others in some parts of the country where corporations may get a boost from having such efforts recognized.

Designers can often build in sustainability by simply by choosing materials that have the least amount of embodied energy and applying an understanding of sun and climate to the design program. These choices

Sustainability is a hot issue with government clients and others in some parts of the country where corporations may get a boost from having such efforts recognized.

TABLE 5.2 (*Continued*) Potentially compatible adjacent uses or mixed uses

Potentially Compatible* Zoning for Adjacent Use (or Mixed Use on the Same Site Development)
*Scale of proposed enterprise, planned site density and local ordinances should be carefully reviewed prior to commiting fund to any development plan. Market forces, such as disparate values may make some marked uses undesireable for the landowner with higher use.
** Compatiblity depends on local definition for this use.

Use Group		Special Use																							Airport		Historic		Hospital		Park		Universit y		Flood	
		SU-1	SU-2	SU-3	SU-5	SU-6	SU-7	SU-8	SU-9	SU-10	SU-13	SU-16	SU-20	SU-28	SU-29	SU-34	SU-35	SU-37	SU-38	SU-39	SU-41	SU-42	SU-43	SU-44	A	A-secondary	HP-1	S	HD-1	HD-2	PK-1	PK-2	UQ-1	UQ-2(B)	FW	FP
Use Description	Use																																			
AIRPORT DISTRICTS																									X											
Airport Special Use District - Permits Public municipal airports Airspace District	A																									X										
A secondary district which consists of Instrument and Non-Instrument Approach Surface Areas	A-secondary																																			
HISTORIC PRESERVATION DISTRICTS																											X									
Historic Preservation District One	HP-1																											X								
Historic Preservation District - Secondary	HP-2, HP-S																																			
HOSPITAL DISTRICTS																													X							
Hospital District One	HD-1																													X						
Hospital District Two	HD-2																																			
PARK DISTRICTS																															X					
Park District One - Permits all sizes and ranges of public park land and facilities	PK-1																															X				
Park Perimeter - Special District Two - Assures that the area peripheral to public parks will be compatible and harmonious with park uses	PK-2																																			
UNIVERSITY QUARTER DISTRICTS																																	X			
University Quarter District One - Permits and facilitates the development, expansion, etc., of a major university complex or campus	UQ-1																																	X		
University Quarter District Two - Permits and facilitates the development, expansion, etc., of University-related group dwelling uses	UQ-2(B)																																			
FLOOD CONTROLS DISTRICTS		-	-	X	-	-	-	-	-	-	-	X	-	-	-	-	-	-	X	X	X	-	-	-	-	X	-	-	-	-	X	X	X	-	X	
Floodway - A secondary district designed to regulate development with floodway areas	FW	-	-	X	-	-	-	-	-	X	-	X	-	-	-	-	-	-	X	X	X	-	-	-	-	X	-	-	-	-	X	X	X	-	X	X
FP Floodway Fringe (Flood Plain) - A secondary district designed to regulate development within flood plain areas as above.	FP																																			

can include building on worn-out or contaminated land and re-using the shells of existing buildings. Sustainability can be incorporated at a more active level with the selection of energy sources and efficient operations equipment and fixtures. Taken to the next level, it involves commissioning, strict maintenance and operations requirements, and active environmental controls. Go one step further and one is actively constructing wetlands, green roofs, roof ponds, and waste and water reclamation systems that may not pay back for years, but demonstrate workable environmental principles. How much sustainability a client will buy into will depend greatly on the tangible benefits to him, the value he places on a sustainable public image, and the degree to which external sources like government or his client base require him to comply.

Security

Improving security is very trendy in the climate of fear that was spawned on 9-11 and is promoted continuously in the press. In some cases the threat to soft targets is very real and well placed:

- Utilities
- Landmarks
- Financial centers
- Assembly occupancies
- Transportation depots
- Government centers

Designers will need to be able to offer hard physical solutions as well as wired or wireless security systems that control, monitor, and communicate instructions for ingress, egress, and emergency signals. The financial scandals of 2002 inspired a desire for transparency, figuratively in transactions, records and management, and literally through architecture with permeable skins, perforated screens, glazing, open plans, multiple points of access, visual monitoring, and security systems. These are seen as the physical manifestations of accountability.

SERVICES FOR FREE

No matter how sophisticated the clients, they will still struggle with why it costs more to provide them with services than the historical percentage of construction cost/building type model would indicate.

The percentage of construction cost/building type model was found to be collusion years ago. The AIA settled the suit in a consent decree. Member firms are advised not use the old reference chart, but I can't and won't tell you how many people I know who hung onto the old chart. Some use it for verification. Others use it discreetly despite the decree and the advisory to members. Members are advised to quote fees to clients based on their reasonable estimate of the time and cost it will take them to perform the services requested.

Sophisticated clients know what they are accustomed to paying for their building type. Our recommendation to designers in this circumstance is to use the list of reasons above to identify issues that make the model inapplicable in specific renovation circumstances, and then tailor your effort and scope to fit within the limits of the client's budget. Be firm when, as work progresses, they ask for services you could have included, but negotiated out of the scope. Few designers have enough leeway in their fee to "give" away services. The relationship need not be adversarial, but a client should know when he's asked for too much. They will not respect designers if you don't set a limit that is fair to the design firm. Know when to walk away from a client that asks for too much for free.

Cognizance of trends in architectural services is needed to compete effectively. These include understanding how to address increased client sophistication, managing complexity successfully, expanding the portfolio of services offered, building in sustainability, and life cycle marketing.

STEP-BY-STEP THROUGH THE REDEVELOPMENT CYCLE

For the investor developer in search of a site, steps in the project re-development process include the following. They are listed in roughly the sequence that they will be needed by the investor/developer:

- Establish the type of property use or uses sought.
- Establish what funds can be raised to execute the project.
- Choose a district that will support the use. Review demographic information if needed.
- Contact the redevelopment authority for tips and suggestions on where to find property that roughly meets the scale requirements and has zoning (or zoning potential) for the desired use.
- Check the comprehensive and district plans for compatible locations.
- Determine if there are financial or other incentives for locating busi-

ness to or rehabilitating existing property within any of the districts being considered.

- Set criteria for the desired property. Start with very broad issues like minimum volume, acreage, required amenities, and required proximities then move to more specific requirements like public sewers, on-site parking, or high bay space.
- List deal stoppers such as flood plains and brownfields.
- Hire a design professional such as an architect or process engineer to help determine the space and volume requirements for the proposed enterprise if this is beyond the investor's ability.
- Find a buyer's broker (See Chapter Six)
- Review prospective properties on paper. Narrow the criteria for selection if the number of prospective properties becomes unwieldy.
- Narrow the field further using several checks
- Zoning data
- Tax rates
- If applicable, existing lease conditions and restrictions
- Lease potential and preferred leasing strategy
- A personal visit to each site for recording observations and impressions
- Professionals to investigate demographics, access, traffic, and visibility as applicable to project needs
- Available documentation including survey, zoning, and as-built document
- A contingent offer on property if needed to tie it up and gain access for site investigation
- Lien status
- Professionals to investigate existing conditions such as site issues, building issues, and program compatibility issues
- Special investigations such as infrared investigation, legal surveys, soils reports, environmental reports and conveyance equipment conditions
- Destructive investigation, if permitted
- A professional like an architect or appraiser to conduct accessibility audits and life safety audits. This is often the same firm hired to investigate building issues.
- The cost impact of issues revealed by the nondestructive site and building investigation

- Compare required development and site programmatic criteria to determine additional development required at the site and building level
- Compare with initial budget for continued compatibility in light of costs relative to discovered issues
- Make a final selection of a re-developable property. Deselect other properties
- Purchase or lease property
- Conduct destructive investigation, if not permitted earlier
- Fit site and building programs to existing site conditions
- Check for budget alignment
- Determine the cost impact of issues revealed by the nondestructive site and building investigation
- Contract design firm to prepare conceptual schematic designs
- Assess the structure and definition of development options and their cost impact
- Select a development strategy from the conceptual designs
- Establish construction phasing, particularly if financing ability or source of funds dictates phased development
- Plan for relocation of on-going operations during construction, if applicable
- Demolition of excess or unstable structures to prepare site for new construction
- Stabilization and protection of existing structures that will remain
- Execution of enclosure and envelope improvements
- Introduction of new utilities and services
- Building systems and circulation improvements
- Building standards for lease-able properties
- Begin or continue leasing process
- If using negotiated contracting, the investor/developer may bring this party to the table as he hires design professionals
- Prepare construction contract documents
- Obtain state required reviews, approvals, and permits
- Bid the work

- Review bids and let contract(s)
- Provide Move Coordination for on-going operations to be temporarily relocated
- Execute contract work
- Commission built work and systems
- Provide Move Coordination to final location
- Owner conducts or contracts maintenance and repair audits
- Design professional or owner executes warranty audit
- The owner or tenant takes occupancy of the finished work
- As the enterprise evolves, new program needs are defined

The method of contractor selection and project delivery required will affect the way that contract documents are prepared. The owner must determine the form of construction contracting to be used for the project. The design professional can define and recommend forms appropriate to his situation. The investor/developer should review these choices with his financiers and attorney.

Design professionals can be hired to perform any or all of the services listed above, provided the professional and the investor are satisfied with his qualifications and fee for service. The sequence of steps changes when the client owns a building and wants to take it to a more profitable use. Most of the steps related to the acquisition of the property can be omitted, but the owner still must investigate zoning issues that relate to development. If he is unsure what use he's likely to develop, he should look at market driven issues like demographics, access, and location of competing enterprises. He should also look at code issues that determine what uses his structure can accommodate based on its existing area, height, and construction type. Then he can follow the steps outlined for building investigation, programming, design selection, phasing, and contracting.

Forms of Contracting and Project Delivery

Contracts to execute the demolition, site preparation, and construction can take several forms. First the owner needs to evaluate his preferred method of contractor selection.

Competitive bidding takes two forms. Open bidding is when all responsive and responsible bids will be reviewed and considered. This form is required for most publicly funded projects above a threshold size. Alternately in private contracts, the developer may choose to invite bidders who have been pre-qualified either by responding to a request for qualifications (RFQ) and interview process or because they are known to the design professional or owner/developer.

Direct selection or negotiated contract is generally not used in public work, except in special circumstances. Privately funded projects often use this method. Contractors may be selected by project type because they are known to the design professional or owner/developer, or because their credentials were preferred among those responding to an RFQ/interview process.

In renovation work there are often so many discovery-based issues that will influence the private owner to be selective among pre-qualified contractors. Contractors who are accustomed to new work may not anticipate discovery issues in the demolition process. Well-articulated contract documents may be the best assurance.

fastfacts

In renovation work there are often so many discovery-based issues that the private owner will consider by being selective among prequalified contractors. Contractors who are accustomed to new work may not anticipate items related to discovery issues in the demolition process, sequencing for accommodating discovery items, and ongoing operations in their price.

Next, the investor/ developer must determine the form of contracting to be used. He must identify the:

- Number of contracts
- Contract type
- Basis of payment

The choices in the number of contracts usually are described as single prime (general) contract or multiple-prime contract. Single prime (general) contract is the most widely used form of construction contract and gives the owner single source responsibility for project delivery. Multiple-prime contracting usually involves three to five prime contractors with direct contracts with the owner. These are usually coordinated by, but not obligated to, a general contractor. Where there are more than a half dozen primes, the multiple-prime contracts effectively require that the owner will act as their own general contractor or construction manager. Many institutional and corporate clients are capable of handling three to five concurrent prime contracts. Very few are capable of coordinating significantly more. When there are more than five prime contracts, the project has evolved into a managed contract. The owner, if he has full time trained staff like facilities engineers, property managers, or in-house architecture and design staff, may self-perform this function, but usually a construction manager is hired for this function. In some states, design firms can take this role on as an extra service.

Quality Assurance and Budget Control Tools

Regardless of the design delivery or contract method used, the design team may use technical specification sections of the project manual to require that subcontractors demonstrate a minimum base of experience on related project types. For some items an engineer's stamp may be required. The owner may elect to pay the design professional to spell out anticipated discovery and sequencing issues in the contract documents. To do this, designers may provide phasing drawings.

The designer may require unit costs on the bid form for items that can be anticipated but not quantified prior to bid. Over-excavation and engineered fill are often required to get to suitable subgrade for a new foundation.

Allowances for items whose quantity can be estimated, but whose quality may be subject to interpretation after bid, are commonly used. It's a good practice for the design professional and the apparent low bidder to sit down and review the bid as soon as possible after it is received to be sure that the bidder has not missed any significant items that would prohibit him from successfully executing the contract. It's a good practice for bidders to attend pre-bid conferences and site walkthroughs to make observations and ask questions that may affect how they structure their bid or proposal.

Alternatives are a cost control tool designers and owners use to accomplish the most program for the funds available. For example, the investor/developer or his consultant discovers he has more program than budget and an estimate is made. The owner then works with his design team to identify packages of work that are in some way discreet. He decides what packages he can't function without. These items become the base bid.

Bid market conditions are sampled. The remaining discreet packages are evaluated for what the market and budget might bear. Some will be dropped. The rest will be listed as alternatives in the bid. Discreet packages in renovation are usually system defined (like remove and replace the roof system on area A base bid; remove and replace the roof system in area B alternative bid; provide a sprinkler system). Alternatives should not be too finely divided or it will be a red flag to bidders that the owner has funding trouble and or is indecisive regarding the real program.

In a competitive or owners market, the owner may be able to get some of the items from his wish list if he packages them discreetly as alternative bid items. In public bids, responding to alternatives is generally mandatory. In private bids it can be optional. Additionally, in private bids, owners may choose to accept voluntary alternates offered by the bidder. Usually these involve equipment substitution.

Expanding the Designer's Portfolio of Services

To grow a firm in the renovation market, consider strategically expanding the portfolio of services. This means firms must start offering a continuum of services that address the life cycle of the built environment. In business-speak, vertical marketing is a method of expanding the professional services offered to one client. These efforts are most suitable for championed clients, such as institutions, governments, and corporations that offer the designer the opportunity for a sustained relationship and multiple projects.

If your firm is called on for bread and butter facilities rehabilitation issues, it should also be perceived as an image giver when it's time for a significantly sized project. Large firms may manage this by dedicating different studio teams or groups for projects with significantly different character.

There are expanded services of design and construction documentation of particular interest to owners of renovation projects. These include:

- Site and location analysis
- Site development planning

To grow a firm in the renovation market, consider strategically expanding the portfolio of services. This means firms must start offering a continuum of services that address the life cycle of the built environment.

- Zoning process assistance
- Pre-design services
- Strategic facility planning- project identification
- Life cycle cost analysis/maintenance forecasting
- Existing facilities analysis
- Accessibility compliance audits
- Code compliance audit systems evaluation/planning-energy audits, energy monitoring
- IAQ services (Indoor Air Quality)
- Security analysis and system design
- Programming and program analysis
- Construction cost estimating
- Feasibility study
- Project phasing assistance
- Design services
- Salvage inventories
- Equipment inventories
- Abatement co-ordination
- Historic preservation
- Space planning
- Environmental graphics (Wayfinding)
- Acoustical design and sound system design
- Lighting design
- Construction cost estimating
- Alternative evaluation/value engineering
- Construction services:
  - Move co-ordination
  - Construction procurement
  - Construction administration services
  - Systems and equipment commissioning
- Construction phase services in increasing order of stake and risk in the project for the design professional—CM Advisor, CM Constructor, Architect/Developer
- Design-Build

- Post-occupancy services:
  - Periodic maintenance reviews
  - Facility management
  - Seismic analysis and improvements design
  - Forensic study

In situations where the design firm's focus is on municipalities, states, utilities, or other institutions, the firm's aim may be to become the provider of choice, i.e. a strategic partner offering vertically integrated services for the life-cycle of the building or the enterprise it houses. It takes a fairly sizable and complex design organization to offer the full array of these services, but consortiums of prime designers and consultants are nothing new to smaller practitioners. It is also important to know

FIGURE 5.11 Part of creating a program for a user is visually quantifying his existing needs for storage, workspace, and special equipment. Observing each area that contains a work function will give the designer insight as to the minimum space to allow in the project.

the limitations of a firm's resources and which services can be offered competitively. For example, if the firm has to hire a consultant to provide a routinely needed service, it may be better to form a strategic partnership or alliance.

I once worked for a Fortune 500 client that had established a facilities consortium of design and constructions firms that did all projects, regardless of size, on its main corporate campuses. In-house design staff managed and coordinated the work of consortium members. Since the work was often speculative and on the fast track, the company negotiated favorable rates with each member firm in exchange for the inside track on a large volume of work. By having the same team with each project, the partners in the consortium gained a delivery time advantage. Because communications between them and with the owner were well established and the owner's construction standards were familiar, documents were abbreviated and material sources rarely had to be searched out and renegotiated. Our firm did projects as small as stamp machines alcoves and as large as process renovations, laboratory wings, and office suites. Other strategic design partners in the design consortium engaged in the high profile image-building work. I discovered yet a third approach to design that this company used. They outsourced off-campus adjacent space needs to a build-to-suit developer who then leased the space to them. It gave the company single point responsibility for dictating their program and the developer had direct control of his design consultants.

DEVELOPMENT TRENDS

Annually, the ULI (Urban Land Institute) evaluates successful projects against the following criteria, "financial viability, resourceful land use, design, relevance to contemporary issues, and sensitivity to the community and the environment." (Alan J. Heavens," When Development Is Done Right", Philadelphia Inquirer, December 15, 2002) Successful projects cited by ULI include many of the following development trends and features. Some of these appear as components on other redevelopment projects that have given themselves a strategic edge in understanding buyers and tenants. From the investor/developer's point of view not all trends are rosy, but they are the kind of things of which the savvy investor will make himself aware. The trends cited are grouped in these categories: Financial, Environmental Change and Protection, Planning Programs, Engineering Lifestyles and Social Trends, and Visual and Functional Impact, based on the area where they have the greatest impact.

Financial

Real Estate Investment Trust's (REIT's), may lose their competitive advantage as a funding mechanism as more non-REIT developers begin to pay dividends. Mutual funds may continue to purchase well- managed REIT's with diverse portfolios as a mechanism to hedge against steep declines in stock investment value.

Developers look to redevelopment authorities to provide subsidies that will enable them to carry the additional negotiated social and infrastructure burden as well as the environmental burden for demolition and cleaning contaminated soil. Cities will sell parcels of vacant or abandoned land for low cost to developers who will subdivide and sell a portion in order to raise the cash needed to initiate development on the remaining portion. Sometimes a developer can simply purchase an option that generates "rent" on undeveloped land and allows the option holder to subdivide and sell the land piecemeal over a longer window of time. Often developers will pick up options on adjacent undeveloped property just to protect their on-going development from pre-emptive competition. Very much like buying a suite on a Monopoly board, this move can keep rents high as the flow of capital increases to complete the development. If an authority enters such a sweet deal with a developer, it is incumbent on them to assert a timetable and milestones for development as a condition of the option contract to assure the desired development will occur or reopen the land to other developers.

Some cities and labor groups go so far as to demand minimum living wage rates as conditions of the deal. Cities and redevelopment agencies recognize the right of residents who are displaced by urban renewal projects to receive suitable opportunities for replacement housing nearby. These entities will press for or require adjacent development or the inclusion of units in a mix of affordability. The unfortunate reality of such aims is that developers often will simply fill a full price unit with a lower income family and subsidize the rent or sales price difference with funds from other units. Historically there were time commitments to offering such units. As soon as the commitment elapsed the units would be raised to full rent. Sometimes these commitments were as little as 5 years. Agreements can be made that cover the life of the use regardless of change in ownership, but this affects the owner's ability to resell.

A planner colleague recently told me of a development scam that goes on in suburban communities, but the same scam could also be used in infill and redevelopment settings. A developer receives subsidy or grants to build affordable housing. He constructs residential units to the minimum standards enforceable or lower if he believes can get away with it. He then markets the development to people who would otherwise not be able to afford the community and offers them financing for loans whose payments are as much as 40% of their income. Sometimes he entices them with relatively low down payments. In most cases it doesn't take long for one of two things to happen. The home falls into disrepair and the owner can't afford the repairs. Bound by development covenant to make them, the developer makes them and takes the property to settle the lien or the owner discovers that paying 40% of his income monthly is more than he can sustain. He falls into default. In either case, the developer ends up owning the property. The developer then dumps the properties in disrepair and leaves a blighted, semi-vacant, and crime-attracting development, making it almost impossible for the remaining residents to move out. In another scenario, the developer fixes up the repossessed units and sells them at market prices, pocketing the difference and raising the assessed value on adjacent properties. This is often the last straw for the remaining owners who lose their property to the county for taxes. Such developers have to continuously relocate and change the name under which they do business, because planning commissions and communities won't be suckered twice by the same grifters.

Community Improvement Districts (CID's) are self-taxing districts that support business improvement districts. Districts may use the generated revenue for public services such as security or maintenance, resolving traffic problems or adding sidewalks or lead and seed money for federal grants. CID money can help commercial property holders maintain peak property values and maximum taxable value for the benefit of the state and local government. Should government be used as the mechanism to raise money to improve local businesses when coalitions of businesses could raise the funds through voluntary means? Some argue that the benefit to the tax base and improved job market speak eloquently. Others argue it is not the proper role of government. Many commercial districts have voted to be self-taxing in hopes of generating a benefit for all proportionate to the contribution of each.

Environmental Change and Protection

Maintaining healthy and adequate water supply is the impetus behind protection of watershed areas and wetlands with conservation easements development. The easements limit or prohibit development opportunities along streams, rivers, and lakes. Wetlands can now be assessed using a points system that rates the property on location, water quality, quantity, and community structure, such as wildlife activity and vegetation. Wetlands with the highest scores have the highest resource values and rate the greatest degree of protection. The points system is a shortcut over the time consuming system used by the Army Corps of Engineers' method of assessment. Using the new shortened system may save money on parcels that are deemed unsuitable for development. In a fast-track method, if the short system shows the property has development potential, the Corps' technique may still follow for verification while development commences.

The use of GIS and mapping technology will better identify areas where floodplains have expanded due to upstream development. Easy access to this information though government databases will allow designers to better select where to develop improved occupied space versus open land development or reserve in flood prone areas of the site. Early identification of potential flood areas should reduce risks for developers and redevelopers as they select sites.

Cities and towns may see growth in the land they own and over which they control development rights. In lieu of conservation trusts, some governments purchase development rights from farms. By controlling these rights, local governments can assemble land for the most profitable sales use or hold land in conservation in perpetuity or for a term. It does bring them into competition with business and private sector groups but it avoids eminent domain issues. Some states, like Massachusetts, have used their environmental agencies to create land designations that halt or limit development of undeveloped land and woodland. In populous states, this will eventually affect property affordability of developed areas.

Urban growth boundaries are another mechanism used to control sprawl. They are a moving target, as incremental annexation allows growth, but only slows it or causes it to leapfrog to development-friendly areas.

Environmentalism and the love of high technology merge in the trend toward ever "smarter" more programmable buildings. Buildings of substantial size already have programmable controls for lighting and HVAC systems; often they have security systems, automatic flush valves, motion activated water flow devices, limit switches, and hand dryers. Refrigerators and dishwashers are capable of notifying their manufacturers when they are in need of repair. There will be increased connectivity and portability of information technology. Wireless technology will also reduce or eliminate some previously hard-wired devices. Equipment that used to be built-in will now become portable. In some cases this level of systems sophistication is appropriate and even essential. In others, it may be more than the level of appropriate technology needed to deliver the comfort and function, but low tech solutions may be discarded in favor of what appears to be the cutting edge. Technology once found only in the office has already become part of the home. With increased telecommuting, this will only increase. The tendency of corporations to outsource their staff will have profound effect on the need for office space and conferencing technology. These changes will trigger changes in the form of residential design, as well. The potential bifurcations in the technology sphere and their impact on building design will be endless. With planned obsolescence and proprietary controls and languages, the challenge and the burden for the design professions to keep current may be great. This will necessarily give rise to additional areas of specialization and consulting.

Planning Programs

Higher density suburban development and urban re-development is a goal of many developers, redevelopment authorities, and even planning departments. Density in many areas will be increased beyond the limits for which existing infrastructure was designed. Mixed-use PUD development (a.k.a. DP zoned properties) can be deceptive. While the number of housing units permitted on a site may not increase, when combined with the collocated commercial development, the built volume of the site may exceed two, three, or four times the residential volume. Infrastructure will necessarily need to be improved to support the additional load. In most cases, the neighbors will be forced to pay a share of development they don't want, when the infrastructure is enhanced. If neighborhood groups are smart and well organized, they will demand that the developer or the redevelopment authority pay as a condition of permitting a rezoning to DP. This may put a strain on the viability of the real estate transaction, if it is contingent on re-zoning, and on the development's viability as a whole. As a reaction to such density grabs, some communities have instituted new zoning ordinances limiting the footprint and land coverage ratios in existing developed neighborhoods.

Not only are cities seeking to re-use existing buildings and building shells attached to existing street infrastructure to stimulate a return of population and redevelopment to the city, they are also looking at ways to revitalize dormant transportation infrastructure to make urban living more attractive. This includes improving transportation stops and reactivating train lines or creating light rail connections to existing commuter lines. This may also have business advantages for prospective employers with high turn-over low-skill jobs to fill. It will reduce the wages they need to pay to cover commuting costs and for employee amenities, like cafeterias. It will bring them closer to neighborhoods that can be mined for workers and reduce travel time and cost for workers. Some cities offer reduced parking requirements as a relocation incentive to cites that locate close to rail lines.

"For purposes of the National Land Trust Census, a land trust has been defined as a nonprofit organization that, as all or part of its mission, actively works to conserve land by undertaking or assisting direct land transactions – primarily the purchase or acceptance of donations of land or conservation easements." (National Land Trust, http://www.lta.org/aboutlta/census.shtml)

While land trusts use a variety of methods to protect land, two of the most commonly used are the purchase or acceptance of donations of land and the purchase or acceptance of donations of a conservation easement, a legal agreement that permanently restricts the development and use of land to ensure protection of its conservation values. Some land trusts acquire land and then convey it to another nonprofit organization or a government agency for permanent protection and stewardship.

Land trusts protect land by other means, including:

- Providing funding to other groups for land acquisition;
- Negotiating with conservation buyers – conservation-minded individuals who are willing to invest in property in anticipation of its ultimate and permanent protection as open space; and
- Facilitating negotiations for land to be acquired by another nonprofit organization or a public agency.

Engineering Lifestyle and Social Trends

The back-to-the-city movement is a movement aimed at enticing empty nesters with assets to move from edge cites and suburbs back to urban neighborhoods. It also involves creating neighborhoods in existing CBD's, where limited housing was originally available. To attract residents for medium to high priced downtown residential real estate development, and stimulate re-gentrification of blighted inner ring neighborhoods, this means introducing lifestyle amenities like parking, grocery stores, and drycleaners in areas that would normally command very high rents. The aim is to redistribute wealth within regions and smooth the beta between tax districts. Convenience and excitement are the draws for the residents who will also have "early adopter" or "influential" personality profiles.

By first attracting predominantly childless households, it allows the city to establish and build a tax base and defer fixing or building public schools, play-parks and day-care facilities in the new downtown neighborhoods where high rents can be crucial to development success. Once the downtown neighborhood is anchored by the well-to-do, supportive middle class and working class residences can be developed in adjacent development to make it easier for downtown services and retailers to retain staff.

Lifestyle malls need to incorporate more than boutique-sized businesses. Multi-level big box integration in repopulated city center mixed

FIGURE 5.12 Screened balconies were created at the Lockerbie Glove Company Lofts, center. The upscale condominiums were carved from a defunct multistory factory. *Photo: Stephen Culbert*

use development is an evolving retail trend. For the franchise, multi-level big box development requires high real estate value and higher-volume traffic projections than suburban stores to offset added expenses such as cart escalators and street level display windows, and interface at garage levels including graphics and wayfinding and security.

Providing sufficient parking is one of the first demands redevelopment authorities make of developers and businesses, and sometimes they require sufficient quotas as to make underground or multistory garages a necessary part of the development package. With low wage jobs predominating in redeveloped areas, particularly retail and entertainment areas, availability of close proximity child care and affordable housing as requirements from businesses in re-development deals in exchange for public subsidy. Sometimes parking revenue is implemented to subsidize the cost of the required worker-friendly project elements.

Human nature searches for competitive advantage and sometimes this means loopholes. In pricey housing districts, affordable housing and public schools will be developed in areas otherwise deemed unsuitable for housing. It will be inserted into abandoned structures, located under flight paths, and built on stilts in flood zones. Most of this will come about by using variance process and PUD. It will happen in the name of economic expediency and social fairness, and even enlightened self-interest. It will meet the letter if not the spirit of ordinances designed to eradicate class-ism in our neighborhoods. No system is perfect, and human nature cannot be engineered; the profit motive is essential to development and there is no limit to the creative ways it will be approached.

Visual and Functional Impact

The emergence of the neo-traditionalist philosophy in architectural design is distinctly different than preservation, which seeks to preserve categories of meaning such as the purity of style, the typicality of the archetype, the fame of the designer, the extent of innovation, and time period, etc. without the transposition of other styles and processes that may have occurred contemporaneously. Preservationists seek to insulate what they value from any interference by the future. The premise of the process is that if something is worthy of preservation, a use will be found for it that will allow it to be preserved. It will be destroyed only if no economically feasible use and no economic substitute for a use can be found.

Neo traditionalists are also distinct from modernists who seek to reduce built form to its essence and consistently apply contemporary materials and methods and who also approach buildings as machines for living or occupy-able art forms.

FIGURE 5.13 School to condominiums, it's elementary. Given the similarity in size and structural bay size between school classrooms (typically 750-900 square feet for general use and 1200 square feet for special purpose classrooms and kindergartens) and condominium units, the reuse of an elementary school for this purpose was so natural that it required few structural alterations of the original structure.

While neo-traditionalists value the work of preservationists, they part company in the use they make of old fabric; they also seek a dynamic interchange between the changing and the enduring. They recognize that towns and cities were built in incremental stages intended to produce a whole, and that traditional patterns can be applied to modern materials and traditional materials can be applied to modern concepts. Hierarchy is important in building types and in the arrangement of spaces. "When adding on to a building, they seek to complement and extend what exists, not stand apart and contrast with it. When given the opportunity to improve the civility of a place by removing something old and building something new and better in its place, they do so. They know that it is better to have better architecture than simply a good example of something from the past. They are willing to make an opportunity to, to innovate on the edge of tradition. This is the process that has built great cities." (Preservation And Traditional Architecture: Friend Or Foe? Presented by

Carroll William Westfall, at the Cornelius O'Brien Conference on Historic Preservation, South Bend, Indiana, Sept 27-29, 2001) Neo-traditionalism is the philosophical expression of the same forces that define new urbanism, sustainability, and the repopulation of the city.

Neo-traditionalism is necessary to relieve the trend toward homophyly, the tendency of all things looking alike and having blurry distinctions between building types. Because people the world over have access to common media and common message, they may tend to think more alike than differently regarding what they build, ruing regional distinctions that give some areas their unique character. The promotion of greater levels of mixed-use promotes such a trend further. This is especially true of buildings in close proximity to one another. (Three Information Age Megatrends, by Watts Wacker, in Architectural Record, March 1998, cited in the AIA Architects Handbook of Professional Practice, pg. 17.)

Neo-traditionalism is also needed to moderate the reaction to homophyly, to create sharply contrasting image-driven buildings with unusual forms and materials that could have the effect, in aggregate, of creating a jarring environmental aesthetic and urban fabric.

Developers can aim mixed-used development at increased 24-hour activity to improve the sense of security and neighborhood vitality with restaurants, convenience stores, 24-hour retail outlets, and transit stops. While not every CBD can be 24-7 convenience Meccas like Manhattan or Hong Kong, 24-hour use will engender the kind of life and vitality in CBS's as neighborhoods in many mid-sized cities that have historically had few downtown residents. To survive CBD's will need to become neighborhoods as well as business centers and entertainment districts. There is immense opportunity for the investor/developer who can bring some of these services into or near downtown.

Closing department stores in older suburbs and downtowns follows a national trend. Downtowns often lack the permanent population to support full service stores. They can't survive on the convenience purchases of office workers and visitors. Outdated malls can't sustain the traffic needed for anchor stores as these move to newer locations. In some places discount retailers move in to fill in the space, but generally this takes the whole mall to gradually down-market in terms of the tenants it attracts.

Mall revival today involves an intricate act of combining renovation and re-tenanting with consumer's demand for "value regional centers" and concepts from outlet centers, traditional regional malls, power centers, and entertainment complexes. It provides a mix of discount, outlet, and off-price retailers, as well as significant food and entertainment offerings. Traditional department stores are usually not part of the mix. Even with the absence of department stores, the number of anchors is high, often between 10 to 15. At 200,000 s.f. plus, these formats are supported by a consumer base that is often larger and more diverse than a power center or traditional mall. Demalling involves conversion from an enclosed regional mall to a power center format (multiple big-box discount retailers attached to or adjoining a strip of smaller stores.) through elimination of ancillary tenant space and replacement by power retailers. For example, Kenwood Mall in Cincinnati replaced its anchors and small stores with big-box tenants such as Barnes & Noble, Computer City, and Old Navy. (Information is drawn from New Retail Concepts, appeared in the 1997 Spring edition of The Strategic Solution, the newsletter of The Strategic Edge http://www.thestrategicedge.com/Articles/rtlcpt97.htm)

Amenities To Incorporate Into Reused Buildings

In light of the new kind of clients and the trends identified above, here's a short list of tenant-attracting improvements to consider:

- Envelope improvements-replace or restore roof, windows, doors, restoring of the skin including rebuilding storefronts, cleaning and pointing masonry and stone, and repairing terracotta details
- Systems and fixture upgrades and refurbishment
- Sprinklering or fire suppression
- Fire alarms
- Security systems
- Compartmentalization to allow mixed uses such as putting apartments over retail stores
- ADA compliance including upgrades or provision of elevators and lifts
- Built in connectivity to Internet, telephone using fiber optic cable
- Fixing up storefronts to improve overall building image
- Outdoor seasonal dining areas
- Common areas such as indoor plazas and atria
- Provide communal amenities, like fitness areas and shared green space
- Turn existing building obstacles into building features

Here are examples of the attractive use of features that were too costly to remove being incorporated as design features:

The Tate Modern is a converted power plant originally designed 1947. The museum's new design incorporates the original boiler as the central feature of the new entry. Pritzker Prize laureates Herzog & de Meuron executed it on London's South Bank.

One of my favorite restaurants in downtown Indianapolis is the Majestic. Built in the lobby of what was once a bank, it incorporates the bank vault as a display feature for the restaurant's fine collection of wine. It is visible from the entry and most areas of the restaurant.

Firms like Target are trying to stay competitive by adding online purchasing and food retailing to their existing businesses. Kroger is expanding into gasoline vending in a similar effort. These national and regional companies may be looking to outsource facilities planning and design to keep their costs down.

Reuse of abandoned manufacturing space is ideal for mixed-use technology incubators, communications hubs, and distribution hubs. With the natural growth in the communications market and in response to recent disasters, there may be some desire to diffuse the locations of these critical communication and distribution structures. Almost certainly these businesses will upgrade security elements in existing structures. Big-box retail/lifestyle malls are another compatible re-use of manufacturing facilities (see above.)

The following chapter will give the investor/developer ideas on how to locate and work with brokers if he is seeking a recoverable property for a use he has determined through his need or research.

FIGURE 5.14 The roof in the foreground shows communications equipment in a small penthouse intended to look similar to existing stair tower penetration.

CHAPTER 6

LOCATING AND SELECTING REDEVELOPMENT PROPERTY WITH INVESTMENT POTENTIAL

BUILDING RELATIONSHIPS WITH REAL ESTATE BROKERS

Working with real estate brokers is a common practice for most investors. Some investors rely on their own abilities to buy and sell real estate, but far more rely on brokers. Real estate brokers have much to offer an investor. Most brokers are part of a Multiple Listing Service (MLS). These brokers can get instant access to properties for sale, buildings that have sold recently, and other valuable information pertaining to the current real estate market. Much of the information is available to the general public, but it's much more difficult to find and use when it has to be sought out on a piece-by-piece basis. Multiple listing services compile the information and make it readily available to subscribers. Having the ability to sit down with brokers and look through their MLS books is a great advantage to anyone seeking to buy or sell real estate.

Licensing requirements for real estate agents and brokers can be very stringent. In almost all cases, some form of education is required and aspiring licensees are typically required to pass a written test before becoming licensed. Many states require licensees to participate in continuing education programs and to maintain an active real estate sales license. A lot of brokers volunteer to take additional courses for specialized training. Since real estate is a complex business, it's important for a licensee to strive for as much quality education as possible. Considering the study that brokers often do, they are normally much better qualified when it comes to real estate issues than an average investor is. Members of the

National Association of Realtors (NAR)® often attend special training courses. Looking for Realtors® is a good starting point when seeking qualified brokers to work with.

It's easy to say that most investors should benefit from working with brokers. However, not all brokers are the same. Some brokers work for the sellers of real estate and work with buyers. This is the traditional role of a broker. If selling property, this is the type of broker that the owner should be working with. But, when buying real estate, a buyer's broker should represent an investor. By retaining the services of a buyer's broker, the investor is the person for whom the broker is working, while the seller's broker is working for the seller. This is important, and we will discuss it later in this chapter.

> It's easy to say that most investors should benefit from working with brokers. However, not all brokers are the same. Some brokers work for the sellers of real estate and with buyers. This is the traditional role of a broker. If an owner is selling property, this is the type of broker that he should be working with. But, when buying real estate, a buyer's broker should represent an investor. By retaining the services of a buyer's broker, the investor is the person for whom the broker is working, while the seller's broker is working for the seller.

Should An Investor Work With A Broker?

Unless the investor is very sophisticated in real estate law, they should be working with a broker when buying or selling real estate. Since most people don't understand the laws and procedures pertaining to real estate, it's difficult to perform well without some guidance. Some people do represent themselves, and some of them do it very well. Most people, however, need help. One can work with an attorney to get answers to legal questions. This is good business even if there's a broker working with the developer. Lawyers are the best solution to legal questions, but they are not usually qualified real estate salespeople. In larger markets, one may find specialty firms where partners are both realtors and attorneys. Developers generally have both a broker and a lawyer, unless they have a much higher level of education in real estate practices and law than most people do.

Good brokers can fulfill many roles for an investor. There are obvious jobs that brokers do and there are other tasks that are not so well known. The public perception of brokers can be misinformed. The principles applied in the business of real estate are often misunderstood. People just don't know what really goes on behind the scenes. Being a broker and a brokerage owner, Roger has expert knowledge in the ways of the business. We're about to share some of the industry's secrets.

Brokers list buildings to sell. This puts them in the business of helping sellers to sell properties. Brokerages advertise properties for sale in hopes of attracting buyers. When buyers respond to the ads, the brokers will work with the buyers to help them find and acquire a suitable property. So, the

FIGURE 6.1 The "hot" location of Monument Circle at the geographic center of the city provides formal outdoor "living space" for tenants of adjacent high-rise buildings and the general public.

basics of the business is offering properties for sale as a representative of a seller and helping buyers to find real estate to purchase. In addition to these obvious roles, good brokers do much more. An experienced broker can assist in finding financing, tracking the closing process, and working with property inspectors, among many things. Brokers can provide valuable research for planning a strategy for an investment property. The list of potential services could go on and on. As a result, brokers can do a lot to help further the goals of a real estate investor.

Brokers' Commissions

Brokers generally earn their money only when a sale closes. Payment for services rendered is usually in the form of a percentage of the sales price. Some sellers resent having to pay a commission for a sale that they feel they could make themselves. Brokerages usually pay for all advertising to attract buyers. Brokers spend hours showing properties that don't sell. For every showing done, only a small percent result in a sale. Brokers spend a lot of time working without getting paid for their efforts. They make up for this by earning commissions on sales that do close. Sellers who resent paying commissions are usually shortsighted. See Figure 6.2.

Some people think that the anticipated commission amount is added on top of the sales price. Usually, a building that is being financed can't be sold for more than its appraised value. The commission comes out of the sales price, but it is not normally an add-on. In some cases a seller might be willing to sell for less if a commission is not being paid, but an appraisal determines the value of a property. Sellers should recognize that the commission is a cost to them for a valuable service. When checking recent sales prices of benchmark properties, one should be clear whether the sales price includes a broker's commission. Agents rarely get rich off commissions for doing nothing. Rich agents are usually motivated in their efforts for the seller. The bottom line is that if the investor is happy with the deal that is made and the money that is spent or earned, there's no reason to resent the commission.

Many people think, incorrectly, that buyer's brokers must be paid directly by the buyer. This is not true. Buyers or sellers can pay buyer's brokers. Most sellers' brokerages that co-broke (work with other brokerages and split commissions) are willing to share commissions with buyer's brokers. It is not unusual for a buyer to pay a buyer's broker directly, but there is no rule or law that requires the buyer to be the one to pay the buyer's broker.

Types of Brokers

Not all brokerages or brokers are alike. The obvious difference is that of a seller's brokerage compared to a buyer's brokerage, but there's more. For example, some brokerages specialize in commercial properties. There are brokers who work only with shopping centers. Others specialize in apartment buildings. Other brokers deal mostly with houses. Finding specialty brokers is a definite advantage. It stands to reason that if a person does the same type of work, day in and day out, they should be good at what they do. Investors need to build a list of qualified professionals to work with and depend on. This includes appraisers, lawyers, lenders, and brokers, not to mention the many other types of professionals that may be required for various types of real estate. What's the bottom line?

> **Many people think, incorrectly, that buyer's brokers must be paid directly by the buyer. This is not true. Buyers or sellers can pay buyer's brokers.**

If ______________________________, broker of the ______________________________, agency procures an acceptable offer for the purchase of my real estate, commonly known as ______________________________, and the property is successfully sold, the real estate agency shall receive a commission equal to __________% of the closed sale price. The listed price of this property is ______________________________ ($__________). This commission agreement will remain in effect from ____________________ to ____________________.
Seller agrees that if the property is sold within six months to anyone the broker has registered with the seller, as a prospective buyer, the broker shall be entitled to the above commission. This does not apply if the seller lists the property with a licensed real estate brokerage on an exclusive basis.

______________________ ______________________
Seller Date Broker Date

____
Seller Date

FIGURE 6.2 Broker commission arrangement

Investors can find a few good brokers to work with in their quest for real estate riches.

What's the difference between a seller's broker and a buyer's broker? A seller's broker works for the seller and with the buyer. This means that the broker's loyalty is to the seller, not the buyer. Law requires the broker to treat a buyer fairly and honestly, but the broker is not required to disclose everything that is known about a seller's position. For example, if a buyer makes an offer to buy a property and tells the broker that he wants to offer $150,000, but that he will go as high as $165,000, the broker is obligated to share the conversation with the seller. On the other hand, if the seller says that $150,000 is not acceptable, counters an offer at $160,000, and tells the broker that a counter of $155,000 will be acceptable, the broker doesn't have to share this information with the buyer.

Buyer's brokers work for buyers and with sellers. Essentially, the role is reversed from what was just described. Buyer's brokers don't list properties for sale, as a rule. Technically, a broker can be both a buyer's broker and a seller's broker, as long as they are not both on the same transaction. In reality, most good buyer's brokers don't list properties. This means that the brokers have more time to search for the types of properties buyers are seeking. Instead of soliciting listings to sell, buyer's brokers can work full-time on finding properties that their clients (buyers) are looking for.

Roles Of Real Estate Brokers

What is the role of a real estate broker? We've already hit the high spots on this issue. In the simplest terms, brokers are paid to arrange the sale of real estate. The expanded version of a broker's role can include anything from playing taxi driver to taking a cake out of the oven. (The aroma of fresh baked food can help sell a house, so some brokers have their sellers put something in the oven before a showing.) Good brokers do perform a number of services for their customers and clients. The job usually starts by answering phone inquires about properties advertised for sale. Getting listings of properties to sell is a role of a seller's broker, but not all seller's brokers go after listings. It's fairly common for some agents to be listing agents while others are selling agents. This doesn't mean that either broker is a buyer's broker.

Some real estate professionals are much more comfortable listing properties than they are with selling them. Since most deals are done on a co-brokered basis, a listing broker gets paid even when another broker makes the sale. Sometimes the best listing brokers are people with deep community roots and a lot of friends and contacts. Being visible within the community helps when seeking listings. Selling brokers don't need to know a lot of people to make money. A selling broker can run ads in a newspaper and then field the calls to make sales. Roger prefers selling to listing, but many brokers are just the opposite.

Once a broker helps a buyer to find a property, it's common practice for the broker to work with the buyer to structure an offer to purchase. The selling agent then delivers the offer to the listing agent, or the owner if the selling agent is also the listing agent. A listing agent will present the purchase offer to the seller and explain the contractual offering. Counteroffers, an example is given in Figure 6.3, may be made from either or both sides of the deal. Sellers may receive offers that are below, at, or even above the listing price.

When a prospective buyer has made an offer, the seller's broker is not required to advise the lower bidder that a higher bid has been made, unless the seller wishes to conduct an "auction" between the interested parties. Some bidders make asking-price bids only to lose out to a higher bid without the opportunity to counteroffer depending on the seller's priorities. A prospective buyer can assert the request to counteroffer with his bid without disclosing the amount. It is however like waving a sign that says, "I'm prepared to go higher."

In other circumstances, a buyer can be more attractive to a seller if he structures his deal with cash or mostly cash. Sellers have been known to prefer ready cash to a higher price that requires financing. A prospective buyer should learn all he can about the seller's priorities before he places an offer. He may get only one chance.

Once a deal is struck, the selling broker might work with the buyer to coordinate property inspections (Figure 6.4 and Figure 6.5). The listing broker is likely to work with an appraiser during the closing process. Both brokers should stay on top of all of the closing procedures to make sure that everything goes smoothly and in a timely fashion.

A lot of selling brokers will assist buyers in finding financing sources. When paperwork needs to get from one place to another, one of the brokers will usually take care of it. Brokers often have to act as sounding boards for buyers during the closing process. Many times buyers get cold feet, or what's called buyer's remorse. It is up to the selling broker to keep the buyers motivated and happy during the closing process, which can take anywhere from about 2 weeks to as long as 6 weeks, or more. When the time comes to close a deal, both brokers are normally at the closing to answer questions that either the buyer or seller may have. Plus, brokers like to be on hand to pick up their commission checks when the deal is done.

Counteroffer

This counteroffer is in response to the purchase and sale agreement dated ______________________________ between the Purchasers, ____and the Sellers, ____ for the sale of the real estate commonly known as ______________________________.

All other terms shall remain the same, Seller retains the right to accept any other offer prior to written acceptance and delivery of this counteroffer back to the Seller. This counteroffer shall expire at _______________ o'clock am/pm on _______________, unless an executed accepted copy is returned to the Seller prior to the above deadline. The following counteroffer is submitted for your review:

____

____

____

____

____

____

____

____

Seller	Date	Purchaser	Date
Seller	Date	Purchaser	Date

FIGURE 6.3 Counteroffer

Inspection Log

Item	*Poor*	*Fair*	*Good*	*Excellent*
Foyer				
Hall				
Kitchen				
Living room				
Dining room				
Master bedroom				
Family room				
Bedroom 2				
Bedroom 3				
Bedroom 4				
Bedroom 5				
Master bathroom				
Bathroom 2				
Bathroom 3				
Half bath				
Closet space				
Floor coverings				
Interior paint				
Plumbing system				
Heating system				
Electrical system				
Basement				
Attic				
Insulation				
Garage				
Deck				
Siding				
Exterior paint				
Lawn				
Roof				

Comments: ______________________________

FIGURE 6.4 Property inspection log

Inspection Addendum

This addendum shall become an integral part of the purchase and sale agreement dated ________________________________, between ____, Purchasers and ____, Sellers of the real property commonly known as __________________________. Within _______ days of acceptance of the above mentioned contract, the Purchaser shall order an inspection of the property located at ____, from a qualified representative of the Purchaser's choice at the Purchaser's own expense. This inspection shall include the items indicated and checked below:

_____ Roof
_____ Heating system
_____ Cooling system
_____ Foundation
_____ Plumbing
_____ Electrical
_____ Appliances
_____ Chimney
_____ Septic
_____ Well
_____ Code violations
_____ Drainage systems
_____ Other: ____

In the event the Purchaser's are not satisfied with the inspection results they may void this contract if written notice is given to the Sellers by ______________________. Seller agrees to allow reasonable access to the property for the purpose of this inspection. Additional terms and conditions are as follows:

____

____

Purchaser	Date	Seller	Date
Purchaser	Date	Seller	Date

FIGURE 6.5 Property inspection addendum

Not all brokers are willing to invest their time in the follow-up work of a sale. There are brokers who feel that once a contract is signed and delivered, the deal is in the hands of others. These brokers often lose deals that could have been saved during the closing process. The investor should find brokers who are willing to put in the extra effort to hold real estate deals together. To do this, ask brokers what their normal procedures are during the process of a sale and closing. Experience will be the best proof of the broker's job performance. Since investors often buy multiple properties over time, they have multiple chances to test different brokers until they find one that they like working with.

Having the right broker on the investor's side can mean the difference between getting fair deals and getting great deals. Investment brokers often build a network of investors. It's common for the brokers to offer new listings to the network of investors before public advertising is done. Some brokers scan new listings from the MLS on a weekly basis and bring suitable properties to the attention of the right investors. This type of arrangement works well for sellers, buyers, and brokers. Brokers save money on advertising and get quick sales. Sellers realize fast sales, and the investors get great offerings early in the marketing process.

fastfacts

Having the right broker on the investor's side can mean the difference between getting fair deals and getting great deals. Investment brokers often build a network of investors. It's common for the brokers to offer new listings to the network of investors before public advertising is done.

Finding and Working with the Right Broker

One can connect with the right brokers in many ways. A very effective way is to create a brochure for the investor/developer. Not many investors do this, but the ones who do, get noticed. If one is serious about buying investment property, he can take the time to create a winning sales piece of his own. This doesn't have to be an expensive process. A simple letter is all that is really needed, but a nice, tri-fold brochure is better. The piece should tell brokers and sellers who is seeking to invest, what kind of investment, the types of properties that they are interested in, and any other special details that might spark their interest. For example, if there is an established line of credit, the investor can close quickly on properties. Once people in the business know that they're dealing with a serious investor, he will probably get a number of special opportunities.

Deliver promotional pieces to suitable real estate brokerages. To buy property in a particular neighborhood, one can also go door to door and leave brochures for property owners to review. Its hard to say when an owner is about to list a property for sale, and sometimes one can get to the seller before a property is listed and negotiate a better price.

After finding the right broker or brokers, one can be faced with more business than he can handle. Investors might be presented with several potential properties on a weekly basis. This can be quite overwhelming and confusing. Don't get too caught up in the excitement. Sort through the properties carefully. Experienced investment brokers can produce a lot of viable deals in a short period of time. Don't feel pressured to act on all of the offerings. Sift through them and look for properties that fit the profile created.

When too many offers come in, refine the criteria and require brokers to adhere to the profile. Any good broker will respect the investor's wishes. For example, one might wish to see buildings with four to eight rental units and price ranges of $150,000 to $400,000. Say so. If a positive cash flow is a requirement, let it be known. Narrowing the criteria will eliminate speculative and capricious offers.

The purchaser needs to develop good relations with experienced, specialized buyer's brokers. If the brokers are seasoned, they will not try to force-feed buildings that don't fit the project profile to their investors. This is not to say that an occasional offering for a stray property won't come in, but these opportunities can be well worth the time to investigate. Professional brokers who take their work seriously will not normally waste a buyer's time with dud properties.

Buying From A Seller's Broker

Buying from a seller's broker can work out okay, but as a buyer, one is better off working with a buyer's broker. Until fairly recently, there were no buyer's brokers in a formal role. Traditionally, all brokers were seller's brokers. Most deals that sell through the traditional manner are fine. But, there are some aspects of buying from a seller's broker that can be risky if one doesn't know the rules of the road.

In dealing with a traditional broker who represents a seller but works with the buyer, one should be careful what he says. Anything that is said to a seller's broker can be, and in some cases is required to be, repeated to the seller. Seller's brokers are required by law to be honest with buyers and to treat them fairly. But, the fiduciary relationship (loyalty) is between the seller and the broker. This puts the buyer at some disadvantage if too much information is disclosed to the broker. In other words, a buyer shouldn't say anything to the broker that he would not want the seller to hear.

Buyer's Responsibilities

Some investors feel that if they have a broker then there is no need to invest personal time in following through on a deal. Don't believe this for a moment. It's like a landlord who hires a management company to run a building. The management company is supposed to take care of day-to-day management duties. But, landlords have to manage their management companies. The same is true with brokers. Making arrangements for representation from a broker is not the end of the story for good investors.

If the broker is good, the buyer's duties in the course of a sale will be minimal. But, if the broker is not so good, the buyer may be the only person who can pull the fat out of the fire. It is in the buyer's best interest to study real estate principles and practices. He should learn what goes on at every step of a transaction. Having some professional level knowledge is a great advantage in managing brokers and investments.

The Reality of a Purchase

To find the reality of a purchase, one may have to dig a lot deeper than the sales hype that is presented to him. Brokers and sellers sometimes embellish their offerings. While fraud, lack of disclosure, and deceit are illegal and uncommon when dealing with reputable brokers, puffing is not so rare. What is puffing? The term puffing refers to taking the truth and expanding on it a bit. In the old days, some people might have described it as a white lie. The process is not truly lying, but it can paint a picture that is a bit more attractive in the mind's eye than it is on a financial statement.

Review building documents carefully. During his years in real estate, Roger has seen an awful lot of omissions. Surely some of them were honest mistakes, but some have seemed questionable in terms of intent. For example, if one is looking at income and expenses for a building, make sure that actual income, not potential income, is reviewed. Confirm that all expenses are accounted for. If a seller neglects to list the cost of water and

Form RD 1955-45
(Rev. 6-97)

UNITED STATES DEPARTMENT OF AGRICULTURE
RURAL DEVELOPMENT
FARM SERVICE AGENCY

FORM APPROVED
OMB NO. 0575-0172

Advice No.

STANDARD SALES CONTRACT
SALE OF REAL PROPERTY BY THE UNITED STATES

1. THE OFFER DATE OF THIS CONTRACT (THE DATE SIGNED BY THE PURCHASER) IS ______________ 19____.
2. THE UNITED STATS OF AMERICA, acting through the ☐ Rural Housing Service; ☐ Rural Utilities Service; ☐ Rural Business-Cooperative Service; ☐ Farm Service Agency, hereinafter referred to as the "Agency", as SELLER, agrees to sell to the PURCHASER named below, and said purchaser agrees to buy, the property identified hereinafter, subject to the CONDITIONS OF SALE on pages 3 and 4 hereof which are incorporated and made part hereof.
3. PROPERTY IDENTIFICATION. Street address, including ZIP code and county:

   Brief Legal Description:

   together with the appurtenances thereunto belonging.
4. EARNEST MONEY DEPOSIT, $______________, (TO BE REFUNDED TO PURCHASER IF THIS OFFER REJECTED OR IF AGENCY CREDIT SALE IS NOT APPROVED) ☐ TO BE REFUNDED TO PURCHASER AT CLOSING ☐ TO BE APPLIED TO CLOSING COSTS, AT CLOSING, WITH ANY BALANCE REFUNDED TO PURCHASER ☐ TO BE APPLIED TO CLOSING COSTS, AT CLOSING, WITH ANY BALANCE APPLIED TO THE PURCHASE PRICE.
5. PRICE: $______________ CASH AT CLOSING: $______________, WITH BALANCE OF $______________ BY CREDIT SALE (SECURED BY MORTGAGE OR DEED OF TRUST) ACCEPTED BY AGENCY PROVIDING FOR EQUAL ______________ INSTALLMENTS OF PRINCIPAL AND INTEREST AT THE AGENCY INTEREST RATE IN EFFECT AS SET FORTH IN RD INSTRUCTION 440.1 (AVAILABLE IN ANY AGENCY OFFICE) AT THE TIME THE APPLICANT IS NOTIFIED THE CREDIT SALE IS APPROVED ☐ WITH ANY BALANCE OF THE LOAN TO BE PAID IN FULL NOT LATER THAN THE ______________ ANNIVERSARY OF THE LOAN.
6. CONTINGENCY. If a credit sale is indicated in paragraph 5 above, this contract is contingent upon the Agency approving a credit sale, satisfactory to and in the name of the following party(ies):
7. CONVEYANCE. Title is to be taken in the following name and style:
8. SIGNATURE. This contract is signed by one or more of those personally named in paragraph 6 or an authorized party or official of the legal entity named in paragraph 6 (called the Purchaser).
9. OCCUPANCY. Purchaser will close with property ☐ vacant; subject to ☐ Purchaser's own occupancy only; ☐ occupancy by other(s).
10. THE PROPERTY DESCRIBED IN THIS CONTRACT ☐ is ☐ is not subject to taxation while owned by the Government. Taxes will be ☐ paid in full ☐ prorated in accordance with Item H, page 3 of form.
11. DEED RESTRICTION. The property ☐ is ☐ is not subject to deed restrictions in accordance with Item O, page 3 of form.
12. SPECIAL STIPULATIONS:
13. The sale shall be closed at ______________ within thirty (30) days after indication by the Seller of readiness to close, unless the parties otherwise agree in writing.

    Purchaser has signed this contract on the date shown in paragraph 1, above.

____
Purchaser's Signature

____
Type or Print Purchaser's Name

____
Purchaser's Signature

____
Type of Print Purchaser's Name

____
Co-Signer's Signature

____
Type or Print Co-Signer's Name

ACCEPTED BY THE UNITED STATES OF AMERICA

BY ______________
(Signature)

____
(Type Name and Title of Official)

____
(Agency)

UNITED STATES DEPARTMENT OF AGRICULTURE

Date Accepted ______________

According to the Paperwork Reduction Act of 1995, no persons are required to respond to a collection of information unless it displays a valid OMB control number. The valid OMB control number for this information collection is 0575-0172. The time required to complete this information collection is estimated to average 30 minutes per response, including the time for reviewing instructions, searching existing data sources, gathering and maintaining the data needed, and completing and reviewing the collection of information.

FIGURE 6.6 Sample sales contract (*Continued*)

sewage services, the rate of return on a building could turn around quickly. Leave nothing to chance. Check out everything. Just because the property lists that the area is served by city sewer doesn't mean that it's connected to it. In most municipalities, property owners are required to pay a sewer fee if a sewer serves the area, even if the property has not been connected.

BROKER'S CERTIFICATION (IF SOLD THROUGH A REAL ESTATE BROKER)

The undersigned Broker certifies that neither he/she nor anyone authorized to act for him/her has declined to sell the property described herein to or to make it available for inspection or consideration by a prospective purchaser because of race, color, religion, sex, age, handicap, national origin or marital status. The undersigned further acknowledges that no commission, as stated on the notice of real property for sale shall be due or earned until and unless this contract is closed and title has passed to the purchaser herein. Earned commissions will be paid in cash at closing and passing of title only where sufficient cash to cover the commission is paid by purchaser; otherwise commission is paid by the Agency in approximately four weeks after closing.

NOTE: The broker must sign this certification.

____
(Broker's Signature)

____
Broker's Social Security or Employer Identification No.

____
(Type or Print Name of Broker)

____
(Co-Broker Signature, if applicable)

____
Co-Broker's Social Security or Employer Identification No.

____
(Type or Print Name of any Co-Broker)

FIGURE 6.6 *(Continued)* Sample sales contract

fastfacts

To find the reality of a purchase, one may have to dig a lot deeper than the sales hype that is presented to him. Brokers and sellers sometimes embellish their offerings. While fraud, lack of disclosure, and deceit are illegal and uncommon when dealing with reputable brokers, puffing is not so rare.

Doing a historical data search on a property may uncover some factors that could concern the investor (Figure 6.9). For example, say that a building is pulling rents of $650 a month in a neighborhood where other rents for similar units are as low as $550. Why is the building able to command such a higher rental rate? Find out. There may be a plausible reason, but it may be that the owner of the building was lucky enough to fill the building with higher rents that will not hold up over time. Don't take anything for granted. While investors may work with brokers, they should not get lazy and feel that they are not responsible for their own good fortune.

ASSESSING POTENTIAL INVESTMENTS

There are a number of ways to look at investments. It's possible for 100 investors to look at the same property with 100 different views. Not all investors are in search of the same goals. While it's true that most investors are motivated by money, their needs for cash vary, as can their desires for how the money is ultimately obtained. Every investor must do a personal assessment of any potential purchase. Real estate must be chosen based on criteria that meet an investment plan. If the investor is looking for quick-

THE FOLLOWING CONDITIONS OF SALE ARE AGREED TO BY PURCHASER AND SELLER BEING THE CONDITIONS OF SALE REFERRED TO IN PARAGRAPH 2, PAGE 1

GENERAL - APPLICABLE TO ALL CONTRACTS EXCEPT AS MODIFIED BY PRIOR PARAGRAPHS

A. Earnest Money Deposit. The earnest money deposit, shall be in the amount set forth in Agency regulations (7 CFR, Part 1955, Subpart C or 7 CFR Part 3550, as appropriate).

B. Deed to the Property. Within thirty (30) days after acceptance of the contract or removal of the contingency of Paragraph 6, page 1 (if applicable), whichever occurs last, the Government shall prepare for the purchaser a quitclaim deed to the property for delivery at the closing. The closing shall occur within thirty (30) days after the Government notifies the purchaser that the sale is ready to be closed. If a credit sale has been approved, the Government will also provide the required promissory note and security instruments. The purchaser shall deliver the executed promissory note and security instruments to the Government at the closing. If the contingency in Paragraph 6 is applicable and the Government disapproves the purchaser's credit, the purchaser shall be notified of the disapproval of credit and the contract shall terminate.

C. Encumbrances or Defects. If the purchaser, before receiving a deed and within thirty (30) days after the Government's acceptance of the bid, submits proof of any encumbrances or title defects, the Government may take any necessary remedial action. If the Government does not elect to exercise the right, the purchaser may, if the encumbrance or title defect affects the marketability of the title, rescind purchaser's purchase obligation and recover all amounts paid by purchaser to the Government on account of the purchase price. However, neither the purchaser nor parties claiming under purchaser shall be entitled, under any circumstances, to recover from the Government any damages, interest, or costs on account of any encumbrance or defect affecting the title of the property. Unless proof of encumbrances or defects, other than any enumerated on Exhibit A, is submitted by the purchaser within the time specified above, any and all encumbrances and defects shall be conclusively presumed waived, and the purchaser and any parties claiming under purchaser shall be forever barred from asserting them against the Government.

D. Abstracts or Title Evidence. The Government is not obligated to furnish any abstracts or other title evidence but will permit purchaser to inspect its title papers at a place selected by, and at no expense to, the Government.

E. Accepting the Property. The purchaser agrees to accept the property as is, in its present condition. No warranty is given on the condition of the property.

F. Loss or Damage to Property. If, through no fault of either party, the property is lost or damaged as a result of fire, vandalism or an act of God between the time of acceptance of the offer and the time the title of the property is conveyed by the Agency, the Agency will reappraise the property. The reappraised value of the property will serve as the amount the Agency will accept from the purchaser. However, if the actual loss, based on reduction in market value as determined by the Agency is less than $500, payment of the full purchase price is required. In the event the two parties cannot agree upon an adjusted price, either party, by mailing notice in writing to the other, may terminate the contract of sale, and the earnest money will be returned to the offeror.

G. Possession Rights. The purchaser will accept the property subject to the rights of any person or persons in possession of or presently occupying the property or claiming a right to occupy the property as indicated in Paragraph 9, page 1.

H. Payment of Taxes. If the property while in Government inventory is subject to taxation, the taxes will be prorated between the Government and the purchaser as of the date title is conveyed. If the property is not subject to taxation while in Government inventory, the purchaser will pay all taxes on the property which become due and payable on or after the date the title of the property is conveyed by the Government.

I. Mineral Rights. The Government will convey to the purchaser all mineral rights to which it has title.

J. Liquidated Damages. If the purchaser fails to comply with any of the terms or conditions hereof, the Government, by mailing notice in writing, may terminate the contract for sale. The earnest money deposit shall be retained by the Government as full liquidated damages except where failure to close is due to non-approval of credit.

K. Representation Regarding Property. Representations or statements regarding the property made by any representative of the Government shall not be binding on the Government or considered as grounds for any claim for adjustment in or rescission of any resulting contract. The purchaser expressly waives any claim for adjustment or rescission based upon any representation or statement not expressly included herein. The Government makes no warranties or representations not set forth in writing herein concerning the condition of title or the permissible uses of the property.

L. Member of Congress. No Member of or Delegate to Congress or Resident Commissioner shall be admitted to any share or part of the contract of which these conditions form a part, or to any benefit that may arise therefrom.

M. Subject to Agency Regulations. All offers and resulting contracts shall be subject to the regulations of the Agency, now or hereafter in effect.

N. Documentary Stamps. The purchaser will be required to purchase and place upon the deed the necessary documentary stamps.

FIGURE 6.6 (*Continued*) Sample sales contract

O. Deed Restrictions (*If Applicable*). This property contains a dwelling unit or units which the Agency has deemed to be inadequate for residential occupancy. The quitclaim deed by which this property will be conveyed to the purchaser will contain a covenant binding the purchasers and the property which will restrict the residential unit(s) on the property from being used for residential occupancy until such time as the dwelling unit(s) is (are) structurally sound and habitable, has a potable water supply, has functionally adequate, safe, and operable heating, plumbing, electrical and sewage disposal systems, and meets the Thermal Performance Standards as outlined in Exhibit D, 7 CFR Part 1924, Subpart A, which are the Agency requirements for a residential unit(s) to meet decent, safe, and sanitary standards. This restriction is required by Section 510(e) of the Housing Act of 1949, as amended, 42 U.S.C. § 1480(e).

P. Entire Agreement. This contract contains the final and entire agreement between the parties hereto and they shall not be bound by any terms, conditions, statements, or representations, oral or written, not herein contained.

APPLICABLE TO CREDIT SALES (LOANS BY THE AGENCY) ONLY

Q. Purchaser Financial Information. The purchaser will submit financial information upon request of the Government within 30 days of such request.

R. Security Instruments. Upon closing all deeds and mortgages or other security instruments incident to the sale shall be on Agency forms and shall immediately be filed for record by the Agency at the expense of purchaser.

S. Insurance. To protect the Government's security in any buildings and appurtenances, the purchaser shall carry insurance against loss by fire, windstorm, flood and any other hazards required by the Government. The insurance shall be in an amount and form, and with an insurer, satisfactory to the Government. The original policy with evidence of premium payment shall be delivered to the Government at the time of delivery of the quitclaim deed to the purchaser.

T. Prepayment. The purchaser may pay at any time all or part of the unpaid balance of the purchase price with no prepayment penalty. *(For Multiple Family Housing sales only, the purchaser may be subject to prepayment restrictions of Section 502(c) of the Housing Act of 1949, 42 U.S. C. §1472(c)*

FIGURE 6.6 (*Continued*) Sample sales contract

> Real estate must be chosen based on criteria that meet an investment plan. If the investor is looking for quick-flips and another looking for retirement property, they may not be interested in the same properties.

flips and another looking for retirement property, they may not be interested in the same properties. What would make one owner/developer jump to a purchase might put another off. Learning how to do investment assessments is something that all wise investors take the time to do.

The owner/developer can hire consultants to help in the assessment work. This is not a bad idea, especially for beginning investors. Finding a good consultant or broker can be just the springboard the owner/developer needs to get off to a grand start in real estate. However, one may discover that consultants and brokers don't share personal feelings for their client's prospective properties. There are certainly times when gut reactions work best, and consultants hired may not be sufficiently in tune with the owners true agenda. Still, professional advice never hurts. The owner/developer may not take it, but if the designer or another consultant on his team offers it, he may at least listen to it and consider its value.

Estimate of Purchaser's Closing Costs

Sales price			________ (A)
Estimated costs:			
Escrow fees	________		
Document preparation fees	________		
Loan origination fee	________		
Legal fees	________		
Loan assumption fee	________		
Transfer tax	________		
Pest control fee	________		
Loan application fee	________		
Recording fees	________		
Points	________		
Trustee's fees	________		
Notary fees	________		
Prorated taxes	________		
Interest	________		
FHA/MIP (mortgage insurance)	________		
Inspection fees	________		
Credit report fee	________		
Hazard insurance	________		
Title insurance	________		
Down payment	________		
Other fees	________		
Total costs	________	(B)	
Credits	________		
	________		
	________		
Total credits	________	(C)	
Total estimated closing costs (B minus C)			$ ________

FIGURE 6.7 Sample purchaser's closing statement

Form RD 1927-10
(Rev. 7-98)

UNITED STATES DEPARTMENT OF AGRICULTURE
RURAL DEVELOPMENT
FARM SERVICE AGENCY

FORM APPROVED
OMB NO. 0575-0147

FINAL TITLE OPINION

LOAN APPLICANT	ADDRESS OR PROPERTY COVERED BY THIS OPINION	
APPLICANT FOR TITLE EXAMINATION	COUNTY	STATE

I. I have examined title to the property described in the security instrument described in paragraph II. B. below. My examination covered the period from the time of termination of title search covered by my Preliminary Title Opinion on Form RD 1927-9; or the time of recordation of the initial loan security instrument if this opinion covers land already owned by the loan applicant in a subsequent loan case, to ________________, ______, at ________ a.m. p.m. (including the time of filing the current security instrument). *(Date)*

II. Based on said title examination, my preliminary title examination if any, and any additional information concerning the title which has come to my attention, it is my opionion that:

A. Good and marketable title, in accordance with title examination standards prevailing in the area, to said property (real estate and any water rights offered as security) is now vested in ____

____

as____.
(Joint tenants, tenants by the entirety, etc.)

B. The United States of America holds a valid __________ *(Priority)* ______________ *(Mortgage, etc.)* lien on said property as required by Rural Development or the Farm Service Agency, or their successor (Agency), which lien was filed for record on ____________ *(Date)*, ______, at _______ a.m. p.m. and is recorded in ________________________ *(Book, page, and office)*.

C. Said property and lien are subject only to encumbrances, reservations, exceptions, and defects which were approved by written administrative waivers of the Agency attached hereto or to my Preliminary Title Opinion.

III. If a water right is involved and is not covered by the current security instrument, it is subject only to the encumbrances, reservations, exceptions, and defects set forth in said administrative waivers and was made available as security in the following manner (Water stock would normally be reissued in the names of said land owners and the United States of America and delivered to the Agency Official at the time of loan closing):

According to the Paperwork Reduction Act of 1995, an agency may not conduct or sponsor, and a person is not required to respond to, a collection of information unless it displays a valid OMB control number. The valid OMB control number for this information collection is 0575-0147. The time required to complete this information collection is estimated to average 20 minutes per response, including the time for reviewing instructions, searching existing data sources, gathering and maintaining the data needed, and completing and reviewing the collection of information.

FIGURE 6.8 Final title opinion form (*Continued*)

The assessment of an investment can be fairly simple. Some investors will simply look at a profit-and-loss statement for the last few years and make a decision. Other investors will want more data to sift through. Having too much information to dig through can be almost as bad as not having enough. Make a plan to make the most of time invested in this analysis. Once the investor has a system for investment analysis, he is more likely to make greater profits from their investments.

IV. The term "encumbrances, reservations, exceptions, and defects" means all matters which would prevent the United States from obtaining the required lien on the property identified in paragraph I, including but not limited to (a) mortgages, deeds of trust, and vendors', mechanics', materialmen's, and all other liens, including any provisions thereof for future advances which could take priority over the said lien to the United States, (b) Federal, State, and local taxes, including county, school, improvement, water, drainage, sewer, inheritance, personal property, and income, (c) State and Federal bankruptcy, insolvency, receivership, and probate proceedings, (d) judgments and pending suits, in State and Federal courts, (e) recorded covenants; conditions; restrictions; reservations; liens; encumbrances; easements; rights-of-way; leases; mineral, oil, gas, and geothermal rights (regardless of the right of surface entry); timber rights; water rights; pending court proceedings and other matters of record which affect the title of the property or the ability of the buyer or seller to convey or accept title.

V. This opinion is issued expressly for the benefit of the above-named applicant for title examination and the United States of America acting through the United States Department of Agriculture Agency which provided the assistance, and I assume liability to each hereunder.

_______________ (Date) _______________ (Attorney's signature)

Attachments _______________ (Address, include ZIP Code)

FIGURE 6.8 *(Continued)* Final title opinion form

Narrowing The Field

Narrowing the field of potential properties to buy can be a daunting task. It doesn't have to be. Start by setting parameters to work within. For example, an investor who is interested in apartment buildings could set the following parameters:

- No one-bedroom apartments
- No buildings with electric heat
- No buildings with less than 6 units or more than 12 units
- No buildings that don't have public water and sewer services
- No buildings that are more than 30 minutes from home
- No buildings taller than 2 stories

When setting up the rules for purchases, one can make the rules any way he likes them. If the developer doesn't want to buy any property that doesn't have a paved parking area, make that one of the rules. Set out stipulations before beginning a property search, and it will save a lot of time. If working with brokers, the investor should give the brokers copies of buying requirements and refuse to look at any building that doesn't fit the profiles of acceptable properties (Figure 6.10). The time saved with this technique can be quite substantial, and the investor's time may well be one of his most valuable assets.

U.S. Census Bureau

Housing Vacancy Survey
First Quarter 1999

Table 11. Percent Distribution by Type of Unit, for the United States and Regions: First Quarter 1999 and 1998

(Percent distribution may not add to total, due to rounding)

	First quarter 1999			
	United States	North-east	Mid-West	South
All housing units	100	100	100	100
Year-round vacant	9.2	6.9	6.6	9.7
For rent	2.6	2.3	2.4	3.1
For sale only	1.1	0.8	0.9	1.4
Rented or sold, awaiting occupancy	0.7	0.6	0.8	0.8
Held off market	4.8	4.2	4.1	6.0
For occasional use	1.7	1.3	0.9	2.4
Temporarily occupied by persons with usual residence elsewhere	0.8	0.8	0.7	0.9
For other reasons	2.3	2.1	2.5	2.7
Seasonal vacant	2.6	3.7	2.4	2.3
Occupied	88.2	88.4	89.4	86.4

Type of housing unit	First quarter 1998			
	United States	North-east	Mid-West	South
All housing units	100	100	100	100
Year-round vacant	8.9	6.9	6.6	9.7
For rent	2.5	2.2	2.2	2.8
For sale only	1.0	1.0	0.8	1.3
Rented or sold, awaiting occupancy	0.7	0.6	0.7	0.9
Held off market	4.6	3.8	3.8	5.9
For occasional use	1.5	1.1	0.8	2.1
Temporarily occupied by persons with usual residence elsewhere	0.8	0.8	0.6	1.0
For other reasons	2.3	1.9	2.4	2.8
Seasonal vacant	2.8	3.9	2.5	2.6
Occupied	88.3	88.5	89.9	86.6

FIGURE 6.9 Housing vacancies

Please inspect all areas of your rental unit carefully. Note any existing deficiencies on the form below. The information on this form will be used in determining the return of your damage deposit. Please be thorough, and complete all applicable items.

Tenant: ______________________________

Rental unit: ______________________________

Item	*Location of Defect*
Walls	______________
Floor coverings	______________
Ceilings	______________
Windows	______________
Screens	______________
Window treatments	______________
Doors	______________
Light fixtures	______________
Cabinets	______________
Countertops	______________
Plumbing	______________
Heating	______________
Air conditioning	______________
Electrical	______________
Trim work	______________
Smoke detectors	______________
Light bulbs	______________
Appliances	______________

FIGURE 6.10 Potential property deficiencies checklist *(Continued)*

Item	*Location of Defect*
Furniture	______
Fireplace	______
Hardware	______
Closets	______
Landscaping	______
Parking area	______
Storage area	______
Other	______
	______

Comments

______

______

______

______

Inspection completed by: ______

Tenant Date

FIGURE 6.10 *(Continued)* Potential property deficiencies checklist

When creating an outline for the types of properties most suitable for the project, don't leave any room for gray areas. Don't hedge on issues, or it will frustrate the screening process. Define project needs and desires and stick to them. If the owner/developer requires that sellers be willing to hold paper as a second mortgage, he should insist upon it. When he doesn't want a property that has a swimming pool, eliminate such properties from the search grid. Weeding out the types of properties that are not wanted before the search begins is a good idea and a real timesaver.

Demographic Studies

Demographic studies can tell a lot about an area. But, they may not mean much to an average investor. When buying or building a shopping center, a strong demographic study can be very helpful. Someone thinking of opening a restaurant might benefit from demographics. When buying an apartment building, a study of demographics will not be of as much importance. For most investors it is easy enough to get first-hand views of an area that tell enough about the demographics.

fastfacts

Demographic studies can tell you a lot about an area. But, they may not mean much to an average investor. If you are buying or building a shopping center, a strong demographic study can be very helpful. Someone thinking of opening a restaurant might benefit from demographics. If you are buying an apartment building, a study of demographics will not be of as much importance. For most investors it is easy enough to get first-hand views of an area that tell enough about the demographics.

Investors who are considering buying a convenience store might well want both a demographics study and a traffic count. This information could be very helpful in determining what the potential income of the property would be. Economic models can be applied to that information to determine if a store is viable, and at what scale. If the investor is purchasing a duplex to rent out, he probably isn't too interested in a traffic count or the demographics of an area. Buying a large apartment building to convert to condos might easily justify the expense of a customized demographic study, but buying a car wash might not. Common sense has to be used in deciding how far to go in the research process. General information on demographics is available free through the Census Bureau and also through many state-run economic development agencies. Major streets and roads may have a traffic analysis available from the DOT or street department.

Let's talk about apartment buildings for a moment. Assume that an investor wants to buy a six-unit building in a neighborhood that he's unfamiliar with. There are several buildings up for sale. Some of them have all one-bedroom apartments in them while others have a mixture of two-

and three-bedroom units. Does this make any difference? Yes, it does. For one thing, one-bedroom apartments tend to have a higher turnover rate than larger apartments do. Most investors consider this to be a negative point. But, investors who like annual turnover so that they can boost rental rates easier and more often, might like the small units. Can the small units be rented? Look at the population of the neighborhood. Are there a lot of single people or couples without children, or is the area full of kids? If the community seems to be kid-driven, the one-bedroom apartments are probably going to be a problem. One should factor the cost to reconfigure at least some of the units into the budget to buy the building.

Since people with children are going to want something larger than a one-bedroom apartment, it may be difficult to rent to the type of people the neighborhood seems to attract. At the same time, single adults who don't have children, who would rent one-bedroom units, may not want to live in an area that is teeming with kids. Buying the one-bedroom units might be a major mistake. It could be why the building is up for sale. Driving through the neighborhood and parking on the street in different places for a few days will tell a lot about the area. By observing the neighborhood, one can get a feel for vandalism, the income ranges of people using the area, police activity, and more. This type of personal inspection can be as effective as a demographic report, and it costs much less.

One should get to know a lot about the area in which he is investing. When getting into commercial real estate, the need for a customized demographic report is stronger than when dealing with residential real estate. It's rare that such reports are needed for residential investments. One can save money by informed observation. Figure 6.11 shows an innovative link between old and new. What one sees for himself will probably reveal much more than a few sheets of paper with numbers on them.

CRUNCHING NUMBERS

Crunching numbers is what some investors enjoy most. Seeing how the numbers work in a wide variety of situations is relaxing. There are investors, however, that despise running numbers. Some investors are totally obsessive when it comes to building spreadsheets or balance sheets. There was a land developer who would spend hours each day plugging in numbers and printing out spreadsheets. The walls of his office were coated with green-bar computer paper. Finding numbers that work is important, but one cannot become so consumed with the numbers that he fails to take care of other responsibilities as an investor.

FIGURE 6. 11 Elevated bridge linking old and new structures at Circle Center Mall

Some investors hire financial analysts to produce financial reports. Many investors do their own number crunching. In some cases, the complexity of the task might require the services of a Certified Public Accountant (CPA). But for most average investments, a reasonably intelligent person can probably do the projections himself. The value of a good spreadsheet is directly related to the quality of the information used to create it. If the numbers are wild guesses, the investor can't depend too heavily on the reports. However, when he puts in solid numbers, the reports can be the map to greater wealth.

Different strategies are needed for the many types of investments available. Putting numbers together for a small apartment building is pretty easy. Doing the same job for a shopping center or a large condo project is not so simple. The first thing that an investor must decide is whether he has the ability to generate his own numbers. If the investor is nervous or uncomfortable about the job, he should hire an expert to help. The chances are good that, once he sees how the pros do it a few times, he will be able to assume more of the responsibility himself.

Every investment can be different, and there are certainly more than enough different types of investments to make running the numbers confusing. For example, the process used to project the profitability of a land

Position 3

FORM APPROVED
OMB No. 0575-0015

Form RD 442-3 (Rev. 3-97)	Name
BALANCE SHEET	Address

	Month Day Year *Current Year*	Month Day Year *Prior Year*
ASSETS		
CURRENT ASSETS		
1. Cash on hand in Banks		
2. Time deposits and short-term investments		
3. Accounts receiveable		
4. Less: Allowance for doubtful accounts	( )	( )
5. Inventories		
6. Prepayments		
7.		
8.		
9. Total Current Assets *(Add 1 through 8)*		
FIXED ASSETS		
10. Land		
11. Buildings		
12 Furniture and equipment		
13.		
14. Less: Accumulated depreciation	( )	( )
15. Net Total Fixed Assets *(Add 10 through 14)*		
OTHER ASSETS		
16.		
17.		
18. Total Assets (Add 9, 15, 16 and 17)		
LIABILITIES AND EQUITIES		
CURRENT LIABILITIES		
19. Accounts payable		
20. Notes payable		
21. Current portion of USDA note		
22. Customer deposits		
23. Taxes payable		
24. Interest payable		
25.		
26.		
27. Total Current Liabilities *(Add 19 through 26)*		
LONG-TERM LIABILITIES		
28. Notes payable USDA		
29.		
30.		
31. Total Long-Term Liabilities *(Add 28 through 30)*		
32. Total Liabilities *(Add 27 and 31)*		
EQUITY		
33. Retained earnings		
34. Memberships		
35. Total Equity *(Add lines 33 and 34)*		
36. Total Liabilities and Equity *(Add lines 32 and 35)*		

CERTIFIED CORRECT	Date	Appropriate Official *(Signature)*

According to the Paperwork Reduction Act of 1995, no persons are required to respond to a collection of information unless it displays a valid OMB control number. The valid OMB control number for this information collection is 0570-0015. The time required to complete this information is estimated to average 1 hour per response, including the time for reviewing instructions, searching existing data sources, gathering and maintaining the data needed, and completing and reviewing the collection of information.

RD 442-3 (Rev. 3-97)

FIGURE 6.12 Balance sheet (*Continued*)

deal where a subdivision will be made would be very different from running the numbers on how profitable a triplex might be. All income and expenses must be accounted for when building a spreadsheet. This includes

INSTRUCTIONS

Present Borrowers

This form may be used as a year end Balance Sheet by Rural Development Community Program and Farm Service Agency Group Farm Loan Program borrowers who do not have an independent audit. Submit two copies within 60 days following year's end to the Agency Official. An independently audited balance sheet will substitute for this form.

Applicants

In preparing this form when the application for financing is for a facility which is a unit of your overall operation, two balance sheets are to be submitted: one for the facility being financed and one for the entire operation. Examples: (a) application to finance a sewage system which is a part of a water-sewage system or municipality, (b) application to finance a nursing home which is part of a larger health care facility.

Preparation of this Form

1. Enter data where appropriate for the current and prior year.
2. Line 35, Total Equity, of this form will be the same as line 26, on Form RD 442-2, "Statement of Budget, Income and Equity", when using the form.
3. The term Equity is used interchangeably with Net Worth, Fund Balance, etc.

BALANCE SHEET ITEMS

Current Assets

1. Cash on hand and in Banks
   Includes undeposited cash and demand deposits.

2. Time Deposits and Short Term Investments
   Funds in savings accounts and certificates of deposit maturing within one year.

3. Accounts Receivable
   Amounts billed but not paid by customers, users, etc. This is the gross amount before any allowances in item 4.

4. Allowance for Doubtful Accounts
   Amounts included in item 3 which are estimated to be uncollectible.

5. Inventories
   The total of all materials, supplies and finished goods on hand.

6. Prepayments
   Payments made in advance of receipt of goods or utilization of services. Examples: rent, insurance.

7 - 8. List other current assets not included above.

Fixed Assets

10 - 12. List land, buildings, furniture and equipment separately by gross value.

13. List other fixed assets.

14. Accumulated Depreciation
Indicate total accumulated depreciation for items 10-13.

Other Assets

16 - 17. List other assets not previously accounted for.

Current Liabilities

19. Accounts Payable
    Amounts due to creditors for goods delivered or services completed.

20. Notes Payable
    Amounts due to banks and other creditors for which a promissory note has been signed.

21. Current Portion USDA Note
    Amount due USDA for principal payment during the next 12 months. Includes any payments which are in arrears.

22. Customer Deposits
    Funds of various kinds held for others.

23. Taxes Payable

24. Interest Payable USDA
    Interest applicable to principal amount in line 21.

25 - 26. List other payables and accruals not shown above.

Long Term Liabilities

28. Notes Payable USDA
    List total principal payments to USDA which mature after one year and are not included in line 21.

29 - 30. List all other long term liabilities such as bonds, bank loans, etc. which are due after one year.

Equity

33. Retained Earnings
    Net income which has been accumulated from the beginning of the operation and not distributed to members, users, etc.

34. Memberships
    The total of funds collected from persons of membership type facilities, i.e., water and sewer systems.

RD 442-3 Page 2 of 2

FIGURE 6.12 (*Continued*) Balance sheet

both hard and soft costs. A hard cost is an expense for something like replacement windows, a new water heater, or a new roof. Designers may refer to these as bricks and mortar or sticks and bricks costs. Soft costs are expenses for such things as building permits, inspection fees, surveys, and so forth. Many investors get a tainted picture of their potential profit because they fail to include all of their expenses. This can be not only disappointing, it can be disastrous to the profit picture.

Investors will be able to project numbers best if historical data for operational costs like taxes, utilities, and maintenance can be used. Hire an architect, engineer, estimator, or contractor with experience in the building type to estimate the construction costs. Be sure the design professional has a sufficient database of similarly sized and scaled construction to provide reliable numbers. If the building will have specialty areas, like a commercial kitchen, a laboratory, or a clean room, it may be a good idea to get price estimates directly from dealers or manufacturers of major lots of equipment. Add to this the soft costs such as permits, design fees, and administration costs of the project.

Very few investors fail to account for their known income from a property deal. But, they sometimes overestimate their anticipated income. One should be conservative when laying out projected income. It's always a relief to make more than projected, but if the project makes less than projected, the results may not be so nice. Try to work with known figures whenever possible and limit guessing to areas where there is no other choice.

When factoring in expenses there can be a lot to consider:

- The cost of borrowing money
- Real estate taxes
- Utility bills
- Maintenance expense
- Vacancy rates
- Management fees
- Insurance
- Engineering and survey costs
- Building permits
- Inspections
- Cost overruns

It's fine to be aggressive in one's mind, but one should be conservative in actions if he wants to survive in the business for many years to come. Investors can take some risks if they make sure that they are calculated risks, and that they can endure any losses that might occur.

Talk

Talk is cheap, so they say, but really, talk can be extremely valuable. The investor should talk to brokers, appraisers, tenants, and other landlords to get a feel for what he is dealing with. Real estate is a competitive business, but many of the players are more than happy to talk about their deals, at least once they are done. Bragging is big fun for a lot of investors. When investors fall into bad deals, they often like to get their feelings out by complaining about what went wrong. Investors can learn a lot from talking to others within the business.

Some investors don't enjoy the social scene. Going to events to talk with fellow investors just doesn't appeal to some people. Investors who fall within this group should consider hiring people to talk to. Appraisers will normally consult with investors for an hourly fee. Brokers generally give their time to investors in hopes of making money on a sale. Tenants in buildings that are for sale frequently volunteer information to prospective buyers. Other building owners may or may not be willing to talk honestly about their successes or failures. Investors should try to build a network of people with whom they can talk. There is much to be learned from the experiences of others.

Investors should try to build a network of people with whom they can talk. There is much to be learned from the experiences of others.

Historical Data

Using historical data to make buying decisions is very sensible. Given enough history on a building or a neighborhood, one can make some fairly safe projections for the future. Getting a list of previous rental rates on a building can be extremely helpful. Studying the cost of fuel oil for a building over the past five years can help one to project the cost for the coming winter. Going over comparable sales in a region will allow one to make a strong assessment of current market values for all types of real estate. Tracking the rise in property taxes or association fees can help the investor pick a figure for future increases. Much about the future can be learned from the past. Historical data can be recovered from a number of sources:

- Records kept by the seller
- The tax assessor's office

- Real estate brokers
- Appraisers
- Property management firms
- Newspapers

An investor can look to see what asking prices for rents and buildings are. This information isn't conclusive in what actual sale and rental prices were, but it helps to create a pattern. One should invest all the time that he can afford in finding out everything that there is to know about real estate in the area where money will be invested.

Combining the findings of research can create a good picture of how things were and how they may be in the future. A visit to the records room where deeds are kept can tell the investor how often properties have changed hands over the years. For example, if one is considering the purchase of a property on Wilson Street, go to the registry of deeds and pull all of the deeds for all of the properties on Wilson Street. See what the average length of ownership has been. If the time that a property is kept is short, it may indicate a troubled neighborhood.

Finding out that tax assessments in a certain area have gone up consistently over the last few years could be enough to either scare the investor away or to make him allow for tax increases when building the spreadsheet. Once the investor has compiled a number of files containing various types of historical data, the pieces of the financial puzzle can be put together. Drawing from personal research will allow the investor to generate a good projection of what to expect from a given property. There are, of course, no guarantees in any speculation, but historical data can take a lot of the guesswork out of the procedure. Investors who work with past facts to project future earnings tend to be more successful than investors who simply roll the dice and hope for the best. In budgeting time for real estate investments, the investor should make sure to allot some time to research. Research should pay off the extra effort with more certain profit.

CHAPTER 7

EVALUATION IS PART OF PLANNING

"BEFORE YOU BUY, VERIFY"

Roger has a saying, "Before you buy, verify." That is good advice for the investor/developer. Covering every concept in this chapter is just not possible. The topic is broad and would require more space than is possible here. Converting from a lower zoned use to a higher one can trigger site work that was not otherwise planned or anticipated. This is especially true when moving from a residential use to a commercial or institutional use. Read the requirements for the proposed use and measure the existing property for the degree to which it complies. Include upgrades in the project's anticipated budget as in Table 7.1 and Figure 7.1

TABLE 7.1 The Rule of 5% indicates the range of budget contingencies appropriate for different types of projects at each phase of the development process.

Project Phase	Suggested Budget Contingency			
	New Construction	Heavy Renovation (gutting)	Selective Renovation	Restoration
Programming/ Pre-design	30%	35%-40%	30%-40%	35%-50%
Schematic Design	25%	30%-40%	25%-35%	35%-50%
Design Development	20%	25%-35%	20%-30%	30%-40%
Construction Documents	15%	20%-30%	15%- 25%	25%-35%
Bid	10%	15%- 25%	10%-20%	20%-30%
Construction	5%	10%-20%	5%-10%	15%- 25%
Project Closeout	0-1%	5%-10%	0-5%	0-10%

USDA-RD
Form RD 440-11
(Rev. 11-96)

ESTIMATE OF FUNDS NEEDED
FOR
30-Day Period Commencing
____

FORM APPROVED
OMB NO. 0575-0015

Name of Borrower _______________

Items	Amount of Funds
Development	$
Contract or Job No. ________	
Contract or Job No. ________	
Contract or Job No. ________	
Land and Rights-of-Way	
Legal Services	
Engineering Fees	
Interest	
Equipment	
Contingencies	
Refinancing	
Initial O&M	
Other	
TOTAL	$

Prepared by _______________
Name of Borrower

By _______________

Date _______________

Approved by _______________
RD County Supervisor/District Director

Date _______________

Public reporting burden for this collection of information is estimated to average 1 hour per response, including the time for reviewing instructions, searching existing data sources, gathering and maintaining the data needed, and completing and reviewing the collection of information. Send comments regarding this burden estimate or any other aspect of this collection of information, including suggestions for reducing this burden, to U.S. Department of Agriculture, Clearance Officer, STOP 7602, 1400 Independence Avenue, S.W., Washington, D.C.20250-7602.Please DO NOT RETURN this form to this address. Forward to the local USDA office only. You are not required to respond to this collection of information unless it displays a currently valid OMB control number.

FIGURE 7.1 Estimate form for roadwork

Converting from a lower zoned use to a higher one can trigger site work that was not otherwise planned or anticipated.

Contingency Clauses and Inspection Provisions

Since inspections can get expensive, the investor/developer should avoid paying for them until he is certain that he wants to acquire a property. He may try to secure the property with a contingency contract and then have the inspectors do their jobs. When the investor/developer puts a building under contract with contingency clauses, he is in control. By doing this, he can lock in the agreed price and terms with the seller prior to paying for professional inspections. If the inspections come back with negative news, he can exercise his rights under the contingency clause and walk away from the deal. (Figure 7.2) Another option is to negotiate a lower price based on the problems turned up from the inspection. In either case, the investor/developer has not spent money on inspections without knowing that he has a deal in place and the property is off the market. Most investors agree that contingency contracts are the smartest way to control property without ownership. If the market for the property is not "hot," most sellers will agree to a contingency contract.

When the investor/developer puts a building under contract with contingency clauses, he is in control.

Sometimes contingency contracts are used if the property needs to be rezoned. Since only the property owner can request a rezoning, there may be a separate contract under which he seeks the rezoning on behalf of the purchaser. Usually the purchaser will provide the owner with the resources to pursue the rezoning. If the rezoning fails, the investor/developer can usually opt out of the deal or purchase at an adjusted price.

Roger has bought and sold a lot of real estate. As a broker, he's moved millions of dollars worth of real estate in a year. In all of his experiences, he's never found a seller who balked at a contingency in a contract for a property inspection. The most resistance encountered involved tight deadlines for the inspections to be performed. An investor/developer shouldn't be afraid to make a purchase offer that contains an inspection contingency. If a seller won't accept your contingency offer, it might very well mean

Form RD 440-34
(Rev. 6-97)

Position 5

FORM APPROVED
OMB NO. 0575-0172

UNITED STATES DEPARTMENT OF AGRICULTURE
RURAL DEVELOPMENT
FARM SERVICE AGENCY

OPTION TO PURCHASE REAL PROPERTY

1. In consideration of the sum of $ ______________________ in hand paid and other valuable consideration, the receipt and sufficiency of which are hereby acknowledged, the undersigned (hereinafter called the "Seller"), who covenants to be the owner thereof, hereby, for the Seller and the Seller's heirs, executors, administrators, successors and assigns, offers and agrees to sell and convey to

____
(Name and Address)

(hereinafter called the "Buyer"), and hereby grants to the said Buyer the exclusive and irrevocable option and right to purchase, under the conditions hereinafter provided, the following-described property, located in ______________________

County, State of ______________________:
(Insert here full and complete legal description, including volume and page where recorded, of the property including any water rights and water stock being purchased.)

According to the Paperwork Reduction Act of 1995, no persons are required to respond to a collection of information unless it displays a valid OMB control number. The valid OMB control number for this information collection is 0575-0172. The time required to complete this information collection is estimated to average 5 minutes per response, including the time for reviewing instructions, searching existing data sources, gathering and maintaining the data needed, and completing and reviewing the collection of information.

RD 440-34 (Rev. 6-97)

FIGURE 7.2 Option to purchase form *(Continued)*

that the seller is trying to conceal some material fact about the building. From my point of view, a seller who is offering a building, and is unwilling to allow the building to be inspected, should be avoided.

I had a client who experienced a horror story regarding a real estate deal and the failure of the seller to disclose information requested. It turned out they did have something to hide, contamination. The remediation required was worth about three times the value of the structure to be erected! Fortunately, the deal was a land lease and, when pressed, the lessors removed the contaminated material from the site at their own expense. The client's loss was limited to the delay related to the clean up.

The title to said property is to be conveyed free and clear of all encumbrances except for the following reservations, exceptions and leases, and no others:
(Insert here a full statement of all reservations, exceptions and leases, including in the case of leases, the date of the termination of the lease, the correct name(s) and address(es) of the lessee(s) and, if recorded, the place of recordation)

2. The option is given to enable the Buyer to obtain a loan made by the United States of America, acting through the ☐ Rural Housing Service; ☐ Rural Utilities Service; ☐ Rural Business-Cooperative Service; ☐ Farm Service Agency, hereinafter called the "Government" for the purchase of said property. It is agreed that the Buyer's efforts to obtain a loan constitute a part of the consideration for this option and any downpayment will be refunded if the loan cannot be processed by the Government.

3. The total purchase price for said property is $____________________ ; said amount

☐ includes ☐ excludes the $____________________ mentioned in paragraph 1.

4. The Seller agrees to pay all expenses of title clearance including, if required, abstract or certificate of title or policy of title insurance, continued down to the date of acceptance of this option and thereafter continued down to and including date of recordation of the deed from the Seller to the Buyer, costs of survey, if required, and attorney's fees; and the Seller agrees that, except as herein provided, all taxes, liens, encumbrances or other interests in third persons will be satisfied discharged, or paid by the Seller including stamp taxes and other expenses incident to the preparation and execution of the deed and other evidences of title. Title evidences will be obtained from persons and be in such form as the Government shall approve.

(Strike inapplicable language above or insert herein any different agreement regarding the paying of title clearance charges)

5. The Seller also agrees to secure for the Buyer, from the records of the Farm Service Agency, aerial surveys of the property when available, all obtainable information relating to allotments and production history and any other information needed in connection with the consideration of the proposed purchase of the property.

6. The Seller further agrees to convey said property to the Buyer by general warranty deed (except where the law provides otherwise for conveyances by trustees, officers of courts, etc.) in the form, manner and at the time required by the Government, conveying to the Buyer a valid, unencumbered, indefeasible fee-simple title to said property meeting all requirements of the Government; that the purchase price shall be paid at the time of recording such deed; and that said lands, including improvements, shall be delivered in the same condition as they now are, customary use and wear excepted.

7. Taxes, water assessments and other general and special assessments of whatsoever nature for the year in which the closing of the transaction takes place shall be prorated as of the date of the closing of the transaction, it being expressly agreed that for the purpose of such proration the tax year shall be deemed to be the calendar year. If the closing of the transaction shall occur before the tax rate is fixed, the apportionment of taxes shall be on the basis of the tax rate for the next preceding year applied to the latest assessed valuation.

(Insert here any different tax agreement)

FIGURE 7.2 *(Continued)* Option to purchase form

It's not unusual for a seller to refuse destructive investigation or testing on or within the building. He has a risk of real property loss from the damage if the deal isn't executed. Non-destructive investigative testing should be permitted to the extent that it doesn't disrupt the occupants' on-going operations.

Inspection Reports and the Investor

Reading inspection reports can be a complicated process. Most inspectors use common language and terms. If you have any questions, ask for

8. This option may be exercised by the Buyer, at any time while the offer herein shall remain in force, by mailing, telegraphing or delivering in person a written notice of acceptance of the offer herein to ______________________________,

at ______________________________, in the city of ______________________________,

County of ______________________________, State of ______________________________,

The offer herein shall remain irrevocable for a period of ______________ months from the date hereof and shall remain in force thereafter until one (1) year from the date hereof unless earlier terminated by the Seller. The Seller may terminate this offer at any time after the ______________ months irrevocable period provided herein by giving to the Buyer ten (10) days written notice of intention to terminate at the address of the Buyer. Acceptance of this option by the Buyer within ten (10) days after such notice is received by the Buyer shall constitute a valid acceptance of the option.

9. Loss or damage to the property by fire or from an act of God shall be at the risk of the Seller until the deed to the Buyer has been recorded, and in the event that such loss or damage occurs, the Buyer may, without liability, refuse to accept conveyance of title, or may elect to accept conveyance of title, in which case there shall be an equitable adjustment of the purchase price.

10. The Seller agrees that, irrespective of any other provision in this option, the Buyer, or the Buyer's assignees, may, if the option is accepted, without any liability therefore refuse to accept conveyance of the property described herein if the foresaid loan cannot be made or insured because of defects in the title to other land now owned by, or being purchased by, the buyer.

11. The Seller agrees to furnish, at Seller's expense, to the Buyer a certificate from a reliable firm certifying that the following described building(s) covered by this option (a) is now free of termite infestation and (b) either is now free of unrepaired termite damage or has suffered unrepaired termite damage which is specifically described in the certificate.

12. The Seller agrees to furnish, at the Seller's expense, to the Buyer evidence from the Health Department or a reliable and competent source that the waste disposal system for the dwelling is functioning properly, and the water supply for domestic use meets State Health Department requirements. This evidence must be in the Agency Office before a loan will be approved.

13. The Seller hereby gives the Government or its agents consent to enter on said property at reasonable times for the purpose of inspecting or appraising it, in connection with the making of a loan to purchase the property.

____

____

14. Insert here conditions peculiar to this particular transaction.

(Sellers Telephone Number)

IN WITNESS WHEREOF, the Seller and the Buyer have set their hands and seals this ______________ day of ______________, 19___.

WITNESSES:

______________	______________ *(Seller)**
______________	______________ *(Seller)**
______________	______________ *(Buyer)**
______________	______________ *(Buyer)**
______________	______________
______________	______________
______________	______________

**(Indicate marital status of Seller as "married", "legally separated", "unmarried", after signature)*

(over)

FIGURE 7.2 *(Continued)* Option to purchase form

clarification. Many times there will be a symbol legend included with a survey. It will help with decoding the information presented. You are paying for a professional service when you retain a property inspection. Soils reports will usually include conclusions that are intended as advice to a structural designer. Well-written reports will have an executive summary that

(For use if Seller is a corporation)

IN WITNESS WHEREOF, the Seller has caused its corporate name to be hereunto subscribed by its ________________ President, and its duly attested corporate seal to be hereunto affixed by its ________________ Secretary, at ________________, State of ________________ on the ________________ day of ________________, 19___.

(CORPORATE SEAL) ________________
(Name of Corporation)

ATTEST: ________________ **By** ________________

________________ ***Secretary.*** ________________ ***President.***

ACKNOWLEDGMENT

FIGURE 7.2 *(Continued)* Option to purchase form

addresses the key issues, so that the owner can look for more detail if desired. When a professional writes a report, he needs to anticipate how the owner intends to use the information. What is his purpose? Is he trying to establish scope? Is he trying to get to cost? Is he looking for options in addressing a particular issue?

FORMS MANUAL INSERT **FORM RD 440-34**

Used by the applicant/ borrower to obtain option on real property to be purchased.

(see reverse)

PROCEDURE FOR PREPARATION	:	**RD HB-1-3550 and RD HB-2-3550. FSA transferred Instructions 1943-A and 1943-B.**
PREPARED BY	:	**Applicant.**
NUMBER OF COPIES	:	**Original and two copies.** ***(Original and three - Extra copy will be prepared for Attorney when the Agency so desires).***
SIGNATURES REQUIRED	:	**Original and one copy by seller and applicant.**
DISTRIBUTION OF COPIES	:	**Original to applicant's loan docket; signed copy to seller; copy to applicant and copy to Attorney, if prepared.**

FIGURE 7.2 *(Continued)* Option to purchase form

Once the investor/developer receives a report, the designer may need to answer his questions to make sure he understand all aspects of it, especially the cost implications. The designer should include this service in his proposal if he knows he's working with a client who is relatively inexperienced

Form RD 442-20
(Rev. 10-96)

UNITED STATES DEPARTMENT OF AGRICULTURE
RURAL DEVELOPMENT

FORM APPROVED
OMB NO. 0575-0015

RIGHT-OF-WAY EASEMENT

KNOW ALL MEN BY THESE PRESENTS:

That in consideration of One Dollar ($1.00) and other good and valuable consideration paid to

_______________________________________ and _______________________________________,

hereinafter referred to as GRANTOR, by _______________________________________,
hereinafter referred to as GRANTEE, the receipt of which is hereby acknowledged, the GRANTOR does hereby grant, bargain, sell, transfer, and convey unto the GRANTEE, its successor and assigns, a perpetual easement with the right to erect, construct, install, and lay, and thereafter use, operate, inspect, repair, maintain, replace, and remove

____

____

____

over, across, and through the land of the GRANTOR situate in _______________________ County,

State of _______________, said land being described as follows:

____

____

____

together with the right of ingress and egress over the adjacent lands of the GRANTOR, his successors and assigns, for the purposes of this easement.

The easement shall be __________ feet in width, the center line of which is described as follows:

____

____

____

____

The consideration hereinabove recited shall constitute payment in full for any damages to the land of the GRANTOR, his successors and assigns, by reason of the installation, operation, and maintenance of the structures or improvements referred to herein. The GRANTEE covenants to maintain the easement in good repair so that no unreasonable damage will result from its use to the adjacent land of the GRANTOR, his successors and assigns.

The grant and other provisions of this easement shall constitute a covenant running with the land for the benefit of the GRANTEE, its successors and assigns.

IN WITNESS WHEREOF, the GRANTORS have executed this instrument this __________ day of ______________

19_____.

_______________________________ (SEAL)

_______________________________ (SEAL)

Public reporting burden for this collection of information is estimated to average 1 hour per response, including the time for reviewing instructions, searching existing data sources, gathering and maintaining the data needed, and completing and reviewing the collection of information. Send comments regarding this burden estimate or any other aspect of this collection of information, including suggestions for reducing this burden, to U.S. Department of Agriculture, Clearance Officer, STOP 7602, 1400 Independence Avenue, S.W., Washington, D.C. 20250-7602. Please DO NOT RETURN this form to this address. Forward to the local USDA office only. You are not required to respond to this collection of information unless it displays a currently valid OMB control number.

RD 442-20 (Rev. 10-96)

FIGURE 7.3 Easement agreement

in building and renovation projects. The service will cost more than when the same designer works with a more sophisticated client, but the inexperienced client will receive an added value that the other client doesn't require.

For example, the investor may see in the report that a roof has a remaining useful life of three years. (Figure 7.4) Is this good or bad? Well, the inspector knows it's not good. (Roofs generally have a useful life of 20 to 25 years when they are new.) But, if the client hasn't built before or has only residential references, he probably won't know this. This is why inexperienced investor/developers need an inspection firm that will spend time with explanations.

Near the end of its service life, the roof should generally be replaced in the course of the redevelopment of the site, even if it is not yet leaking. Ideally, re-roofing should occur contemporaneously with the installation of rooftop equipment and roof penetrations for new (or improved) mechanical, electrical, and plumbing systems.

In another example, a question arises. Is a 500-gallon septic tank large enough? The answer depends on the use, but in all cases, a 500-gallon tank is small. Most residential septic tanks have a capacity of 1,000 gallons. An investor who doesn't know this might think that a 500-gallon tank is plenty big; it certainly sounds big. Can you see how a lack of clarity creates an understanding gap that can cause trouble when assessing a property report?

FIGURE 7.4 Inspection reports include an estimate of the remaining roof life.

Maintaining Your Roof Asset Saves Money

Working the Numbers

[A]	**Total Number of Buildings**	= 6
[B]	**Total Roof Area of Buildings**	= 113,294 SQ. FT.
[C]	**Average Roof Replacement Cost**	= $ 8.50 / SQ. FT.
[D]	**Total Roof Asset Value (B x C)**	= $ 962,999

Annualized Program Budgets

No Maintenance Program		Maintenance Program
Years 10 =	**[E] Reroofing Time Cycle**	= 20 Years
SQ. FT. 11,329 =	**[F] Annual Reroofing Area (B / E)**	= 5,665 SQ. FT.
/ Year $ 96,300 =	**[G] Annual Reroofing Cost (F x C)**	= $ 48,150 / Year
/ Year $ 5,778 =	**[H] Annual Design/QA Fee** (6% x G)	= $ 2,889 / Year
/ Year $ ____ =	**[I] Annual Average Maintenance** First Year: Survey $ 0.08 Repairs $ 0.50 Subsequent Years: Survey $ 0.03 Repairs $ 0.05	= $ 11,301.08 / Year
/ Year $ 102,078 =	**[J] Total Annual Reroofing, Design & Maintenance Budget (G + H + I)**	= $ 73,641.10 / Year
	[K] Maintenance Program VS. No Maintenance Program Savings	= $ (28,436.79) / Year* **28%**

* This amount does not take into account hard and soft cost (e.g., consequential damage to interior construction and equipment, maintenance/janitorial staff time for clean-up and interrupted time from leaks)

FIGURE 7.5 Maintaining your roof asset

Good inspection firms don't assume that their clients have extended knowledge in the field of construction. These companies write good reports with easy explanations and comments. Investors who go to a cheap service may receive a form with little boxes checked off and nothing more. It can leave him just as much in the dark as before the inspection was done. Before you hiring an inspection firm, it's wise to ask to see sample reports from some of their previous jobs. What you are shown will give you an idea of what to expect. Top-notch inspection firms will have sample inspections

fastfacts

Once the investor/developer receives a report, the designer may need to answer his questions to make sure he understand all aspects of it, especially the cost implications. The designer should include this service when he plans his proposal if he knows he's working with a client who is relatively inexperienced in building and renovation projects.

to share that are accompanied by a legend list that explains marks, symbols, and comment sections. Getting this type of explanatory data up front can be a relief to the investor and will make him more knowledgeable in understanding and addressing building-related design issues with the architect/engineer. This is even truer when the same firm that does the design documents does not perform the inspection work.

Beginning with Consultants

Having experts do preliminary checks is a critical part of the development process. There are times when mobilizing the teams will be similar to a general deploying troops. Large development plans can require a small army of experts to confirm the viability of a project. Even small developments often require several types of experts to be involved in the preliminary development work. Usually the developer will be the person in charge of all of the experts, although the inexperienced investor may delegate this to one of the prime consultants, such as the architect/engineer or the general contractor. An investor can have a project manager handle the work for him, but most small developers do a majority of their own project management. Most large developers have sophisticated in-house staff or at least regular consultants.

Timing can be a major consideration when the troops are mobilized. When working against deadlines to remove contingencies, the developer will keep steady pressure on the people researching the project. Developers who do

Having experts do preliminary checks is a critical part of the development process.

not develop a voice and a level of professional performance with their development teams often suffer the consequences. When consultants are well screened, the developer will know if he can depend on them. Establishing a working relationship in advance of a project will let both parties know basically what to expect from each other.

Which Experts?

Once a property is under option or contract, it is time to roll out the experts. The attorney is usually the first expert to be called into service. Normally, a lawyer is retained to review legal agreements before they are signed. After getting control of a property, you must then call upon the various people you need to make verifications for you. The types of people that you need will depend on your skills and the type of development that you are doing. While it is not feasible for me to guess what your needs will be, I can give you a good overview of how the preliminary process might work for a development project. With this in mind, let's go through some of the steps that you might require on your job.

Your Lawyer

Your lawyer should be involved during the process when you are gaining control of a property. Once you have a property locked up, the lawyer should move into a research mode. This would include doing a title search and checking out the deed of the property for any potential problems such as liens, outstanding taxes, and pending probate. Alternately, if working with a buyer's agent, he can contract a title search and surety company for the investor. Some developers do this work themselves, but unless you are very comfortable in your expertise to catch minor items that could amount to major problems, having a top-notch real estate attorney do the research is a good idea. If your lawyer works fast, you might want to have this work done before you start sending the rest of your team into action. There is no point in running up expensive bills with other experts if your lawyer shoots the deal down in the first day or two.

A Survey Crew

A survey crew should normally be dispatched quickly to confirm what you think you are buying. A simple boundary survey in developed areas doesn't take long to complete. In rural areas, the same type of survey can be time consuming, as benchmarks and other reference points may be difficult to locate. You will probably want the survey crew to do an elevation survey in addition to the boundary survey. An elevation survey makes it easy to see how building placement and drainage issues will come into play with a development.

If the land to be redeveloped will not be touched by the renovation, it will usually be enough to rely on a certified survey of the previous owner if there has not been significant site development since the survey was done. If outbuildings, parking, or utilities will be altered or added in the development process, get the survey. Always have the utilities located before breaking ground. In some states, it's the law.

The slope of the land can affect many aspects of a development. For example, there are recommended slope percentages that are normally used in developing land. In the case of a lawn, a slope of up to three percent would be considered good. A lawn that has a five-percent slope would be considered too steep by many developers. Road areas, on the other hand, may have a slope of up to eight percent. Elevation surveys and topographical (topo) maps make it possible to read the slope of land. Topo maps are readily available from many sources, which range from the United States government to local sporting goods stores. Many map companies now offer topo maps on CD-ROM for computer use. Surveyors will create site plans in conjunction with engineers. (Figure 7.6)

Soil Tests

Soil tests are used to confirm that land for a private septic system can perk sufficiently. The soil test can dictate the type of septic system that may be used and how it must be installed. Additionally, soil studies can reveal

> **fast**facts
>
> A survey crew should normally be dispatched quickly to confirm what you think you are buying. A simple boundary survey in developed areas doesn't take long to complete. In rural areas, the same type of survey can be time consuming as benchmarks and other reference points may be difficult to locate. You will probably want the survey crew to do an elevation survey in addition to the boundary survey. An elevation survey makes it easy to see how building placement and drainage issues will come into play with a development.

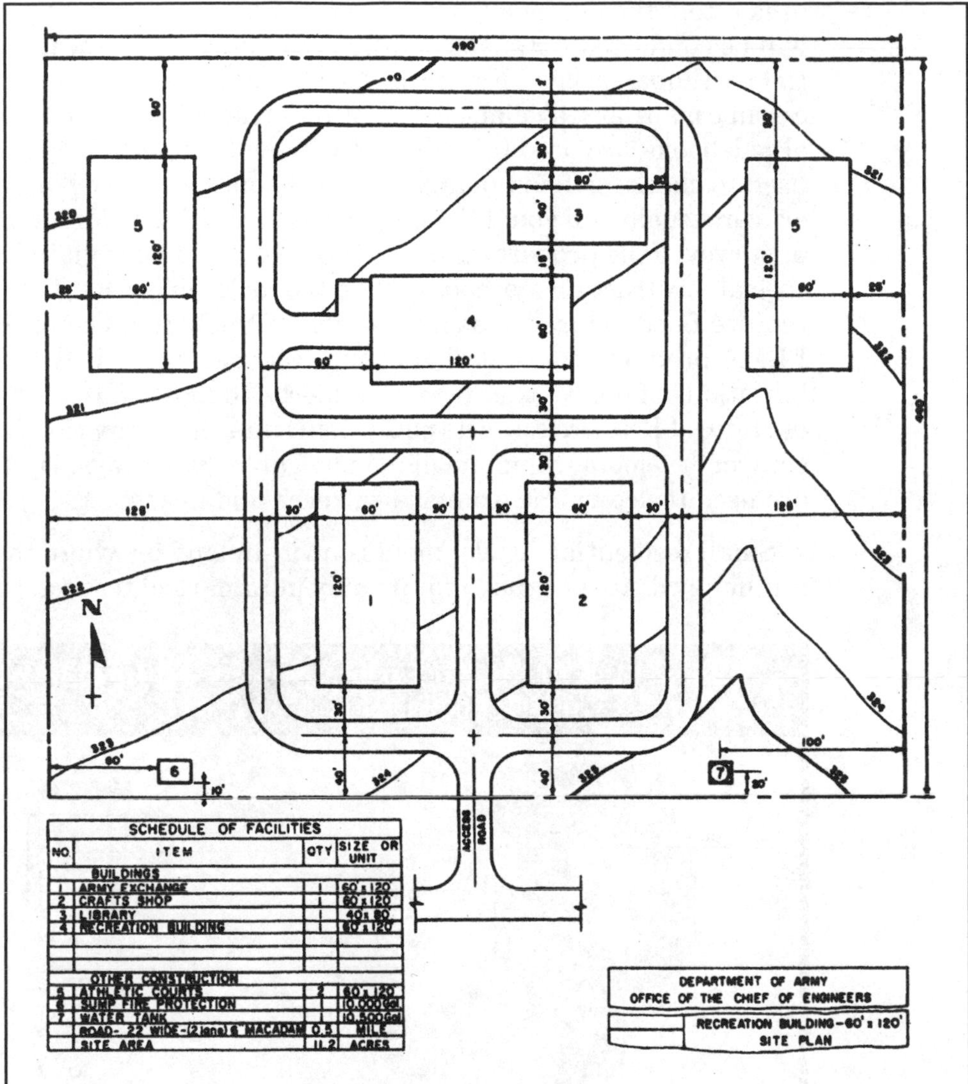

FIGURE 7.6 Typical site plan

facts about how well land will compact during development. Drainage issues can also be addressed when soils are tested. Independent geotechnical engineers or soil scientists are usually retained to perform soil tests.

Soil engineers will review soil maps for the area being researched. Government maps are available to the engineers and local maps may also be available. If you are working with an engineer who works in the site area often, the engineer may have in-house maps to work with. Studies will be conducted for such conditions as underground waterways, potential earthquake risks (Figure 7.7), compaction, absorption, and so forth. Seismic maps, also available from the government and incorporated in model codebooks, are used to evaluate the risk of earthquakes. Topo maps are used to check for flood plains and flood zones. County plan commissioners can usually tell you if the property is in the flood plain with an address or survey. If the property is in the 100-year or 50-year plain it will require special construction methods that add considerable project cost. It will also require flood insurance as a condition of financing. Generally speaking, FEMA prohibits construction in the 100-year plain. It will permit rehabilitation of flooded existing real property. In most states the Department of Natural Resources (or its equivalent) and the Army Corp of Engineers control development in and along navigable waterways. Hydrology maps are used to determine drainage patterns and needs.

Small residential developments on virgin land or where the site will be minimally disturbed may require only minimal soil testing. In some areas

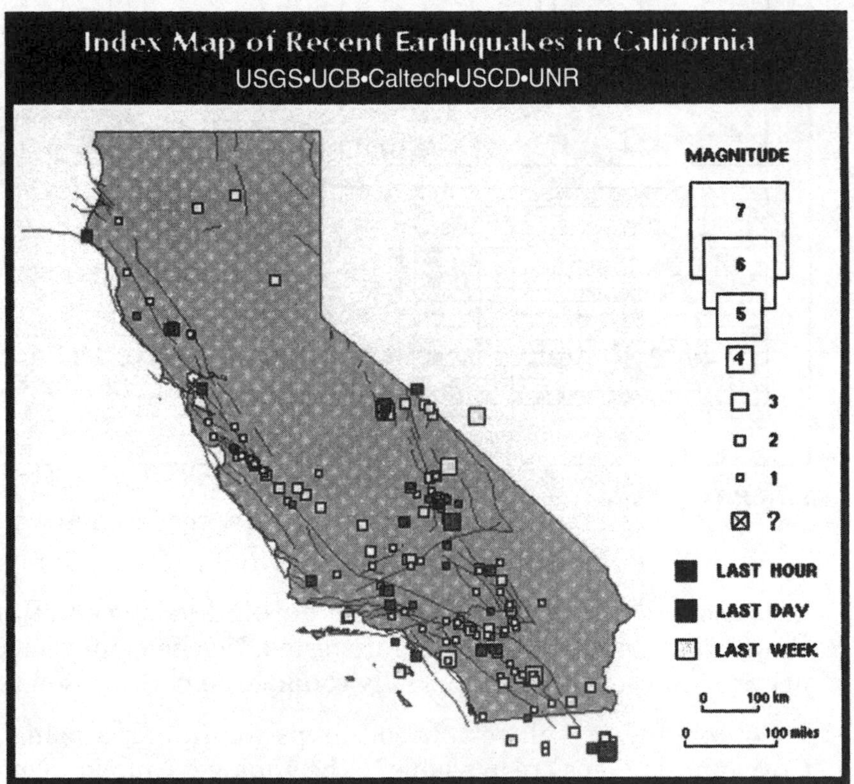

FIGURE 7.7 Earthquake map

> **Drainage issues can also be addressed when soils are tested. Independent geotechnical engineers or soil scientists are usually retained to perform soil tests.**

like these, builders may make their own assessments. Local code officials may render opinions on the need for drainage control. Geotechnical engineering work is expensive and can take a considerable amount of time to complete, but it is generally needed on larger developments and in redevelopments on sites with existing development or a history which includes underground storage tanks or landfill.

While not quite a horror story, an engineer I knew once lived to regret the decision to defer soil testing until after construction began. The project was a small addition to an existing multistory building. There were other known borings taken in areas on a site which was known to have been a landfill. He decided not to disturb the existing paved area until construction began and designed to a conservative 1500-psi bearing stated on the documents. The contract contained unit prices for compacted fill and necessary over-excavation. It also required the contractor to demonstrate that he had reached the required bearing capacity. The headache came when the contractor opened the ground and water poured in from beneath an adjacent levee and beneath an adjacent tank. There was a piece of yard piping bisecting the area that had broken in the process of excavation. The over-excavation was only two or three feet. The contractor, looking to save a few dollars, would not pay to have cores drilled. Instead, he opted to go with the only geotechnical engineer that would certify without them and performed only a compaction test and a hand auger test. Since the document language was vague and did not stipulate the type of test, the owner had to pay extra for the additional test or accept the results. The point is, don't scrimp on proper geotechnical testing if there will be new foundation work. Soil is not forgiving.

Environmental Studies

Environmental studies may be needed to obtain approval for development. The increased awareness of preserving wetlands and other natural features can destroy a developer's plans quickly. Having water on a site can make the development more valuable. People often enjoy living and working around lakes, streams, and rivers. But, aside from flood issues, environmental concerns must be evaluated. It doesn't take much water for a section of land to be considered wetlands. Vegetation is one measuring stick used by environmental agencies. If you are thinking of developing land that shows any hint of potential wet spots, you had better insist on an environmental study. This is a good thing to require on all properties.

If it is not a "wetland," water can also be an attractive nuisance. The building program and operation must consider ways to mitigate that. Still or slowly moving water can also be a health hazard if it serves to breed insects. Introducing aeration may address this in small ponds.

The increased awareness of preserving wetlands and other natural features can destroy a developer's plans quickly.

There are state and federal standards that must be observed in terms of environmental issues. Normally, a phone call to your local environmental agency will get an inspector to your site for a free inspection. This may not always be the case, but it has proved to be true during my development projects. Violating an environmental law can be extremely costly, so don't take any chances on this detail of development.

Zoning

Zoning is a key issue in any development. Without the proper zoning, obtaining permits to develop land will not be possible. An attorney should look into the zoning laws for the owner. Sometimes the owner will delegate this to the design professional, since they can respond with alternative solutions to zoning requirements. This effort is outside the effort of a schematic design contract, and the architect or engineer should be compensated. Some of the elements that should be checked include:

- Permitted uses
- Design standards
- Density regulations
- Conditional uses
- Special uses
- Contiguous property restrictions

Zoning is a key issue in any development. Without the proper zoning, obtaining land development permits will not be possible.

Building Codes

The design professional should look into the requirements of local building codes. Issues here could run from permits for street entrances to drainage for storm water. Fire codes should also be considered. You may be required to provide fire hydrants that you were not counting on or some other similarly expensive proposition. A full code analysis should be included before selecting the final design scheme and moving into design development drawings.

Utilities

Utilities are often taken for granted—they shouldn't be. Just because a subdivision at the other end of the street has city water and sewer doesn't mean that your piece of land has the necessary utilities running in front of it. You might be required to pay for an extension of a sewer line or water main, and this can be very expensive. An existing sewer may be too small to handle the increased demands that your project will put on it, and upgrading the sewer could be your responsibility.

fastfacts

Utilities are often taken for granted—they shouldn't be. Just because a subdivision at the other end of the street has city water and sewer doesn't mean that your piece of land has the necessary utilities running in front of it. You might be required to pay for an extension of a sewer line or water main, and this can be very expensive. An existing sewer may be too small to handle the increased demands that your project will put on it, and upgrading the sewer could be your responsibility.

Constructing streets and sidewalks might turn out to be a lot more than you bargained for. These improvements may be imperative and you might be required to build them to state standards, which could cost much more than a private type of installation. Your land planner and engineers should be able to steer you safely around these potential obstacles.

As you can see, there is no shortage of work and many types of duties in a typical development project. If you are going to be your own project manager, you will have to arrange for the needed services, coordinate them, and keep all of your information organized. This is not a small task, but it is one that most people can manage.

Managing Your Experts

Managing your experts and their reports is a responsibility that you should not take lightly. Most people like to think that when they hire professionals, they can leave all the work to them and wait for their results. Sometimes this is true, but more often than not, some prodding is needed to keep everything on track. Calling and scheduling a survey should be all that is needed to get a survey done. It probably is enough to get the job done, but getting the job done when it is promised to you is another matter altogether.

Developers who have years of experience know what to expect from their development teams. The odds are that over the years a good working relationship has evolved. Rookie developers don't have this luxury. Even established developers have to keep their fingers in the pie to make sure that everything turns out correctly and on time. Some phases of the developing process require more attention from a developer than others. But all aspects of the work should be tracked and managed by the developer or the project manager. See the figures that follow. If a project manager is used, the developer should manage the project manager.

Land developing is not a business that is well suited to hands-off people. Getting involved is what makes the business both fun and successful. Taking an active role in all phases of development will also make you a better developer. You will learn from the start to finish what is required to turn a piece of raw land into a sparkling development. Learning how to motivate, push, manage, and manipulate your experts may take some time, and you are sure to make some mistakes along the way. If you don't go around with a chip on your shoulder and don't pretend to be a know-it-all, you shouldn't have many bad encounters. The players on a development team are usually willing to work together and to work with the

Freddie Mac LoanProspector **Quantitative Analysis Appraisal Report** File No.

THIS SUMMARY APPRAISAL REPORT IS INTENDED FOR USE BY THE LENDER/CLIENT FOR A MORTGAGE FINANCE TRANSACTION ONLY.

SUBJECT

Property Address City State Zip Code
Legal Description County
Assessor's Parcel No. Tax Year R.E. Taxes $ Special Assessments $
Borrower Current Owner Occupant: ☐ Owner ☐ Tenant ☐ Vacant
Neighborhood or Project Name Project Type: ☐ PUD ☐ Condominium HOA $ /Mo.
Sales Price $ Date of Sale Description / $ amount of loan charges/concessions to be paid by seller
Property rights appraised ☐ Fee Simple ☐ Leasehold Map Reference Census Tract

NEIGHBORHOOD

Note: Race and the racial composition of the neighborhood are not appraisal factors.

								Single family housing	Condominium housing
Location	☐ Urban	☐ Suburban	☐ Rural	Property values	☐ Increasing	☐ Stable	☐ Declining	PRICE $ (000) AGE (Yrs)	PRICE (if applic.) $ (000) AGE (Yrs)
Built up	☐ Over 75%	☐ 25–75%	☐ Under 25%	Demand/supply	☐ Shortage	☐ In balance	☐ Over supply	Low	Low
Growth rate	☐ Rapid	☐ Stable	☐ Slow	Marketing time	☐ Under 3 mos.	☐ 3–6 mos.	☐ Over 6 mos.	High	High
								Predominant	Predominant

Neighborhood boundaries ....

SITE

Dimensions .... Site area .... Shape ....
Specific zoning classification and description ....
Zoning compliance: ☐ Legal ☐ Legal nonconforming (Grandfathered use) ☐ Illegal, attach description ☐ No zoning
Highest and best use of subject property as improved (or as proposed per plans and specifications): ☐ Present use ☐ Other use, attach description.

Utilities	Public	Other		Public	Other	Off-site Improvements	Type	Public	Private
Electricity	☐	☐ ______	Water	☐	☐ ______	Street	______	☐	☐
Gas	☐	☐ ______	Sanitary sewer	☐	☐ ______	Alley	______	☐	☐

Are there any apparent adverse site conditions (easements, encroachments, special assessments, slide areas, etc.)? ☐ Yes ☐ No If Yes, attach description.

IMPROVEMENTS

Source(s) used for physical characteristics of property: ☐ Interior and exterior inspection ☐ Exterior inspection from street ☐ Previous appraisal files ☐ MLS ☐ Assessment and tax records ☐ Prior inspection ☐ Property owner ☐ Other (Describe):
No. of Stories Type (Det./Att.) Exterior Walls Roof Surface Manufactured Housing ☐ Yes ☐ No
Does the property generally conform to the neighborhood in terms of style, condition, and construction materials? ☐ Yes ☐ No If No, attach description.
Are there any apparent physical deficiencies or conditions that would affect the soundness or structural integrity of the improvements or the livability of the property? ☐ Yes ☐ No If Yes, attach description.
Are there any apparent adverse environmental conditions (hazardous wastes, toxic substances, etc.) present in the improvements, on the site, or in the immediate vicinity of the subject property? ☐ Yes ☐ No If Yes, attach description.

QUANTITATIVE SALES COMPARISON ANALYSIS

I researched the subject market area for comparable listings and sales that are the most similar and proximate to the subject property.
My research revealed a total of ______ sales ranging in sales price from $______ to $______.
My research revealed a total of ______ listings ranging in list price from $______ to $______.
The analysis of the comparable sales below reflects market reaction to significant variations between the sales and the subject property.

FEATURE	SUBJECT	SALE 1		SALE 2		SALE 3	
Address							
Proximity to Subject							
Sales Price	$	$		$		$	
Price/Gross Liv. Area	$ ☐	$ ☐		$ ☐		$ ☐	
Data & Verification Sources							
VALUE ADJUSTMENTS	DESCRIPTION	DESCRIPTION	+(-) $ Adjustment	DESCRIPTION	+(-) $ Adjustment	DESCRIPTION	+(-) $ Adjustment
Sales or Financing Concessions							
Date of Sale/Time							
Location							
Site							
View							
Design (Style)							
Actual Age (Yrs.)							
Condition							
Above Grade Room Count	Total | Bdrms | Baths	Total | Bdrms | Baths		Total | Bdrms | Baths		Total | Bdrms | Baths	
Gross Living Area	Sq. Ft.	Sq. Ft.		Sq. Ft.		Sq. Ft.	
Basement & Finished Rooms Below Grade							
Garage/Carport							
Net Adj. (Total)		☐ + ☐ −	$	☐ + ☐ −	$	☐ + ☐ −	$
Adjusted Sales Price of Comparables			$		$		$
Date of Prior Sale							
Price of Prior Sale	$	$		$		$	

Analysis of any current agreement of sale, option, or listing of the subject property and analysis of the prior sales of subject and comparables: ______

Summary of sales comparison and value conclusion: ______

This appraisal is made ☐ "as-is", ☐ subject to completion per plans and specifications on the basis of a hypothetical condition that the improvements have been completed, or ☐ subject to the following repairs, alterations or conditions:

BASED ON AN ☐ EXTERIOR INSPECTION FROM THE STREET OR AN ☐ INTERIOR AND EXTERIOR INSPECTION, I ESTIMATE THE MARKET VALUE, AS DEFINED, OF THE REAL PROPERTY THAT IS THE SUBJECT OF THIS REPORT TO BE $______, AS OF ______.

Freddie Mac Form 2055 Page 1 of 3 11/97

FIGURE 7.8 Appraisal form (*Continued*)

LoanProspector **Quantitative Analysis Appraisal Report** File No.

P U D

Project Information for PUDs (If applicable) — Is the developer/builder in control of the homeowners' association (HOA)? ☐ Yes ☐ No

Provide the following information for PUDs only if the developer/builder is in control of the HOA and the subject property is an attached dwelling unit:

Total number of phases ________ Total number of units ________ Total number of units sold ________

Total number of units rented ________ Total number of units for sale ________ Data Source(s) ________

Was the project created by the conversion of existing buildings into a PUD? ☐ Yes ☐ No If Yes, date of conversion: ________

Does the project contain any multi-dwelling units? ☐ Yes ☐ No Data Source: ________

Are the common elements completed? ☐ Yes ☐ No If No, describe status of completion: ________

Are any common elements leased to or by the homeowners' association? ☐ Yes ☐ No If Yes, attach addendum describing rental terms and options.

Describe common elements and recreational facilities: ________

C O N D O M I N I U M

Project Information for Condominiums (If applicable) — Is the developer/builder in control of the homeowners' association (HOA)? ☐ Yes ☐ No

Provide the following information for all Condominium Projects:

Total number of phases ________ Total number of units ________ Total number of units sold ________

Total number of units rented ________ Total number of units for sale ________ Data Source(s) ________

Was the project created by the conversion of existing buildings into a condominium? ☐ Yes ☐ No If Yes, date of conversion: ________

Project Type: ☐ Primary Residence ☐ Second Home or Recreational ☐ Row or Townhouse ☐ Garden ☐ Midrise ☐ Highrise ☐ ________

Condition of the project, quality of construction, unit mix, etc.: ________

Are the common elements completed? ☐ Yes ☐ No If No, describe status of completion: ________

Are any common elements leased to or by the homeowners' association? ☐ Yes ☐ No If Yes, attach addendum describing rental terms and options.

Describe common elements and recreational facilities: ________

PURPOSE OF APPRAISAL: The purpose of this appraisal is to estimate the market value of the real property that is the subject of this report based on a quantitative sales comparison analysis for use in a mortgage finance transaction.

DEFINITION OF MARKET VALUE: The most probable price which a property should bring in a competitive and open market under all conditions requisite to a fair sale, the buyer and seller, each acting prudently, knowledgeably and assuming the price is not affected by undue stimulus. Implicit in this definition is the consummation of a sale as of a specified date and the passing of title from seller to buyer under conditions whereby: (1) buyer and seller are typically motivated; (2) both parties are well informed or well advised, and each acting in what he considers his own best interest; (3) a reasonable time is allowed for exposure in the open market; (4) payment is made in terms of cash in U.S. dollars or in terms of financial arrangements comparable thereto; and (5) the price represents the normal consideration for the property sold unaffected by special or creative financing or sales concessions* granted by anyone associated with the sale.

*Adjustments to the comparables must be made for special or creative financing or sales concessions. No adjustments are necessary for those costs which are normally paid by sellers as a result of tradition or law in a market area; these costs are readily identifiable since the seller pays these costs in virtually all sales transactions. Special or creative financing adjustments can be made to the comparable property by comparisons to financing terms offered by a third party institutional lender that is not already involved in the property or transaction. Any adjustment should not be calculated on a mechanical dollar for dollar cost of the financing or concession but the dollar amount of any adjustment should approximate the market's reaction to the financing or concessions based on the appraiser's judgment.

STATEMENT OF LIMITING CONDITIONS AND APPRAISER'S CERTIFICATION

CONTINGENT AND LIMITING CONDITIONS: The appraiser's certification that appears in the appraisal report is subject to the following conditions:

1. The appraiser will not be responsible for matters of a legal nature that affect either the property being appraised or the title to it. The appraiser assumes that the title is good and marketable and, therefore, will not render any opinions about the title. The property is appraised on the basis of it being under responsible ownership.
2. The appraiser has provided any required sketch in the appraisal report to show approximate dimensions of the improvements and the sketch is included only to assist the reader of the report in visualizing the property and understanding the appraiser's determination of its size.
3. The appraiser will not give testimony or appear in court because he or she made an appraisal of the property in question, unless specific arrangements to do so have been made beforehand.
4. The appraiser has noted in the appraisal report any adverse conditions (such as, but not limited to, needed repairs, the presence of hazardous wastes, toxic substances, etc.) observed during the inspection of the subject property or that he or she became aware of during the normal research involved in performing the appraisal. Unless otherwise stated in the appraisal report, the appraiser has no knowledge of any hidden or unapparent conditions of the property or adverse environmental conditions (including the presence of hazardous wastes, toxic substances, etc.) that would make the property more or less valuable, and has assumed that there are no such conditions and makes no guarantees or warranties, expressed or implied, regarding the condition of the property. The appraiser will not be responsible for any such conditions that do exist or for any engineering or testing that might be required to discover whether such conditions exist. Because the appraiser is not an expert in the field of environmental hazards, the appraisal report must not be considered as an environmental assessment of the property.
5. The appraiser obtained the information, estimates, and opinions that were expressed in the appraisal report from sources that he or she considers to be reliable and believes them to be true and correct. The appraiser does not assume responsibility for the accuracy of such items that were furnished by other parties.
6. The appraiser will not disclose the contents of the appraisal report except as provided for in the Uniform Standards of Professional Appraisal Practice.
7. The appraiser must provide his or her prior written consent before the lender/client specified in the appraisal report can distribute the appraisal report (including conclusions about the property value, the appraiser's identity and professional designations, and references to any professional appraisal organizations or the firm with which the appraiser is associated) to anyone other than the borrower; the mortgagee or its successors and assigns; the mortgage insurer; consultants; professional appraisal organizations; any state or federally approved financial institution; or any department, agency, or instrumentality of the United States or any state or the District of Columbia; except that the lender/client may distribute the report to data collection or reporting service(s) without having to obtain the appraiser's prior written consent. The appraiser's written consent and approval must also be obtained before the appraisal can be conveyed by anyone to the public through advertising, public relations, news, sales, or other media.
8. The appraiser has based his or her appraisal report and valuation conclusion for an appraisal that is subject to completion per plans and specifications on the basis of a hypothetical condition that the improvements have been completed.
9. The appraiser has based his or her appraisal report and valuation conclusion for an appraisal that is subject to completion, repairs, or alterations on the assumption that completion of the improvements will be performed in a workmanlike manner.

FIGURE 7.8 (*Continued*) Appraisal form

Freddie Mac | **Loan Prospector** **Quantitative Analysis Appraisal Report** File No.

APPRAISER'S CERTIFICATION: The Appraiser certifies and agrees that:

1. I performed this appraisal by (1) personally inspecting from the street the subject property and neighborhood and each of the comparable sales (unless I have otherwise indicated in this report that I also inspected the interior of the subject property); (2) collecting, confirming, and analyzing data from reliable public and/or private sources; and (3) reporting the results of my inspection and analysis in this summary appraisal report. I further certify that I have adequate information about the physical characteristics of the subject property and the comparable sales to develop this appraisal.
2. I have researched and analyzed the comparable sales and offerings/listings in the subject market area and have reported the comparable sales in this report that are the best available for the subject property. I further certify that adequate comparable market data exists in the general market area to develop a reliable sales comparison analysis for the subject property.
3. I have taken into consideration the factors that have an impact on value in my development of the estimate of market value in the appraisal report. I further certify that I have noted any apparent or known adverse conditions in the subject improvements, on the subject site, or on any site within the immediate vicinity of the subject property of which I am aware, have considered these adverse conditions in my analysis of the property value to the extent that I had market evidence to support them, and have commented about the effect of the adverse conditions on the marketability of the subject property. I have not knowingly withheld any significant information from the appraisal report and I believe, to the best of my knowledge, that all statements and information in the appraisal report are true and correct.
4. I stated in the appraisal report only my own personal, unbiased, and professional analysis, opinions, and conclusions, which are subject only to the contingent and limiting conditions specified in this form.
5. I have no present or prospective interest in the property that is the subject of this report, and I have no present or prospective personal interest or bias with respect to the participants in the transaction. I did not base, either partially or completely, my analysis and/or the estimate of market value in the appraisal report on the race, color, religion, sex, age, marital status, handicap, familial status, or national origin of either the prospective owners or occupants of the subject property or of the present owners or occupants of the properties in the vicinity of the subject property or on any other basis prohibited by law.
6. I have no present or contemplated future interest in the subject property, and neither my current or future employment nor my compensation for performing this appraisal is contingent on the appraised value of the property.
7. I was not required to report a predetermined value or direction in value that favors the cause of the client or any related party, the amount of the value estimate, the attainment of a specific result, or the occurrence of a subsequent event in order to receive my compensation and/or employment for performing the appraisal. I did not base the appraisal report on a requested minimum valuation, a specific valuation, or the need to approve a specific mortgage loan.
8. I estimated the market value of the real property that is the subject of this report based on the sales comparison approach to value. I further certify that I considered the cost and income approaches to value, but, through mutual agreement with the client, did not develop them, unless I have noted otherwise in this report.
9. I performed this appraisal as a limited appraisal, subject to the Departure Provision of the Uniform Standards of Professional Appraisal Practice that were adopted and promulgated by the Appraisal Standards Board of The Appraisal Foundation and that were in place as of the effective date of the appraisal (unless I have otherwise indicated in this report that the appraisal is a complete appraisal, in which case, the Departure Provision does not apply).
10. I acknowledge that an estimate of a reasonable exposure time in the open market is a condition in the definition of market value. The exposure time associated with the estimate of market value for the subject property is consistent with the marketing time noted in the Neighborhood section of this report. The marketing period concluded for the subject property at the estimated market value is also consistent with the marketing time noted in the Neighborhood section.
11. I personally prepared all conclusions and opinions about the real estate that were set forth in the appraisal report. I further certify that no one provided significant professional assistance to me in the development of this appraisal.

SUPERVISORY APPRAISER'S CERTIFICATION: If a supervisory appraiser signed the appraisal report, he or she certifies and agrees that: I directly supervise the appraiser who prepared the appraisal report, have examined the appraisal report for compliance with the Uniform Standards of Professional Appraisal Practice, agree with the statements and conclusions of the appraiser, agree to be bound by the appraiser's certifications numbered 5 through 7 above, and am taking full responsibility for the appraisal and the appraisal report.

APPRAISER:

Signature ____________

Name ____________

Company Name ____________

Company Address ____________

____

Date of Report/Signature ____________

State Certification # ____________

or State License # ____________

State ____________

Expiration Date of Certification or License ____________

ADDRESS OF PROPERTY APPRAISED:

____

____

APPRAISED VALUE OF SUBJECT PROPERTY $ ____________

EFFECTIVE DATE OF APPRAISAL/INSPECTION ____________

LENDER/CLIENT:

Name ____________

Company Name ____________

Company Address ____________

____

SUPERVISORY APPRAISER (ONLY IF REQUIRED):

Signature ____________

Name ____________

Company Name ____________

Company Address ____________

____

Date of Report/Signature ____________

State Certification # ____________

or State License # ____________

State ____________

Expiration Date of Certification or License ____________

SUPERVISORY APPRAISER:

SUBJECT PROPERTY:

☐ Did not inspect subject property

☐ Did inspect exterior of subject property from street

☐ Did inspect interior and exterior of subject property

COMPARABLE SALES:

☐ Did not inspect exterior of comparable sales from street

☐ Did inspect exterior of comparable sales from street

FIGURE 7.8 (*Continued*) Appraisal form

> **Land developing is not a business that is well suited to hands-off people. Getting involved is what makes the business both fun and successful. Taking an active role in all phases of development will also make you a better developer.**

developer of a project. So, let's take a step-by-step tour of how you might go about managing your experts for faster turnaround, high quality work, and bigger profits.

Develop A System

Your first step should be to develop a system for keeping track of what is going on with your project. A lot of developers use computers to organize their management duties. Computers are great, but not everyone likes to work with them. Using a combination system might work best for you. What is a combination system? It is a system that uses computerized files and old-fashioned paper trails. Personally, I favor a combination system and I have one that has worked very well for me over the years.

My system involves the use of corkboards and a computer system. I do my day-to-day tracking on corkboards and maintain an ongoing record of activities on my computer. There are people who would say that my system is too simple, but simple systems are sometimes the best. Let me give you a brief overview of how I operate.

I use multiple corkboards in my office. One of the boards has headings for days of the week. Under each of these heading I keep small pieces of paper that tell me what I'm required to do on a particular day. When I complete a task, I remove the piece of paper. This not only keeps me organized, but also gives me a sense of accomplishment as each piece of paper comes off the board.

Another board that I use has headings with expert specialty areas listed, such as: surveyors, soils tests, zoning, and so forth. The pieces of paper under these headings may duplicate what is on my daily board, but each piece of paper keeps me informed of what I need to accomplish.

A third board that I maintain is my think-tank board. This is where I post pieces of paper with my ideas on them. Whenever I think of something that is or might be of value during the development of a project, I jot down a note and post it on the think-tank board. When I have time, I review the

Form RD 1922-15
(Rev. 6-97)

ADMINISTRATIVE APPRAISAL REVIEW
FOR SINGLE FAMILY HOUSING

1. Rural Development Office	2. Appraiser Name
3. Borrower/Former Borrower/Applicant	4. Date of Appraisal
5. Property Address	6. Borrower Case Number

The purpose of this review is for loan underwriting, processing a conditional commitment for a dwelling to be built, rehabilitated, or developed as a manufactured home package, issuance of a conditional commitment for a Guaranteed Rural Housing loan, and/or loan servicing purposes. The reasons for disagreement by the reviewer to any of the following statements are to be documented and attached herewith.

1. Uniform Residential Appraisal Report for the subject property is attached. The report correctly identifies the property and has been completed, signed, and dated by the appraiser.

2. The mathematical calculations and adjustments are correct, or errors, if any, have been noted and determined to have no significant impact on the final market value conclusion of the appraisal.

3. In preparing this report, the appraiser has used three comparable properties sold within the past twelve months from the date of the report. The comparable properties appear to be similar to the subject and are from the same or like market. The market value appears to be reasonable.

4. The appraiser has used both the comparable sales and the cost approach in preparing the appraisal report as prescribed in RD Instruction 1922-C or the Direct Single Family Housing Handbooks, as appropriate.

5. For Guaranteed Rural Housing only, the land value (does, does not) exceed 30% of the value of the total package. (circle one)

6. The appraisal is acceptable for the intended purpose and I recommend: (check one)

____ Authorization of payment to contract appraiser.

____ Acceptance of appraisal for Guaranteed Rural Housing Loan.

____ Issuance of a Conditional Commitment under 7 CFR 3550.70.

____ Other: (explain) ______________________________

SIGNATURE OF REVIEWER	TITLE	DATE OF REVIEW

RD 1922-15 (Rev. 6-97)

FIGURE 7.9 Appraisal review form

notes and think more about them. Sometimes I look at them while I'm talking on the telephone. By keeping the ideas in front of me, I can digest them day by day. This, I believe, is an edge for me, and it is something that would be more difficult if I had all of my information on a computer.

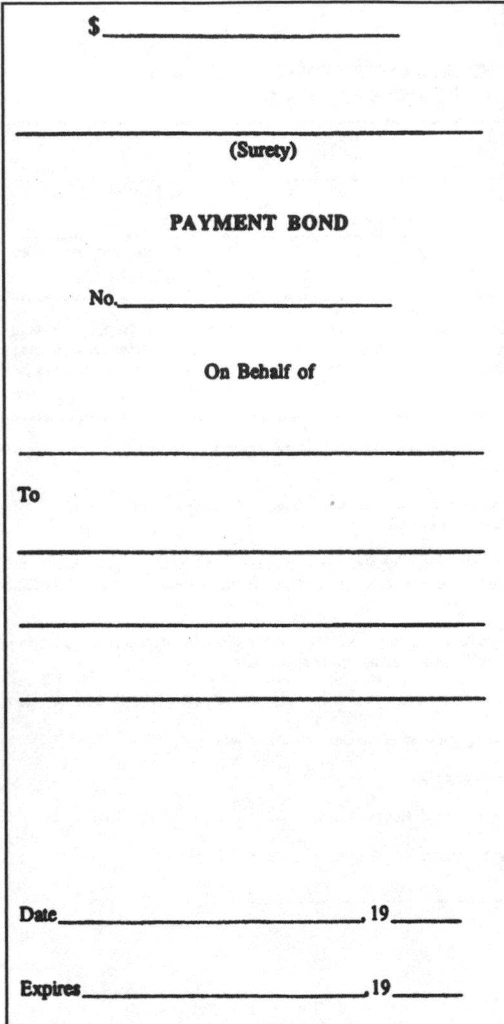
$______________

____
(Surety)

PAYMENT BOND

No.______________

On Behalf of

____

To

____

____

____

Date______________, 19____

Expires______________, 19____

FIGURE 7.10 A payment bond (*Continued*)

The computerized version of my organizational procedure is a weekly recap of what I've done and what I need to do. Of course, there are spreadsheets on the computer that keep me in touch with my development budget. It's common for me to print reports from the computer and pin them to my office walls. I find that the more often I see what I'm doing, the better prepared I am to accomplish my goals. To some people, my system is clumsy, but it has worked well for me over the years. You have to define your own system, and it can be anything that you are comfortable with and that works. But, you must have a system for tracing your efforts and your requirements.

Tickler Files

Most developers have some version of tickler files. These are files that remind the developers to do something at a specific time. A tickler file can be as simple as a stack of index cards and a small box to hold them. The important aspect of the files is to make sure that nothing of importance is forgotten or not followed up on. For example, if a survey is due in on Wednesday, the tickler file should alert you to check for it on Thursday. If the survey has not arrived, you will know to call the survey firm and find out what the delay is. Tickler files are invaluable when it comes to staying on top of a development project.

Phone Calls

Phone calls can keep your project on time. Unfortunately, it is usually necessary to follow up on work that you have scheduled. This can take a big

Payment Bond

U.S. Department of Housing and Urban Development Office of Housing Federal Housing Commissioner

(This Bond is issued simultaneously with Performance Bond in favor of Owner conditioned on the full and faithful performance of the contract)

Know All Men By These Presents, that we, ______

of ______

as Principal, (hereinafter called the Principal) and ______,

a ______ as Surety, (hereinafter called the Surety) are held and firmly bound unto ______ as Obligee, (hereinafter called the "Owner"), for the use and benefit of claimants as hereinafter defined, in the sum of ______ Dollars ($), lawful money of the United States of America, for the payment of which Principal and Surety bind themselves, their heirs, executors, administrators, successors and assigns, jointly and severally, firmly by these presents.

Whereas, Principal has entered into a Construction Contract dated ______ with Owner for the construction of a Housing Project designated as ______ a copy of which Construction Contract is by reference made a part hereof; and is hereinafter referred to as the Contract.

Now, therefore, the conditions of this obligation is such that, if Principal shall promptly make payment to all claimants as hereinafter defined, for all labor and material used or reasonably required for use in the performance of the Contract, then this obligation shall be void; otherwise it shall remain in full force and effect, subject, however, to the following conditions:

1. A Claimant is defined as one having a direct contract with the Principal or with a subcontractor of the Principal for labor, material, or both, used or reasonably required for use in the performance of the contract, labor and material being construed to include that part of water, gas, power, light, heat, oil, gasoline, telephone service or rental of equipment directly applicable to the Contract.

2. The above name Principal and Surety hereby jointly and severally agree with the Owner that every claimant as herein defined, who has not been paid in full before the expiration of a period of ninety (90) days after the date on which the last of such claimant's work or labor was done or performed, or materials were furnished by such claimant, may sue on this bond for the use of such claimant, prosecute the suit to final judgment for such sum or sums as may be justly due claimant, and have execution thereon. The Owner shall not be liable for the payment of any costs or expenses of any such suit.

3. No suit or action shall be commenced hereunder by any claimant:

a) Unless claimant, other than one having direct contract with the Principal, shall have given written notice to any two of the following: The Principal, the Owner, or the Surety above named, within ninety (90) days after such claimant did or performed the last of the work or labor, or furnished the last of the materials for which said claim is made, stating with substantial accuracy the amount claimed and the name of the party to whom the materials were furnished, or for whom the work or labor was done or performed. Such notice shall be served by mailing the same by registered mail or certified mail, postage prepaid, in an envelope addressed to the Principal, Owner or Surety, at any place where an office is regularly maintained for the transaction of business, or served in any manner in which legal process may be served in the state in which the aforesaid project is located, save that such service need not be made by a public officer.

b) After the expiration of one (1) year following the date on which Principal ceased work on said Contract, it being understood, however, that if any limitation embodied in this bond is prohibited by any law controlling the construction hereof, such limitation shall be deemed to be amended so as to be equal to the minimum period of limitation permitted by such law.

c) Other than in a state court of competent jurisdiction in and for the county or other political subdivision of the state in which the project, or any part thereof, is situated, or in the United States District Court for the district in which the project, or any part thereof, is situated, and not elsewhere.

4. The amount of this bond shall be reduced by and to the extent of any payment or payments made in good faith hereunder, inclusive of the payment by Surety of mechanics' liens which may be filed of record against said improvement, whether or not claim for the amount of such lien be presented under and against this bond.

Signed and Sealed this ______ day of ______, 19____.

Witness as to Principal: ______ (Seal)

(Principal)

______ By: ______

______

(Surety)

By: ______

form HUD-50052-A (11/89)

FIGURE 7.10 *(Continued)* A payment bond

The important aspect of the files is to make sure that nothing of importance is forgotten or not followed up on. For example, if a survey is due in on Wednesday, the tickler file should alert you to check for it on Thursday.

BID BOND *(See instruction on reverse)*	DATE BOND EXECUTED *(Must not be later than bid opening date)*	OMB NO.: 9000-0045 Expires: 09/30/98

Public reporting burden for this collection of information is estimated to average 25 minutes per response, including the time for reviewing instructions, searching existing data sources, gathering and maintaining the data needed, and completing and reviewing the collection of information. Send comments regarding this burden estimate or any other aspect of this collection of information, including suggestions for reducing this burden, to the FAR Secretariate (MVR), Federal Acquisition Policy Division, GSA, Washington, DC 20405.

PRINCIPAL *(Legal name and business address)*	TYPE OF ORGANIZATION *("X" one)* ☐ INDIVIDUAL ☐ PARTNERSHIP ☐ JOINT VENTURE ☐ CORPORATION STATE OF INCORPORATION
SURETY(IES) *(Name(s) and business address(es))*	

PENAL SUM OF BOND					BID IDENTIFICATION	
PERCENT OF BID PRICE	AMOUNT NOT TO EXCEED				BID DATE	INVITATION NO.
	MILLION(S)	THOUSAND(S)	HUNDRED(S)	CENTS	FOR *(Construction, Supplies, or Services)*	

OBLIGATION:

We, the Principal and Surety(ies) are firmly bound to the United States of America (hereinafter called the Government) in the above penal sum. For payment of the penal sum, we bind ourselves, our heirs, executors, administrators, and successors, jointly and severally. However, where the Sureties are corporations acting as co-sureties, we, the Sureties, bind ourselves in such sum "jointly and severally" as well as "severally" only for the purpose of allowing a joint action or actions against any or all of us. For all other purposes, each Surety binds itself, jointly and severally with the Principal, for the payment of the sum shown opposite the name of the Surety. If no limit of liability is indicated, the limit of liability is the full amount of the penal sum.

CONDITIONS:

The Principal has submitted the bid identified above.

THEREFORE:

The above obligation is void if the Principal - (a) upon acceptance by the Government of the bid identified above, within the period specified therein for acceptance (sixty (60) days if no period is specified), executes the further contractual documents and gives the bond(s) required by the terms of the bid as accepted within the time specified (ten (10) days if no period is specified) after receipt of the forms by the principal; or (b) in the event of failure to execute such further contractual documents and give such bonds, pays the Government for any cost of procuring the work which exceeds the amount of the bid.

Each Surety executing this instrument agrees that its obligation is not impaired by any extension(s) of the time for acceptance of the bid that the Principal may grant to the Government. Notice to the surety(ies) of extension(s) are waived. However, waiver of the notice applies only to extensions aggregating not more than sixty (60) calendar days in addition to the period originally allowed for acceptance of the bid.

WITNESS:

The Principal and Surety(ies) executed this bid bond and affixed their seals on the above date.

PRINCIPAL

SIGNATURE(S)	1. *(Seal)*	2. *(Seal)*	3. *(Seal)*	*Corporate Seal*
NAME(S) & TITLE(S) *(Typed)*	1.	2.	3.	

INDIVIDUAL SURETY(IES)

SIGNATURE(S)	1. *(Seal)*	2. *(Seal)*
NAME(S) *(Typed)*	1.	2.

CORPORATE SURETY(IES)

SURETY A				
NAME & ADDRESS		STATE OF INC.	LIABILITY LIMIT $	
SIGNATURE(S)	1.	2.		*Corporate Seal*
NAME(S) & TITLE(S) *(Typed)*	1.	2.		

AUTHORIZED FOR LOCAL REPRODUCTION
Previous edition is usable

STANDARD FORM 24 (REV.)
Prescribed by GSA - FAR (48 CFR) 53.228(a)

FIGURE 7.11 A bid bond (*Continued*)

bite out of your workday, but it is essential if you want to keep your project on schedule. Don't wait days to follow up on work that should be done. Every day you lose is costing you money. Be aggressive. Avoid being a pest, but don't hesitate to make polite inquires pertaining to the status of work

CORPORATE SURETY(IES) ***(Continued)***

SURETY B	NAME & ADDRESS		STATE OF INC.	LIABILITY LIMIT $	Corporate Seal
	SIGNATURE(S)	1.	2.		
	NAME(S) & TITLE(S) *(Typed)*	1.	2.		
SURETY C	NAME & ADDRESS		STATE OF INC.	LIABILITY LIMIT $	Corporate Seal
	SIGNATURE(S)	1.	2.		
	NAME(S) & TITLE(S) *(Typed)*	1.	2.		
SURETY D	NAME & ADDRESS		STATE OF INC.	LIABILITY LIMIT $	Corporate Seal
	SIGNATURE(S)	1.	2.		
	NAME(S) & TITLE(S) *(Typed)*	1.	2.		
SURETY E	NAME & ADDRESS		STATE OF INC.	LIABILITY LIMIT $	Corporate Seal
	SIGNATURE(S)	1.	2.		
	NAME(S) & TITLE(S) *(Typed)*	1.	2.		
SURETY F	NAME & ADDRESS		STATE OF INC.	LIABILITY LIMIT $	Corporate Seal
	SIGNATURE(S)	1.	2.		
	NAME(S) & TITLE(S) *(Typed)*	1.	2.		
SURETY G	NAME & ADDRESS		STATE OF INC.	LIABILITY LIMIT $	Corporate Seal
	SIGNATURE(S)	1.	2.		
	NAME(S) & TITLE(S) *(Typed)*	1.	2.		

INSTRUCTIONS

1. This form is authorized for use when a bid guaranty is required. Any deviation from this form will require the written approval of the Administrator of General Services.

2. Insert the full legal name and business address of the Principal in the space designated "Principal" on the face of the form. An authorized person shall sign the bond. Any person signing in a representative capacity (e.g., an attorney-in-fact) must furnish evidence of authority if that representative is not a member of the firm, partnership, or joint venture, or an officer of the corporation involved.

3. The bond may express penal sum as a percentage of the bid price. In these cases, the bond may state a maximum dollar limitation (e.g., 20% of the bid price but the amount not to exceed dollars).

4. (a) Corporations executing the bond as sureties must appear on the Department of the Treasury's list of approved sureties and must act within the limitation listed therein. Where more than one corporate surety is involved, their names and addresses shall appear in the spaces (Surety A, Surety B, etc.) headed "CORPORATE SURETY(IES)." In the space designed "SURETY(IES)" on the face of the form, insert only the letter identification of the sureties.

(b) Where individual sureties are involved, a completed Affidavit of Individual Surety (Standard Form 28), for each individual surety, shall accompany the bond. The Government may require the surety to furnish additional substantiating information concerning its financial capability.

5. Corporations executing the bond shall affix their corporate seals. Individuals shall execute the bond opposite the word "Corporate Seal"; and shall affix an adhesive seal if executed in Maine, New Hampshire, or any other jurisdiction requiring adhesive seals.

6. Type the name and title of each person signing this bond in the space provided.

7. In its application to negotiated contracts, the terms "bid" and "bidder" shall include "proposal" and "offeror."

STANDARD FORM 24 (REV.) **BACK**

FIGURE 7.11 (*Continued*) A bid bond

that you have requested. If you are timid on the phone, get over it. You have to learn to call people and push them to make your project come out on time.

Your Company Name
Your Company Address
Your Company Phone and Fax Numbers

REQUEST FOR SUBSTITUTIONS

Customer name: ______________________________

Customer address: ______________________________

Customer city/state/zip: ______________________________

Customer phone number: ______________________________

Job location: ______________________________

Plans and specifications dated: ______________________________

Bid requested from: ______________________________

Type of work: ______________________________

The following items are being substituted for the items specified in the attached plans and specifications: ______________________________

____

____

____

____

____

Please indicate your acceptance of these substitutions by signing below.

______________________________ ______________________________
Contractor **Date** **Customer** **Date**

____
Customer **Date**

FIGURE 7.12 Request for substitutions form

Files

Office files must be kept as projects are developed. Plan on making a lot of photocopies of documents. Some developers make copies of every check that they write and receive. Maintaining copies of all correspondence is essential. Written records are indispensable if you ever have to go to court to resolve differences with others. Not only are the records important

Your Company Name
Your Company Address
Your Company Phone and Fax Numbers

PROPOSAL

Date: ____________________

Customer's name: ____

Address: ____

Phone number: ____

Job location: ____

DESCRIPTION OF WORK

Your Company Name will supply, and/or coordinate, all labor and material for the above-referenced job as follows: ____

____

____

____

____

____

____

PAYMENT SCHEDULE

Price: ____________________________________ **dollars ($____________)**

Payments to be made as follows: ____

____

____

All payments shall be made in full, upon presentation of each completed invoice. If payment is not made according to the terms above, Your Company Name will have the following rights and remedies. Your Company Name may charge a monthly service charge of ____________ (_____%) percent, ____________ (_____%) percent per year, from the first day default is made. Your Company Name may lien the property where the work has been done. Your Company Name may use all legal methods in the collection of monies owed to it. Your Company Name may seek compensation, at the rate of $_____ per hour, for attempts made to collect unpaid monies.

(Page 1 of 2. Please initial _______.)

FIGURE 7.13 Sample proposal (*Continued*)

during litigation, they make doing business much easier. There is so much involved in a development project that keeping your thoughts clear can be very difficult. If you can turn to a file and find your answers, you are way ahead in the game.

Your Company Name may seek payment for legal fees and other costs of collection, to the full extent the law allows.

If the job is not ready for the service or materials requested, as scheduled, and the delay is not due to Your Company Name's actions, Your Company Name may charge the customer for lost time. This charge will be at a rate of $________ per hour, per man, including travel time.

If you have any questions or don't understand this proposal, seek professional advice. Upon acceptance, this proposal becomes a binding contract between both parties.

Respectfully submitted,

Your Name
Title

ACCEPTANCE

We, the undersigned, do hereby agree to, and accept, all the terms and conditions of this proposal. We fully understand the terms and conditions, and hereby consent to enter into this contract.

Your Company Name	**Customer**
By: ____________________	____________________
Title: ____________________	**Date:** ____________________
Date: ____________________	

Proposal expires in 30 days, if not accepted by all parties.

FIGURE 7.13 *(Continued)* Sample proposal

Personal Involvement

Personal involvement is instrumental in making a project profitable. You can have an associate perform many of the tasks for you, but someone close to you must be willing to stay on top of all aspects of your work. Leaving your fate in the hands of subcontractors and vendors is risky business. You have to rely on outside help, but it is up to you to make sure that the people working with and for you are doing their jobs properly and on time. There is no substitute for first-hand management. If you don't already possess good organizational and management skills, work on them. Consider going to some seminars. Read more books and develop the skills as quickly as you can. The sooner you learn to run your business well, the better the business will do.

Form RD 1924-7
(Rev. 2-97)

OMB NO. 0575-0042

UNITED STATES DEPARTMENT OF AGRICULTURE
RURAL DEVELOPMENT AND
FARM SERVICE AGENCY

CONTRACT CHANGE ORDER

ORDER NO. ____

DATE ____

STATE ____

COUNTY ____

CONTRACT FOR ____

OWNER ____

To ____
(Contractor)

You are hereby requested to comply with the following changes from the contract plans and specifications:

Description of Changes (Supplemental Plans and Specifications Attached)	DECREASE in Contract Price	INCREASE in Contract Price
	$	$
TOTALS	$	
NET CHANGE IN CONTRACT PRICE	$	

JUSTIFICATION:

The amount of the Contract will be (Decreased) (Increased) By The Sum Of: ____

____ Dollars ($ ____).

The Contract Total Including this and previous Change Orders Will Be: ____

____ Dollars ($ ____).

The Contract Period Provided for Completion Will Be (Increased) (Decreased) (Unchanged): ____ Days.

This document will become a supplement to the contract and all provisions will apply hereto.

Requested ____ *(Owner)* ____ *(Date)*

Recommended ____ *(Owner's Architect/Engineer)* ____ *(Date)*

Accepted ____ *(Contractor)* ____ *(Date)*

Approved by Agency ____ *(Name and Title)* ____ *(Date)*

Public reporting burden for this collection of information is estimated to average 15 minutes per response, including the time for reviewing instructions, searching existing data sources, gathering and maintaining the data needed, and completing and reviewing the collection of information. Send comments regarding this burden estimate or any other aspect of this collection of information, including suggestions for reducing this burden, to U.S. Department of Agriculture, Clearance Officer, STOP 7602, 1400 Independence Avenue, S.W., Washington, D.C. 20250-7602. Please DO NOT RETURN this form to this address. Forward to the local USDA office only. You are not required to respond to this collection of information unless it displays a currently valid OMB control number.

POSITION 6

Form RD 1924-7 (Rev. 2-97)

FIGURE 7.14 A change order

Your Company Name
Your Company Address
Your Company Phone and Fax Numbers

EARLY TERMINATION AND MUTUAL RELEASE OF CONTRACT

For good and valuable consideration had and received and the mutual promises and releases herein contained, the parties known as ______________________________ (Contractor) and ______________________________ (Customer) do hereby release each other, now and forever, in and from all further promises, liabilities, warranties, requirements, obligations, payments, and performance of the contract dated ____________________, 19 ________, entitled ______________________________ and made for the purpose of ______________________ ______________________________ as reflected in said contract between them.

The parties each acknowledge all matters between them regarding the said contract have been satisfactorily adjusted between them, and the contract has been terminated prior to its entire fulfillment and performance, as the parties have agreed such early termination is mutually desirable.

Accordingly, said contract is hereby SUPERSEDED AND ABSOLUTELY TERMINATED.

Each party warrants each's own full power and authority to enter into this Early Termination and Mutual Release of Contract, which shall become effective only upon the signature of both parties.

Date: ______________________________ Date: ______________________________

Customer: ______________________________ Contractor: ______________________________

by: ______________________________ (Seal) Title: ______________________________

by: ______________________________ (Seal)

State of ______________________________ of ______________________________

The foregoing Early Termination and Mutual Release of Contract was sworn to and acknowledged before me by ______________________________ and ______________________________ on ______________________________, 19 ______.

____
Notary Public

My commission expires:____________ (Notary Seal)

FIGURE 7.15 Early termination and mutual release of contract

ARCHITECT-ENGINEER CONTRACT	1. CONTRACT NO.
	2. DATE OF CONTRACT
3a. NAME OF ARCHITECT-ENGINEER	3b. TELEPHONE NO. *(Include Area Code)*

3c. ADDRESS OF ARCHITECT-ENGINEER *(Include ZIP Code)*

4. DEPARTMENT OR AGENCY AND ADDRESS *(Include ZIP Code)*

5. PROJECT TITLE AND LOCATION

6. CONTRACT FOR *(General description of services to be provided)*

7. CONTRACT AMOUNT *(Express in words and figures)*

8. NEGOTIATION AUTHORITY

9. ADMINISTRATIVE, APPROPRIATION, AND ACCOUNTING DATA

NSN 7540-00-181-8326
PREVIOUS EDITION NOT USABLE

STANDARD FORM 252 (REV. 10-83)
Prescribed by GSA - FAR (48 CFR) 53.236-2(a)

FIGURE 7.16 Architect-engineer contract (*Continued*)

10. The United States of America (called the Government) represented by the Contracting Officer executing this contract, and the Architect-Engineer agree to perform this contract in strict accordance with the clauses and the documents identified as follows, all of which are made a part of this contract:

If the parties to this contract are comprised of more than one legal entity, each entity shall be jointly and severally liable under this conract. The parties hereto have executed this contract as of the date recorded in Item 2.

	SIGNATURES	NAMES AND TITLES *(Typed)*
11. ARCHITECT-ENGINEER OR OTHER PROFESSIONAL SERVICES CONTRACTOR		
A		
B		
C		
D		
12. THE UNITED STATES OF AMERICA		
		Contracting Officer

STANDARD FORM 252 (REV. 10-83) BACK

FIGURE 7.16 *(Continued)* Architect-engineer contract

Maintaining copies of all correspondence is essential. Written records are indispensable if you ever have to go to court to resolve differences with others.

Form RD 1942-19
(Rev. 10-96)

UNITED STATES DEPARTMENT OF AGRICULTURE
RURAL DEVELOPMENT

FORM APPROVED
OMB NO. 0575-0015

AGREEMENT FOR ENGINEERING SERVICES

This Agreement, made this ______________ day of ______________________________, 19 _____ ,

by and between ____, hereafter referred to as the OWNER,

and ____, hereinafter referred to as the ENGINEER:

THE OWNER intends to construct a ____

____________________ in ____________________ County, State of ____________________

which may be paid for in part with financial assistance from the United States of America acting through Rural Development of the United States Department of Agriculture, pursuant to the consolidated Farm and Rural Development Act, (7 U.S.C. 1921 et seq.) and for which the ENGINEER agrees to perform the various professional engineering services for the design and construction of said system.

WITNESSETH:

That for and in consideration of the mutual covenants and promises between the parties hereto, it is hereby agreed:

SECTION A - ENGINEERING SERVICES

The ENGINEER shall furnish engineering services as follows:

1. The ENGINEER will conduct preliminary investigations, prepare preliminary drawings, provide a preliminary itemized list of probable construction costs effective as of the date of the preliminary report, and submit a preliminary engineering report following Rural Development instructions and guides.
2. The ENGINEER will furnish 10 copies of the preliminary engineering report, and layout maps to the OWNER.
3. The ENGINEER will attend conferences with the OWNER, representatives of Rural Development, or other interested parties as may be reasonably necessary.
4. After the preliminary engineering report has been reviewed and approved by the OWNER and by Rural Development and the OWNER directs the ENGINEER to proceed, the ENGINEER will perform the necessary design surveys, accomplish the detailed design of the project, prepare construction drawings, specifications and contract documents, and prepare a final cost estimate based on the final design for the entire system. It is also understood that if subsurface explorations (such as borings, soil tests, rock soundings and the like) are required, the ENGINEER will furnish coordination of said explorations without additional charge, but the costs incident to such explorations shall be paid for by the OWNER as set out in Section D hereof.
5. The contract documents furnished by the ENGINEER under Section A-4 shall utilize Rural Development-endorsed construction contract documents, including Rural Development General Conditions, Contract Change Orders, and partial payment estimates. All of these documents shall be subject to Rural Development approval. Copies of guide contract documents may be obtained from Rural Development.
6. Prior to the advertisement for bids, the ENGINEER will provide for each construction contract, not to exceed 10 copies of detailed drawings, specifications, and contract documents for use by the OWNER, appropriate Federal, State, and local agencies from whom approval of the project must be obtained. The cost of such drawings, specifications, and contract documents shall be included in the basic compensation paid to the ENGINEER.
7. The ENGINEER will furnish additional copies of the drawings, specifications and contract documents as required by prospective bidders, material suppliers, and other interested parties, but may charge them for the reasonable cost of such copies. Upon award of each contract, the ENGINEER will furnish to the OWNER five sets of the drawings, specifications and contract documents for execution. The cost of these sets shall be included in the basic compensation paid to the ENGINEER. Original documents, survey notes, tracings, and the like, except those furnished to the ENGINEER by the OWNER, are and shall remain the property of the ENGINEER.

Public reporting burden for this collection of information is estimated to average 4 hours per response, including the time for reviewing instructions, searching existing data sources, gathering and maintaining the data needed, and completing and reviewing the collection of information. Send comments regarding this burden estimate or any other aspect of this collection of information, including suggestions for reducing this burden, to U.S. Department of Agriculture, Clearance Officer, STOP 7602, 1400 Independence Avenue, S.W., Washington, D.C. 20250-7602. Please DO NOT RETURN this form to this address. Forward to the local USDA office only. You are not required to respond to this collection of information unless it displays a currently valid OMB control number.

Position 6 RD 1942-19 (Rev. 10-96)

FIGURE 7.17 Agreement for engineering services (*Continued*)

(Section A - continued)

8. The drawings prepared by the ENGINEER under the provisions of Section A-4 above shall be in sufficient detail to permit the actual location of the proposed improvements on the ground. The ENGINEER shall prepare and furnish to the OWNER without any additional compensation, three copies of a map(s) showing the general location of needed construction easements and permanent easements and the land to be acquired. Property surveys, property plats, property descriptions, abstracting and negotiations for land rights shall be accomplished by the OWNER, unless the OWNER requests, and the ENGINEER agrees to provide those services. In the event the ENGINEER is requested to provide such services, the ENGINEER shall be additionally compensated as set out in Section D hereof.

9. The ENGINEER will attend the bid opening and tabulate the bid proposals, make an analysis of the bids, and make recommendations for awarding contracts for construction.

10. The ENGINEER will review and approve, for conformance with the design concept, any necessary shop and working drawings furnished by contractors.

11. The ENGINEER will interpret the intent of the drawings and specifications to protect the OWNER against defects and deficiencies in construction on the part of the contractors. The ENGINEER will not, however, guarantee the performance by any contractor.

12. The ENGINEER will establish baselines for locating the work together with a suitable number of bench marks adjacent to the work as shown in the contract documents.

13. The ENGINEER will provide general engineering review of the work of the contractors as construction progresses to ascertain that the contractor is conforming with the design concept.

14. Unless notified by the OWNER in writing that the OWNER will provide for resident inspection, the ENGINEER will provide resident construction inspection. The ENGINEER'S undertaking hereunder shall not relieve the contractor of contractor's obligation to perform the work in conformity with the drawings and specifications and in a workmanlike manner; shall not make the ENGINEER an insurer of the contractor's performance; and shall not impose upon the ENGINEER any obligation to see that the work is performed in a safe manner.

15. The ENGINEER will cooperate and work closely with Rural Development representatives.

16. The ENGINEER will review the contractor's applications for progress and final payment and, when approved, submit same to the OWNER for payment.

17. The ENGINEER will prepare necessary contract change orders for approval of the OWNER, Rural Development, and others on a timely basis.

18. The ENGINEER will make a final review prior to the issuance of the statement of substantial completion of all construction and submit a written report to the OWNER and Rural Development. Prior to submitting the final pay estimate, the ENGINEER shall submit a statement of completion to and obtain the written acceptance of the facility from the OWNER and Rural Development.

19. The ENGINEER will provide the OWNER with one set of reproducible record (as-built) drawings, and two sets of prints at no additional cost to the OWNER. Such drawings will be based upon construction records provided by the contractor during construction and reviewed by the resident inspector and from the resident inspector's construction data.

20. If State statutes require notices and advertisements of final payment, the ENGINEER shall assist in their preparation.

21. The ENGINEER will be available to furnish engineering services and consultations necessary to correct unforeseen project operation difficulties for a period of one year after the date of statement of substantial completion of the facility. This service will include instruction of the OWNER in initial project operation and maintenance but will not include supervision of normal operation of the system. Such consultation and advice shall be furnished without additional charge except for travel and subsistence costs. The ENGINEER will assist the OWNER in performing a review of the project during the 11th month after the date of the certificate of substantial completion.

22. The ENGINEER further agrees to obtain and maintain, at the ENGINEER'S expense, such insurance as will protect the ENGINEER from claims under the Workman's Compensation Act and such comprehensive general liability insurance as will protect the OWNER and the ENGINEER from all claims for bodily injury, death, or property damage which may arise from the performance by the ENGINEER or by the ENGINEER'S employees of the ENGINEER'S functions and services required under this Agreement.

FIGURE 7.17 (*Continued*) Agreement for engineering services

(Section A - continued)

23. The services called for in the Section A-1 and A-2 of this Agreement shall be completed and the report submitted within ______________________ calendar days from the date of authorization to proceed. After acceptance by the OWNER and Rural Development of the Preliminary Engineering Report and upon written authorization from the OWNER, the ENGINEER will complete final plans, specifications and contract documents and submit for approval of the OWNER, Rural Development and all State regulatory

agencies within ______________________ calendar days from the date of authorization unless otherwise agreed to by both parties.

If the above is not accomplished within the time period specified, this Agreement may be terminated by the OWNER. The time for completion will be extended by the OWNER for a reasonable time if completion is delayed due to unforeseeable causes beyond the control and without the fault or negligence of the ENGINEER.

SECTION B - COMPENSATION FOR ENGINEERING SERVICES

1. The OWNER shall compensate the ENGINEER for preliminary engineering services in the sum of

____ Dollars ($ ______________________)
after the review and approval of the preliminary engineering report by the OWNER and Rural Development.

2. The OWNER shall compensate the ENGINEER for design and contract administration engineering services in the amount of: (Select (a) or (b))

(a) ____ Dollars ($ ______________________) or

(b) As shown in Attachment 1

When Attachment 1 is used to establish compensation for the design and contract administration services, the actual construction costs on which compensation is determined shall exclude legal fees, administrative costs, engineering fees, land rights, acquisition costs, water costs, and interest expense incurred during the construction period.

3. The compensation for preliminary engineering services, design and contract administration services shall be payable as follows:

(a) A sum which equals seventy percent (70%) of the total compensation payable under Section B-1 and 2, after completion and submission of the construction drawings, specifications, cost estimates, and contract documents, and the acceptance of the same by OWNER and Rural Development.

(b) A sum which, together with the compensation provided in Section B-3-(a) above, equals eighty percent (80%) of the compensation payable immediately after the construction contracts are awarded.

(c) A sum equal to fifteen percent (15%) of the compensation will be paid on a monthly basis for general engineering review of the contractor's work during the construction period on percentage ratios identical to those approved by the ENGINEER as a basis upon which to make partial payments to the contractor(s). However, payment under this paragraph and of such additional sums as are due the ENGINEER by reason of any necessary adjustments in the payment computations will be in an amount so that the aggregate of all sums paid to the ENGINEER will equal ninety-five (95%) of the compensation. A final payment to equal 100 percent shall be made when it is determined that all services required by this Agreement have been completed except for the services set forth in Section A-21 hereof.

SECTION C - COMPENSATION FOR RESIDENT INSPECTION AS SET FORTH IN SECTION A-14

When the ENGINEER provides resident inspection, the ENGINEER will, prior to the preconstruction conference, submit a resume of the resident inspector's qualifications, anticipated duties and responsibilities for approval by the OWNER and Rural Development. The OWNER agrees to pay the ENGINEER for such services in accordance with the schedule set out in Attachment 1. The ENGINEER will render to OWNER for such services an itemized bill, once each month, for compensation for such services performed hereunder during such period, the same to be due and payable by the OWNER to the ENGINEER on or before the 10th day of the following period.

Under normal construction circumstances, and for the proposed construction period of ______________________ days, the cost of

resident inspection is estimated to be $ ______________________.

FIGURE 7.17 *(Continued)* Agreement for engineering services

SECTION D - ADDITIONAL ENGINEERING SERVICES

In addition to the foregoing being performed, the following services may be provided UPON PRIOR WRITTEN AUTHORIZATION OF THE OWNER and written approval of Rural Development.

1. Site surveys for water treatment plants, sewage treatment works, dams, reservoirs, and other similar special surveys as may be required.

2. Laboratory tests, well tests, borings, specialized geological, soils, hydraulic, or other studies recommended by the ENGINEER.

3. Property surveys, detailed description of sites, maps, drawings, or estimates related thereto; assistance in negotiating for land and easement rights.

4. Necessary data and filing maps for water rights, water adjudication, and litigation.

5. Redesigns ordered by the OWNER after final plans have been accepted by the OWNER and Rural Development, except redesigns to reduce the project cost to within the funds available.

6. Appearances before courts or boards on matters of litigation or hearings related to the project.

7. Preparation of environment impact assessments or environmental impact statements.

8. Performance of detailed staking necessary for construction of the project in excess of the control staking set forth in Section A-12.

9. The ENGINEER further agrees to provide the operation and maintenance manual for facilities when required for

   $______________________.

   Payment for the services specified in this Section D shall be as agreed in writing between the OWNER and approved by Rural Development prior to commencement of the work. Barring unforeseen circumstances, such payment is estimated not to exceed

   $______________________. The ENGINEER will render to OWNER for such services an itemized bill, separate from any other billing, once each month, for compensation for services performed hereunder during such period, the same to be due and payable by OWNER to the ENGINEER on or before the 10th day of the following period.

SECTION E - INTEREST ON UNPAID SUMS

If OWNER fails to make any payment due ENGINEER within 60 days for services and expenses and funds are available for the project then the ENGINEER shall be entitled to interest at the rate of ____________________ percent per annum from said 60th day, not to exceed an annual rate of 12 percent.

SECTION F - SPECIAL PROVISIONS

FIGURE 7.17 (*Continued*) Agreement for engineering services

SECTION G - APPROVAL BY RURAL DEVELOPMENT

This Agreement shall not become effective until approved by Rural Development. Such approval shall be evidenced by the signature of a duly authorized representative of Rural Development in the space provided at the end of this Agreement. The approval so evidenced by Rural Development shall in no way commit Rural Development to render financial assistance to the OWNER and is without liability for any payment hereunder, but in the event such assistance is provided, approval shall signify that the provisions of this Agreement are consistent with the requirements of Rural Development.

IN WITNESS WHEREOF, the parties hereto have executed, or caused to be executed by their duly authorized officials, this Agreement in duplicate on the respective dates indicated below.

(SEAL)

ATTEST ________________________

Type Name ________________________

Title ________________________

OWNER:

By ________________________

Type Name ________________________

Title ________________________

Date ________________________

(SEAL)

ATTEST ________________________

Type Name ________________________

Title ________________________

ENGINEER:

By ________________________

Type Name ________________________

Title ________________________

Date ________________________

APPROVED:

RURAL DEVELOPMENT

By ________________________

Type Name ________________________

Title ________________________

Date ________________________

FIGURE 7.17 (*Continued*) Agreement for engineering services

INTERIM AGREEMENT

(For use only when OWNER is not legally organized on the date the Agreement for Engineering Services is executed.)

In lieu of the execution of the foregoing Agreement for Engineering Services dated the ______________________ day of ______________________, 19___, by the party designated as OWNER therein, the undersigned, hereinafter referred to as INTERIM PARTIES, have executed this Interim Agreement in consideration of the services described in Section A-1 through A-3, inclusive, of said Agreement for Engineering Services to be performed by the ENGINEER, and the ENGINEER agrees to accept this Interim Agreement as evidenced by ENGINEER'S execution hereof contemporaneously with the execution of the Agreement for Engineering Services. The ENGINEER also agrees to perform the services set forth in Section A-1 through A-3, inclusive, of said Agreement in consideration of the sum stated in Section B-1 of said Agreement be paid in the manner set forth therein.

It is anticipated that the OWNER shall promptly become a legal entity with full authority to accept and execute said Agreement for Engineering Services and that the OWNER, after becoming so qualified, shall promptly take such action necessary to adopt, ratify, execute, and become bound by the Agreement for Engineering Services. The ENGINEER agrees that upon such due execution of the Agreement for Engineering Services by the OWNER, the INTERIM PARTIES automatically will be relieved of any responsibility or of liability assumed by their execution of this Interim Agreement, and that the ENGINEER will hold the OWNER solely responsible for performance of the terms and conditions imposed upon the OWNER by the Agreement for Engineering Services, including the payment of all sums specified in Section B-1 of said Agreement.

If the OWNER is not legally organized, or if after being duly organized it fails or refuses to adopt, ratify, and execute the Agreement for Engineering Services within 30 days from the date it becomes legally organized and qualified to do so, or if for any other reason the project fails to proceed beyond the preliminary stage described in Section A-1 through A-3 inclusive, of said Agreement, the INTERIM PARTIES agree to pay ENGINEER for such preliminary engineering services, an amount not to exceed the sum specified therefor in Section B-1 of said Agreement.

IN WITNESS WHEREOF, the parties hereto have executed, or caused to be executed by their duly authorized officials, this Agreement in duplicate this ____________ day of ______________________, 19___.

______________________	______________________
OWNER	ENGINEER

FIGURE 7.17 (*Continued*) Agreement for engineering services

CHAPTER 8
SITE PLANNING AND EVALUATION

THE IMPORTANCE OF EVALUATION

The evaluation of sites and facilities helps an investor select a property for development. These decisions can be guided by many factors. Incentives for redevelopment versus new construction need to be considered. Preliminary legwork makes a big difference in the success of any project. The following sections outline the various factors that influence investors' decisions.

FACTORS THAT MAKE A DIFFERENCE

Investors need to determine the existence of covenants and restrictions, flood zones, liens, mechanic's and materials liens, along with the potential cost implications, prior to commitment to a property. These are serious issues in the decision to acquire and maintain the subject property. Market demand is another consideration. For instance, the characteristics of a property can affect the market demand. Using a form like the one in Figure 8.1 can be helpful in keeping track of critical information about a property considered for purchase.

Covenants and Restrictions

Covenants and restrictions in a deed can ruin project development plans. It is not uncommon in many situations for developers to incorporate their own rules and regulations in property deeds before they are transferred

Comparative Property Data Sheet

Address ______________________________

Style ______________ Rents ______________

Amenities ______________ Number of Rooms ______________

Number of Bedrooms ________ Number of Bathrooms ________

Siding ______________ Heat Type ______________

Type of Hot Water ________ Water (public/private) ________

Sewer (public/private) ________ Basement (yes/no) ________

Utilities paid by landlord ______________________

Security ______________ Storage ______________

Laundry facilities ______________________

Deposit required ______________ Pets allowed ______________

Parking facilities ______________________

Proximity to shopping ______________________

School system ______________________

General condition of rental units ______________________

Floor Plan

	1st	*2nd*	*3rd*	*Basement*
Living Room				
Dining Room				
Family Room				
Bedrooms				
Bathrooms				
Kitchen				
Comments				

Other Pertinent Information

____

____

FIGURE 8.1 Property information sheet

to buyers. These types of restrictions can cover almost anything. For example, you may find that commercial vehicles, like a plumbing van, cannot be parked in the driveway of a property for more than a set period of time. The restrictions may limit the size, type, and color of any mailbox used on the property. It is not uncommon for deed restrictions to dictate a group of colors for the exterior siding of buildings. The list of possibilities is almost endless, so check the deeds very carefully before you buy any property.

Covenants and restrictions in a deed can ruin project development plans. It is not uncommon in many situations for developers to incorporate their own rules and regulations in property deeds before they are transferred to buyers.

Flood Zones

Properties located in flood zones and flood plains can be a very poor investment. There are times when these properties are nearly worthless due to difficulty in obtaining flood insurance. Construction or improvements to a levee can favorably affect the buyer's ability to get flood insurance. Buildings that may appear to be well away from any threat of flooding could be considered at risk. Federal flood maps are usually used to locate flood-risk areas. The best way to protect against buying a property that may be in a flood-hazard zone is to engage a professional land surveyor. Often the county planning commissioner will also keep flood control maps and can tell, given a survey or an address, if a tract is in a flood plain. The surveyor can do an elevation survey to determine if the property is safe to buy at normal market prices.

Mechanic's and Material Man's Liens

Mechanic's and material man's liens are dangerous. They can escape detection in a title search and pop up the next week. These liens cloud a title and can cause you financial pain. These liens occur when work has recently been

Buildings that appear, to the untrained eye, to be well away from any threat of flooding could be considered at risk. Federal flood maps are usually used to locate flood-risk areas.

done on a property. If the workers or the material suppliers are not paid as they should be, they have lien rights. These rights can extend for months, so it is possible that you could buy a property and discover a month later that your new property is encumbered by liens. If an investor is considering buildings where obvious work has been done recently, he can talk to the contractors and suppliers to see that everyone has been paid prior to purchase of the property. He can also require a waiver of lien affidavit from the seller as a condition of purchase. This will give him some recourse should a lien be discovered. The liens run with the property, not the property owner, so you could inherit someone else's problems. If you don't think this could happen, consider this story from Roger's experience.

Roger sold a multi-family building a few years ago. A real estate agent owned the building. He had listed the property with a different real estate agency than his own. Roger's real estate company was the one to bring a buyer to the table. In fact, he was the broker who produced the buyer. During the inspection of the property many deficiencies came up. There were roof leaks in an apartment where the buyer had not been allowed access until just a day or so before closing. Fortunately, he had written the purchase offer in a way to protect all parties, and the buyer was not hurt by the roof leaks and other building-related problems. There was, however, another problem that the buyer was not so lucky with.

Roger noticed probable evidence of an underground oil tank. His suspicion turned out to be correct. Due to the local environmental rules and regulations, the tank had to be removed. By law, if the broker had knowledge of the tank, he was required to disclose its presence. Being a real estate professional, both the owner/broker and the listing brokers should have noted the oil tank and disclosed it, but neither of them did. Not wanting to get sued, Roger raised the question and got the answer he suspected. The seller agreed to have the tank removed. This type of work is not cheap, but the seller did contract for the removal of the tank.

The buyer went to the closing table thinking all was well. So did the listing and buyer's brokers. The seller sat through the closing, signed the papers, and took his check. On his way out of the closing room, he looked back at the group and told them not to forget to pay the contractor for removing the oil tank. Words can't express how flabbergasting that was. The buyer had just taken possession of the property. The bank had issued a check for the full amount due to the seller, and now some contractor had lien rights against the buyer's new building. The listing broker and Roger split the cost of paying the contractor. This appeased the buyer and the seller walked free and clear. If the brokers hadn't paid the contractor, and they didn't have to since they had not done anything wrong, the buyer would have been stuck with a big bill to pay and a potential lien on his building. So, you see it can happen and a buyer must work hard to protect himself. See Figure 8.2 and Figure 8.3.

PRELIMINARY LEGWORK

As previously mentioned, preliminary legwork is one of the most important steps in successfully negotiating a deal. It might seem difficult and time-consuming. However, the time spent is worth it if the investor is to avoid any surprises in the final stages of the purchase. The two major components are researching market demand and checking for any existing leases.

Market Demand

An important consideration in buying a property for conversion is the market demand. This applies to projects such as conversion of an old motel into condominiums, a house into a duplex, or an abandoned warehouse into retail space. Market demand can change quickly, sometimes before a conversion project can be completed. This adds a little risk to becoming a conversion investor, but the risk can be managed in most cases. If there has been enough research before purchasing a property, the odds are good the investor will not get caught in a bind.

For example, assume the investor is considering the purchase of a duplex and converting it to a four-unit building. Will the area provide a steady stream of potential tenants? Checking today's newspaper will indicate what type of competition is presently on the market. This information may be helpful, but it is not conclusive. A friendly banker might share the bank's vacancy-rate statistics for the area. This will be helpful and the information will be based on historical data that should be dependable. Another approach is to go to a library and research advertisements in old newspapers. By tracking the past, one may predict the future with startling accuracy.

How long did rental ads run? They probably were not canceled until the rental unit was leased. This will give historical data on what to expect in rent-up time. It is smart to pay attention to the size of the units being rented. Efficiency and one-bedroom units normally have a much higher turnover rate than larger units do. In what location were the units that rented the fastest? This information can help an investor gauge what part of town to buy in. The investor should garner as much information as possible from the old advertisements and create a written log. These notes will help now and later.

Your Company Name

Your Company Address

Your Company Phone and Fax Numbers

SHORT-FORM LIEN WAIVER

Customer name: ____________________

Customer address: ____________________

Customer city/state/zip: ____________________

Customer phone number: ____________________

Job location: ____________________

Date: ____________________

Type of work: ____________________

Contractor: ____________________

Contractor address: ____________________

Subcontractor: ____________________

Subcontractor address: ____________________

Description of work completed to date: ____________________

____

____

____

____

Payments received to date: ____________________

Payment received on this date: ____________________

Total amount paid, including this payment: ____________________

The contractor/subcontractor signing below acknowledges receipt of all payments stated above. These payments are in compliance with the written contract between the parties above. The contractor/subcontractor signing below hereby states payment for all work done to this date has been paid in full.

The contractor/subcontractor signing below releases and relinquishes any and all rights available to place a mechanic or materialman lien against the subject property for the above described work. All parties agree that all work performed to date has been paid for in full and in compliance with their written contract.

The undersigned contractor/subcontractor releases the general contractor/customer from any liability for nonpayment of material or services extended through this date. The undersigned contractor/subcontractor has read this entire agreement and understands the agreement.

____

Contractor/Subcontractor **Date**

FIGURE 8.2 Short-form lien waiver

Licensed real estate appraisers know how to run down all the information needed for market research. Consulting appraisers have their fingers on the pulse in most real estate markets. It is, after all, their job. You may spend a few hundred dollars for information supplied by an appraiser, but it is a great investment.

Your Company Name
Your Company Address
Your Company Phone and Fax Numbers

CERTIFICATE OF SUBCONTRACTOR COMPLETION AND ACCEPTANCE

Contractor: ____________________

Subcontractor: ____________________

Job Name: ____________________

Job Location: ____________________

Job Description: ____________________

____

____

____

Date of completion: ____________________

Date of final inspection by contractor: ____________________

Date of code compliance inspection and approval: ____________________

Defects found in material or workmanship: ____________________

____

____

____

ACKNOWLEDGMENT

Contractor acknowledges the completion of all contracted work and accepts all workmanship and materials as being satisfactory. Upon signing this certificate, the contractor releases the subcontractor from any responsibility for additional work, except warranty work. Warranty work will be performed for a period of ________ from the date of completion. Warranty work will include the repair of any material or workmanship defects occurring between now and the end of the warranty period. All existing workmanship and materials are acceptable to the contractor and payment will be made, in full, according to the payment schedule in the contract, between the two parties.

____________________ ____________________
Contractor Date Subcontractor Date

FIGURE 8.3 Certificate of completion

Who else can help the investor? Companies who manage rental properties can. Talk with enough management companies, and one can come up with some solid numbers for vacancy rates in almost any area. The companies may, however, fluff over their vacancy rates a little. Since management companies don't like customers to believe they have high vacancy rates, it is possible that the reported numbers may not be deadly accurate.

Efficiency and one-bedroom units normally have a much higher turnover rate than larger units do.

fastfacts

Licensed real estate appraisers know how to run down all the information needed for market research. Consulting appraisers have their fingers on the pulse of most real estate markets. It is, after all, their job to know what's going on in the world of real estate. You may spend a few hundred dollars for information supplied by an appraiser, but it is a great investment.

Check Existing Leases

Before buying an existing rental property, the investor should check all existing leases very closely. He may find that a tenant has a long-term lease that doesn't allow for rent increases. It is even possible that there is a tenant with a life estate in the property and provisions for no rental increases. Some investors use this tactic to buy buildings cheaply or to finance them creatively. You might even want to have your attorney review the leases before you commit to buying a building. Security deposits are another issue to check. Buying a building where the tenants have leases that tie your hands could be financial suicide.

THE PRE-PURCHASE INSPECTION PROCESS

Site and building issues are the next level of investigation. These include surveys, property lines, and inspections. The prospective investor should make a careful assessment of all these factors before sealing the deal. Any negative results can be dealt with well before the closing instead of coming as a surprise just as the papers are going to be signed.

Surveys and Property Lines

Surveys are a form of inspection, so to speak, that some buyers don't put enough stock in. Many lenders require a full-blown survey for a property before any money will be allowed to change hands, but this is not

fastfacts

Before buying an existing rental property, the investor should check all existing leases very closely. He may find that a tenant has a long-term lease that doesn't allow for rent increases. It is even possible that the building has a tenant who has a life estate in the property with provisions for no rental increases.

always the case. If your lender doesn't require a survey, you should. Neglecting this important step could result in damaging consequences. The issue of parking, Figure 8.4, is an essential component.

As a broker, Roger had a buyer who placed a four-unit building under contract. The building had a nice, paved parking lot on two sides. To look at the property, it seemed safe to assume that the parking area was a part of the parcel of land. But the survey proved differently. This, however, didn't come out until the last minute at the closing table.

FIGURE 8.4 Providing traffic access and adequate parking makes or breaks the viability of most commercial sites. If parking is off-site, the investor should be sure it's adequate and within a reasonable distance. *Photo: Stephen Culbert*

When the purchase offer was written, Roger had included some standard contingencies, one of which involved survey and engineering studies. The buyer was very lucky that this clause was in his contract. The listing broker was asked on many occasions for a copy of a survey, but to no avail. On the day of the closing, as all were seated around the closing table, the listing agent passed him a copy of the survey. In shock, Roger immediately interrupted the closing and took the buyer outside. After showing the buyer what was wrong, he had two options. He could cancel the purchase, or he could negotiate for better terms. You see, about one-half of the paved parking area belonged to the city, not to the building owner. To make a long story short, the buyer negotiated better terms with the seller and closed on the property. This situation, however, could have been quite a blow to the new buyer had he not been protected with a formal survey.

Inspecting The Grounds

Inspecting the grounds of a potential conversion project can be as important as inspecting the structure itself, yet many novice investors fail to do this. Most real estate buyers tend to look for the obvious. They inspect the building's exterior and then move right inside to look for problems. Very few newcomers to the conversion business spend enough time outside. The following scenario illustrates this point.

You are a prospective purchaser. Upon meeting with your real estate broker, a buyer's broker, you are riding together in his vehicle to inspect properties. The first stop of the day is a large, rambling residential home located in a commercial zone. The building's size is awesome. You plan to convert the building into a dental clinic, and your mind is racing with ways to lay out the interior of the building. You envision several dental offices being located in the building, some for general dentistry and some for specialists. Dollar signs are running though your head. You are so taken with the size, and consequently the potential for the number of rental units, that you are oblivious to anything else.

Since the buyer's broker represents you, it is his duty to bring you back down to earth and point out other features, benefits, and obstacles associated with the building. Now, if he were a seller's broker, he wouldn't be obligated to relate his professional opinions to you and could capitalize on your excitement to get you to sign on the dotted line. This is a very important concept. Whenever possible, it should be in your best interest to deal with a buyer's broker, not a seller's broker. There isn't room go into all of the details behind the advice in this book, but investors should look into the benefits of using a buyer's broker for real estate transactions.

fastfacts

Inspecting the grounds of a potential conversion project can be as important as inspecting the structure itself, yet many novice investors fail to do this. Most people who look for real estate look for the obvious. They inspect the building's exterior, perhaps the overall exterior appearance, and then move right inside the building to look for problems. Very few newcomers to the conversion business spend enough time outside.

Upon inspecting your potential purchase, a few questions come to mind. Will there be enough room to create adequate parking space for patients and staff? Will local zoning affect the size of the parking area? Can signs be erected to mark the presence of dental offices? Is the building on municipal utilities for water, sewer, and natural gas? How much land surrounds the building? Is the building lot graded properly, or will you have to invest in extensive soil work? What are the neighboring properties like and will they detract from a building that houses professional space? The list goes on and noting these points can indicate potential problems that you might overlook. When inspecting the grounds of a building, one must look below the surface. Parking and utilities are two primary considerations. Other aspects of the building lot come into play, depending on the type of use planned for the property. For example, if a client is planning some type of enterprise that would require an additional access to a main road, he will likely need a permit for the new access. Depending on visibility, traffic, and other factors, he may not be able to obtain additional access. This could destroy his plan for some types of uses. It is information like this that makes a buyer's broker invaluable to you.

SITE WORK

Many investors and building designers fail to think about site work when assessing the value of a potential project, but that can be an expensive mistake. Site work isn't an issue in many projects, but it can be a major expense in some jobs. One cannot afford to overlook the cost of earth moving, paving, utilities, and other expenses that might be necessary to make your conversion dream a reality.

Site work can involve any number of jobs on the outside of a building. See Figure 8.5. The site work for new construction is generally somewhat different than it is for remodeling and conversion projects. However, if you are making a substantial change of use in a property, you could be looking at a high percentage of the project cost in site work.

The common forms of site work involved in most projects include:

- Preparation
  - Building demolition
  - Tree and brush removal
  - Re-grading
  - Utility accesses
- Regulatory and functional alterations
  - Paving and sidewalks
  - Pavement patching and site restoration
  - Drainage
  - Parking

FIGURE 8.5 An effort to screen and protect a transformer and service meters isn't fully successful. This elevation was opened to wider view after the demolition of other structures on the opposite side of the alley. *Photo: Stephen Culbert*

Your Company Name
Your Company Address
Your Company Phone and Fax Numbers

LETTER SOLICITING BIDS FROM SUBCONTRACTORS

Date: ____________________

Subcontractor address: ___________________________

____

____

Dear: _______________________

I am soliciting bids for the work listed below, and I would like to offer you the opportunity to participate in the bidding. If you are interested in giving quoted prices for the labor / material for this job, please let me hear from you. The job will start ____________. Financing has been arranged and the job will be started on schedule. Your quote, if you choose to enter one, must be received no later than ____________________.

The proposed work is as follows: ____

____

____

____

Thank you for your time and consideration in this request.

Sincerely,

Your Name
Title

FIGURE 8.6 Form letter for soliciting bids from contractors

- Accessibility improvements
- Site enhancement
- Security building

Your Company Name

Your Company Address

Your Company Phone and Fax Numbers

BID REQUEST

Contractor's name: ______________________________

Contractor's address: ______________________________

Contractor's city/state/zip: ______________________________

Contractor's phone number: ______________________________

Job location: ______________________________

Plans and specifications dated: ______________________________

Bid requested from: ______________________________

Type of work: ______________________________

Description of material to be quoted: ______________________________

____

____

All quotes to be based on attached plans and specifications. No substitutions allowed without written consent of customer.

Please provide quoted prices for the following: ______________________________

____

____

____

____

All bids must be submitted by: ______________________________

FIGURE 8.7 Bid request form

- Signs
- Landscape lighting
- Seeding
- Sodding
- Trees

– Landscaping

As shown in Figure 8.8 and Figure 8.9, projects with unique site conditions, large budgets, complex scope, or special uses may also include more atypical needs such as these:

- Establishing suitable subgrade conditions
- Dewatering
- Decontamination or containment of polluted soil or water
- Tank removal
- Removal of non-building structures and features
- Regulatory and functional alterations
- Erosion control and soil retention
- Wetlands preservation
- Sewage treatment plant
- Power generation plant
- Altering or providing curb-cuts and site access

FIGURE 8.8 A temporary support for a field drain discovered during an excavation. Here, the field drain will be re-routed and reconnected. *Photo: Nick Fredericks*

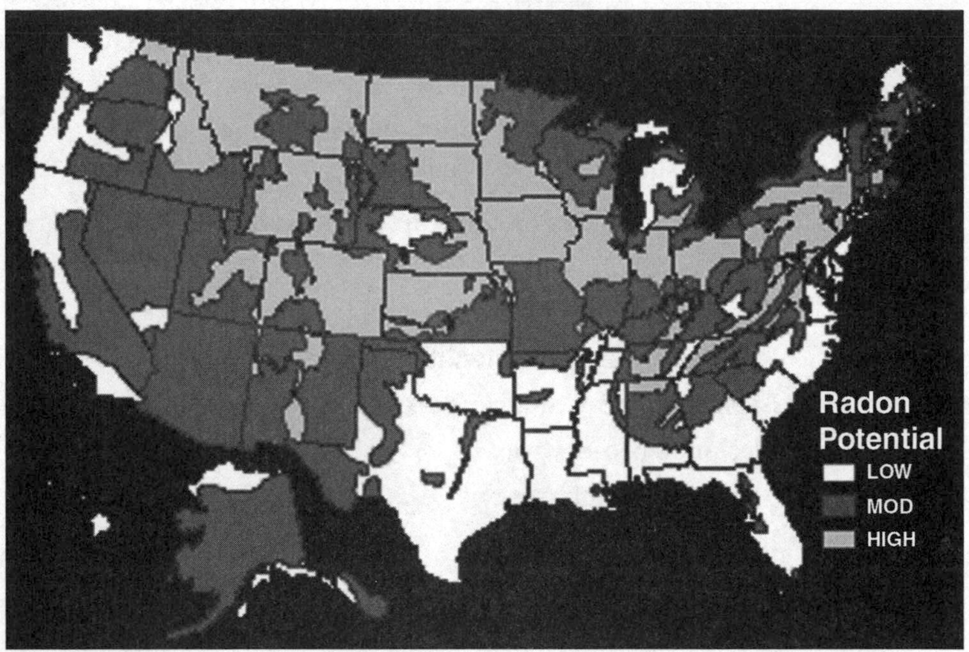

FIGURE 8.9 Geologic Radon Potential of the United States. The best defense against the build-up of radon is adequate ventilation; adding it to the construction program should be considered in the budget. *Source: United States Geological Service*

- Fences
- Lifts and docks
- Fire suppression systems
- Right-of-way and alterations
- Site enhancement
  - Way-finding devices and site signs
  - Ponds, pools, and fountains
  - Site furnishings
  - Exterior sound systems
  - Monuments, markers, and site art
  - Exterior monitoring and security systems
  - Security access gates and devices
  - Site hardening
  - Irrigation systems

– Historic site restoration or reconstruction

– Decks, patios, and awnings

Projecting Site Work — What To Look For

Knowing what to look for is half the battle with site work. Many projects lose profit to site work because it wasn't considered until after commitments were made to a project and its budget. Figure 8.10 shows an example. If a phase of work is omitted from the budget, it is obviously going to put stress on any profit picture. It is easy to forget site work on an existing building project because there will be some level of existing site development. It's easy for investors to be caught off guard, so it's nearly always appropriate for the design professional to inquire who will be addressing site issues before proceeding with design.

For example, a project could involve converting a single-family use into a multi-family use. What conditions might cause a need for grading? Anything that adds additional exterior space will likely trigger the need to re-grade adjacent to the structure. For example, adding a parking area, drives, access walks, building additions, or outbuildings (like garages and carports) will trigger re-grading. Providing deck areas, pools, patios, and other developed exterior spaces will also trigger grading and site devel-

FIGURE 8.10 Ground water can vary seasonally and may not always be present when soils reports are prepared. It is important to cover contingencies when bidding the project. *Photo: Nick Fredericks*

opment work.

Poor drainage may need to be corrected with fill dirt and fine grading. Moisture problems in the existing building may require trenching and regrading to establish efficient perimeter drains. Below grade moisture problems due to a high water table may need to be corrected with excavation and negative side waterproofing and grade restoration.

Increasing utility capacity or adding a service or connecting to a service may trigger the need for utility trenches and grade restoration. Adding access or egress to an existing lower level will require considerable excavation and regrading. If the soil has not been worked, adding topsoil for lawns and planted areas may also trigger some finish grading work. Depending on the scope needs of the project, the developer may involve a landscape architect, landscape designer, civil engineer, and/or site contractor. If these specialties are not involved at this phase, the investor developer will turn to the architect or general contractor to discuss major site issues. An experienced eye can discern essential and optional site issues to address and estimate before design scope has been determined.

Demolition, Paving, and Landscaping

Conversion projects frequently need some site demolition work. Site clean up can be an issue if the project is in a blighted area or has been unoccupied. Location and the history of a site may yield some surprises. Conversion projects also often require that driveways and parking areas be enlarged, reconfigured, and landscaped. This involves site work. The extent of the work will vary with the individual project according to programmatic need and local zoning ordinances.

Demolition and Salvage

When a major public housing project was constructed on a small site of just a few acres, small retail outlets had been razed from the site some years prior in urban renewal. The lot sat fallow until construction began. When the general contractor did his site clean up, excluding trees and brush that were cleared, there were 1155 steel drums of which ten were filled with bottles and one with needles. Demolition is not just a matter of clearing natural materials.

Building demolition work should be preplanned and included in the site preparation budget in order to cover contingencies such as these. It must be executed under OSHA rules. Disposal of the debris is controlled chiefly by the EPA. Only qualified demolition contractors should undertake it.

Building demolition is not the same as selective demolition or gutting of the structures to remain on site. Demolition means that entire structures have to be removed. Where those structures have massive concrete basements or tanks below grade, and new site development will not occur in that location, they are sometimes removed to about a foot below grade, filled with sand or drainage fill, and then re-covered. Where there will be site development, the removal will need to go deep enough not to affect the new development.

Most structures that are dismantled with a wrecking ball and crane can be removed with earth moving equipment. Larger or more massive structures may require weakening at connections and implosion. Items with resale salvage value may be selectively removed prior to building demolition. Historic fittings, fixtures, finishes, and built-in furniture are favorite salvage items. Construction debris also has salvage value when separated into recyclable elements. For example, structural and miscellaneous steel, metal decks, skin panels, and pipe can be melted down. Concrete can be ground for drainage fill and asphalt can be recycled.

fastfacts

Building demolition work should be preplanned and included in site preparation. It must be executed under OSHA rules. Disposal of the debris is controlled chiefly by the EPA. Only qualified demolition contractors should undertake it.

Some environmentally friendly specifiers require construction waste streaming to maximize recycling. On a contaminated site, contractors must separate products that must be handled by different types of landfills; the disposal costs alone dictate that. When disposal requirements are unstated, or legal disposal is the only stipulation, it is the contractor's option to maximize the salvage value of the demolition waste.

Smart contractors look for salvage value to lower their bid or improve the project's profitability. If the owner has salvage requirements for elements within structures to be demolished, he needs to remove those elements from the structure before the contractor gets control of the site, or he must stipulate in the contract that they be salvaged. Cleaning, protection, and storage of salvage items will be the owner's responsibility unless that is also delegated in the documents.

Paving

Conversion projects often require that driveways and parking areas be

> **Items with resale salvage value may be selectively removed prior to building demolition. Historic fittings, fixtures, finishes, built-in furniture, and specialties are favorite salvage items. Construction debris also has salvage value when separated into recyclable elements.**

enlarged or reconfigured. This involves site work. The extent of the work will vary with the individual project according to programmatic need and local zoning ordinances. If you are converting a small building from residential to commercial use, parking costs may be significant relative to the total project cost. On the other hand, taking a single-family building to multi-family may require that a little stone and asphalt be added along an existing drive to create a few extra spots.

Conversion uses don't normally result in decreased parking requirements. Plan on adding some parking when you renovate. It is rare that a higher or more intense use will require fewer spots than the existing lower use. If the original use was a factory, mall, or assembly space, the property might be taken to a use or mix of uses that have lower parking requirements.

Landscaping

Site development such as providing additional parking can trigger the requirement that some trees be removed. Tree removal specialists can be hired for unique conditions or where a tree has impacted an existing foundation, but usually a general contractor or site demolition contractor can adequately address this need. In some communities, mature trees larger than a certain girth cannot be removed without permission of the planning commission or neighborhood association. As a matter of practice, some developers require tree marking in their survey requests so their site design will minimize the destruction of mature trees.

Seeding, sodding, and landscaping a conversion project can transform a marginal property into a special one. Almost all conversion projects can benefit from some additional landscaping. Watch out though; it can get expensive quickly. When funds are tight, and they usually are, put trees and shrubs where they will have the greatest visual impact. If the project is to be leased or resold, select rapidly maturing species to enhance curb

FIGURE 8.11 A railroad abutment was too costly to demolish so the garage accommodates it.

fronts, entrances, and common areas. Include sod only where lawn traffic is expected soon after the project is occupied, such as near an entry or patio. If the property is to be owner occupied, zoning ordinances may require sod or seed to protect from erosion. Other landscaping is frequently deferred for a season or two to reduce front-end costs.

Utilities

Utilities are not normally a problem in converting small buildings from one use to an incrementally higher one, but they can be. Connection to city sewer and water services is usually sufficient to move up the intensity of use without major improvements. For example, most plumbing codes allow a 3-inch sewer pipe for houses that do not contain more than two toilets. If the property has a 3-inch sewer, but the developed property will have four toilets, the line will need to be replaced with a larger one or a second service connection could be added. A second service might result in a new tap fee. Professionals inspecting the building will check the size of existing services to determine if they are sufficient for continuing the existing use. If a change of use is contemplated, it is important for the inspecting professional to know what uses are being considered because each use has different plumbing fixture requirements.

There was once a client with a large commercial building originally built for retail. The client was looking to lease space in the basement of this downtown property to maximize the rent the building could yield. Since basements are less attractive space for offices and retail, the building manager considered leasing to a beauty school.

After examining the space, the lease was determined to be an unsuitable deal for the managers because the sewers were above the elevation of the number of sinks the salon would require. The city would not grant a permit to cut into a large existing sewer on an arterial street that had just undergone major infrastructure and image improvements such as new curbs and paving. The city would allow connection into a sewer under an alley that was smaller and already overloaded. The project's budget was broken by the cost of the pump, sump, odor control equipment, and backflow preventor that were required to connect to the alley sewer. The space was eventually leased as less demanding storage occupancy. It is also a good idea to check the size of the incoming water service. It is less likely that the service is going to have to upgraded to a larger size, but why risk surprise?

Electrical service is another issue to consider. When a building is altered to accommodate multiple tenants, it is normal to install electrical services that can be separately metered for each tenant. The job could also require site work if the supply cable is run underground. Even with an overhead connection, obstacles like tree limbs might have to be removed to bring in service.

As a case in point, a building constructed as a one-story shell office space was being renovated. When the owner recognized that the office market was glutted, he looked to fill his building with mixed uses. He leased a large section of the building to a rapidly growing church group (an assembly occupancy) and an adjacent area to a daycare center.

The change in the intensity of the use of the building triggered the need for a new electrical service main connection that had not been anticipated by the owner when he made his lease agreement. To save the deal, the owner elected to cut most of the landscape enhancements, reduce the quality of light fixtures and HVAC equipment, and cut back on finishes and hardware quality.

Septic systems can create a lot of problems when converting to a higher or more intense use. Overloading a system is illegal because of the health hazard it can present. Sometimes a larger septic tank can be installed and the field enlarged to accommodate the new demand on the system. In most cases a soil scientist will have to be consulted to determine if the soil can

Electrical service is another issue to consider. When a building is altered to accommodate multiple tenants, it is normal to install electrical services that can be separately metered for each tenant.

handle the increased volume of leachate.

Dorothy was once involved with the conversion of a small branch bank to an out-of-plant conference and training center for a large corporation. The soil wouldn't hold the added volume for an expanded septic system, and the only remaining unpaved area of the site was in the right-of-way. The corporate owner was forced to pay a share of the cost of extending the distance to the nearest sewer when government funds were withdrawn in a budget cut. The clients chose to proceed because the project had already partially progressed and they saw the sewer extension as something that would give them options in developing the remaining portion of their land for industrial and research use.

Site contractors often do septic fieldwork. A reputable site contractor or a civil engineer should be able to offer professional advice prior to purchase. Consulting with an expert or two can be well worth the effort. Be careful when considering a property where a public sewer is not available.

Gas piping is normally run underground. Guess who's going to be needed if the building's gas supply must be increased? The site contractor, once again. In commercial conversions, especially to a use that includes a commercial kitchen, laboratory or some other gas-guzzling use, an increased service capacity is likely to become an issue, especially on a keeper. If the building is intended for quick resale, electric fuel might be used as an alternative source.

In some central business districts and campus sites, steam and chilled water are available as an industrial by-product. Tapping these sources in high-rise and mid-rise renovation can increase leaseable area on existing floor plates because less space needs to be devoted to mechanical systems. In Indianapolis, a combination of trash and coal is burned to generate the steam used for one of the most extensive systems in the country. The steam is available from the gas company.

The disastrous consequences of poor planning can be avoided by good preliminary legwork. Many unexpected situations can arise which shock the investor into realizing that the project is turning out very differently than what was planned. Sometimes the consequences can be life threatening or sometimes just plain expensive. Renovation that results in danger to public health will not be tolerated by governmental authorities and, most likely, will be put on hold until an acceptable plan is developed. Expensive alterations to a plan can also derail a project indefinitely. These setbacks can be avoided by an excellent development plan.

CHAPTER 9

BUILDING PLANNING AND EVALUATION

This chapter introduces the myriad ways to evaluate existing buildings with respect to the potential program(s) and physical issues. Evaluation extends from the foundation to the roof. All structural and mechanical systems are mentioned. However, professional advice is recommended when necessary. Evaluation by the investor can go to a certain point and then the experts will need to be called in.

THE PRE-PURCHASE INSPECTION

Personal inspections should be the only requirement for first-time inspections. Since this phase of inspection hinges on personal preference, you are the best person to perform it. As you move to the second inspection, it may be time to call in professionals. As a contractor, you probably have a depth of knowledge in some areas and a general knowledge of many other aspects of construction. It is not enough, however, to possess only a little knowledge in various fields. Unless you are well versed in all aspects of construction, you should call in selected professionals to assist you in the second inspection.

Let's say that your trade strength is in carpentry. You are familiar with mechanical trades from seeing these trades work, but you are not a licensed electrician, plumber, or HVAC mechanic. It is very likely that you could spot glaring problems in any of these fields, but it also likely that you would overlook what might be some serious problems. For this reason, you should seriously consider having a plumber, an electrician, and an HVAC contractor inspect the property. You might also have other specialists take a look at the premises. By working together with these experts, you can limit your exposure to potentially serious problems.

UNDER THE OCCUPIED SPACE

Many types of buildings have space of some sort under the living space. This space could take the form of a basement, crawlspace, or cellar. Start your inspection in this location.

One of the first things to look for is dampness, mold, and standing water. Inspect the foundation walls to see if they are wet or have marks left by standing water. Water marks often expose leaky basements even when water has not been present for some time. Take a screwdriver and probe the sill plates and the floor joists to see if they are rotting. Next, look over the mechanical equipment: plumbing, heating, electrical wiring, heating systems, water tanks, etc. If anything is stored on an elevated platform, you may be looking at a water problem. Moisture can do a lot of damage in a building. Assuming that the basement, cellar, or crawl space check out, you can move upstairs.

FIGURE 9.1 Crawlspace observations can reveal a great deal about a building.

> Many types of buildings have space of some sort under the living space. This space could take the form of a basement, crawlspace, or cellar. Start your inspection in this location. If the building is built on a slab foundation, you can eliminate this step.

IN THE OCCUPIED SPACE

There are a multitude of potential problems hiding in the living space. Some of these problems are not easily detected. For example, if the walls are not insulated or the insulation has lost its insulating value, you can't see the problem easily. You can check the wall insulation by removing the cover plates from electrical switches and outlets on outside walls. Be careful not to come into contact with hot wires. Once the covers are removed, you can inspect the wall cavity to see if insulation is present and what type it is. It is also helpful to ask for fuel and utility bills for the last year or two to see if the building is costing more than normal to maintain climatic control.

FIGURE 9.2 This classroom with an exposed duct, surface mounted speakers and conduit, a TV with a VCR on a cart, is under-lit with unshielded surface mounted lights. A room like this begs for an overhaul and interior upgrades. *Photo: Stephen Culbert*

Old single-pane windows might be drafty and some may leak. No acoustical materials may be present. Wall surfaces can be rough and uneven. These demonstrate a knee-jerk approach to systems improvements over the history of the space. Checking floor coverings, interior wall coverings, and assorted building components is not very difficult. Usually if these items look good, they are. You can check windows and doors to see if they are of good quality and installed properly. A quick check of the plumbing and light fixtures will tell you if everything appears to be in working order. If the lights come on and the plumbing fixtures fill and drain, they are probably all right. Heating and air conditioning is easy enough to test. Just move the thermostat to desired levels and check to see that both systems are working.

A lot of interior cosmetic issues may not be of importance to you. As a conversion contractor, you will probably rip out much of the existing structure, so fancy wall coverings and little dings in the drywall won't make much of an impact on a property's value. You need to concentrate on structural issues and mechanical systems. This is where big money can be lost or spent; so don't leave anything to the imagination on these items.

OVERHEAD

In the attic, you may find a huge problem, wood-infesting beetles. In some areas, beetles, termites, and other wood-infesting creatures can require a building to be tented and fumigated. This is a high-dollar expense, and you may still have to pay to repair the damage caused by the little wood-eating creatures. Most pest control companies will inspect properties for such problems without cost.

While you're in the attic, check the insulation and ventilation. Inspect the ceiling joists, the rafters, and the roof sheathing. If the roof is leaking badly, there will be evidence of it in the attic. Poke around a little. You might find some electrical problems, plumbing problems, or other problems that have been hidden with insulation as in Figure 9.3.

ONE THAT DIDN'T FLY

Here's a story of a project where, after inspection, the project didn't fly. Roger had a dentist friend who wanted to convert a residence into a dental office. The dentist located a property that had frontage on a busy road, compatible zoning, and enough land to add the needed parking.

FIGURE 9.3 Interstitial zones are crowded with ducts, conduit, pipe, supports, primary structure, light boxes, and ceiling framing. When proposing new ceiling heights, accommodating these elements must be considered. *Photo: Stephen Culbert*

fastfacts

In the attic, you may find a huge problem - wood-infesting beetles. In some areas, beetles, termites, and other wood-infesting creatures can require a building to be tented and fumigated. This is a high-dollar expense, and you may still have to pay to have the damage repaired. Most pest control companies will inspect properties for problems without cost.

On the surface this looked quite good. Inside, the building needed a lot of work, but the dentist was prepared to gut the interior and add new finishes and partitions. Contractors had provided him with prices to execute the planned work. When Roger reviewed the plans, he noticed a few minor problems in the layout on the neatly presented plans. Next he looked at the estimates from the contractors, and he and the dentist walked the site. Roger kept notes as they walked.

He noticed the windows were old, large, and leaky. Replacing them was not on the estimate. There were some framing obstacles such as a stairway and a chimney. The cost of adjusting the plan and new framing to work around these obstacles would have used a considerable portion of the budget, and they were not included in the estimate. The dentist had requested a new central HVAC system, but space for vertical chases and the required interstitial space for horizontal ductwork had not been considered.

In short, when all the discovered hidden costs were included, it wasn't feasible to include the extensive modifications required to make the project work within budget. The dentist recognized that it wouldn't get off the ground without expanding the budget and dropped the project.

FOUNDATION WORK

Some foundations have obvious problems that are readily observable to the untrained eye. The easiest one to spot is a building without a foundation. Yes, they exist. Old buildings, and sometimes not so old buildings, (usually found in rural or low income areas) sometimes are constructed with wood sills resting directly on the ground or a pile of stones. Most often, the sills and floor assembly have been weather exposed and have dry rot.

Raising a building and putting a new foundation below it can be costly and complex. It adds cost in at least four ways. Materials and details may be expensive to acquire and install. Installation may require a specialty contractor. In most cases, plans and details will also require the stamp of a design professional which adds a design fee, and plan review by the local authority which adds filing fees.

When such a costly issue is discovered prior to sale, the expense to convert it to a commercial use could be a negotiating chip for the investor/developer with the seller. While he's unlikely to eat the whole expense, he may

Except in unusual circumstances, it is unwise to buy a building that needs a new foundation. Everything rests on it, and is subject to damage during repair.

reduce his asking price. Except in unusual circumstances, it is unwise to buy a building that needs a new foundation. Everything rests on it, and is subject to damage during the foundation installation.

LEAKING FOUNDATION

Foundations frequently leak, and this is perhaps the most commonly observed problem with them. Mold and mildew can form even if surfaces are only damp. This will create health problems for occupants. Condensation may form on exterior wall surfaces when the basement is uninsulated and the interior space is conditioned with moist warm air. Problems with mold and mildew are only exacerbated when the foundation is wet. Intermittent moisture will also rot or rust framing members. If there are cracks and the foundation is exposed to freeze/thaw cycles, the framing members will expand over time, eventually causing the wall to shift and not bear as it was designed. If water flow is seasonal, standing water may develop, stop mechanical and electrical equipment, and become a death trap. If the foundation is wet, first look for cracks. If you don't find any, and the property doesn't have a high water table, perimeter drains or a sump pump can be installed to carry water at the foundation away from its perimeter.

It is best to install foundation waterproofing products on the exterior face or positive side of the foundation. There are negative side water proofing products, but unless one chooses from expensive industrial systems coatings, the negative side products will periodically fail and need to be reinstalled. Waterproofing products rarely stop ground water from running through foundation cracks. A few membrane systems will bridge very small nonstructural cracks.

Depending on the plumbing code in force and the occupancy, the owner may be permitted to install an interior trench drain to resolve foundation moisture issues where excavation and positive side drainage is impractical. A trench is cut around the interior face of the foundation perimeter, and then it's partially filled with drainage material. Perforated pipe is then pitched to drain to an interior sump. The trench is backfilled with more drainage fill. A sump pump is added to the sump to pump water to the sewer system.

Alternately, removal of oversized plant material, excavation on the exterior side of the foundation, installation of perimeter drain tile, drainage fill and waterproofing, and foundation insulation may fix leaky walls. This more costly approach will tear up the landscape at the base of the building. Downspouts and roof conductors can be filled. Roof drainage can be re-routed to run over ground or through soil to daylight, avoiding undersized sewers and combined sewers that may overload and back up.

Mold and mildew can form even if surfaces are only damp. This will create health problems for occupants.

SINKING FOUNDATION

A sinking foundation can cause a lot of problems. Fortunately they are not very common. Usually they occur when the subgrade was insufficient at the time the building was built. Sometimes this is because the fill was improperly compacted. Small sinkholes are a problem in some regions. If the site was a landfill or had a history of highly organic soil and the designer didn't know it, this can happen easily. The soil under a footing may recede or wash away below the footing, leaving a portion of the footing unsupported.

Signs of a sinking or shifting foundation, for example Figure 9.4, include sticking doors and windows, nail pops, and cracking at the joint between ceiling and wall. One might see some sway in the roofline. Measuring with a transit may help determine if the shift is slight or great. In a low-tech approach, a plumb bob and line level can also be used.

For example, sometimes the foundation can be shored and undercut. Weak soil can then be removed and concrete fill pumped in to stabilize it. See Figure 9.5. The existing structure must also be realigned and anchored to prevent further creep caused by the momentum of its misalignment.

fastfacts

Signs of a sinking or shifting foundation include sticking doors and windows, nail pops, and cracking at the joint between ceiling and wall. One might see some sway in the roof line.

FIGURE 9.4 The visible bow in the conduit and the long lateral crack indicate the foundation has shifted.

In some soil conditions with low or uncertain bearing capacity, the engineer may elect to underpin the foundation or use horizontal connections to prevent differential settlement between structures by forcing them to move as one.

FOOTINGS AND FOUNDATIONS

Footings and foundation walls are elements of construction that builders and remodelers have to work with on a regular basis. You might be installing a pier foundation for a deck, a full foundation for a house, or sealing a foundation to prevent water leakage. Bedrock, or ledge as it is often called, can

FIGURE 9.5 Dewatering was indicated before the matt foundation could be placed at this river edge site. *Photo: Nick Fredericks*

provide a footing for a foundation. However, footings are generally made of concrete that is poured in a hole or trench that is at least six inches below the local frost line. Let's start our discussion of foundations with ledge.

LEDGE

In parts of the country, such as Maine, there is a lot of rock. When it is bedrock, it is sometimes called ledge. This ledge can be deep in the ground or it can protrude up above ground level. It is frequently only a few feet below the grade level. This situation can ruin plans for a full basement. The only way to deal with ledge is to blast it out, and this gets extremely expensive. However, most code authorities recognize bedrock as a natural footing that can be built on. Check with your local code officers before making this assumption, but you will probably find that bedrock can be used as a footing.

TYPES OF FOOTINGS

There are two basic types of footings for foundations. Pier footings are created by digging holes in the ground and filling them with concrete. Support posts later rest on the concrete in the holes and provide a stable foundation for a building. It is common for pre-formed tubes to be used when pier foundations are made. The tubes resist frost heaves and result in less seasonal movement than what would occur if the concrete was poured directly into a hole in the earth.

Continuous or running footings are created by digging a trench and filling it with concrete. The trench provides a full boundary for the structure being built. When a full foundation wall is wanted, a continuous footing is needed. All footings should be installed at least six inches below the local frost level.

Continuous footings are normally used when full-size structures, such as homes, are being built. Pier foundations are frequently used for decks and porches. However, there are many homes that are supported on pier foundations. Since pier foundations are less expensive than full foundations, they are often used on camps, cottages, decks, porches, and other buildings where a full foundation is not required.

TYPES OF FOUNDATIONS

There are many types of foundations. Each type has its place in construction, and some are better than others depending upon their uses. Remodelers are often hired to add living space onto homes. This involves the installation of new foundations. Choosing the best, and most cost-effective, type of foundation for your jobs will make your bids more competitive and your customers happier.

Slab Foundations

Slab foundations are about the least expensive type to use for living space. This doesn't necessarily mean they are the best, but they usually cost the least. Since a slab foundation gives you footings and a sub floor all in one package, the cost of constructing a room addition on a slab is quite affordable, when compared to other foundation options.

There are some disadvantages to slab foundations. For one thing, underground installations, such as plumbing, electrical wiring, and heating and air conditioning systems, are not accessible once the floor is poured. Some people don't mind this, but others can't stand the idea of not being able to get to their mechanical installations.

Slab floors tend to be cold. Customers might not think of this when planning a job, but they will think of it when they walk around on the finished floor without shoes on. Carpeting helps to combat the cold, but there is a noticeable difference between a concrete floor and a wood floor. There is also the issue of concrete floors being harder than wood floors.

Moisture sometimes seeps into slab floors. This isn't a routine problem, but it can occur. If moisture invades a slab, it can cause floor covering to come unglued. It can also make carpeting damp, musty, and in the long term it can destroy it. In-floor radiant heat is gaining popularity and is a very good option for a builder with a slab.

fastfacts

There are some disadvantages to slab foundations. For one thing, underground installations of plumbing, electrical wiring, and heating and air-conditioning, are not accessible once the floor is poured. Some people don't mind this, but others can't stand the idea of not being able to get to their mechanical installations.

Storage under a slab floor is nonexistent. There is no room for mechanical equipment, such as a heat pump or water heater. This may not be much of a factor in remodeling work, but it is something to consider when building a new home.

Pier Foundations

Pier foundations can be very cost-effective for certain types of projects. They are an obvious choice for decks, but they can be used for several types of additions. Screen porches do very well when built on pier foundations. Sunrooms can also be built on piers. Other types of rooms can be placed on piers, but they generally look more out of place and present some difficulties with mechanical installations.

If the room being built on piers is not equipped with mechanical installations, there is little need to block off the underside of the addition. I'm not saying that the floor joists shouldn't be insulated, but there will be no need to protect pipes from freezing or air ducts from exposure. Installing lattice around the perimeter of the piers will enclose the foundation to enhance its eye appeal.

When plumbing, heating, or air ducts are installed under the structure that is built on piers, additional precautions may need to be taken. Since exposure to outside elements often affects the performance of these systems, you may have to build an enclosed chaseway under the addition to protect the systems. This is still much less expensive than constructing a full foundation.

Crawlspaces

Houses built on crawlspaces are common. There should be at least eighteen inches of height between the ground and any floor joists, but other than that, a crawlspace can have as much height as is needed. Crawlspace foundations cost much less to build than full basements. Additions built over crawlspaces make it relatively easy to install mechanical systems, and the enclosed foundation protects the systems from outside elements.

Having a crawlspace foundation allows access to mechanical systems and framing systems. This gives a lot of customers peace of mind. They know if anything ever goes wrong under their floor, it can be accessed. If new mechanical equipment, such as a heating system, is required to handle a new addition, it can often be tucked into the crawlspace.

From an appearance point of view, crawlspace foundations normally beat out slabs and piers. The exterior can be veneered with brick or it can be swirled with a stucco pattern and painted. Unlike a slab, where exterior siding must be installed low to the ground, additions built on crawlspaces can have their siding start well above ground level, avoiding some moisture problems. Most room additions work very well on crawlspace foundations.

Basements

Basements are nice from several standpoints. They make installing mechanical equipment easy. Access to building components is excellent in a basement, and an unfinished basement provides significant room for storage. Most people never seem to have enough storage, so this is a major selling point for a basement. Refer to Figure 9.6.

fastfacts

Having a crawlspace foundation allows access to mechanical systems and framing systems. This gives a lot of customers peace of mind. They know if anything ever goes wrong under their floor, it can be accessed. If new mechanical equipment is required to handle a new addition, it can often be tucked into the crawlspace.

FIGURE 9.6 Low ceiling height can be a difficult issue to resolve, especially when there is a complex web of building services, communications lines, and process services threaded through a basement. Running systems in parallel, wherever possible, helps reduce crossover conflicts. *Photo: Stephen Culbert*

The drawbacks to basements include possible moisture problems and considerable expense during construction. Some basements fill with water on a regular basis. Subsoil drains, sumps, drain tile, and sump pumps can be installed to correct most water problems, but the effort and expense has to be accounted for. Excavation for a basement gets expensive, and so does the additional height of the foundation walls. If money is no object, then a basement is rarely a bad choice.

fastfacts

Basements are nice from several standpoints. They make installing mechanical equipment easy. Access to building components is excellent in a basement, and an unfinished basement provides significant room for storage. Most people never seem to have enough storage, so this is a major selling point.

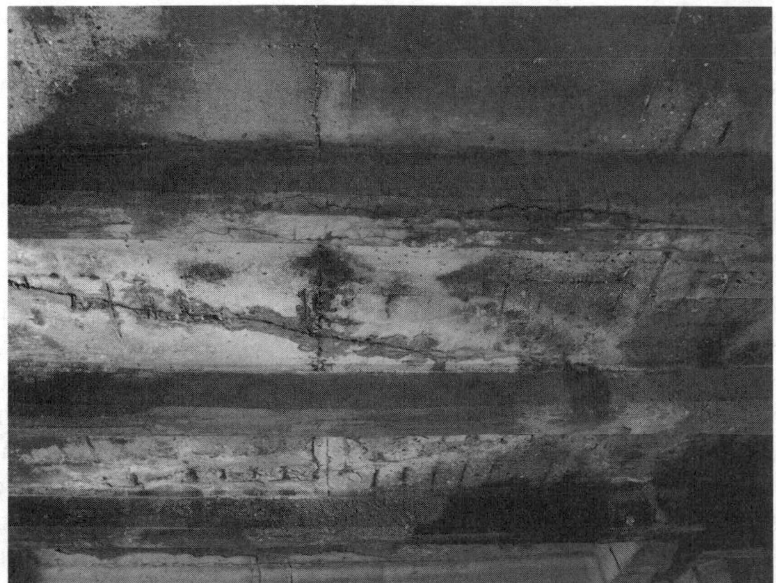

FIGURE 9.7 Concrete deck with leaking old patches and exposed rebar needs substantial concrete restoration to maintain its structural integrity. *Photo: Stephen Culbert*

ROOFING REPAIRS

Roofing repairs are more common than major roofing changes in conversion projects. There can be all sorts of repairs with older buildings. The work could be as simple as replacing one or two shingles that have blown away, or as complicated as resurfacing a complete built-up roofing system. It is up to you and your property inspector to determine what type of work and expense will be involved with your project.

Missing Shingles

A few missing shingles are nothing to lose sleep over. It will require a trip up onto the roof to replace the shingles, but the work is not extensive or expensive. You may have trouble finding replacement shingles that will match the color of existing shingles, but you can probably come close to making a match. I wouldn't worry about a few missing shingles.

Flashing Leaks

Flashing leaks are common in older buildings. Depending on the age of a building, the flashing could be made of any number of materials, such as copper, aluminum, or lead. Replacing leaky flashing is not a very big deal for an experienced roofer. It is usually better to replace leaking flashing than it is to try to repair it. Sometimes a quick fix is appropriate, but it is normally better to invest in a good fix.

Rotted Sheathing

Rotted roof sheathing doesn't come up very often, but when it does, the cost of repairs is notable. If an attic doesn't have proper ventilation, it is not unusual for condensation to occur. When this happens, moisture invades roof sheathing from within the attic. When this condition goes unchecked, serious rotting can take place. If the roof sheathing has to be replaced, you are looking at some major money. Roof coverings will have to come off and so will the sheathing. This isn't work that adds to the income potential of a building, it is a full-out expense, and one that you don't want to encounter. When plywood gets wet, it turns black. This is a pretty sure sign that big trouble is brewing.

Other Roofing Problems

Other roofing problems can crop up. For example, a flat roof may not be equipped with roof drains. This can cause water to collect on the roof. A flat roof should have some arrangements for draining excess water. These arrangements may be as simple as weep holes or as extensive as roof drains. One way or the other, you should make sure that a flat roof has some way of draining water which may collect on it.

There are a number of various problems that may turn up with a roof. Shingles can become brittle. They can also blow off. Cedar shakes can be affected by too much moisture. Slate roofs can work themselves loose and create a safety hazard. They can also grow greenery if they stay too wet. Tin roofs can peel off or just leak. Every type of roof offers some type of potential problem. For this reason, you should have all roofs checked out by professionals before you make a commitment to purchase a building. See the following figures.

INSULATION

There are two schools of thought when it comes to conversion projects and insulation. You can either take steps to insulate the building to modern standards, or you can leave well enough alone. Deciding which path to take

FIGURE 9.9 An existing nearly level roof retains rain and snow. Wrinkles in the surface of the roof material demonstrate that water has gotten between the plies and turned to vapor. Vapor forces plies to delaminate and tear. The owner chose to replace this roof.

FIGURE 9.10 The top of this chimney needs to be repaired. The cap brick should be reset and flashed; the brick should be cleaned and repointed. The stack should be raised to increase draw and eliminate re-sooting of the surfaces.

FIGURE 9.11 The presence of moss is unmistakable evidence of a low spot on the roof.

will depend on your individual circumstances. If you are going to replace exterior siding or open up exterior walls from the inside, you will be ahead of the game to go ahead and bring the insulation up to current standards. When the siding and interior of exterior walls do not require any major work, you might be better off to leave the wall insulation alone.

The chances are good that when you buy a building, if a real estate broker is involved, you will receive a written disclosure statement. One category on the statement will be about insulation. Many sellers simply state that they do not know what quantity or type of insulation is installed in exterior walls. If you receive this type of disclosure, you're free to make the same statement, assuming that you don't, in fact, have knowledge of what is in the walls. This is your ticket out of having to upgrade the wall insulation, but it doesn't mean you shouldn't invest in additional insulation.

Buyers and tenants who pay their own utility expenses commonly want to know what the R-values are for insulation in a building. Saying you don't know what the R-values are may be acceptable, but being able to provide a statement which shows that the insulation meets current industry standards gives you a stronger case in making a sale or rental.

FIGURE 9.12 There is inadequate curb height to keep out the weather at a skylight that was removed and patched with a lightly fastened hatch cover. A new curb and a new skylight were added in this renovation.

Of all the many phases of work involved in a conversion project, insulation is one of the least expensive, and it is one that can pay for itself over time. Increased insulation will result in savings from heating and cooling costs. A lot of people are willing to pay a little more up front in order to save a lot in the long run.

If you decide to upgrade the insulation in a building, you have several options available as shown in Table 9.1. Choosing the right one will depend heavily on the type of building you have and the conditions under which the new insulation must be installed. Some contractors blow insulation into exterior walls and attics. A lot of contractors use fiberglass batts to insulate habitable space. There are, without a doubt, many types of insulation to choose from and many methods available for installing it.

Energy codes may specify minimum average R-value for wall assemblies, roof assemblies, and exposed decks. Depending on the existing construction to remain, and the scope of the renovation, different types of insulation may be appropriate. When adding insulation and vapor barriers it is

TABLE 9.1 Insulation types and equivalent R-value per inch of material thickness

Existing Insulation type	R-value per inch
Fiber glass blanket or batt	2.9 to 3.8 (use 3.2)
Faced fiber glass blanket or batt	3.7 to 4.3 (use 3.8)
Loose-fill fiber glass	2.3 to 2.7 (use 2.5)
Loose-fill rock wool	2.7 to 3.0 (use 2.8)
Loose-fill cellulose	3.4 to 3.7 (use 3.5)
Perlite or vermiculite	2.4 to 3.7 (use 2.7)
Expanded polystyrene board	3.6 to 4 (use 3.8)
Extruded polystyrene board	4.5 to 5 (use 4.8)
Polyisocyanurate board, unfaced	5.6 to 6.3 (use 5.8)
Polyisocyanurate board, foil-faced	7
Spray polyurethane foam	5.6 to 6.3 (use 5.9)

fastfacts

Of all the many phases of work involved in a conversion project, insulation is one of the least expensive and can pay for itself over time. Increased insulation will result in savings from heating and cooling costs. A lot of people are willing to pay a little more up front in order to save a lot in the long run.

vital to calculate the location of the dew point in the wall assembly. Altering the location and thickness of new insulation materials may prevent the buildup of moisture within the wall assembly.

Insulation Options

Insulation options available to a conversion contractor are numerous enough to create some confusion. Should you use rock wool or cellulose? Is fiberglass better than perlite? What's the best insulation for my budget? How difficult will it be to install loose-fill insulation? These are just some of the questions that might come up when planning the insulation phase for your building. Perhaps, taking a look at various types of insulation on an individual basis will help to clear the murky water.

Foam

Foam insulation doesn't have much of a place in remodeling conversions. Liquid foam can be injected into existing walls with a special machine, but there is little need for it unless a building has a brick exterior. Urethane foam insulation was very popular for a while, but then it fell in popularity. It was discovered to offer health hazards, and many locations restricted or banned its use. Refer to Figure 9.13. When this form insulation is used, it is extremely efficient, but it is flammable. If burned, urethane gives off cyanide gas. This deadly gas is one of the primary reasons for some areas to restrict the use of urethane. Foam insulation can only be used in conjunction with a minimum ½" thick thermal barrier (usually gypsum board) or in an otherwise locally approved tested assembly.

Loose-fill Insulation

Loose-fill insulation is sold in bags. It is meant to be spread over an area or blown into a space. The loose-fill material may consist of cellulose, glass fiber, mineral wool, perlite, or vermiculite. All of these are available in loose

FIGURE 9.13 Pipes project into space for new furring and insulation. Loose fill insulation will be stuffed into spaces not suitable for polystyrene boards. A more costly but more effective insulation method would be the use of expanding foam. *Photo: Nick Fredericks*

form. This type of insulation is frequently blown into existing walls and attics, and it can be a good friend to a conversion contractor.

Blowing insulation into an attic is very simple, assuming that you have a machine designed for the job. These machines can be rented from tool rental centers, but many suppliers will loan you a blower if you buy enough insulation. If you have plenty of space to move around in an attic, you don't need a blowing machine. You can simply walk around and distribute insulation out of the bags it is sold in.

Blowing insulation into walls is a bit more difficult. Fire-stopping can get in the way and cause only half the wall to get insulated. To overcome this, assuming that fire-blocking is in place, you have to make two entry holes in each stud bay to introduce the insulation into the wall. There is one problem with blowing insulation into exterior walls from the outside that I don't enjoy. It is plugging the holes needed for access to the wall cavities. In the case of a conversion project, I would make the holes on the inside. Patching the holes will be easier and more attractive on the inside than it would be on the outside.

Cellulose

Cellulose is a common form of loose-fill insulation. It can be made of recycled paper. The insulation is inexpensive and easy to install. However, if it gets wet, cellulose loses much of its insulating value. Untreated, cellulose presents a high fire risk, but a treatment can be applied to retard the fire hazard. I recommend installing only fire-treated cellulose.

Since cellulose insulation is made from paper, it doesn't irritate a person's skin or respiratory system in the way that some types of loose-fill insulation can. This is one reason why I have used cellulose every time that I have installed loose-fill insulation personally. There are no environmental risks involved with cellulose that I know of, and this added benefit keeps people happy.

Mineral Wool

Mineral wool offers some irritation complications similar to fiberglass insulation. A mask, gloves, and full body protection should be worn when installing it. The insulating qualities of mineral wool are good, but if I am required to install loose-fill insulation myself, I choose cellulose.

Vermiculite and perlite are both used in loose-fill insulation. Neither of these insulators is flammable, and both of them are considered to be free of any harmful fumes and gases. Either of these materials may be well worth your time to investigate when converting buildings and insulating them.

Vapor Barriers

Vapor barriers play an important role in the insulation of a building. For example, rigid insulation boards which are installed without a vapor barrier can lose up to half of their R-value to moisture. When insulation is installed in walls and crawlspaces, a vapor barrier should also be installed. If you are using glass-fiber insulation, it can be purchased with a vapor barrier already installed. Another way to create a vapor barrier is to wrap the interior of outside walls with plastic.

In temperate climates, the faced side of the insulation, or the vapor barrier, will be located on the interior face of the wall. In hot humid areas, this should be reversed. Air barriers like Tyvek applied to the outside of the structure are meant to exhale vapor, allowing it to exit the wall assembly. They function as an air barrier against drafts. Moisture retained in walls will not only damage the structure, it can also promote the growth of mold and mildew, sources of health problems for many people.

When insulation is installed in walls and crawlspaces, a vapor barrier should also be installed.

If you use faced insulation, the facing should be installed on the heated side of the wall. The goal is to keep moisture from the house from entering the wall cavity. If this goal is not met, rotting of the sole plates, siding, and studs can occur. Many modern contracting firms install unfaced fiberglass batts in exterior walls and then cover the interior of the walls with plastic to act as a vapor barrier.

Icynene foam is a proprietary technology manufactured in Canada and relatively new in the U.S. market. The manufacturers claim R-values are comparable with high performance polyisocyanurate, except a thermal barrier is not required. It doesn't lose R-value with age and, like other foams, it forms a complete seal in the cavity. Its cost can be several times higher than polyisocyanurate board, but it can be applied vertically or horizontally with only a sprayer and without significant prep work.

Autoclaved expanded concrete, also relatively new as an insulation material, can be used as an exterior cladding material in lieu of masonry or EIFS. It should only be located where it will not be subject to impact or scratching or gouging. It has thermal properties that exceed perlite and is through-colored. It is routable, can be custom colored, and very lightweight. While its sculptural properties make it a desirable substitute for stone, designers must use caution not to locate it where it will be subject to projectiles, impact, and gouging. Existing urea formaldehyde foam insulation (UFFI) or asbestos-containing insulation, usually a rock wool material, can reduce a building's value because of the abatement cost associated with removing it.

The envelope of a building includes the material that covers the roof and the systems that support them, the materials that cover the walls (also called skin) and the systems that support them, and the openings in the walls (also called apertures) which generally mean doors and windows, although it can include openings of other types.

MOISTURE

The greatest enemy to the envelope is the penetration of moisture. If flashings are absent or badly installed, water that should drain away from a cavity assembly will stay within the construction and wreak havoc. Anywhere the surface of the building skin is breached by damage, weather, or structural movement or where sealants have failed, moisture will get in. Always look at these systems carefully. Although some things like sealants may be affordable to replace, other systems, like brick veneer, are not.

As shown in the following figures, masonry cleaning and restoration or epoxy concrete patching, depending on the method specified, can be a significant cost factor in re-using an old building. The largest share of salvageable urban non-residential buildings seems to involve concrete and masonry construction of various types. It is also one of the most easily dismissed areas of renovation when the budget gets tight. Leaving the patina of age (a.k.a. old dirt) on a building won't necessarily exacerbate on-going deterioration, provided the skin is mended sufficiently to restore its water-tightness.

Sometimes when exiting masonry has begun to fail, but is structurally intact, it will be protected by cement plaster parge covered over with lightweight materials like EIFS or siding. The effect of such a change must be considered in light of the context of the building and its renovated use.

In other cases where face brick has begun to fail, the veneer may be stripped and a new skin provided over both old and new construction.

Other types of skin besides masonry are subject to weathering and loading and thermal stresses with age and exposure. Provided they are watertight and have structural integrity, they are fit to stay if the look is compatible with the desired aesthetic vision.

FIGURE 9.14 Early signs that this brick needs to be repointed are visible holes at the joints and hairline cracks between brick and mortar.

FIGURE 9.15 When masonry walls crack and the gap exceeds 1/16 inch in width, cracks should be injected. Cracks of this size are a tip that the foundation may have shifted.

FIGURE 9.16 Damaged brick masonry repair at the historic head house at Union Station. Cleaning the masonry was deferred. Sometimes harsh cleaners or strong water jets can exacerbate damage by making the surface more porous. Brick can then take on additional water. Thermal cycles will cause the moisture to expand and open new avenues for moisture. This can break down the brick.

FIGURE 9.17 Spalled stone, poorly patched, will allow moisture to gain entry. The patch should be ground out and patched with materials that are matched in color and texture to the original stone. Epoxy cements are used for this purpose.

FIGURE 9.18 Veneer has been removed from the original building. It will be skinned to look like the new construction, right. To the left, a new wall has been constructed to obscure the old. Such methods are employed when a seamless exterior is desired and brick matching or style matching of the original structure is prohibitive or undesirable.

FIGURE 9.19 Failed concrete parging exposed building brick to moisture that caused it to spall. Building brick doesn't always have the moisture resistance of face brick or hard-burned brick, thus it must be protected when a structure at a party wall is removed.

Panels such as those shown in Figure 9.20 can be salvaged from eventual self-destruction if relieving support can be added. Addressing the problem may require removing panels, adding anchors that tie back to structure, or reinstalling the panels. Another approach is to installing lighter weight panels of alternate materials. Many owners will ignore such a problem-in-the-making until an incident, such as spalled concrete causing damage below, forces it to their attention.

CURTAIN WALL SYSTEMS

Some old curtain wall systems contain transite and this is a red flag, especially if transite panels will be penetrated or otherwise compromised during the renovation. Transite frequently contains friable asbestos. It can sometimes be encapsulated rather than abated if the new building skin is anchored to the curtain wall framing or the structure. Design professionals should not rely on their skills to determine if there are asbestos-

FIGURE 9.20 Creeping concrete panels show greater degree of material shift on panels at the bottom that carry the greatest load. In full light the problem is not readily observable. *Photo: Stephen Culbert*

containing building materials. An abatement report is better. Better still is an owner who has dealt with abatement as a removal issue prior to contracting designers.

LEAKY WINDOW SYSTEMS

The cost difference between repairing and refinishing or removing and replacing old leaky window systems is usually a no-brainer, except when the window materials have historic or artistic value worth preserving as in Figure 9.21. Then specialty contractors can be a great resource in eval-

FIGURE 9.21 An affordable approach to historic materials restoration (not preservation) is exhibited in this window restoration. *Photo: Stephen Culbert*

uating costs and options. Doors are similar to windows, except that hardware is a more significant consideration since it has a role in life safety. In preservation, operating devices like hinges and locks may be removed and rebuilt. Steel doorframes may be puttied, sanded, or even recast. Sometimes historic glass can be replaced with thin units of insulating glass. In other installations, historic windows are left in place and new insulated windows are installed behind them.

DOORS

In most cases, it is more economical to get new doors with new hardware than to piece patch and refinish existing doors and provide them with new hardware. However, wood panel doors and other special types of doors may be worth preserving. Pre-finished doors offer the advantage of quick installation, but on a job where at least some of the doors from the original occupancy will be re-used, field finishing is more appropriate to get the best match in finishes.

Often the renovation program will call for window area to be reduced or eliminated. Often this exercise is done badly, especially on the nonpublic exposure. A bit more consideration in this matter and consistency in the choice of infill material can have a unifying effect on the building and neighboring structures. See Figure 9.22. In urban areas, alley exposures today may become more exposed tomorrow when adjacent structures are razed. As areas are renovated, what were alleys may become side streets. Newer, taller structures may be able to view tops and backs of buildings.

Some details of the envelope, like marquees, tiles, terracotta, and mosaics, were built of materials no longer manufactured or very hard to find. Sometimes the work is one of a kind. These are irreplaceable and possibly worthy of preservation. If the budget won't allow the restoration of such pieces, one should consider protecting them with the hope of later restoration. In interior locations one can consider exhibiting them "as is."

On a factory renovation that converted to mixed uses, the aluminum letters that spelled the company name of the seller were salvaged, rearranged, and remounted over the front door. Another bronze logo piece from the first owner of the factory was turned into a table with a glass top. The same factory has a large heavy sliding door that was painted an accent color and re-commissioned as a space divider. Care was taken to allow legal egress from either side of the door in any position.

FIGURE 9.22 This alley view shows assorted aperture infill materials, efflorescing masonry, exposed conduit, battered concrete, roof conductors that spill into the alley, missing glass panes, leaking windows, rusting lintels, and an outmoded badly maintained fire escape. Exits do not lead to grade. The improvements required to rehabilitate this envelope are considerable. *Photo: Stephen Culbert*

DRYWALL

If the building you are rehabbing has walls and ceilings covered with drywall, you have very few problems to contend with. Drywall is easy to cut and easy to patch. New drywall can be blended into existing drywall very well. A coat of sealer and a coat of paint is all that is needed to camouflage

FIGURE 9.23 Original firehouse doors were restored and then blocked with planters so that they would not be used. The Victorian era firehouse was converted to a professional photographic studio in a downtown fringe neighborhood. The business has recently moved.

any disruption of the walls or ceilings. However, not all buildings offer the advantage of existing drywall. Some of them can be much more difficult to work with.

PLASTER

Plaster was a common covering for walls and ceilings at one time. There are still plenty of buildings in use that have walls and ceilings covered with plaster. If you buy one of these buildings, repairing cuts, cracks, and holes

FIGURE 9.24 Restored polychrome terra cotta details co-exist with brick that needs re-pointing.

in the plaster will be substantially more difficult than it would if you were working with existing drywall.

Plaster can throw you some curves, and I mean this literally. When plaster is applied to lathe, it seldom comes out smoothly. There are rises and depressions that create an uneven surface. Trying to work to this type of surface with drywall for a repair is not easy. It can be done, but some skill will be needed to make a good match of the patch.

The wood strips and wire used in conjunction with plaster make life difficult for the person who has to work around it. A plumber can take a hammer and knock out a channel for a pipe in drywall in moments. Creating the same opening in a plaster wall will require the use of a saw and a lot more time. There will also be considerably more dust created, and probably a few nicks, cuts, and scratches on the hands and arms. Basically, what I'm saying is that plaster is harder to work with for people in the trades during installations, and it is much more difficult to patch properly than drywall is. You must factor this into your overall production schedule and budget.

MASONRY WALLS

Masonry walls are rare in modern residential construction, but there are a lot of buildings available where brick and block have been used for the exterior walls. These types of walls present challenges to the mechanical trades, and to the people who are in charge of repairing and covering them. Exterior walls made of masonry can be worked with, but expect higher production costs.

FIGURE 9.25 Destructive discovery reveals the source of water inside the building. Here a roof conductor has been disconnected.
Photo: Stephen Culbert

PANELING

Wood paneling has seen bursts of popularity from time to time. It has been used in family rooms, bedrooms, bathrooms, and probably every other type of room. If your building has walls covered with paneling, budget in enough money to replace it if it will be disturbed. Trying to repair or match old paneling is next to impossible.

TILE

There was a time when ceramic tile was used heavily in bathrooms. Floors were covered with it, showers were made out of it, and tile routinely ran about halfway up the bathroom walls. Tile is a good wall covering, but old tile is hard to match. If you are going to be doing bathroom remodeling that will probably cause tile to be damaged, budget for a complete replacement. If you try to get by with a little patch here and there, the quality appearance of your conversion project will suffer.

> Tile is a good wall covering, but old tile is hard to match. If you are going to be doing bathroom remodeling which will probably cause damaged tile, budget for a complete replacement.

CEILINGS

Ceilings in modern buildings usually consist of painted drywall. The ceilings are frequently covered with a texture to hide flaws in the finish work of the drywall. There is nothing wrong with this type of ceiling. In fact, it is cost-effective, desirable by a majority of people, and well accepted in the real estate market. Since cost of construction is a key factor in the conversion business, a simple drywall ceiling is usually the best choice available.

Lay-in Acoustical Board

Drop-in tiles and the framework that holds them sometimes become a part of a conversion project. This type of ceiling is accepted readily in commercial circles, but it is generally looked down upon in residential properties. There are times when this type of dropped ceiling is needed to conceal wiring, pipes, and heating and air-conditioning components. And, the use of a dropped ceiling can reduce your conversion costs. How? Well, let me explain.

Let's assume that you have bought an old house that has plaster walls and ceilings. The ceilings are close to ten feet high. You want to add bathrooms on the second story, and you will also need new electrical work up above. There is also the task of extending new heating and cooling ducts to the upper level. How are you going to do this?

You could cut out the ceiling and work all of your equipment, in some way or another, through the ceiling joists. This, of course, would be time consuming and expensive. There would also be the trouble and expense of repairing the ceiling. Is there an alternative? Yes, you could run all of your mechanical components below the existing ceiling and hide them with a dropped ceiling. The building has plenty of ceiling height to allow such an installation and drop, so you might be very wise to consider this option.

You could install a dropped ceiling consisting of removable tiles and a gridwork of framing. One advantage to this approach is that the new installation would remain accessible. They could be reached by removing the tiles. Not a bad idea! However, if you dislike the look of drop-in tiles, you could frame a new ceiling system and cover it with drywall. Either way, you create an easy installation path for your mechanical equipment.

WOOD FLOORS

Wood floors were abundant in the houses of yesteryear. If your building has wood floors, you should try to save them. You should look under any carpeting or vinyl that is in your building. It was not uncommon for contractors to cover up perfectly good wood floors with the trendy materials of their time. You may discover a gold mine of hardwood flooring that you didn't know existed.

Old floors that have discolored can be brought back to a vibrant life. It will require some sanding and refinishing, but wood floors can endure a lot and still come out looking good. With the high cost of installing wood floors, you would be foolish to destroy such a floor during your conversion.

Installing wood floors will not normally pay for itself in rental conversions. The expense is just too great to recoup. I suppose that if the rental unit has a small, separate dining room, you might do all right by putting wood floors in it. But, in general, I would not install any wood flooring in an average conversion project.

fastfacts

Old floors that have discolored can be brought back to vibrant life. It will require some sanding and refinishing, but wood floors can endure a lot and still come out looking good. With the high cost of installing wood floors, you would be foolish to destroy such a floor during your conversion.

BUILT-INS AND MILLWORK

You can save some money by giving old cabinets a new look. This can be done by refinishing the existing cabinets. Just changing the doors on cabinets can make a big difference. Follow that lead with new drawer fronts and new pulls, and your cabinets take on a new personality. Finish the job with a new veneer and the cabinets look good as new, but at a fraction of the cost. Well, this scenario can certainly work for the remodeler who is concerned with simply upgrading an existing kitchen, but what about you, the conversion contractor? Chances are good that you are not only going to have one kitchen to remodel, but that you will be adding new kitchens. This means you are going to have to buy new cabinets. Ah, there had to be a catch.

Refinishing old cabinets and installing new fronts is fine if you have old cabinets to work with. But when you frame up new kitchens, you have to start shopping for affordable cabinets and counters. This chore is not as simple as it might seem. Price and quality vary greatly in cabinets. When it comes to counters, you have some other decisions make. Will you have the counters made up on site, or will you order pre-formed counters? Which way is cheaper? Is one better than the other? See how the questions can just keep coming at you? Well, let's stop the rush of questions and address them one at a time. This will allow us to work through the tough subject of cabinets and counters with good results.

Custom Counters

Custom counters should cost more than production counters. Sometimes they do, but they often don't cost more. I'll give you a quick example. I just finished building a new house for myself. The kitchen has a double-bowl, corner sink in it. With the location of the sink, I didn't want to use a pre-formed top that would place seams under the sink drains. As it worked out, that is exactly where the joints between sections of countertop would have fallen. I didn't like the risk of having seams under the sink, so I sought alternative options.

If I were willing to use a pre-form counter, it would cost in the neighborhood of $320. Well, I didn't want to do this, so my next step was to investigate how much a pre-formed top with a different seam configuration would cost. It was quoted to me at around $600. Not wanting to pay double to avoid two seams, I talked to my carpenters. Ultimately, I had the counter built right in my kitchen. I got a stronger, better counter for a little more than a stock unit would have cost, and a lot less than what a custom preformed unit would have been. The total cost was around $400.

Existing Trim

Depending upon the type of building you're buying, its age, and your conversion plans, you may want to salvage the existing trim. Old houses often have very ornate trim, and this can add to the charm of some types of conversions. Assuming that the existing trim, even if it isn't anything special, is in good shape, you have a decision to make. Conversion jobs frequently require the removal of some walls and the addition of others. Attempting to use existing trim for baseboards can be a bother.

Removing existing trim without damage is time consuming work. It also isn't easy to get old trim off without damaging some of it. So, will you be able to match the trim you salvage with new trim? You might very well be able to, but this is something you should verify before you cast your budget numbers in stone. It may be that the old trim is not of a type that is easily matched, and this can mean buying all new trim, an expensive proposition.

In cases where the existing trim is something of an antique nature, you can seek out special suppliers who can help you. There are sources that sell replica trim. This stuff's expensive, but it is available. Ordinarily, it is not cost effective to go to such an extreme as this, but there may be occasions when the expense is justifiable. For example, if you are adding three

Depending upon the type of building you're buying, its age, and your conversion plans, you may want to salvage the existing trim. Old houses often have very ornate trim, and this can add to the charm of some types of conversions.

new interior doors to your project, and all the other doors have old-fashioned trim, it would probably pay to buy replica trim for the new doors. You do have to be careful, though, of how much money you are pumping into a conversion project. The budget can get out of hand quickly.

When most of the windows and interior walls will be kept intact, you should be able to leave existing trim in place. It will probably need some attention with a paintbrush, but that's a minor cost in the scheme of things. If you can get by without replacing interior trim, you will save a considerable amount of money.

In cases where the existing trim is of an antique nature, you can seek out special suppliers who can help. There are sources that sell replica trim.

Scribed and set on splashes can help address irregular existing wall surfaces. Post-formed edges are more durable than self-edges and less subject to damage and delamination through normal use. Some post-formed edges can be configured with a slight bevel that makes them "no-drip". Stained wood edges can add warmth and a milled profile and are easily touched up between leases. Metal edges can give industrial, high-tech or retro looks with minimal added cost. Reserve tile and stone accents and special shapes for walls where they will have greater visual impact. Laminates or light gauge metal sheets can be adhered to walls for hygiene and visual impact at moderate cost.

More expensive options in countertop surfaces, such as solid surface materials, stone, copper, stainless steel, tile, and epoxy resin, are unlikely to be worth the considerably greater cost unless they are for a high-end tenant or buyer and custom made for their particular use. Vinyl and linoleum have been used on countertops and may be suitable for writing surfaces in particular.

ELEVATORS

Existing elevators are generally covered by grandfather clauses in the building code. It allows them to remain in service provided they are maintained. Freight elevators are intended for freight, not passengers. When the use of an elevator will change from freight to passenger, full compliance to current code will be required.

fastfacts

Reserve tile and stone accents and special shapes for walls where they will have the greatest visual impact. Laminates and light gauge metal sheets can be adhered to walls for hygiene and visual impact at moderate cost.

A change-of-use can trigger the requirement to provide an elevator if the building is over three stories. If the new use will house one of the non-exempt Title III uses under ADAAG (this specifically includes health care providers and public accommodations), providing an elevator will also be required. If the facility houses government tenants, even local ones, Title II applies and the three-story exemption may not be used. An elevator must be provided with just two stories if all functions housed on the top floor are not accessible at grade.

A change-of-use can trigger the requirement to provide an elevator if the building is over three stories.

Only the undue burden clause, equal to 20% of gross construction cost or structural impracticability of the required alteration of the primary structure, will relieve the owner from the burden to remove this accessibility barrier. A specialist should examine elevators that have been out of service for some time. Most architects are not qualified to make a detailed assessment of the extent of rehab possible and the comparative cost of replacement.

Sometimes, historic elevators have custom doors, cabs, and finishes. They may have their controls and annunciation devices upgraded and surfaces cleaned leaving the historic fabric substantially undisturbed.

Otherwise compliant existing passenger elevators can be refit to appeal to new clientele. In most of the Midwest, replacing an elevator in an existing shaft begins around $50,000 for a basic holeless hydraulic two-stop model. Estimate $10,000 per stop for up to four floors or 50 feet. Beyond this height, full extension hydraulic units, electric cable, and traction units must be considered. Check with manufacturers not only for material costs but also for installed costs. In strong union towns, wage rates for elevator workers are among the highest of all union professions.

ESCALATORS

Escalators are notoriously prone to maintenance problems. I have worked on projects where owners of renovated property elected to have them removed. Since traffic with the new use was projected to be lighter, the owners were able to claim valuable leaseable area by restoring floors in the escalator wells.

Here's a tip: Escalators can be very useful in fitting "big box occupancies" into existing multi-story space. Yes, designers can find escalators that handle shopping carts. MulvannyG2 Architecture specified Verma-Port cart for two such Target store renovations in Portland (http://mulvannyg2.com/updates/target.asp). Darrott makes several models (http://www.darrott.com/vermaport_sc_english.html.) Cartveyor is another of this type made by Pflow (http://www.cartveyor.com/Pages/operatn.html) We mention these since cart elevators are somewhat unusual and hard to find. We found these with a limited search. There may be other manufacturers of similar products.

ROGER'S ADVICE

Roger has had extensive experience in construction and remodeling. He brings a hands-on perspective to the problems of conversion projects. The latter part of this chapter contains information and advice taken from his years on the job.

PLUMBING SYSTEMS

Site assessments of plumbing systems can be difficult. Much of the piping is normally concealed and not accessible for inspection. You can flush toilets, drain sinks, and run water from faucets, but you can't see inside walls, floors, and ceilings. It may be possible to inspect some of the plumbing systems from within a basement, cellar, or crawl space. Even if you can only see small sections of piping, you can get a good idea of what to expect from the entire system. Another location that can reveal some clues is found under cabinets. If you look under cabinets where plumbing is located, you can probably tell what type of material has been used for water pipes, drains, and vents. This information can prove to be very helpful.

If you made the right moves when buying your project, you had the plumbing system checked out by a competent professional. Hopefully the reports given to you were accurate and your work with the plumbing system will go as planned. However, don't count on things going just the way you want them to. There can be an awful lot of surprises involved with a plumbing system. See Figure 9.26. For example, you might look under a sink and see plastic pipe being used for the drain. If you assume that all of the drains are plastic, you could be way off base. It's possible that the plastic pipe under the sink was installed as a replacement for an old galvanized steel pipe that had given up its usefulness. When you open the wall, expecting to see plastic drains, you could be confronted with cast-iron and steel pipe. A surprise like this could get expensive.

When you are in the process of converting a building from one use to another, you can usually count on some plumbing changes. They may be minor, but they can be major. For example, if you are converting a single-family home into a duplex, you may have to do nothing more than add a kitchen sink to the new duplex. If the existing house has at least two bathrooms and one kitchen, you might get off cheap. But, suppose you were converting this same property to use as a hair salon? Think of all the sink locations needed in a beauty shop. Consider the amount of hot water need-

FIGURE 9.26 Existing pipes had to be relocated so they would not conflict with electrical panels slated to be located below them. The exact location of the pipes wasn't known until the ceiling was removed. *Photo: Nick Fredericks.*

When you are in the process of converting a building from one use to another, you can usually count on some plumbing changes.

ed on a regular basis. Will you need to have a public restroom in the shop? Do handicap plumbing codes come into effect with this type of conversion? See how quickly the plumbing needs for a building can change, depending upon the use?

There is a lot to consider when assessing your plumbing requirements. First, the plumbing system must be solid and in good working order. Secondly, local codes will probably require you to bring the system up to current code standards if you embark on extensive rehab work. And, of course, you may have to relocate, add, delete, or reconsider plumbing to accommodate the new use of the building. With all of this in mind, let's talk about the various phases and situations that are most likely to affect you and the plumbing in your building.

The primary service of your plumbing system is the first concern. This is something that you should address before buying a building:

- Is the sewer large enough for your new use of the building?
- Will the water service be adequate?
- Does the building have a water supply that will fulfill the occupant's needs?
- Will sewage disposal be a problem with the new use of the building?

These are the questions you need answers to. Who can answer them? You may be able to answer them yourself. A general knowledge of plumbing and some research can go a long ways in making a person capable of answering typical plumbing questions. If the issue is over your head, you can consult with a licensed plumber. The local plumbing inspector can also be consulted. Your local utilities office should be able to shed some light on issues pertaining to water mains and sewers. Before you get too involved with a building, you should have all of the key questions answered.

Local codes will probably require you to bring the system up to current code standards if you embark on extensive rehab work.

Existing Drains And Vents

Existing drains and vents will probably be acceptable for continued use. They may have to be altered or relocated, but the materials, overall, should be salvageable. One exception to this is galvanized steel pipe used for drains. This pipe is notorious for its ability to clog up and rust out. If the building has galvanized pipe used for drainage, I would replace it. You might get by with leaving the pipe in place, but there will come a time when replacement will be mandatory. It is better to head off the problem early and avoid tearing up the walls and ceilings of a recently renovated building.

Many older buildings will have cast-iron pipe used for drainage. This pipe is normally satisfactory for continued service. The life of cast-iron pipe is long, and few problems are associated with it. Schedule-40 plastic pipe is the material used in modern plumbing systems. If your building has this type of pipe, you should have no need to replace it. Lead pipe will turn up occasionally in old houses. If you discover any lead bends, traps, or pipes, replace them. The soft lead deteriorates over time, and problems are sure to follow. Aside from these tips, the remainder of what you should look for is leaks and slow-running drains.

Leaks in drainage and vent systems are hard to find once piping is concealed as in Figure 9.27. However, if there is a significant leak, it will usually show up somewhere. If you can do a visual inspection of a drain, do it. Fill a fixture with water and then allow the fixture to empty into the drain you are observing. If a leak is present, you should be able to spot it. Another telltale sign of a drainage leak can be the discoloration of a ceiling. Leaks under and around bathtubs are common. So are leaks around the bases of toilets. When these fixtures are installed above a ceiling, the ceiling is usually the first place where evidence of a leak will appear.

Slow drains are easy to test for. All you have to do is flush toilets and drain fixtures to see if the water flows down the drain promptly. Hair clogs are common in lavatories and bathtubs. These minor clogs can give the appearance of a much bigger problem. If you experience problems with either of these types of fixtures, check the fixture outlet and trap before you condemn the drainpipe. Multiplying the anticipated number of occupants by the loads listed in Table 9.2 can make an estimate of requirements.

Old Plumbing

Old plumbing can present a lot of problems for remodelers. For instance, old galvanized steel pipe tends to clog up with rust and other deposits. This happens whether it has been used to convey potable water or drainage. Anytime you authorize your plumber to tie into existing galvanized pipes,

FIGURE 9.27 Moisture from plumbing fixtures above has repeatedly wet the surface of this joist causing the early stages of dry rot to be visible. In this case, repairing the plumbing leak is sufficient to remove the source of moisture and stop the process without triggering structural intervention.

you could be setting yourself up for call-backs. My experience has shown that all galvanized pipe should be replaced with modern plumbing materials. The up-front savings of tying into old steel pipes is generally lost in unbillable time for call-backs. And this doesn't even take into account the frustration of homeowners who have just paid handsomely for quality remodeling work that doesn't function properly. My advice is this, if you see galvanized pipe on a job, talk the customer into replacing it.

To illustrate how you can become responsible for existing piping problems, let me share some of my past experience. I've done a lot of kitchen remodeling. Many of the jobs have entailed the addition of garbage disposers. In my earlier years, I used to work right from the trap arm (the pipe that sticks out under the kitchen sink). If the trap arm was galvanized, I would have my people connect to it. It didn't take more than a couple of jobs for me to change my philosophy on this issue.

I discovered that old galvanized drains that would adequately drain a sink full of water would not necessarily take on the discharge of a garbage disposer. This experience came at a high price. The sinks would test out okay when they were installed, because only water was going down the

TABLE 9.2 Potential sanitary flow by type of establishment (*Continued*)

Type of establishment	Gallons
Schools (toilet and lavatories only)	15 per day per person
Schools (with above plus cafeteria)	25 per day per person
Schools (with above plus cafeteria and showers)	35 per day per person
Day workers at schools and offices	15 per day per person
Day camps	25 per day per person
Trailer parks or tourist camps (with built-in bath)	50 per day per person
Trailer parks or tourist camps (with central bathhouse)	35 per day per person
Work or construction camps	50 per day per person
Public picnic parks (toilet wastes only)	5 per day per person
Public picnic parks (bathhouse, showers, and flush toilets)	10 per day per person
Swimming pools and beaches	10 per day per person
Country clubs	25 per locker
Luxury residences and estates	150 per day per person
Rooming houses	40 per day per person
Boarding houses	50 per day per person
Hotels (with connecting baths)	50 per day per person
Hotels (with private baths, 2 persons per room)	100 per day per person
Factories (gallons per person per shift—exclusive of industrial wastes)	25 per day per person
Nursing homes	75 per day per person
General hospitals	150 per day per person
Public institutions (other than hospitals)	100 per day per person
Restaurants (toilet and kitchen wastes per unit of serving capacity)	25 per day per person
Kitchen wastes from hotels, camps, boarding houses, etc. serving 3 meals per day	10 per day per person
Motels	50 per bed space
Motels with bath, toilet and kitchen wastes	60 per bed space
Drive in theaters	5 per car space
Stores	400 per toilet room
Service stations	10 per vehicle served
Airports	3 to 5 per passenger
Assembly halls	2 per seat

TABLE 9.2 *(Continued)* Potential sanitary flow by type of establishment

Type of establishment	Gallons
Bowling alleys	75 per lane
Churches (small)	3 to 5 per sanctuary seat
Churches (large with kitchens)	5 to 7 per sanctuary seat
Dance halls	2 per day per person
Laundries (coin-operated)	400 per machine
Service stations	1000 (first bay) 500 (each add. bay)
Subdivision or individual homes	75 per day per person
Marinas:	
Flush toilets	36 per fixture per hr
Urinals	10 per fixture per hr
Wash basins	15 per fixture per hr
Showers	150 per fixture per hr

drain. But, as customers used their disposers, the drains would begin to clog up. Snaking the drains would punch holes in the clogs and get the drainage running again, but the repairs didn't last long. Invariably, the galvanized pipe had to be cut out and replaced with plastic pipe. This, of course, frequently involved cutting into walls and messing up brand-new remodeling jobs. Customers don't appreciate this type of action. Anyway, I learned quickly to have all galvanized drains replaced, even if it had to be done at my own expense. It was cheaper to replace them during the remodeling work than it was after, and the customers never got mad under these conditions.

Some other types of old drainage pipes that you are likely to run across are DWV copper and cast iron. Both of these materials make good drains, and they last for a very long time. Unless circumstances are unusual, there will be no need to replace either of these types of drains.

Lead pipe is not found in a lot of homes today, but it still turns up from time to time. The most common locations are near the traps of bathtubs and the bends under toilets. If you notice any lead pipe, plan on replacing it. This material is soft and does not adapt well to remodeling work. Vibrations from cutting out floors and building new walls are likely to make the old lead joints leak. Even the lead itself is likely to crack and leak. Count on replacing any lead you find.

Brass pipe was used to convey potable water in the years past. This pipe is not all bad, but it is not as desirable as modern materials. I won't say that you have to replace all brass pipe that you find, but if you have to tap into a brass system, you should be prepared for some problems. The screw joints along the system may develop leaks as you monkey around with fitting in new tees. If I saw brass pipe on a job, I would make sure that the customer was not going to hold me responsible for stress leaks down the line.

Galvanized steel pipe that is used for water pipe is just about as bad as the same pipe used for drains. I've seen galvanized water lines seize up with so much debris, such as rust, that water would only trickle out of the end of it. If you plan to ask your plumber to work with old galvanized water piping, be prepared to pay a steep price.

Old cut-off valves can complicate your plumber's life. If the main cut-off valve in a house won't stop the flow of water, your plumber may be forced to cut the water off at the street. This usually isn't a big deal, but it can add up a little in labor. If you know that you will have to tap into existing water lines, you can test the main cut-off while you are doing your estimate inspection. Refer to Figure 9.28. Finding out ahead of time that a valve is defective can save you money and your plumber some time and trouble.

Used Materials

Not many homeowners request contractors to install used materials, but occasions arise where this is the case. I've had homeowners who wanted my company to install plumbing fixtures that they had purchased at yard sales and such. In my time in the trades, I've had requests to install just about every type of used residential fixture in remodeling jobs. I don't have a blanket policy against doing this, but I don't like it, and I don't do it very often.

Used fixtures can be trouble just waiting for a place to happen. If you have your plumber install some of them, you might be the lucky one to win the honor of being the place where the trouble surfaces. Old toilets can have hairline cracks that can't be seen easily, but that can leak profusely. Sinks offer the same risks. Used water heaters can leak, be full of sediment, have burned-out elements, and a host of other problems. Bathtubs and showers can also harbor unseen defects. If you want to be safe, refuse to install used plumbing fixtures.

Claw-foot tubs are one type of used fixture that seems to be very popular in some remodeling jobs. A case can be made for installing these units, since they are not common. I urge you, however, to approach any job where used fixtures are requested with care. Write a liability waiver that limits

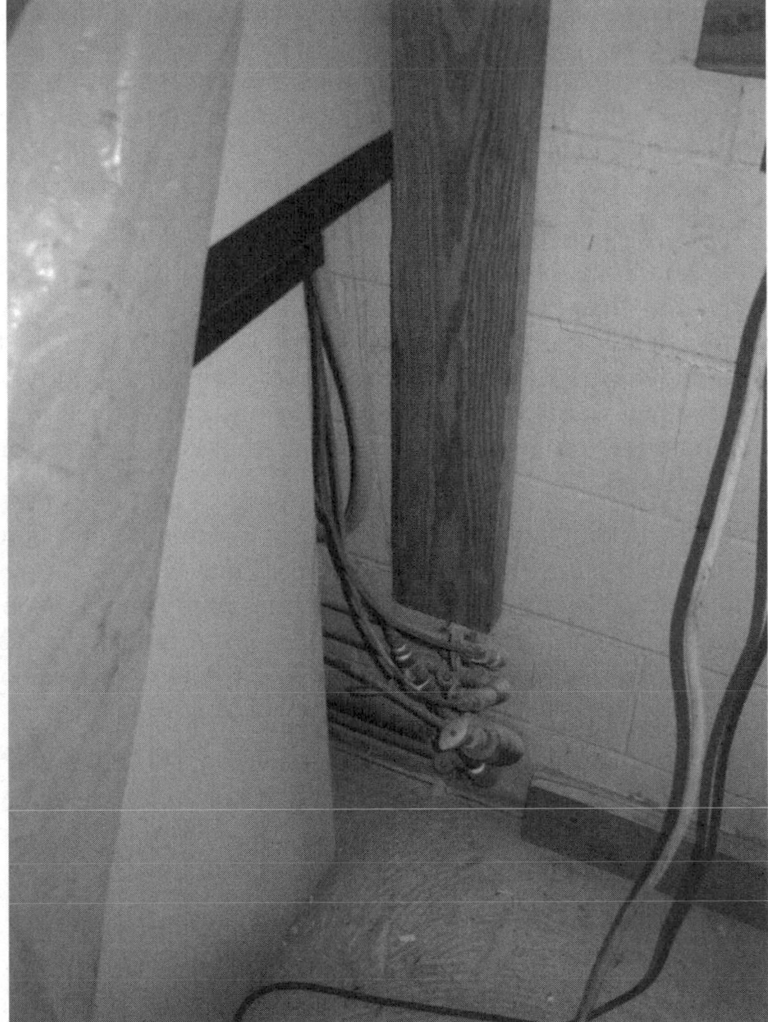

FIGURE 9.28 Access to existing valves must be maintained. These valves will be incorporated within a horizontal chase. *Photo: Nick Fredericks*

your exposure to the connections made to the fixture. By doing this, if the fixture itself is defective, you and your plumber won't be under the gun.

Keep Your Eyes Open

When you are estimating a job where plumbing work will be needed, keep your eyes open. If copper pipe is stained green, beware. The pipe might be on the verge of rupturing, due to too much acid in the water. When your plumber tries to cut into the pipe, an entire section may have to be replaced. If the building sewer is too small, you could lose all of your profit installing a new one. Whenever major work is done on a system, most codes require that the entire system be brought into compliance with current codes. This can get extremely expensive. A 40-gallon water heater might be doing just fine under existing conditions, but if you are building an in-law addition where additional people will be putting demands on the water heater, the heater may not meet the demands.

You should always involve experts in your estimating process before you give any firm prices to customers. It is possible for you to spot some obvious trouble spots with plumbing systems, but you need a seasoned plumber, one who has experience in remodeling, to make sure that you stay out of hot water. It may be a little inconvenient to have your plumber tag along with you on estimates, but it can save you a lot of money and embarrassment.

If you are bidding new construction, get a few prices from reputable plumbing companies before you submit a bid. There is a tendency for contractors to assume that plumbing is about the same from one job to the next. This can be the case, but don't count on it. Plumbing is often an expensive and potentially dangerous part of a job, so don't leave yourself out on a limb.

The plumbing code is a complex subject. It is not one that we can delve into, in depth, in this chapter. However, I will provide you with pages upon pages of information that will answer your most-often-asked questions pertaining to the plumbing requirements. Study the following information to make yourself more aware of the plumbing needs in your jobs:

- Will a force main or backflow preventor be required?
- Will the city permit new service?
- Can one connect to existing storm system?
- Can sewers or site handle added contribution of paved area or addition?
- If not, where does the water go?
- Is there room for on-site detention or constructed wetland?

EVALUATING EXISTING (HVAC) SYSTEMS

If you are a remodeler, you are going to be forced into working with heating and air conditioning, and you are going to find yourself evaluating existing systems. Unless you have a lot of experience in this field, you should take an expert with you when inspecting existing units. A boiler that looks perfectly fine may have a cracked section. The heat exchanger on a heating system can be bad and very difficult for untrained eyes to detect. If you are adding space to a house, you will have to determine if existing heating and cooling systems can be tapped into. They may not be large enough to handle the increased demand of extra living space. If you forget to factor in a new heating system when doing your cost estimates, you may lose a lot of sleep trying to figure out how to worm your way out of the mistake. It is definitely in your best interest to take a professional along with you on routine inspections of existing systems.

Some contractors will say just about anything to get work. Others are just ignorant enough to make statements that put qualified contractors up against a wall. Let me give you an example of what I'm talking about. Let's say that you are estimating an attic conversion. As part of your estimate, you are concerned about getting heat to the upstairs living space. You're not comfortable that the forced hot-air furnace and existing ductwork will be adequate. On top of this, the customer wants you to install a new air-conditioning unit and tie it into the existing ductwork that is used by the furnace. After listening to the customer, you express your concerns about the existing equipment not being suitable for the job. You recommend installing a one-piece heat pump in the attic, since it will be all one big room, used as a studio.

After making your feelings known, the customer replies by saying that two other contractors didn't have any problem with doing the job the way it was specified. The homeowner starts to question your knowledge and ability. In reality, you are right and the other contractors are wrong, but the homeowner is choosing to side with the previous contractors. This may be because two independent contractors didn't raise the same concerns that you have, or it could be that the customer doesn't like to be wrong. Either way, you're in the hot seat.

Now that you've got your potential customer questioning your experience, what are you going to do? If you're right, and in this case you are, you should stand your ground. This may cost you a sale, but it is better to lose the sale than to take it and wind up in a big mess. If you had an expert with you who knew heating and air conditioning as well as you know general remodeling, you could sway the customer. While it's true that two remodelers didn't voice concerns over the mechanical equipment, having an expert back you up could be all it would take to win this job. You are in a difficult position. If you tell the customer that the job requires more than a simple mechanical tie-in, you could lose the job. It's possible that you are being too cautious, but it's better to be safe than sorry. If you throw in with the other two contractors and bid the job against your better

FIGURE 9.29 Pumps that were not in code compliance when installed block the required clear space at an electrical panel and must be moved. Designers should be observant of such requirements and advise the owner of such discoveries.

FIGURE 9.30 Red mold growing on a re-roofed commercial building amidst new air handlers shows that moisture has collected on the roof for some time. The microclimate is altered by the air handlers. The situation that is attributed as the cause of the ill-famed Legionnaire's disease was not vastly different. *Photo: Stephen Culbert*

FIGURE 9.31 When you can't go out, go up, but watch your step. The property line limits where this owner can locate mechanical equipment and roof conductors. Generally speaking, a door where the landing has been removed must be permanently closed, or better yet, infilled.

judgment, you could be setting yourself up for a lawsuit when the systems don't perform properly. What are you going to do?

In this position, I would suggest that the homeowner either allow me to return with one of my experts, or that some expert be contacted by the homeowner directly. I would explain my concerns and the repercussions of putting too many demands on an undersized system. If the homeowner chose to argue with me after this type of educational explanation, I would decline any interest in bidding the job.

Does this story sound a little farfetched? Well, it's not. I've run into circumstances similar to those in the story. My background gives me a broader knowledge of mechanical equipment than what most remodelers have. This advantage has proved useful over the years. There have been several times when customers have told me that contractors had assured them that existing ducts for their heating systems could be used to convey cool air from a new air conditioner. This is rarely the case. Oh, the air will find its way through the ducts, but cooling will not be efficient. Duct sizes are larger for air conditioners than they are for furnaces. A forced-air furnace could be tied into ducts serving an air conditioner, but the reverse is rarely true.

The size of ductwork is not the only potential problem that remodelers run into. There are many times when an existing heating or cooling system will be adequate to tap into, but there are also plenty of times when they won't be. How can you tell if an existing system is suitable for expanded use? The best way is to have a couple of experts check the system out. They will have to do a heat-gain, heat-loss worksheet to determine accurately what size system will be needed. Experienced heating-and-cooling mechanics can often make very educated guesses, but be careful not to accept these guesstimates as gospel. I know that many good contractors can eyeball a system and tell if it is capable of taking on extra duty. But, if you don't want to wind up in a bind, get the experts to do a full-blown worksheet on the job and ask for their recommendations in writing. This type of action will help keep you off the hook if things don't work out just the way you would like for them to.

There is no rule-of-thumb method used for sizing heating and cooling systems. Some contractors size them with tight limits. This is especially true in track housing, where every dime counts. A lot of contractors, like myself, install systems that are a little larger than they need to be. This provides a margin of error to compensate for any miscalculations. These oversized systems can often handle some extra load, but don't expect any existing system to be substantial enough to take on a large addition or an attic conversion. It is possible that an existing system can manage these types of improvements, but the occasions will be rare.

I've seen contractors push heating and cooling systems to the max. This isn't a good idea. If you overload a system, there is going to come a time

There are many times when an existing heating or cooling system will be adequate to tap into, but there are also plenty of times when they won't be.

when the system doesn't work to its expected performance. When this happens, some angry homeowner is going to be calling you with complaints. This problem can be avoided by simply doing the job right the first time. If you have to go back, at your own expense, to do a retrofit, your profit will be out the window.

It is common for homeowners to put remodelers in tough spots. How many times have you gone out to look at a job and had the homeowners ask you for a guess on what the estimate will amount to? Is it feasible for a contractor to give someone an off-the-cuff price for a basement conversion, an attic conversion, a complete kitchen remodel, or any other type of major work? No, it isn't. Yet, a lot of contractors do it. Why do they feel compelled to make rash comments? I don't know, but I've seen a lot of contractors do it.

There is a big difference between making a rough estimate on the spot and having a pre-planned price in mind. Some types of home improvements can be sold right on the spot. Decks, for example, can be figured on a square-footage basis with enough accuracy to make selling one right on the spot feasible. Room additions can even be figured out in advance, but you have no way of knowing what to expect from a heating or cooling system until you see it. If your company uses a per-square-foot price for room additions, it must be based on being able to tie into existing mechanical systems. If you quote a price for an addition and then find that the existing mechanical systems won't handle it, who do you think is going to be forced into paying for a new system? Probably your company.

DUCTWORK

Ductwork will be one of the first considerations when evaluating an air-conditioning system or a forced hot-air heating system. Someone is going to have to determine if the existing ducts can be tied into effectively to serve new living space. This someone should be an expert, and preferably the one who is giving you a firm quote for doing the work. Don't attempt to evaluate ductwork on your own, unless you have a much higher level of knowledge about such systems than an average remodeling contractor.

There are some basics about ductwork that you can look for. When ductwork leaves a plenum (this is the ductwork located in the immediate area of the furnace), it will normally leave either as a trunk line or as individual ducts. If the ducts coming off the plenum are small, you are looking at individual supply ducts. More likely, you will see a large, rectangular duct extending for some distance. Smaller ducts will take off from this main trunk. As the trunk line becomes longer, it should also become smaller. To maintain a proper air flow, the size of a trunk line has to be reduced as it becomes longer in length. If you see a trunk line that is not reduced as it runs most of the length of a building, you can expect to have air-flow problems. It would seem that this problem would be rare, but it is not all that uncommon.

I recently rented a house while building my new home. The house I rented suffered from an oversized trunk line. Whoever installed the ductwork did a poor job. Since the trunk line was not reduced progressively, rooms at the far end of the main duct were never heated as well as rooms closer to the origination point of the trunk line. Because the duct was too big, there was no opportunity for a volume and pressure of air to exhaust through the heat registers. This resulted in cold rooms. To get the cold rooms warm, the thermostat had to be set so high that other rooms in the house were too hot.

If you run into a house like the one I had rented and added to the existing trunk line, your new installation would not perform well. The customer

FIGURE 9.32 Above street level, this exterior HVAC retrofit is visible from adjacent structures. *Photo: Stephen Culbert*

fastfacts

Duct work will be one of the first considerations when evaluating an air-conditioning system or a forced hot-air heating system. Someone is going to have to determine if the existing ducts can be tied into effectively to serve the new living space. This should be an expert, and preferably the one who is giving you a firm quote for doing the work.

might accept its performance, since some of the other parts of the home would probably be affected similarly, but you shouldn't set yourself up for the risk. If you see a major trunk line that is running full size for a long length, call in an expert to evaluate the needs for making the job right and discuss the problem with your customer before any work is done.

The main trunk line is the only portion of ductwork that should have an effect on any new work that you do. However, if the seams on the trunk line are not sealed properly, air can escape. This reduces the airflow and the effectiveness of the trunk line. Ultimately, it can affect your new tie-ins. They will not receive the amount of air that they should. If you see gaps at seams in the trunk line, discuss the problem with your customer and detail a release of liability for the potential problems associated with existing conditions.

Ductwork for an air-conditioning system is usually larger than that used for a heating system. This is, perhaps, one of the most likely traps for a remodeler to fall into. If a customer wants you to tie a new air-conditioning system into existing ducts, have the size of the ducts evaluated by an expert. Taking a job on face value, without accurate sizing data to go by, can result in major problems for you.

THE MAIN UNIT

The main unit of a heating or air-conditioning system is an expensive component. While you should not be responsible for the overall condition of this unit, you could be held accountable for not knowing or notifying the customer that the existing unit is inadequate for the additional load you are creating for it. This is, again, a time to call in an expert. Whether the main unit is a boiler, a furnace, or a heat pump, you should have a qualified professional evaluate it. Even if you are making only modest increases in living space, you could be setting yourself up for big trouble if you don't document that the existing unit can handle the new load.

RADIATORS

Depending upon where you work, radiators may still be very much in use. Older houses frequently depend on radiators for their heat. If you are estimating a job where the customer wants radiators installed, be careful. Radiators are sometimes hard to come by, and they are never cheap. Before you make any commitment for installing radiators, confirm their price and availability.

ELECTRIC HEAT

Electric heat is simple enough to understand. It's so simple, in fact, that some remodelers find themselves in trouble because of it. Let's say that you are doing an estimate for a basement conversion. All of the upper level of the building is heated with electric baseboard heat. You've discussed heating options with the customer, and they are willing to stick with electric heat for the new living space. Your job seems simple. Hang a few baseboard units, run a little wire, and bingo, the heat work is done. This may be true, but don't count on it. Suppose the main electrical service is full and will not accept any new circuits? Who is going to pay for adding a new set-up for the additional heat? If you take the job before discovering that the box is filled to capacity, you may very well be eating the cost of an additional service. Check the panel box to make sure there is room to grow before you commit to installing new electric heat.

HOW MUCH DO YOU KNOW?

How much do you know about heating and air-conditioning systems? Unless you are a skilled technician in these fields, you should plan on hiring competent subcontractors to work with these systems for you. For one thing, a special trade license is usually required in this area of work. For another, amateur attempts at either heating or air conditioning can result in very costly lessons of experience.

You've already been told to have your potential buildings checked out before committing to buying them. Hopefully, you will do this. However, confirming that existing systems are in good working order is not enough in the conversion business. Since you will be changing the use of a property, you will most likely be altering the needs of both the heating and air-conditioning systems. Savvy conversion contractors cover this issue with their experts before buying properties. But, there are always some people who either don't remember or don't bother to investigate expansion possibilities. These people generally lose money. Since your goal is to make money, have at least one professional review the systems in buildings you are buying before you buy them. Ask for a report that will cover both the current condition of the equipment as well as what will be involved with upgrading the systems to meet the demands of your building's new use.

COST FACTORS

There are two cost factors to consider when altering, replacing, or installing heating and air-conditioning systems. The first is the cost of installation. Some types of systems cost much less than others to install. This is certainly a factor for anyone wishing to make a few extra dollars on a conversion deal. However, it is not wise to look only at the cost of acquisition and installation. You should also consider the cost of operating various systems. If you plan to keep the property for yourself, the long-range effect of high operating costs will make you wish you had spent a little more at the time of conversion so that you wouldn't be spending so much in the cost of operating the system. Even if you are going to sell or rent the property, prospective buyers and tenants (who will be paying their own utility expenses) may frown upon systems where the cost of operation will be high. Before you take the cheapest way out on installation costs, weigh all of the options and potential scenarios.

As a real estate broker, I've been involved in the selling and leasing of all types of properties. One of the most common questions asked pertains to the type of heating and cooling systems in use. I've shown properties to people who were on the verge of making commitments to buy them, only to lose the deal to electric baseboard heat. The same as proved to be true with prospective rental tenants. The sight of electric heat and the vision of high monthly utility bills can send good, qualified prospects running in search of another property. This is only one example, but we will explore others as we delve into the various types of systems to be considered.

TYPES OF HEATING SYSTEMS

Numerous types of heating systems exist. The type found in your building is likely to be determined by your geographical region and the age of the property. Different types of heating systems vary in their fuel usage, performance, and cost. To bring this overall picture into better focus, let's concentrate on each of the major heating systems that you may find yourself working with.

Forced Hot Air

Forced hot-air furnaces were very popular for a lot of years. They are still in production and in use. Overall, a forced hot-air system provides good service in any climate. One drawback to this type of system is the dust that is being moved around almost constantly by the furnace. People who suffer from allergies frequently have trouble living in homes where forced hot-air systems are in use.

Hot-air furnaces can be purchased to run off of a variety of fuels, such as oil, gas, or electricity. The efficiency of hot-air furnaces is acceptable, and aside from noise and dust, there isn't a lot of bad information to consider in regard to them. There are, however, some factors that make these systems less than ideal for a conversion contractor.

Hot-air furnaces rely on heat ducts to convey warm air to living space and to return cold air to the furnace. If your conversion will require new space to be heated, such as an attic conversion might create, the duct sizing for the heating system will probably have to be enlarged. The furnace will also have to be enlarged in most instances. This gets expensive. Another downside is that you will have to get both supply and return ducts into the new space being created. Unlike plumbing and electrical components, which can sometimes be snaked through existing walls, heat ducts require a good deal of space. This will mean building chase ways or opening walls and ceilings to allow the installation of new ducts.

Some people take a look at buildings equipped with hot-air furnaces and get excited about using the existing ducts to distribute cool air from new air-conditioning equipment that is planned for the project. This normally won't work very well. Both heating and cooling systems can share common ductwork, but the ducts should be sized based on cooling needs, rather than on heating needs. Ductwork for air conditioning is typically larger than that required for a heating system. With this being the case, tying a new air conditioner into existing heat ducts will usually result in poor performance.

fastfacts

Forced hot-air furnaces were very popular for a lot of years. They are still in production and in use. Overall, a forced hot-air system provides good service in any climate. One drawback to this type of system is dust being moved around almost constantly by the blown hot air.

Forced hot-air furnaces operate at reasonable energy costs, but they don't combine the advantage of having both heating and air conditioning in one package, like a heat pump can. There are a lot of forced-air furnaces in operation, but I don't feel they are the best type of system to install when converting a building. If you have to go to the expense of buying a larger furnace, you might be better off to switch the type of system serving the property.

Heat Pumps

Heat pumps are extremely popular in many parts of the country. A heat pump can provide both heating and cooling from a single source. This is a big advantage. Heat pumps use ductwork and forced air, similar to the way that a hot-air furnace does. Dust and airborne irritants can still be a problem when using a heat pump. There are, however, many misconceptions in the minds of people when the subject of a heat pump is brought up.

Many people think that heat pumps are not effective in cold climates. To some extent this is true, but the case against a heat pump in frigid regions is not as clear-cut as some people would lead you to believe.

Heat pumps do perform at their best when installed in regions with moderate temperatures. An average balance point for a heat pump tends to be just a little below freezing temperature. If the outside temperature dips below a heat pump's balance point, supplementary heat comes on to offset the change in temperature. This heat is usually created with electric elements, and the operating cost can get expensive when the electric heat is kicking in. However, in many areas, such as Virginia, heat pumps are extremely efficient. All of the new homes I built in Virginia were equipped with heat pumps.

fastfacts

Heat pumps are extremely popular in many parts of the country. A heat pump can provide both heating and cooling from a single source. This is a big advantage. Heat pumps use duct work and forced air, similar to the way that a hot-air furnace does. Dust and airborne irritants can still be a problem when using a heat pump.

In very cold locations, such as Maine, heat pumps are not popular in residential applications. There are different types of heat pumps and some work just fine in cold regions. Air-to-air heat pumps are best suited to moderate temperatures. Water-based heat pumps can be cost-effective in their operating expenses in areas where extreme cold sets in for long periods. The installation cost of a water-based heat pump is, at times, prohibitive, but the operating cost is attractive.

Regardless of where your building is located, you should be able to match a heat pump to its heating and cooling needs. The biggest drawbacks in areas with extreme temperatures are the acquisition and installation cost. But once that is behind you, the low operating cost can keep you happy for a long time to come.

Heat pumps normally require two major pieces of equipment, an inside unit and an outside unit. Space limitations are rarely a problem, however. The ductwork used with an air-type system is more difficult to install in conversion projects than some other types of heat. This is due to the bulk of the ducts and the lack of places to conceal them. This can be overcome by opening walls and ceilings or building chases. Ducts for heat pumps are sized for their cooling requirements, so performance from both the heating and air conditioning is normally satisfactory.

If you are doing a conversion that involves a minimal space, such as a garage or attic conversion, a single-unit heat pump may be the answer to your heating and cooling needs. If you've stayed at many motels, you've probably seen this type of unit. Part of the unit sits in the living space with the other part extending to the outside. Basically, the heat pump sits in an outside wall where it works very well. Using this type of unit can help you avoid problems associated with extending ductwork, and you can continue to use existing systems for the unaltered space. A one-piece heat pump is not inexpensive to buy, but again, the operating costs are affordable.

Forced Hot-Water

Forced hot-water heat is unquestionably popular in areas where winter temperatures are brutal. When it comes to beating extreme winter temperatures, it's hard to find a better heating system. But this type of system doesn't do one much good in the summer months, since there is no air conditioning combined in it. Buildings with hot-water heat require a separate system for air conditioning, if cooling is desired.

Buildings where hot-water heat is in use are often friendly towards conversion contractors. Many boilers are oversized to a point where an extra zone of heat can be added without having to upgrade the size of the boiler. This is not always the case, so don't assume that you can heat additional space without the expense of a larger boiler.

The copper tubing used to carry water from a boiler to heating units is small, usually it has a diameter of only three-quarters of an inch. This makes snaking the piping through existing space much easier than trying to hide bulky ductwork. The baseboard heating units normally used with forced hot-water heat attach directly to existing walls. There are no registers or returns to cut in, therefore eliminating some potential risk of damaging existing walls and ceilings.

Another advantage to the use of a boiler and hot-water system can be the expense of hot water for domestic use, such as cooking and showers. Boilers can be set up to heat domestic water with the cost being much less than that of an electric water heater. People in Florida and other Deep-South states will have little need for hot-water heat. A heat pump will probably serve their needs much better. But, if your building is in the north, hot-water heat is hard to beat.

fastfacts

Forced hot-water heat is unquestionably popular in areas where winter temperatures are brutal. When it comes to beating extreme winter temperatures, it's hard do find a better heating system. But this type of system doesn't do one much good in the summer months, since there is no air conditioning combined in it. Buildings with hot-water heat require a separate system for air conditioning.

Electric Heat

Electric baseboard heat is the most economical type of heat to install. It is also easy to install in conversion projects, because electrical wire is all that has to be snaked to the heating units. So it's cheap and easy to install, but there is a problem. Historically, electric heat is expensive to operate. This is not such a big deal in areas where the winters are mild and short, but it can be a serious expense in colder climates.

I installed electric heat in my first home. The cost was too good to pass up, but I later regretted it. The operating cost for heat in that house was horrendous. When I first moved to Maine, I rented a house. Guess what? It had electric heat. Houses in Maine with electric heat are not very sought after, and I found out why. Even using wood stoves as my primary source of heat, the electric bills during the heating season hit $300. The range in the kitchen was fueled with gas, so that was not even a part of the electric bill. As you might imagine, I moved when the lease expired.

Electric heat is viewed as being very expensive to operate. In some regions, where temperatures are mild, electric heat makes a lot of sense. It easy and inexpensive to install, and if it isn't used very often, the operating costs are not a big factor. Areas where the winter temperatures are mild enough to allow this are generally pretty hot in the summer. This calls for air conditioning. You might find that it makes more sense to simply have a heat pump installed.

AIR CONDITIONING

When you are thinking of adding air conditioning to your conversion project, you have three basic options. You can install a heat pump that will provide both heating and air conditioning, and this is usually a good choice. Another option is to keep whatever the existing heating system is and install an independent air-conditioning system. This can be sensible. Your third option is to install individual air conditioners on a room-by-room basis. This eliminates the need for ductwork, but it is not as attractive and it may not be as efficient. What will you do?

Heat Pumps

You've already heard about heat pumps. In many areas they are an ideal combination system. In some areas it costs so much to get a unit that will perform well in winter conditions that you may not be able to justify the expense. If your building has an existing heating system that is sufficient, tearing it out to put in a heat pump might be considered radical. However, the long-range savings in operation costs might prove otherwise. You will have to do some research and see how the numbers work out for your individual building.

Straight Air-Conditioning Units

Straight air-conditioning units are far from being inexpensive when installed. Your building may require such an expense, but the cost will be significant. I would try to avoid this situation, personally.

Individual Units

Individual units have merit in many ways. For one thing, occupants of the conditioned space can control their own comfort. If a central unit is used, some people will be chilly while others are warm. Another advantage to independent units is their ease of installation. Unlike central units that require extensive ductwork and time to install, independent units can be put in place quickly and inexpensively. There is another advantage, too. If a central system goes out of order, your whole building is uncomfortable. When an independent unit shuts down, only a portion of your property is affected.

There are so many variations and possibilities linked to conversion projects that you must assess your needs on a personal basis, even on a building-by-building basis. My best advice to you is to set aside time to look into all of your options carefully. Don't jump into anything. Once you have narrowed the field, talk to experts. When you have all the facts, you can make a safe, informed decision.

ELECTRICAL SYSTEMS

The unasked questions pertaining to electrical work are often more important than the ones which are presented. Most buyers don't know enough about electrical systems to understand what questions to pose. This is where your knowledge and expertise shines. If you can point out key issues to potential customers before they are even aware that such issues exist, you have a much better chance of making a sale. With this in mind, let's peruse some of the unasked questions that you can capitalize on.

Is Your Electrical Service Adequate?

Is your electrical service adequate for all of these changes? This is a question you should ask whenever a customer is requesting the addition of new circuits. A garbage disposer or dishwasher may seem innocent enough, but if there is no room left in the panel box for a new circuit, an easy job can turn into an expensive mistake. You should always check the electrical panel before you make any firm commitments to providing additional circuits.

Are You Aware Of The Code Requirements?

Are you aware of the code requirements pertaining to this work you want done? This question should always be asked. Honest homeowners will almost always say that they are not aware of code requirements. This is your chance to show off a little and to impress the homeowner. For instance, you can quote the need for GFI (Ground Fault Interrupter) protection. This can be followed with code requirements on outlet spacing. Essentially, wall outlets cannot be more than twelve feet apart. The code

FIGURE 9.33 Is the existing structure able to support new equipment? If original design calculations are not part of the owner's records, and they rarely are, structural engineers may have to evaluate the existing structure. *Photo: Stephen Culbert*

requires a light or appliance with a six-foot electrical cord to be placed in any location along a wall without having to use an extension cord to reach an outlet. Along kitchen counters, the spacing is reduced to four feet. These types of statistics impress people, and if you can impress them, you can sell them. However, don't take the code regulations that I'm giving you here for gospel, check your local code for current requirements.

Have You Thought About Your Switch Locations?

Have you thought about your switch locations and which switches will control which lights? This question can be very important during the planning stage of a job. By showing people how they can specify the location of switches, within reason, and how they can suggest what lights the switches operate, you can give the customer a better job. People pick up on these types of questions, and they identify them with caring and concern on your part. This is a big step towards closing a sale.

Have You Set A Budget?

Have you set a budget for your light fixtures? Electrical contractors sometimes bid design-build jobs without including the price of light fixtures. On bid jobs there is often an allowance for fixtures. Often electrical specifiers will writer their specifications around the product lines available from a local product rep's lines, stating a standard of design product for each item specified. Then they will permit packages by competing product rep's lines. If a rep doesn't have a line for each item in the spec this can work against him, since he will have to go to the manufacturer or a competitor for pricing. They will typically detail a fixture allowance in their bid, but their price may not include any allowance for fixtures. If you forget to mention this fact to your customers, someone might have to come up with hundreds of dollars that they hadn't planned on. One fixture, such as a dining room chandelier, can cost several hundred dollars. It is also possible to buy fixtures for less than ten dollars. Before you can bid a job successfully, you must establish a lighting allowance with your customer.

This list of questions could continue for several more pages, but you should be getting the idea of what I'm telling you. Don't wait for your potential customers to ask all of the questions. It is not fair for you to expect them to know what questions to ask. You should prompt them with questions that are pertinent to the job. In doing this, you head off problems before they develop, you win more jobs, and you have happier customers.

There are so many variations and possibilities linked to conversion projects that you must assess your needs on a personal basis, even on a building-by-building basis. My best advice to you is to set aside time to look into all of your options carefully. Don't jump into anything. Once you have narrowed the field, talk to experts. When you have all the facts you can make a safe, informed decision.

Existing Conditions

Existing conditions with electrical remodeling do not normally create as many problems for a remodeler as plumbing can. This is not to say that existing electrical systems can't cause trouble for you. The primary concern for contractors in most remodeling jobs, pertaining to electrical work, is the electrical service. If the panel box is in compliance with code requirements, has adequate room for any additional circuits being created, and is in satisfactory condition, the remainder of existing wiring does not necessarily affect you. Unlike plumbing, where old pipes are being tapped into, old wiring is left alone during remodeling. By this, I mean that new circuits are not tied into existing circuits. Naturally, your electrician may have to reroute existing wires. This can get you involved in existing conditions. But, if you are doing an attic conversion, a basement conversion, or building an addition, you should not have any reason to work with old wiring. All of your work will be focused on running new wires to the existing panel box.

Since the panel box is so critical, this is one of the first things that you should look at during your estimate inspection. If the service is a fuse box, you can expect some trouble. When the box is a 100-amp circuit-breaker box, you should still expect some trouble. With today's houses, a 100-amp electrical service is considered small. If you are doing any significant additional wiring, a 100-amp box may not be sufficient. A 200-amp service will generally be large enough to avoid major electrical upgrades in the service panel, but you can't just assume this. If a house is large or has a number of separate circuits, even a 200-amp panel can become full quickly. If you look in a panel box and see that it is full, or nearly full, you should be aware that costly modification to the electrical service for the home may be needed before your work can be completed. This is a good time to have your electrician look over the job to give you firm price quotes.

I don't want to give you the impression that the electrical service is the only place where existing electrical conditions can affect you. It is not. For

fastfacts

The primary concern for contractors in most remodeling jobs is the electrical service. If the panel box is in compliance with code requirements, has adequate room for any additional circuits being created, and is in satisfactory condition, the remainder of existing wiring does not necessarily affect you.

an example, you may be replacing an existing water heater as a part of your remodeling job. This is certainly not unusual. Neither is it unusual for older electric water heaters to be connected to wires that are, by present code requirements, too small. It was common for years to run 12-gauge wire to a water heater. Under today's code requirements, the wire must be no less than 10-gauge. The current code also requires an independent disconnect box to be located near the water heater. This has not always been the case. So, if you stumble onto a water heater that is wired with 12-gauge wire and no disconnect box, your cost to replace the heater will have to include upgrading the wire and installing the disconnect. A job like this can get expensive, and it can eat away at your anticipated profit.

Kitchens

Are you aware that major kitchen appliances are required to have their own electrical circuit? Well, they are, and many older homes were not wired in this manner. If you are doing extensive kitchen remodeling, there are several code upgrades that may be needed. Your electrician may have to run a whole new circuit for kitchen outlets. Kitchen outlets are required to be installed on two separate circuits. GFI protection will be required in the kitchen, and appliance wiring may have to be reworked to provide individual circuits. All these new circuits can fill a small panel box quickly, so you have to be able to evaluate these existing conditions during your estimate phase.

Bathrooms

Let's talk about bathrooms for a moment. If you are gutting and redoing a bathroom, there are a couple of electrical issues to be aware of. A bathroom is required to have GFI protection. Many old bathrooms don't have this, so you will have to plan on the expense to provide it. If the bathroom does not have an operable window, a ventilation fan will be required. This will cause you to run new wiring, buy and install the fixture, and extend a vent hose for the fan. Finding a way to vent a fan that is located in a bathroom can be tricky. If the bathroom doesn't have attic space above it or isn't built on an outside wall, getting the vent to open air space can require extensive work. If you fail to pick up on this during your estimate, the cost for doing the job may come out of your pocket.

When you remodel a bathroom, your work may very well include the installation of a whirlpool tub. If it does, you will need to wire the motor for this fixture with a GFI circuit. This isn't particularly difficult, but a GFI breaker costs about ten times what a regular breaker does, and then there is the cost for more wire than you might have thought would be needed. On top of this, there is the labor for a licensed electrician to run the wire and install the breaker. These are both little jobs that you might not have figured on. All in all, not knowing that a whirlpool needs to be GFI protected can cost you a few hundred dollars.

Electrical Improvements

Before you can budget for electrical improvements, you must have a starting point. This should be established prior to purchasing a building. Your inspector should inform you of all the existing electrical conditions. If you know what your plans for a building are before you buy it, and you should, the inspector can also give you a good idea of what to expect as you begin the conversion process. For example, if you are making three apartments out of a single-family home, the inspector should be able to tell you that two additional electrical services will be needed. If the wiring is extremely old and will need to be replaced entirely, your inspector should file a report to that effect. To realize profits in the conversion business, you must learn to have plenty of facts to work with before making financial commitments. Otherwise, you could lose your shirt on the first deal you do.

Electrical Services in Rental Units

Electrical services are needed for all of your residential rental units. Each apartment should have its own electrical service. The same is true for commercial tenants. The expense of installing individual electrical services can get steep. There is the cost of a panel box, the circuit breakers, a weather head, assorted other items, and the labor of a licensed electrician. It is not difficult to spend considerable money for each service installed. Regional differences may make this cost lower or higher, but at any rate, the money needed for a new electrical service will be enough to get your attention.

When it comes to new electrical services, there is more to consider than just cost. You, or your electrician, will have to find suitable locations for each service panel. The location chosen will have bearing on the cost of wiring your new units, so choose it carefully. You want the panel box as close to your wiring paths as possible.

Old houses might have fused electrical systems. It is not unusual to find 60-amp services installed at older homes. These electrical services are not nearly adequate for modern electrical demands. A 100-amp service should be considered a minimum size for each residential rental unit. 200-amp services are best for houses, but a 100-amp service can usually handle the requirements of an apartment. If you get into commercial conversions, you may have to switch to 200-amp services. In either case, you should upgrade your building to circuit breakers if it is presently protected by fuses.

The upgrading and addition of electrical services should, in my opinion, only be done by experienced, licensed electricians. An electrical permit is usually required for this work, and these permits are normally issued only to master electricians. The power present in a panel box is enough to kill a person on the spot. This is no place for learning by experience. Your experience could terminate your career and your life.

I wired my new home, but I didn't get very involved in the installation of the electrical service. I mounted the panel and assisted a master electrician, but I kept my fingers well away from the power cables. Doing my own wiring was pretty simple, but I had no desire to fry myself at the panel box. All of the wires and devices that I worked with were cold. The main breaker at the panel box was turned off during my activity with the electrical system.

Old Wiring

Old wiring in buildings can present conversion contractors with some challenges. Depending upon the age of your building and the condition of its wiring, you may be faced with replacing all of the wiring. Most jurisdictions require all electrical, plumbing, and heating systems to be brought up to current code requirements if extensive work is being done to the systems. This can affect your budget in a negative way. To protect yourself, you have to establish the rules and regulations on a local level and plan accordingly.

There may be times when existing wiring is on the verge of being in violation of current codes. This may put the ball in your court, as to making a judgment call on whether to upgrade or not. Some people will take the path of least resistance and cost by not doing anything. I would upgrade any wiring that is questionable. Money is money, but people's lives could be at stake. Given a borderline situation, the call is yours, but I would heartily recommend that you take the wiring to a safer level.

Conversion projects usually involve an increase in the use of mechanical systems, such as electrical wiring. While a house might have functioned flawlessly as a home, its wiring could be far too inadequate in the use you have planned for the building. Electrical systems can start fires, and fires can kill people and destroy property. New electrical wiring may not be one of the best cash-on-cash returns you can invest on in a building, but it certainly is good for your piece of mind.

Wiring codes have changed over the years. As new products have become available, the need for better wiring has increased. Think back to the time you spent in your grandparent's home. Do you remember a lot of little extension cords being used on a daily basis? I know I do. Can you remember when fuses blew frequently as your grandparents began to accumulate modern appliances? I can't talk for you, but I certainly remember such times. In fact, I can remember electrical situations in my grandparent's house that today would scare me to death. I was too young at the time to know about the dangers, but now that I understand what's going on, I realize how likely a devastating fire could have been. You want to know what is even scarier? Well, I'll tell you.

The memories I hold from my grandparent's house go way back, probably thirty years. It is understandable how the conditions in that house came to be. What I can't understand is how similar situations can still be present in today's homes. Less than five years ago, I was pretty active in the multi-family market as a broker. My time spent listing and showing apartment buildings was considerable. During this time, I saw many of

fastfacts

Old wiring in buildings can present conversion contractors with some challenges. Depending upon the age of your building and the condition, you may be faced with replacing all of the wiring. Most jurisdictions require all electrical, plumbing, and heating systems to be brought up to current code requirements if extensive work is being done to the systems.

the same problems that existed in the home of my grandparents some twenty or thirty years ago.

The rental properties I'm telling you about were not slums. They were not top-notch units, but the cities where they were located were not in the Dark Ages. Yet, people lived with minimal electrical services. 60-amp fuse boxes were common, and so were six-outlet power strips plugged into thin extension cords. More times than not, the buildings were not even equipped with three-prong plugs. Ground Fault Interrupters were nonexistent, and very few of the buildings had operational smoke detectors. These buildings should have been being inspected periodically by local authorities, but there was no sign of intervention to bring the apartments up to a safe level of living conditions. What does this tell us? Well, it tells us a lot, so much in fact that we don't have time to debate it all in this chapter. The key to this information, as it pertains to you, is that there are still a lot of buildings out there where extensive work should be done on the electrical systems.

Bringing Buildings Into Compliance

Bringing buildings into compliance with current electrical codes can be very expensive. Depending upon how bad the existing wiring is, it may be necessary to strip all walls and ceilings to replace the old wiring. It is not normally necessary to go to such an extreme, but it can be. There are, however, many smaller jobs that often have to be done. This work is easier and less expensive than rewiring an entire building, but the cost can still be prohibitive to making a sizable profit.

Water Heaters

Electric water heaters in older buildings were typically wired with 12-gauge wire. This was considered adequate at the time, but current codes require that a 10-gauge wire be used. You may not have to make this change until a time comes when the water heater must be replaced, but you should check with your electrician or electrical inspector to determine your status and liability on this issue.

Current electrical regulations require that a disconnect box be installed near an electric water heater. This is another rule that was not in effect several years ago. There are a lot of electric water heaters in use where no disconnect box has been installed. Like wire sizing, this obligation may be overlooked until a water heater is replaced, but you should check to make sure.

Smoke Detectors

Under current code regulations, smoke detectors are required in various locations of living space. One is required near bedrooms and another is needed in a kitchen. Other locations, such as halls, can be required to have smoke detectors installed. Requirements can mandate that the smoke detectors be hard wired and connected so that if one detector goes off, they all sound an alarm. You might be able to get by with battery-powered detectors, but this is something you should check out with local authorities or a licensed electrician.

Ground Fault

Ground fault interceptor (GFI) circuits are required in all wet areas. Such areas include kitchens, bathrooms, laundry rooms where a sink is installed, garages, and outside outlets. There are two options when faced with ground-fault rules. You can install a GFI outlet in each of the wet locations so that it is the first power outlet fed onto the circuit. This will provide ground fault protection to the entire circuit. Another option is to install a GFI circuit breaker for the circuit. GFI breakers are expensive, but they are sometimes less of a hassle to install than an outlet would be. The difficulty experienced by installing a GFI outlet is in determining with outlet is the first outlet to be fed on the circuit. If you can tell which outlet is the first, you can simply replace it with a GFI outlet.

Enough Outlets

Many buildings do not have enough outlets. This is a code issue that will not normally have to be brought into compliance unless major work is being done with the electrical system. The chances are good that you will have to correct this deficiency in order to make your converted space suitable for sale or lease. This is especially true if the conversion will be used as an office environment.

A broad-brush description of how the code determines outlet spacing is that a lamp with a six-foot cord should be able to be plugged into an

Ground Fault Interrupter (GFI) circuits are required in all wet areas. Such areas include kitchens, bathrooms, laundry rooms, outside outlets, and garages where a sink is installed.

outlet from anyplace along a wall. This essentially means that outlets should not be spaced more than twelve feet apart. A lamp with a six-foot cord could be placed in the center of the outlets with the cord being capable of reaching either outlet. Spacing in a kitchen is set at four-foot intervals. There are some variations and exceptions to the rules I've just given you, but these examples cover most outlet situations.

If you will be converting a building into professional office space, you should install more outlets than what is required by the electrical code. It is also helpful to supply some split-circuits on the outlets. With the massive amount of electrical equipment used in offices today, it is easy to overload a single circuit. Split circuits are required in kitchens, and they are a good idea in any location where a lot of electrical devices will be in operation simultaneously.

fastfacts

If you will be converting a building into professional office space, you should install more outlets than what is required by the electrical code. It is also helpful to supply some split-circuits on the outlets. With the massive amount of electrical equipment used in offices today, it is easy to overload a single circuit.

Overhead Lights

Overhead lights are not installed as often in modern homes as they once were. I suppose this is done to lower construction costs. To me, however, rooms with overhead lighting are much more useful than those which depend on light from lamps. My feelings have been shared by a multitude of customers. It is my opinion that a majority of the public prefers overhead lighting to lamps. You might want to consider this when setting a budget for your electrical work.

Older buildings generally have ceiling lights. If the wiring is safe and adequate, it is a simple matter to upgrade the old fixtures. Rooms which are not equipped with existing overhead lights can present a problem. Depending upon the direction of the ceiling joists, it may be impossible to snake wires through the ceiling to a suitable switch location. The ceiling could, of course, be opened to allow easy access for wiring, but this gets into higher costs. When the joists are running in the direction of a switch location, it is very feasible that wiring could be snaked through the ceiling and walls with minimal damage.

Lighting in office buildings and professional service buildings must be plentiful. The odds are that ceilings will have to be opened to allow adequate installations. This isn't all bad, however, since such a conversion project will probably require massive wiring work. As long as you plan your electrical work in advance and budget for it properly, you can do just about anything you want to.

While You Are Wiring

While you are wiring a building, there are several thoughts to consider for the future. For example, telephones will be needed in certain rooms. This makes it logical to pre-wire the phone jacks. The same is true of cable television. Running future-use wires when walls are open is a lot easier than working with them after everything is sealed up. Some considerations include:

- Security systems
- Door chimes
- Thermostat wires
- Telephone wires
- Television cables

Electrical Fixtures

Electrical fixtures frequently carry a high mark-up. It is not unusual for a fixture that costs $20 to be sold for $40 or more. If you have access to wholesale fixtures, you should be able to save yourself a few hundred dollars. I have sources where I can buy light fixtures for less than $10. These are not the type of fixtures that you would install in a high-end, custom home, but they're not junk either. Fixtures don't have to cost a fortune to look good and work well. Shopping is the key to affordable light fixtures. You might do okay buying fixtures through your electrician, but there are probably less expensive fixtures available.

Two of my suppliers are long-distance suppliers. I buy from them with the use of a catalog. My savings on a myriad of items is phenomenal. Light bulbs, light fixtures, accessories, plumbing fixtures, hardware, and a long list of other items are available to me through the catalogs at prices which are up to about 30 percent less than the cost at my local wholesalers. The service from these catalog distributors is great. I call one day, and in no more than two days, my order is delivered to my door. This type of outfit is well worth looking into. Effective price shopping can lower the overall cost of your conversion job by a considerable amount.

Electricians

Electricians are a lot like plumbers in terms of specialties. You want electricians who are experienced in old work and remodeling. Their abilities to work wires through walls and ceilings will be much appreciated. Since electrical work does require a trade license, you should make sure that any electricians you are considering are properly licensed and insured. Once you have found a seasoned, master electrician that you are comfortable with, you should be able to work your way through the wiring phase with a minimal of difficulty.

SECURITY

Security is required to relieve or mitigate an owner's or tenant's perception of risk related to threat(s). In establishing appropriate security, the threat(s) must be defined. Some uses have higher exposure than others. While all tenants have a fiduciary responsibility for life safety that are controlled by fire and building codes, many have additional needs based on the nature of the enterprise or the type of occupants. Ask your client:

- Are physical phenomena like earthquakes, floods and fires considered threats?
- Are there environmental threats like critical power outages, radiation, or toxic gasses?
- Might threats result from deliberate human actions like observation, infiltration, contamination, theft, shots, or physical attack?
- Are there inherent threats from accidents, health incidents, or equipment failure?
- What kind of security protection is needed for people, flora and fauna, valuable property, irreplaceable records, hazardous material, delicate or archival materials, proprietary secrets, sensitive equipment, or critical processes?
- If the tenant is a business, what hours do they operate?
- Who is present when open and when closed?
- Who is allowed access and to which areas?

- In addition to access control, is exit control required? The need for this on a mental health ward and in detention is obvious. It may be less obvious, but also necessary, in a museum, library, back-of-house, or large shift employer attempting to control inventory shrinkage, larceny and time theft.
- Are there standards from insurers or accreditation organizations that must be met? For example, some insurers require fire suppression in property areas, even when it is not otherwise required for life safety. Organizations like FDIC require specific levels of access security and fire ratings for banking operations that exceed the requirements of most building codes.
- From which direction(s) can these threats come?
- How should potential threats be monitored?
- What type of alarm or notification is required?

Answers to these questions may add considerable costs to an anticipated tenant build out and should be determined before a development agreement is penned. Addressing these can also be the source of added service for the design professional or the security specialist(s). These needs are so project-specific that a detailed discussion is not appropriate, but asking questions early in the development process will serve all parties well. Reponses to these considerations may be integrated or anticipated in the construction documents, even if security issues will be handled under a separate contract.

In new construction, the greater cost of deadlocking mortise hardware is offset by the greater security it offers than cylindrical or rim devices with the same function. It is, however, more difficult to retrofit this type of hardware into existing doors. Selectively using mortised hardware on exterior doors and tenant access doors is one way to offset its greater cost. In lower-end applications where security issues are moderate, cylindrical devices may be sufficient.

Clients with high security needs may require additional security measures:

- Highly sensitive alarms that sense pressure or temperature
- Establishing vehicular perimeters
- Vehicle barriers in landscape or building design
- Access controlled gates and vestibules
- Garage alarms
- Panic buttons
- Silent alarms

- Reinforcing wall construction with blast straps and liners
- Blowout panels and crumple zones into wall construction
- Safe rooms with blast resistant walls
- Filtered HVAC
- Emergency generators
- Munitions
- Medicines
- Communication
- First aid equipment

Rarely does a client have the need (and the funds) to support these measures, but governments, defense, embassies, and other high risk-high profit enterprises or individuals may.

Simple building hardening may require the selective use of bullet or blast resistant glass, glass block, and wall linings, such as where high volumes of cash, drugs, or liquor are handled. Security grilles are appropriate for pharmacies, jewelry stores, and similar occupancies. Even small businesses often need wall, floor, and building safes or vaults. Time locks and request to exit mechanisms may only be used in special circumstances.

SITE VISIT INSPECTIONS—TIP OFFS TO TROUBLED BUILDINGS

There are certain tip-offs to troubled buildings that experienced investors know how to look for. The signals can be subtle. For example, an apartment building that doesn't have light bulbs in the hall light fixtures could indicate a problem. It could be that the person responsible for routine maintenance is doing a poor job. More likely, it means that either someone is vandalizing the building or that tenants are stealing the light bulbs for use in their own apartments. Something as simple as light bulbs can tell you a lot about a building. See Figure 9.34.

Other little things to look for can include the condition of the common areas, such as hallways, lawns, and so forth. If the grounds of a building are littered, it's not a good sign. Halls that are untidy might mean very little, but it could mean that the residents of the building have little respect for the property. Floors that are clean and halls that are neat generally indicate a better building.

Are there fire extinguishers in all the proper places? Like the light bulbs, missing fire extinguishers can point to problems. Inspect the halls to see if fire prevention equipment is present. Look in the basement or mechanical rooms to confirm that all of the areas meet fire codes. If fire extinguishers are missing or if there is graffiti on the walls and equipment, you could be looking at a building that suffers ongoing maintenance problems.

Once you start touring individual apartments, pay attention to the kitchens and bathrooms. Do you see plungers sitting around the toilets? If you do, it might mean that the drains stop up frequently. Is the general condition of the apartments good? Sloppy apartments might mean that the tenants are not the type of residents you will want in your building. Is the kitchen range clean? A dirty range can indicate a lack of interest by tenants. Since the tenants are the ones who live in the building that may become yours, you will probably want the best tenants that you can find. If most of the apartments are kept poorly, you might decide to bring in new tenants. This can mean some downtime and lost income during the replacement process. Any little thing that you notice might be a hint of what's to come.

FIGURE 9.34 Observe how the building will be maintained by observing the owner or tenant in situ. Here, the owner approached maintenance as a last resort. A designer should not assume this behavior will change when he relocates. *Photo: Stephen Culbert*

Site Visit Inspections

Sizing up potential maintenance problems is part of a site visit. Not all average people have the ability to size up maintenance problems. But, many do. You don't have to be a licensed plumber to see some plumbing problems. Neither do you have to be a foundation contractor to spot water stains on basement walls. Many investors hire professional inspectors to look over properties before a purchase is made. This is good business, but there are some times when you might save yourself some money if you are paying close attention to detail during a site visit. In other words, if you learn some of what to look for on your own, you might be able to rule out buildings on your own, before calling in professional inspection teams. I'm not suggesting that you buy buildings without the use of qualified inspection services. But there is nothing wrong with removing properties from your consideration before paying professionals. Sometimes you may be able to do just this.

When you walk through a building, look at more than the number of bedrooms or the amount of retail square footage that a building has to offer. You shouldn't try to do everything all at once. Some investors attempt to do site visits and inspections all at the same time. This is often a mistake. You should make your first site visit to gain a general understanding of the property that you are thinking of buying. Concentrate on the features and benefits of the property. Don't worry about duct tape on plumbing traps or water stains on ceilings during your initial visit. Of course, if you see some type of glaring problem, make a note of it. But you should spend your first visit getting a feel for the property. Gut reactions are often very strong if you allow yourself to be open to them.

If you are thinking of buying a rental property, look at the property through the eyes of a prospective tenant. Is it the type of space that you would rent? Once you have checked a building out with your tenant's hat on, put on your landlord's hat and take another look. Landlords and tenants don't look at rental property through the same eyes. Once you have completed these two views, go back through the property with your focus on potential maintenance problems. Once you get the benefit of the three types of views, you will be in a better position to make a wise buying decision.

There are a number of things to look for when you are on your inspection duty. Here are a few examples:

- Look for water stains on basement walls and on ceilings.
- Check the cover plates on electrical outlets and switches.
- If you notice black spots on the plates it may indicate electrical problems.

fastfacts

When you walk through a building, look at more than the number of bedrooms or the amount of retail square footage that it has to offer. You shouldn't try to do everything all at once. Some investors attempt to do site visits and inspections all at the same time. This is often a mistake.

- Fill up sinks and lavatories and then let them drain.
- Check plumbing faucets to see if any of them are leaking.
- Run showers to see if they drain okay.
- Fill up bathtubs and release the water to see how they drain.
- Flush toilets and see if the bowl empties well.
- Inspect the flooring in buildings to see if it's in good repair.
- Open and close doors to see if they fit well and lock as they should.
- Turn on lights to see if they all work. Find the electrical service and inspect it.
- If the building is old and has a fuse box, look for spare fuses. Too many spare fuses could indicate electrical problems.
- Look on cement floors to see if there are any stains from water leaks.
- Open and close windows to see that they function properly.
- Basically, go through every room of every building and inspect all that you have the ability to evaluate.

Take notes of your findings. If the building passes your test, then you should call in professional inspectors to look for trouble that you may have missed.

STRUCTURAL PROBLEMS

Structural problems can be difficult to locate and very expensive to repair. Buying a building that suffers from structural problems can be all it takes to ruin an investor's career. Most investors are not qualified to identify a lot of structural problems. Refer to Figure 9.35. This is why you should hire a professional inspection team to go over every building that you are thinking of buying. It's very possible that you might spot some structural problems on your own, but don't count on your own ability to make sure a building is not subject to expensive structural problems.

If you are going to attempt to look for structural problems on your own, you will need a few things. Crawling under a building might be required when looking for a structural problem. Getting into attics is another step that is required when searching for structural problems. A pair of coveralls and a flashlight should be part of your inspection kit. Gloves are a good idea, too. Additionally, a screwdriver and some other basic tools are helpful. If you act as your own inspector, you may be looking for everything from termite damage to roof leaks.

This is not a property inspection book, and there is not enough room here to go into great detail, but there is room for a few tips. Start your inspection in the basement or crawlspace. Use your screwdriver to probe sills and joists. This can tell you if the structural members have rotted or been damaged by wood-investing insects. Look at the joists to see if they

FIGURE 9.35 The obvious defect in this parapet portends poorly for what the bearing walls will reveal. Note the star Dutchman. This is another sign that the structure is in trouble. *Photo: Stephen Culbert*

are peppered with little holes. If they are, it probably means that powder-post beetles have been feasting on them. Look for mud tunnels on the foundation walls. Existence of such tunnels usually means termites are present.

Inspect the subflooring from below. If it's black, there is probably a water leak somewhere above. Do you see any cracks in the foundation? Is there a lot of mold or fungi under the floor? This indicates a moisture problem. Did you notice any peeling paint on the exterior of the building? Moisture problems can cause paint to peel. Do a visual inspection of all support timbers. Are any of them bowed? If so, there's a problem.

When you are finished under a building, go to the attic. Look to see if there is any sign of water damage in the roof sheathing. Beware of any small sawdust piles on the attic floor. This is a sign of wood-infesting insects and may mean that the building will have to be covered with a special type of tent and fumigated. Are the rafters or trusses in good shape? How is the insulation in the attic? Do you see any sagging? Be careful when in attics because stepping in the wrong spot can cause you to crash through a ceiling. All in all, you should probably leave structural inspections up to the experts.

NEGOTIATING POWER

If you find problems with a building, you can use the deficiencies to your advantage. The problems give you reason to offer a lower purchase price. Sellers will sometimes accept a lower price just because one is offered. However, the power of offering a lower price is enhanced when you can provide logical reasons for your offer. Most sellers are willing to be reasonable about repairs that are needed, assuming that the need for the work was not taken into consideration when a price was put on the property.

Since any type of defect might be valuable in lowering a price, you should keep a detailed list of every complaint that you or your inspectors turn up. Missing light bulbs is hardly worth using as a negotiating tool, but the lack of a fire escape or cracks in a paved parking lot could well be worth a considerable price reduction. In some cases, the price break you get will be offset by the actual cost of repairs. But, some conditions that are used as pricing prods may not have to be fixed or may be something that you can fix yourself. This can result in having more money in your pocket, or at least less money tacked onto a mortgage.

Another good reason for documenting every item that you find to be unsatisfactory is that the process will help you to evaluate a building for

> If you find problems with a building, you can use the deficiencies to your advantage. The problems give you reason to offer a lower purchase price. Sellers will sometimes accept a lower price just because one is offered. However, the power of offering a lower price is enhanced when you can provide logical reasons for your offer.

purchase. If you have one building that has a four-page list of problems and another similar building that has no problems, you will probably be able to make a quick decision on which building to act on first. Time spent looking buildings over closely is not wasted. The effort can save you thousands of dollars. Take the time to inspect all potential purchases closely and record your findings. This is a good habit to get into, and you are much more likely to be a successful investor when you follow this procedure.

CHAPTER 10

IDENTIFYING COST EFFECTIVE IMPROVEMENTS AND BASIC AESTHETIC APPROACHES

OVERVIEW

Although the decision to renovate an existing building for a new use is not entirely economic, a potential property developer has to answer the question, " Is it worth it?" With this thought in mind, one must consider a myriad of questions. One might first look at the nature of the potential purchaser/ lessee. Conversions tend to attract businesses and other enterprises that need a break on the cost of their real estate expenditures. This is hardly true of every project, but the location combined with the level of upgrade the developer is willing to fund will affect the amount of rent the property will eventually command. At the low end of the conversion market, developers might seek only to make the space weathertight and maintenance legal for the new occupancy. At the high end of the market, the building might be carefully preserved with careful integration of modern systems, or receive an overhaul so complete as to make the original use obscure. The budget necessarily affects the degree of change that can be designed and executed. Aesthetics and budgets are factors in any design project, so what makes renovation design issues any different?

> **fast**facts
>
> Conversions tend to attract businesses and other enterprises that need a break on the cost of their real estate expenditures.

DESIGN CONSIDERATIONS

When developing "naked land", the building can be almost anything. Design considerations may include the natural environment such as weather, topography, orientation, exposure, and views. Considerations of the manmade environment include existing streets, neighboring buildings and structures, site access points, and utility locations. Legal issues such as code requirements, zoning requirements, and operations limitations are important. Programmatic concepts are scope, scale, minimum clearances and accommodations, and spaces shaped for special purposes. In renovation, aesthetically, there is at least one more factor. The existing site improvements are defined dominantly, in most cases, by the building. Existing elements can be a foil that a designer works with and uses as features and celebrations within his design. Existing elements can also be constraints he strives to mitigate. Most renovation projects will have some elements of both. Usually the budget is not deep enough to address both to the full level that one might prefer in ideal circumstances. Renovations are a messy business, especially if there is a need to be highly selective in the degree of demolition. Renovations are also interesting because buildings that are at the same time both old and new can inform the cultural consciousness and aesthetic experiences of those who inhabit them. Budget and attitude of the parties funding the project will determine in large part what is possible aesthetically and spatially.

The clients' experience and resources in other construction projects will be key in their understanding of how far their budget can actually go towards reaching their strategic aims. There is a vast difference in the legal and programmatic requirements for large-scale projects relative to residential and light commercial projects. Often experience at this scale, while helpful to a general understanding, is not sufficient to make informed decisions at a larger scale. Renovation offers twists that complicate the basic model of new construction, even in larger scale projects.

SCOPE OF PROGRAM

One must consider what the future of the building will be when determining if renovation for change-of-use is feasible. One also has to consider the starting point. How drastic is the change-in-use from the original use? If it's incremental, more of the same budget may be allocated to beauty, function, and comfort. If it's a significant leap, more of the budget may be needed just to make structural and systems alterations necessary to meet the basic program. Generally, incremental changes will not require significant amounts of effort in resizing structural bays, bringing in new utility services or trunks, or adding vertical circulation structures.

The condition of the existing facility, property acquisition costs, and the cost of relocating existing operations are the other factors that may eat up project budget that might be devoted to program aesthetics before design has progressed. With that said, the designer needs to understand the priorities of the owner and maximize the impact of the elements most important to him.

> One must consider what the future of the building will be when determining if renovation for change-of-use is feasible. One also has to consider the starting point. How drastic is the change-in-use from the original use?

Commodity Architecture

Commodity architecture leaves minimal room for innovations and image-driven aesthetic elements. If a client perceives design services as a commodity, the opportunity to create uniqueness will almost necessarily suffer. Sometimes clients are willing to have their understanding of what design services can do for their enterprise broadened, sometimes the budget for the services and their view of what they want has been locked in long before they ever interview the designers. Good designers can do a lot with spatial organization and relationships, incorporating existing features, and making utilitarian elements beautiful, or at least pleasant. Good designers with a larger design budget can simply do more for the same program, even if the construction budget remains more or less fixed. Putting additional money into design can fund the effort it takes to research elements and detail solutions that will save money and maximize the use of the construction dollar. Investing in design and pre-design, like investing in site selection and project evaluation, can make or break the success of a project, especially if it is speculative or designed for leasing.

Designing for Client Satisfaction

Designing for client satisfaction (or tenant enticement) is not always an aesthetic issue. If the client is one person, identifying priorities is a simpler

fastfacts

Commodity architecture leaves minimal room for innovations and image-driven aesthetic elements. If a client perceives design services as a commodity, the opportunity to create uniqueness will almost necessarily suffer.

matter than when the client is defined as a consensus body, a group of unequally weighted partners, or where operations, marketing, and budget agendas at the client level are in conflict. With these larger groups, discerning which individuals must be greatly satisfied and which individuals must be somewhat satisfied will vary according to why the owner is seeking to execute a project in the first place and the relative positions of the decision makers in the power structure of the client's entity. From a practice point of view, if the client has a project point person, for example, a facilities manager or an operations manager, satisfying this person may be as important as satisfying the CEO if the designer sees the opportunity for ongoing or repeat work.

The appeal and value of specific improvements will be weighted by clients differently, but let's look at personality issues combined with the nature of enterprise in a very simplified way to understand how these affect the client's thought process. While nearly every project is a blend of these drivers, and has spaces or elements within them that fit each of these models, generalizing about the most essential aspect can be crucial in establishing design development priorities.

Visual image and prestige-driven clients are chiefly concerned with how their enterprise is esteemed externally and how their peers, clients, and community personally view them. Project types that might fall into this category include:

- Government centers
- Municipal visitors' centers

Investing in design and pre-design, like investing in site selection and project evaluation, can make or break the success of a project, especially if it is speculative or designed for leasing.

- Corporate headquarters
- Research centers
- Financial institutions
- Product marketing centers
- Professional design services for clients in this category
- High-end personal and corporate legal services
- Luxury residences
- Tourist sites that involve chiefly historic or government features
- Higher education facilities with significant endowments or resources

Most clients of this type want to project solid and respectable images that display their success and pride. Clients of this type might be drawn towards traditional and classic design elements and proportions. They will prefer durable, better than average finishes and appointments, and technology, equipment to the extent their resources permit. Features and trim should be most evident in public areas of the design. Entrances, public circulation, showrooms, conference rooms, and executive offices are the best places to focus the design opportunities, special features and highest level of finish materials and trim. Clients like these may leverage the project's finances, and generally have a strong ability to financially execute the project. However designers should be prepared to deal a dose of reality to wannabe's and pretenders.

Visual image and prestige-driven clients are chiefly concerned with how their enterprise is esteemed externally and how their peers, clients, and community personally view them.

Practicality and budget-driven clients highly value space that functions to serve their core enterprise and essential needs. They may reject appearances of luxury or high image. Project types are usually places where the billable activities of the enterprise are actually executed, support services for core enterprises like fulfillment centers and billing services. Project types include:

- Public utilities
- Distribution businesses
- Manufacturing and assembly

- Clinics
- Government branch offices
- Corrections sites
- Municipal courts
- General and criminal legal services
- Middle and low-end commercial retail and development
- Industrial core business enterprises
- Insurance claims processing centers
- Finance centers
- Testing laboratories
- Strategic planning and logistics operations
- Military installations
- Public and private schools with limited resources
- Low and middle income residential projects
- Interposal passenger transportation station

These types of projects often require a high degree of separation and organization of different activities and systems. Efficient process flow and layout are the most essential elements in plan organization. Incorporation of passive environmental systems and off-peak energy storage, energy efficient equipment, and fixtures will be attractive to many of these clients. Durability and minimizing maintenance costs are usually the drivers in selecting finishes and enclosure materials. Many of these projects have public funding or resources of an established corporation or utility. Clients generally have the financial ability to execute these projects, however when public funds are involved, the likelihood of remonstrance or the limits of bonding may have significant impact on prioritizing the elements in the scope and level of construction quality.

Environmentally conscious and comfort-driven projects and clients seek to make nurturing environments where users feel as relaxed and comfortable as possible. Such enterprises might include:

Practicality and budget-driven clients highly value space that functions to serve their core enterprise and essential needs. They may reject appearances of luxury or high image.

- Physicians' offices
- Psychological services
- Family support centers
- Physical and occupational rehabilitation centers
- Nursing homes
- Sanitariums
- Assisted living
- Child care
- Houses of worship
- Neighborhood club facilities
- Training centers
- Conference centers
- Think tanks
- Recycling businesses
- Corporations and organizations with green agendas
- High tech manufacturing, research, or assembly
- Recreation and participatory sports centers
- Casual and family restaurants
- Neighborhood pubs
- Family entertainment venues
- Hotels targeted for tourists and business travelers
- Airports and intermodal passenger transportation hubs
- Retail aimed at the middle-market
- Groceries and sundries
- Administrative support offices
- Tourist attractions that chiefly involve enjoyment of, or interaction with, natural features
- Middle and upper income residential projects

Clients like these will focus the project's resources on enhancing comfort, usability, and conveniences. While finishes and furnishings may need to be durable and cleanable, they also need to be inviting, relaxing, and comfortable. Skylights, windows, passive environmental controls, and appropriate incorporation of systems and communications technology will likely be attractive to this type of client. Because many of these enterprises

Environmentally conscious and comfort-driven projects and clients seek to make nurturing environments where users feel as relaxed and comfortable as possible.

exist on government or institutional support, the ability and schedule of funds available to the client to financially execute his plans should be well understood and considered by designers in planning and contracting.

Sensually driven clients' focus is how the users feel and seek to create places where users seek to be stimulated. These enterprises and their leadership tend to follow or initiate trends in marketing and entertainment and spatial use. They are innovators and are early adopters of technological developments:

- Merchandising centers
- Convention centers
- Research & development centers
- High tech businesses
- Software developers
- Live entertainment venues
- Cinemas
- Contemporary museums
- Arts centers
- Spas, destination resorts, luxury travel accommodations
- High style retail and personal services
- Luxury residences
- Contemporary galleries
- Nightclubs

The external architecture will be used to initially sell the activities housed; the internal architecture will affect client retention. Unusual images, dramatic shapes, surfaces and juxtapositions, and adaptive reuse of exiting objects may inspire such decision makers. Reflective surfaces, transparent and translucent partitions, irregularly shaped spaces, high texture surfaces, water in fountains or reflecting pools, focused and point light sources, active and "smart" environmental systems controls, and incorporation of cutting edge communications technology will influence these client types. Environmental acoustics may be more important with this client type than any other. Positive aromas or active odor elimination can also factor into design solutions. Entrances, public circulation, showrooms, conference rooms, dining rooms, auditoriums, and hospitality guestrooms are excellent places to focus the special features of the design. A high level of finish will be required in all public spaces. Because of their trendy and fashion-driven nature, businesses like these may have a high volatility in their ability to pay. (Charles J. Clarke III, "Lambs, Tigers And Bulls-Oh My! Using The Bolt System To Develop True Customization For Today's Homeowners", *Design Build Business*, Cygnus Business Media, Ft. Atkinson, WI, Vol. 68, No. 4, April 2003, pp. 30-33)

Understanding the nature of the client and the priorities for the facility will determine the success of the designer in identifying appropriate design questions and in prioritizing the design responses to the questions. The questions defined, answered, and prioritized will inform the design process.

> Sensually-driven clients' focus is how the users feel and seek to create places where users seek to be stimulated. These enterprises and their leadership tend to follow or initiate trends in marketing and entertainment and spatial use.

What Are The Appropriate Questions?

When the owner owns the subject building already, he may ask, what is the useful remaining life span of the building if alterations are not done? Is there a continued need for the building? Is the need based on the use for which it was built originally, or is there a new need? How can it be used efficiently? To what degree will renovation of the existing building disrupt its existing occupants? These are also very proper questions for the design firm to consider when making recommendations to an owner on how to proceed in satisfying their program needs.

Contract document development issues such as: How critical is occupancy by a given date? How much lost revenue can be attributed to each day of lost use or production? What time period is available for the construction? Will seasonal factors, such as the weather, adversely affect the ability to complete the work? Will working within an existing shell speed construction and reduce finance costs? Will working within an existing shell allow project completion to take place during cold winter months and for a savings to the project? All factor into answering the essential questions:

What will it cost to renovate the building versus the cost to tear it down and build a new structure on the same site?

How does that compare with building a new structure on an alternate site where demolition is not required and infrastructure is available?

IS RENOVATION WORTH THE TIME, EXPENSE, AND RISK FOR THE ADVANTAGES IT MIGHT OFFER?

Subordinate, but important, specific questions that inform the answers to these questions are also very important. Environmentally, how much energy would be required to refurbish the new building compared to building a new structure? This sort of question is relevant when the owner has an interest in demonstrating environmental or social responsibility to the community, particularly with ordinances or regulations that require it. Energy use, on the other hand, is an economic issue to the owner. So even if an owner is not concerned about depletion of natural resources, the commercial availability of new energy sources is an economic incentive to reduce the energy costs associated with the operation and maintenance of his property. Any system that has a payback is economically worth considering. Alternative sources of energy should be evaluated even where there's an existing system. To what extent is improvement required to off-site amenities and utilities in order to support the proposed new use?

There needs to be an analysis of existing infrastructure available to support the new use of the building:

- Do sewers need to be enlarged or extended?
- Do new services for water, electricity, gas, and steam need to be brought to the existing structure? This includes utilities, sewers, parking, mass transportation, road access, and available related services.
- Will existing roads support the traffic generated by the new use? Most importantly, will it bear the costs of improvements?
- Can costs for these improvements be borne by taxpayers, redevelopment agencies, or utilities, instead of directly by the owner or his tenants?

Because questions like these are not necessarily quantifiable in and of themselves, it can be useful to implement a system of weighted analysis. An issue as important as project feasibility or site selection warrants the use of such a system. On small projects, only the repair/replacement of major building systems would be appropriate objects of similar analysis. Figure 10.1 is a form designed to aid in selection between material choices that serve the same purpose. It can easily be adapted to make decisions between features of roughly equal construction value by listing the owner's priorities in rank order, assigning each priority a relative value. For example, Goal 10 is the prime driver, Goal 7 is essential to the operation, and Goal 2 would be nice to achieve also. This is shown as a spreadsheet version that the user can quickly make on Table 10.1. Then the designer can assign each competing feature a value according to how well it meets each priority. Multiplying the values in the array for priority by the values for feature qualities, and then summing the products will yield weighted value for each competing feature.

Selection Criteria to Meet									
	Most important criteria					**Least important criteria**			
	Criteria	initial cost	durability	maintenance cost	in-service time	warranty	aesthetics	**Score**	
	Criteria Value: VALUE 10-1 for degree to which the criterion is valued by the owner for the subject product class	10	9	7	6	4	2	Score Value: (sumproduct: criteria value array, product performance array for each option)	
Product Option									
A		10	7	7	8	10	7	314	**Best score**
B		10	7	7	6	10	9	306	Medium score
C		8	9	8	6	10	4	301	Worst score
	Product Value: VALUE 10-1 for degree to which the product option meets the criterion above								
An owner with a different set of priorities, might rate the same 3 products with a different outcome.									
	Criteria Value: VALUE 10-1 for degree to which the criterion is valued by the owner for the subject product class	3	4	6	8	9	10	Score Value: (sumproduct: criteria value array, product performance array for each option)	
Product Option	Product Value: VALUE 10-1 for degree to which the product option meets the criterion above								
A		10	7	7	8	10	7	324	Medium score
B		10	7	7	6	10	9	**328**	**Best score**
C		8	9	8	6	10	4	286	Worst score

FIGURE 10.1 System and material comparison method

TABLE 10.1 Weighted evaluation master form. *Courtesy: Luther Mock*

Weighted Evaluation

Question ______________________

Criteria
Criteria Scoring Matrix

How Important?
4 - Major Prefere
3 - Medium Prefe
2 - Minor Prefere
1 - Letter/Letter
No Preference, E
Scored One Poin

A.
B.
C.
D.
E.
F.
G.

	G.	F.	E.	D.	C.	B.	A
Raw Score							
Weight of Importance (0-10)							

Alternative
Analysis Matrix

1.	0	0	0	0	0	0	
2.	0	0	0	0	0	0	
3.	0	0	0	0	0	0	
4.	0	0	0	0	0	0	

A PROJECT PLAN

A project, like a business, should have a plan. Here are the key elements that should be included in a business plan:

- Write an executive summary outlining fundamental goals and objectives for the enterprise. (Stick to these.)

fastfacts

So even if an owner is not concerned about depletion of natural resources, the commercial availability of new energy sources is an economic incentive to reduce the energy costs associated with the operation and maintenance of his property.

- Provide a brief outline of how the company began.
- Clearly state the company's goals, both strategic and fiscal.
- Include biographies of the management team, demonstrating their qualifications for the role they will have in the enterprise.
- Show the service or product plan to be offered.
- Identify market potential for the service or product.
- Demonstrate the marketing strategy.
- Detail the plan showing the method designed to fulfill the expected demand.
- Make a three- to five-year financial projection.
- Develop an exit strategy, in case plans don't work out on a timely basis.
- Identify and use benchmarks to know when to bail out.
- Determine the amount of start-up capital required.
- Establish a contingency or margin.

You do need to identify potential sources of capital. At regular intervals, revisit the plan and update each key element as required.

ESTABLISHING THE BUDGET

Budgeting is a process that will be revisited at regular intervals at each stage of project development. As the design scope becomes more defined and as unknowns are uncovered and resolved during construction, the budget will be continuously adjusted. The process is nearly the same at each phase, although data that are more specific will be available at each level of definition in the form of cost estimates, bid documents, and contractors' proposals.

Estimating Project Costs

Each estimate of project costs must include known hard costs and soft costs. Hard costs include:

- Land acquisition costs
- Property acquisition costs
- Purchase of property rights or easements from adjoining property owners
- Construction costs for labor, materials, mobilization, equipment, utilities permits, and testing
- The contractor's soft costs including overhead, profit, bonding costs, insurance, and security
- Building demolition
- Selective demolition
- Site preparation
- Landscaping

Hard costs also might also include:

- Furnishings and selected loose equipment, although usually an owner will prefer to pay for these separately because they depreciate at a faster rate. It is generally unwise to finance with a building loan or bond because interest on the basic cost of these items will continue to be paid after the useful service life has been exhausted.
- Hazardous materials abatement, if not transferable in total to other parties
- Site remediation, if not transferable in total to other parties
- The cost to provide and maintain off-site amenities, for example, parking or tenant storage, if they are not provided on the site

Soft costs include:

- Site selection and property evaluation costs
- Real estate options
- Service and title fees for land and property acquisition
- Project promotions and advertising
- Owner's insurance
- Legal counsel

- Owner's project and contract administration
- Design and construction services
- Finance application fees, points, closing costs, recording fees, and title search fees
- Administrative review fees

Other costs the owner/developer will be considering include life cycle costs and operations costs if he plans to hold the property for any length of time.

Life cycle costs include:

- Building maintenance costs for cleaning, adjusting, servicing, and repairing building elements intended to continue in service for the life of the building
- Grounds maintenance costs for cleaning, adjusting, servicing, and repairing hardscape elements and costs to maintain plant materials and lawns
- System replacement costs for any essential building element that wears out before the life cycle
- Utility costs for ongoing use of building systems

The owner must also evaluate the expense potential of the building through operations costs:

- Property management, leasing, and promotions costs
- Loss recovery costs on vacated leases
- Losses on unleased or unused space
- Trash and waste removal

CONTROLLING PROJECT COSTS

A large gap exists between the costs of renovation and the financial resources available to many projects. Few lenders will permit sweat equity, however some neighborhood redevelopment corporations do. Some lenders will permit loans based on phased improvements grouped in bid packages.

The first package will contain the elements required to establish a salable property. The work might include removal of hazardous material from the site and basic structural stabilization. It will also include measures required to keep the building watertight, at least in the short-term. This may include replacing or restoring existing windows and doors or the roof. Even at this stage of development, small decisions should be considered in light of long-range plans for the property. For example, consider the patching techniques in Figure 10.2.

fastfacts

A large gap exists between the costs of renovation and the financial resources available to many projects. Few lenders will permit sweat equity, however some neighborhood redevelopment corporations do.

FIGURE 10.2 Two patching techniques, toothed masonry and concrete grout infill, are visible at joist pockets on this former party wall. If the material will be exposed to weather and view, the former is the preferred technique. If the wall will be covered with another material or an addition with new finishes, the latter is not unreasonable. *Photo: Stephen Culbert*

The next step may be gutting of clearly obsolete elements, such as antiquated building systems, finishes, and perhaps nonbearing partitions. See Figure 10.3 and Figure 10.4. It may also include establishing basic building infrastructure. In a potentially multi-tenant building, the developer will establishing heating and cooling plant location(s), vertical shafts, and trunk lines. Electrical service will be assessed and location for additional service set aside, if additional needs are anticipated. Water and sewer connections will be similarly assessed and chases provided. Standpipes and sprinkler mains may be run. Loading docks and elevators may be repaired or replaced.

Rehabilitation of existing stairs and exit systems to code compliance is the next step. Mezzanine floor levels may be added, but probably not subdivided at this phase. Corridors, vestibules, and communications closets may or may not be incorporated before tenants have signed. Sometimes transfer of ownership occurs after phase two or three.

Next, facelift elements will be added to the exterior and to common areas inside. Marquee signs or awnings may be added to demonstrate that a renovation is taking place. Building accessible entrance ramps and oth-

FIGURE 10.3 The owner gutted the interior of this building in order to make it more attractive for resale. It is presently being converted to a chain hotel. *Photo: Stephen Culbert*

FIGURE 10.4 Utility entrance is near the downspout. Exposed conduit and old style insulators should be eliminated. Water has migrated from the roof edge into the soffit materials and deterioration has begun. *Photo: Stephen Culbert*

er required elements to accommodate patrons under the American Disabilities Association (ADA) will be incorporated. Often, with an existing structure, the site is grandfathered and barriers will not be removed until new work is triggered by repairs or demonstrated need. Restoration of significant features in common areas and on the exterior may be done to increase marketability, or it may be deferred until time for the tenant build-out. Redefining existing openings, as in Figure 10.5 is one cost effective way to use an existing shell to its best advantage.

Lastly, tenant space will be built-out to suit the tenant's budget and program specifications. Building signs or other exterior identity for tenants will be added, if agreed. Restoration or protection of significant features in tenant spaces will be addressed at this phase per the tenant agreement.

This scenario is based on speculative development. It varies only when the tenant's build-out uses their own forces and designers, where there is a single tenant, or when the owner acts as his own developer and tenant. In these cases, development may be a little more expeditious if the timed delivery of project funds permits.

In general, before marketing to tenants, the developer should do the least renovation possible to still sell (lease) the space because most tenants will want to build to suit. Incorrect assessment of the market potential for a given use is less likely the cause of market failure than ineffective cost control. According to developer Robert Silverman of Atlanta, "Most failures have resulted from underpricing the cost of construction and inadequate contingency funds, contractors who are inexperienced in renovation, adaptive use, and restoration." (William Hudnut III, " Promoting Reuse", *Urban Land*, November/December 1999)

To control development costs, tenant agreements must be very specific in quantifying the project scope to include allowances and unit costs for incremental changes. There should be strict limits on the number and schedule of tenant reviews and revisions to design documents. Changes made late in the design/ construction process or those that exceed building standard materials and quantities per square foot should cost more than early stage revisions.

To appeal to lenders in renovation of any type, there are many uncertainties in establishing predictable construction costs. These can be

FIGURE 10.5 Windows replaced loading doors, improving the exterior image of this building as well as enhancing the commercial function within. Re-using the existing opening saved money by taking advantage of an existing lintel. *Photo: Stephen Culbert*

overcome with careful cost estimation and the elimination of as many unknowns as possible. Obtaining financing will be aided significantly by the attainment of a prospective purchaser agreement and leases with known stable businesses. Establishing a project scope and sets of solutions that meet construction budgets is critical. Identifying probable unknowns early will allow for some budgeting of these items. Using an appropriate contingency in budgeting will further alleviate the burden that unknowns pose. Requiring unit prices for items likely to be of unknown value levels provides the fairest pricing when they are encountered as work progresses.

For large cost items valued at more than 5% of the budget, bids can be placed with alternates, especially if the alternative can be expressed or enumerated succinctly without additional drawings. Where an alternative requires extensive documentation or alternate design, the professional should establish and communicate the cost of designing and documenting the alternative prior to incorporating it into the project.

If public bidding does not apply, voluntary alternates can be included with a bidder's proposal. These can take two forms, either spelled out in the bid documents or spelled out by the bidder. The basis of award, ethically, should be the base (required) bid, unless the bidding conditions stipulate that required alternates will be considered. The basis of consideration may have a prioritization, or the owner may elect any or all alternates. The method will depend on the competitiveness of the bid environment and the owner's reason for considering the alternatives. Where public bidding rules do apply, if voluntary or mandatory alternates are used, they must be directly stated in the documents. The base bid plus the mandatory alternates must be the basis of contractor selection unless otherwise permitted by state law. If established in the bid conditions, the owner may elect to accept any, all, or none of the mandatory alternates. If voluntary alternates are accepted, this is done after selection. Some jurisdictions prohibit the use of voluntary alternatives.

Hidden Cost Factors

Costs that won't show up on the project estimate include those that result from the basic approach to the project. They include project phasing, contract selection methods, project delivery methods, and managing risk.

Project Phasing Cost Implications

Project phasing has cost implications. The more phases and the longer the construction period, the higher the construction cost will be and the higher the cost of design services. This is because the administrative and mobilization costs are duplicated in each phase. Inflation also will contribute to costs. Multiple phases may be required because of the funding distribution schedule, bond size, ability to raise funds over time, delivery time issues, ongoing use of existing facilities, and seasonal use of premises. Phasing work may allow source principal in funding accounts to accrue to meet actual project goals, provided the rate of return on the escrow account exceeds the rate of inflation in the construction industry and escrowed funds don't have to be spent in the time period when they are allocated. In this scenario, the extended time value of the principal money may work to the developer's advantage. Many public funding scenarios now prohibit this maneuver.

Selection and Delivery Methods as a Source of Savings

Implementing the appropriate method of contractor selection, design team selection, and project delivery method can be a source of savings. "When design firms are forced to compete for the lowest project cost, creativity is stifled. An application, design or concept that may save more money over time is abandoned because the initial cost is slightly higher. Qualification Based Selection allows owners to review the best applicable project solution without the price factor." (Daniel R. Wolf P.E. , "Qualification Based Selection", http://www.spicergroup.com/principle.htm). Because the proposals design professionals might make for their services may differ greatly in scope and services, qualifications-based selection is more appropriate during the design phase, unless the program is highly defined and stipulated to all responders. Rarely is it cost effective for most owners to do this, since a great deal of the design and planning effort in a project is expended in the pre-design phase. Sophisticated owners, like the military services, have sufficient internal staff, institutional design standards, and experience with multiple projects of similar scale and scope to execute the required effort to prepare an RFP (request for proposal) that puts design teams on a level playing field. But for most projects, the amount of time an engineer or architect needs to create project plans and specifications for the contractor can only be estimated based on the scope articulated

> **Project phasing has cost implications. The more phases and the longer the construction period, the higher the construction cost will be and the higher the cost of design services.**

and known site conditions. Adjustments in priorities, preferences, scope, and the revelation of unknown conditions make it challenging to provide a fixed project price before design commences. Many professionals will sell their services incrementally as each phase of the design project draws to a close. If price of services is the sole basis of professional selection, one might consider this question, "Would you feel comfortable driving over the Mackinaw Bridge if you knew it was designed based on the lowest price as opposed to the qualifications of the designing engineer?" After all, engineering is actually only a small percent of the total project cost. (Wolf)

In contractor selection, since there are bid documents, the playing field has been leveled. In a private bid situation, it is worthwhile to invite bidders based on their pre-qualifications. These should demonstrate experience in several projects of similar scale, estimated cost, complexity, building type, construction type, and project delivery method. This will tend to mitigate some of the negatives of open bidding. This method of pricing will keep contractors competitive, but also reduce the amount of competition to knowable odds, making it an attractive place to focus their bidding efforts. If there are too many bidders, some contractors won't waste their time, since the odds of success are low. Negotiated Contracts or Qualification Based Selection in contracting can be worthwhile if the project has a high degree of specialization (hospitals, labs, preservation).

Time and Materials

Time and materials, also known as cost plus fee, is a contracting arrangement that is suitable for projects where there are a great number of unknowns, either in the renovated property itself or within the owner's decision making process. This allows work to commence on the basic design knowing there will likely be significant changes. In this situation, the owner is willing to accept some risk for the timing of his decisions and

fastfacts

Time and materials, also known as cost plus fee, is a contracting arrangement that is suitable for projects where there are a great number of unknowns, either in the renovated property itself or within the owner's decision making process.

the amount of discovery-based issues that might be encountered. When the source of unknown quantities is understood and predictable, unit price contracts can be an effective way to go. This is the form of contracting most often used on civil engineering projects and is an excellent choice for site development, remediation, abatement, and buildings demolitions contracts, especially when this work is contracted separately.

DESIGN-BUILD AND TRADITIONAL DESIGN DELIVERY METHODS

Traditionally, projects are designed, then bid, and then built. This is the most common form of design delivery, also known as design-bid-build. This approach allows the design to be fully developed and periodically reviewed by the owner before bidding and construction begins. A known design with readily quantifiable elements becomes the tool for pricing. This design delivery formula is ideally suited to fixed price contracts regardless of the method of contractor selection.

Design/Build

Design/build has been used successfully with simple, non-custom project types such as storage buildings, or to bid packages that represent simply defined units of work like building demolition or envelope upgrades, which may proceed without tenant/owner input after the price is agreed. It has also been used with varied success to deliver very large complex projects that can be defined in phased bid packages. Often these will involve building purposes and uses that are likely to be fixed over the life of the building. On projects of such scale it is a good idea to involve a construction manager (usually a contractor) and a program manager (usually a design professional). What the owner may give up in the ability to fine-tune the design of the spaces, he gains in savings by reducing the length of construction loans and a sooner start-up for his money-generating operations associated with use of the project.

Maintaining the schedule can be the greatest challenge to the design/build contract. Early in the design process, the team must identify long lead items early and the date by which they must be ordered. They must coordinate this information with the shop drawing and submittal schedule. Allow sufficient time to process items that require additional permits, inspections, or approvals (like HVAC equipment, electrical meters and transformers, elevators). During peak building periods, standard building materials like steel, brick, and gypsum board can be in short supply. Sometimes an owner can lock in a manufacturing order with a pre-selected material and intent to purchase letter. Specialty non-stock material, equipment, or finishes always adds time to the minimum. When a fast track is essential, go with standard units and finishes wherever practical. When a custom finish or unit is critical, call the manufacturer to establish adequate lead-time and allow for it in the construction schedule.

> **Maintaining the schedule can be the greatest challenge to the design-build contract. Early in the design process, the team must identify long lead items early and the date by which they must be ordered.**

The advantage of this delivery system, for the owner, is that it can compress the timeline for completing a project. Some design activities can overlap construction activities. In a Guaranteed Maximum Price (GMP or at risk) contract, the owner knows in advance what the costs of the project will be for him. He should still budget a reserve if he plans to initiate any fine-tuning of the program or design, or if the site or structures have any unknowns that may not be uncovered until demolition or construction has commenced.

Design/build is not recommended for contracts involving a high degree of selectivity or variability. Basic site work, service connections, demolition, and envelope upgrades may be well suited to this delivery method. In some cases, even these may be too much. Such work might include individualized space definitions, configurations, and finish requirements. Design-build GMP contracts should be used only to deliver projects requiring complex systems and relationships or projects where discovery, selectivity, or extensive owner/tenant feedback are required to define the scope. In these cases it may require much greater pre-design effort, including program definition and site/building evaluation, before proceeding to the design phase. It may also be worth configuring a design and construction team experienced in the particular building type being delivered.

In return for the advantages of a fixed price and schedule, the owner gives up the contractual relationship with the design team and interpretive control over the quality, materials, and methods beyond the level of description stipulated to define the contract scope and price. Design direction to the design team will come through the contractor, even if the team is included in owner meetings. The owner must be comfortable with this level of input and service. Each party should be clear on the differences in the roles and relationships of the contract.

Since the design team has a contract with the contractor, their ability to interpret the contract beyond their legal fiduciary responsibility may be compromised. The designers always hold a fiduciary responsibility to the owner and public to protect them through application of minimum design standards required by codes. Construction services by the design team may be limited beyond what is customary. The architect may not directly hire consultants. They may hold separate contracts with the contractor. If the architect is responsible for interdisciplinary co-ordination, this arrangement is ill-advised for the architect.

OBTAINING FAIR PRICING ON CHANGES IN SCOPE

There are several methods an owner or owner's representative or design professional can use to assure that the contractor offers fair pricing when additional work is requested or work is deleted from the contract to keep the budget intact.

First, all parties should establish a fair and reasonable attitude from the beginning.

Good communications, and always through the design professional as conduit, will keep everyone in the loop and identify cost and time issues as they arise. Some call this attitude partnering, but generally, it's just business habit that is likely to result in repeat projects and referrals. The conditions of the contract can identify a specific method for evaluating proposals for scope changes. Sometimes this is articulated with a formula for contractor's material, labor, and subcontractor costs plus a multiplier for his overhead.

Where the codes and conditions of the contract permit, the design professional can allow alternative construction techniques that meet the same performance requirements. He can use his interpretive powers to permit minor deviations in the work where they will not adversely affect project performance or aesthetic requirements without triggering the need for a contractor's proposal.

He can review and recommend action on pay requests and scope changes promptly. This may be the best assurance of a positive owner-contractor relationship. The payment process should not create undue burden for the contractor.

He should be reasonable in evaluating the time and cost proposals the contractor makes for changes in contract scope and requests for additional time for acts of God such as weather-related delays.

One should have a back-up strategy for executing the change in scope if the contractor's proposal is unacceptable. The owner may execute a change using his own forces or by a separate contract. This may result in extra work for the design professional to issue a document that coordinates revisions to the contract, so the owner should contemplate design cost to him when evaluating whether it is worth it to separately contract for a change.

Where the proposed change involves a reduction in scope, and the contractor's price is unacceptable, the design professional can require justification documents such as invoices and restock charges from the contractor and may consider industry averages or quotes from other contractors for providing the work to inform him as to the reasonableness of the contractor's valuation of the proposal. The conditions of the contract may also permit mediation or arbitration to settle such disputed amounts if the professional's determination is unacceptable to either party.

He should bundle contractor's proposals for review and action as a contract change so that there is not more than a benchmark amount at any time. Often the threshold amount from 1% to 5% of the contract will be used as a guideline.

In establishing project contract conditions, the designer can recommend options available to the owner such as electing to pay for stored materials or reducing retainage after a benchmark level of completion is reached. This will enhance the contractor's ability to pay his subs and suppliers. Waivers of lien and documentation of acceptable storage conditions for materials should be tied to these provisions for the owner's protection.

MANAGING RISK

To help owners and designers to manage their exposure to risk, center any contract negotiations on standardized documents that are designed for the delivery of this type of contract. Even if the contract is one of the contractor's

Where the proposed change involves a reduction in scope and the contractor's price is unacceptable, the design professional can require justification documents such as invoices and restock charges from the contractor.

own, the documents could be full of cues to the designer of where his risk may be increased over the traditional contractual relationship. Articles in these documents spell out basic services, extended services, the design/builder's responsibilities, ownership of documents, scheduling, payments, reimbursables, and dispute resolution. Lacking clarification in a contract, the parties may be liable for the level of service described in these documents because they exist as standards of the industry. Designers should consult their legal counsel and their E & O (errors and omissions) insurer before entering a design/build agreement. It is unusual for the design firm to be the lead entity in a design/build venture, because the contractor usually has higher bonding ability and deeper pockets, therefore he will be less risk averse. (Robert J. Erikson, "Design Risk in Design/Build", American Institute of Architects, 6-21-01). Documents referenced include A191, Standard Form of Agreements Between Owner and Design Builder; A201, General Conditions of the Contract for Construction; A491, Standard Form of Agreements Between Design/Builder and Contractor; and B352, Duties, Responsibilities, and Limitations of Authority of the Architect's Project Representative.

fastfacts

To help owners and designers to manage their exposure to risk, center any contract negotiations on standardized documents that are designed for the delivery of this type of contract.

Insurance

To help the owner/developers manage their exposure to risk, they should evaluate their need for several types of insurance. Usually they will take this matter under advisement of their counsel and insurance broker. Insurance can cover losses incurred through fire, flood, title exposure, and general liability. Financial institutions may require mortgage insurance to cover the loan's exposure should the borrower default. Riders can be attached to expand a policy to cover an array of extended coverage losses, building replacement cost insurance, loss-of-rents insurance, and nonbuilding property.

Insurance is a word that may chill your spine with resentment, and the premiums may be high, but you can't afford to operate without it. Insurance is a cost of doing business and a necessity of the rental profession. What type of insurance do you need? Well, in this world of lawsuit-happy individuals, the more coverage you have, the safer you are. Today's tenants may try to make their fortune by taking yours in a lawsuit. Let's review the various types of insurance and their place in a landlording enterprise.

Fire insurance is self-explanatory. It protects you from losses incurred from fire damage. If your property is financed, the lender will require fire insurance. They will insist on coverage in an amount at least equal to the loan amount. The lender will stipulate themselves as the beneficiary of benefits until the loan is satisfied. If the proceeds from the insurance claim exceed the pay-off amount of the loan, you will be entitled to the remaining money.

In addition to the minimum required coverage, you should have coverage to protect your equity. Don't try to overinsure your building. If you have replacement cost insurance, you will only be awarded money to replace the building. You cannot insure the building for an extra $50,000.00 and put the additional money in your pocket. When determining how much fire insurance is needed, don't include the land value in your cost estimates. Land is not a factor in fire insurance; it will still be there when the smoke clears.

Investigate extended coverage for your insurance policy. For small additional premiums, you can benefit from a variety of protection. Some of this additional coverage might include:

- Falling trees
- Freeze damage
- Hail
- Explosion
- Glass breakage
- Ruptured plumbing
- Vandalism
- High winds

These and additional riders are worth looking into. Their cost may be minimal when combined with your fire insurance policy.

Flood insurance is rarely purchased unless the property is situated in a flood zone or flood plain. The same applies to earthquake insurance. It is an uncommon purchase for investors in average areas. These two types of insurance are specialized and will not normally be needed. If you feel your investment is at risk by flooding, earthquakes, or other unusual forms of peril, consult your insurance agent.

Loss-of-rents insurance could benefit any landlord. These policies vary in content and conditions, but they are desirable. If your rental units become uninhabitable, you will have some retribution from the insurance company. In a serious case, such as a fire, these policies can save your property and your credit rating. Investigate the types of coverage available and evaluate the benefits to you.

A policy for belongings housed in the property may be in order. If you keep lawn care equipment or tools on-site, get a policy to cover them. Your homeowner's insurance may not cover the personal property under these conditions. Premiums for this coverage will not amount to much, and if something happens, you will be glad you have it.

Mortgage insurance is mostly a thing of the past. The purpose behind this insurance is to satisfy the loan upon your demise. These policies carry steep premiums and are often cost prohibitive. The same result can be achieved with an inexpensive, decreasing-term life insurance policy. If you die, the proceeds from the policy can be used to satisfy the property's mortgage. This method leaves your heirs with a choice. They can pay off the mortgage or make some other use of the pay-off.

Title insurance is a requirement of lenders in most locations. This insurance protects against claims from unidentified, alleged owners of the property. Title inspections are required before this insurance is issued. The person checking the title will perform an extensive search. They will look for liens, attachments, old and outstanding loans, and a chain of title. These searches are very effective and problems rarely arise after title insurance is issued. In a worst-case scenario, you could lose the property, but the title company would reimburse you financially for your loss.

If an old and undiscovered heir claimed ownership of your property, they could be granted possession. The same is true of old, but perfected, liens, judgment attachments, and related clouds of title. Any outstanding lien or judgment can cloud a title to where it may not be marketable without added title insurance. The title insurance cannot guarantee you will not lose possession of the property. It is designed to protect you financially if the property is lost. When the property is financed, the lender will be the first beneficiary. After the loan is satisfied, you will receive the residual money.

Liability insurance falls into the must-have category. You cannot afford to own property without liability insurance. Liability insurance will protect your assets from a multitude of lawsuits. People falling on your icy sidewalk will not take your personal residence. Loose shingles blowing off the building onto a classic Corvette will not put you in debtor's prison. You need to protect yourself and your assets from any conceivable eventuality.

When shopping liability insurance, look for quality coverage. Demand the best and buy enough of it to cover potential losses. With most insurance carriers, a million dollar policy will not be much more than a policy with a quarter-million-dollar cap. You may have trouble envisioning being sued for more than a few hundred thousand dollars. This is a common response, but it is not rational. Today's legal system encourages people to exploit the smallest liability claim. If someone is permanently crippled or killed, you could be faced with a massive lawsuit. Don't gamble everything you have worked for to save a few bucks on insurance.

Some lenders and grant makers may stipulate minimum coverage as a condition of the loan. Publicly funded projects may also legally require the owner be covered. The general conditions of the contract allow the contractor to satisfy himself that the owner has coverage. It is unusual for a contractor to demand this evidence unless there has been a claim, since the question should arise during project mobilization. Some owners will offer proof of insurance in good faith, as a matter of practice.

When shopping liability insurance, look for quality coverage. Demand the best and buy enough of it to cover potential losses.

PROJECT SCHEDULE

The project schedule begins when the owner/developer first recognizes the need for a project. The sequence in new construction generally follows this slogan: Build it from the bottom up; finish it from the top down. In the world of renovation, the sequence of construction generally moves from exterior to interior and from essential to elective improvements.

CSI's UniFormat is a classification system for construction systems and assemblies. It is used to develop preliminary project descriptions, preliminary cost classifications, and detail filing where a detail involves the interface of multiple building elements and systems. UniFormat facilitates the use of square foot or systems-based cost databases in the early stages of design and permits the same organization to be further defined as design progresses. The groupings can be articulated in design development by inserting a decimal point and using the project manual's section numbers to distinguish bodies of work. Section numbers are derived from CSI's MasterFormat and are the basis for the most commonly used specifications and estimating databases. MasterFormat numbers are also used to organize the information in a construction cost estimate and for filing design related project data.

Build it from the bottom up; finish it from the top down.

Using such a structure helps the design team and estimators avoid costly omissions and identify cost intensive areas of development early in the design process. This approach can be used to refine scope to fit the budget or refine the budget to fit the required scope or both.

UniFormat defines eight basic organizing systems described below:

- Substructure are the below-grade improvements that comprise building foundations and basements.
- Shells include improvements to the building envelope, roof, exterior walls and openings, cleaning, patching, and super structure.
- Interiors include items such as walls, partitions, millwork, acoustical systems, stairways, building specialties such as signs and toilet room accessories, and finishes.
- Services include mechanical, electrical, plumbing, fire protection, conveying systems, communications, and security systems.
- Equipment and Furnishings may appear to be self-explanatory. Essentially furniture includes everything that is not nailed down like desks and artwork and items such as pre-fabricated casework and metal lockers that are secured to the building. Equipment includes vehicular equipment, sports equipment, laboratory equipment, commercial kitchen equipment, and filing systems.
- Other Building Construction involves selective demolition and special construction such as prefabricated building systems or modules, mezzanines, special controls, and instrumentation.
- Building Site Work includes tasks such as building demolition, site preparation, and improvements like paving, utilities, and furnishings such as tanks, building signs, and benches.
- General Requirements including bidding requirements, contracts, contract conditions, and estimates. This would include elements that the contractor requires to mobilize the site such as toilets, temporary power, or job trailers. It also includes special requirements that may affect the contractor's costs such as required testing, accommodating on-going use of the facility and phased work, selective demolition, and waste disposal requirements such as waste streaming.

A bar graph or critical path document may be useful to illustrate the project schedule. In the critical path method, benchmarks are identified for desirable dates of completion and schedule-busting dates.

Maintaining the Project Schedule

Once a schedule is established, maintaining it is best done by revisiting the schedule frequently; on commercial scale projects, this is usually monthly. The general contractor may be the prime source of schedule updates but the owner may also contract with the design firm or another design professional to offer construction supervision. One of many tasks this person will offer is a proactive check on the contractor's schedule and a lever to assure that submittal review schedules are met so that the contractor will not have claims for time due to delays by third parties.

Contractors can establish submittal schedules and construction schedules that identify long lead-time items. Contractors can use the schedule to keep the design professional informed of the hot submittals that require the priority attention, the need for multiple party review, permitting, and testing or lead times for the evaluation of proposals and mock-ups. They can also avoid inundating the designer with a stack of submittals at one time. Some submittals require more than one review. Depending on the experience and qualifications of the subcontractors, submittals such as doors, hardware equipment, and masonry are often ticklish points in the review process.

Finishes, especially on bid projects where they are not pre-selected, can be another sticking point. This is not because they are particularly complex, but because major finish elements must be considered together. Until finishes have been selected, equipment and materials can't be ordered or fabricated. The contractor should bundle exterior and interior finish submittals into groups for evaluation.

Sometimes the design professional will issue a color schedule in advance of reviewing the accompanying submittals, with the caveat that the specified criteria must be met. Selections for minor elements will be derived from the major selections and may be deferred until later in the project. Sometimes furniture selection will be tied to the interior finish selection package.

Penalty and Bonus Clauses

Design/build contracts frequently employ liquidated damages or penalties for failure to meet the schedule. See Table 10.2. Some will also offer bonuses for early completion. This is also used on design-bid-build contracts where a delay may produce a quantifiable economic hardship for the owner. Generally, if used, a penalty clause must be accompanied by a bonus clause for early completion, although the amount for each need not be equal. In many jurisdictions, a penalty clause is unenforceable, even with the related bonus clause.

Penalty clauses are not the same as liquidated damages which represent a number reflecting real loss, such as loss of operations, additional lease charges, late fees, and loss of rental income that could be quantified. Usually these costs are about ½% to 1% of the contract amount. In EJCDC (National Society of Professional Engineers Joint Contract Documents Committee) and AIA (American Institute of Architects) general conditions documents, they do not take effect in the case of an act beyond the contractor's control for which he has made a timely claim.

fastfacts

Generally, if used, a penalty clause must be accompanied by a bonus clause for early completion, although the amount for each need not be equal. In many jurisdictions, a penalty clause is unenforceable, even with the related bonus clause.

SELECTING AND PRIORITIZING THE IMPROVEMENTS

Cost-effective building improvements can prove profitable for real estate investors whether they are selling a building or renting it out. The right improvements make a building more desirable, and buildings with desirability are usually more profitable. Putting money into a building can be risky. Money invested in cosmetic upgrades doesn't always yield the rate of return on the money you spent. Some investments offer a much higher chance of a profitable return than others do. Using light small-scale conversions as an example, let's examine the thought process and exercises needed to select between specific scope elements. In the light commercial and residential conversion scales of projects, the analysis exercises may be somewhat less structured and formalized than when making similar evaluations for projects of more demanding scale and complexity. Fee and schedule normally associated with small scale projects necessarily limit the hours that can be devoted to this analysis.

TABLE 10.2 Summary sheet, payment application with explanatory footnotes (*Continued*)

Laboratory Expansion and Envelope Upgrades at the A.W.T. Building

Owner's name

Project Location

Partial Payment Request No. 000
Period Covered: date - date
Job No. XXX0000

	Period	Cumulative
SUMMARY		
Original Contract Work Completed to Date	$0.00	$0.00
Extra Work Completed to Date	$0.00	$0.00
Total Work Completed to Date	$0.00	$0.00
Less Retainage in Escrow Account 10%	$0.00	$0.00
Less Retainage Released	$0.00	$0.00
Subtotals	$0.00	$0.00
Less Stored Materials Installed (Period Only)	$0.00	
New/Current Stored Materials	$0.00	$0.00
Net Amount Due This Payment/Subtotal	$0.00	$0.00
Less Previously Paid		$0.00
Net Amount Due This Payment	$0.00	
CONTRACT RECAP		
Original Contract Amount		
Approved Change Order No. 1		
Approved Change Order No. 2		
Current Contract Amount		$0.00
PAYMENT RECAP		
Net Amount for Work Completed	$0.00	$0.00
Retainage for Work Completed	$0.00	$0.00
TOTAL PAYOUT	**$0.00**	**$0.00**

For example, in a single-family home, kitchen remodeling is the best place to put improvement money. Bathroom remodeling is the second most likely area of a home to replenish your remodeling dollars. Adding a deck or a garage to a home can also make a house more profitable. Other types of improvements, however, like replacing carpeting or drapes may

TABLE 10.2 (*Continued*) Summary sheet, payment application with explanatory footnotes

CERTIFICATION OF CONTRACTOR

Contractor's Corporation

The undersigned contractor certifies that to the best of their knowledge, information and belief the work covered by this payment estimate has been completed in accordance with the contract documents, that all amounts have been paid by the contractor for work for which previous payment estimates were issued and payments received from the owner, and that current payment shown herein is now due.

By ______________________________ **Date** ______________

signatory, title

CERTIFICATION OF ARCHITECT or ENGINEER

Design professional's corporation

By ______________________________ **Date** ______________

signatory, title

APPROVAL OF OWNER

By ______________________________ **Date** ______________

signatory, title

Owner's name

CERTIFICATION OF QUANITIES OF INSTALLED WORK IF BY PARTY OTHER THAN ARCHITECT OR ENGINEER

By ______________________________ **Date** ______________

signatory, title

Owner's Representative

not make financial sense. Deciding on which improvements make the most sense can be more difficult for investors who work with retail space or office space.

Knowing how to assess the value of an improvement is instrumental in making money. Sometimes it's best not to make any improvements. For example, if an office building has acceptable carpeting in it, it probably won't pay to upgrade it to a carpet that is more plush, unless it will raise the space from grade B space to A space and command more rent from a different class of tenant. There are other times when putting money into a building can make the property much more valuable. How value is determined depends on the investor involved.

Some investors see the value of an improvement only when a building is sold and a profit is gained. Other investors assign value in terms of the pull for tenants and the amount of rent that can be charged for a property. These strategies work with all types of construction. One can create an aura about an office building that will attract first-class professional tenants. Creating a warm environment for tenants can make an apartment building much easier to rent to the best tenants for the highest prices. But, you have to learn how to recognize what the best improvements for various motivations are.

You can increase the return on an investment by improving a property. The question is to decide if the improvements add to your investment. Some investors have an eye for improvement projects, but most depend on appraisers to determine if an improvement is worthwhile. When there is big money at stake, one should involve experts to help make the right decisions. Average investors should always consult with appraisers before making major improvement investments.

Types of Improvements Made to Buildings

Types of improvements made to buildings can be broken down into four main categories. The first category includes improvements that are made to enhance the sales price of a property, Investment Enhancing Improvements. Improvements that are used to attract tenants, or Marketability Improvements, create the second category. The third are improvements made to reduce operations and management costs or to facilitate the operations of the core enterprise. These may be called Operations Improvements. The last are Legally Mandated Improvements. These include work required by maintenance codes that demand working plumbing, weathertightness, and structural soundness in occupied property. Building codes, fire codes and other codes require physical changes to support a new use or the removal of barriers based on use. Sometimes the improvements cross over from one category to another. For example, remodeling the kitchens in an apartment building might increase both its sales value and its draw for tenants. These, or course, are the most desirable types of improvements to make.

If you invest in improvements to pull in more tenants, better tenants, or increase rents, you have to weigh the amount of time required to regain the cost of the improvements. When investments are made for sales value, the return on the investment may not be realized until the property is sold, and it might not be seen then. Ideally, concentrate on improvements that can boost tenant appeal and sales value at the same time.

Smart improvements can be almost anything, but they usually involve improvements that add both desirability and value to a property. For example, having built-in dishwashers installed in your apartments could be considered a dual-benefit improvement. The dishwasher should increase the building's value and attract more tenants. This doesn't mean that the value of your building will escalate in an amount equal to what you spend on the dishwashers, but some of the investment should be shown in appraised value. But putting designer hardware on the doors, windows, and cabinets would not normally fill both needs. It might influence some tenants, but it probably would not increase the property value.

Investment-Enhancing Improvements

There are many ways to determine what types of improvements fall into the smart investment category. The most reliable way is to have before-and-after appraisals done on your property before making the improvements. Talking to lenders can be quite enlightening. Most lenders who are willing to make improvement loans have a better-than-average awareness of which improvements are financially feasible. Real estate brokers can also help you to assess potential improvements, but temper what you are told by brokers. Not all brokers are savvy in terms of the return on improvements, and some brokers may tell you what you want to hear in hopes of getting your business in buying and selling real estate. Ideally, talk to some investors who have first-hand experience to draw from. While you may be a competitor of other investors, you might still find it mutually beneficial to share thoughts. Best of all, get a number of opinions to evaluate. Give the most weight to the opinion offered by the professional appraiser, but also factor in what you learn from the others with whom you discuss the matter.

Capturing Space

One way to gain a lot of additional square footage in a building, while working with the most reasonable cost estimates possible, can be done by building up. A lot of contractors think of expanding horizontally when adding an addition to a house. If you go up instead of going out, you could save a lot of money. Remove all existing roofing and build a second story on top of the existing building. Or, perhaps all you will want to do is convert the attic into occupied space, which may not require such extensive roofing and framing work.

Suppose you take a one-story building and add a full second story, as well as a modified attic for additional space. Think of the square footage you gain to lease out on an annual basis. Going up can definitely be better than building out.

When you elect to build up rather than out, you eliminate the need for site work, footings, foundation, and some other expensive aspects of construction. The cost of construction, on a per-square-foot basis, is much lower. In some cases ground-floor space may rent for more then upper-story space, but this is something you will have to research on a local level. While it may make sense to spend more money to get ground-level space, depending upon your circumstances, there are some properties where there is not enough surrounding land on which to build out. For these buildings, going up is the only way to go. And this means messing with the roof.

One way to gain a lot of additional square footage in a building, while working with the most reasonable cost estimates possible, can be done by building up.

There is no question that attic conversions can offer the best use of affordable space. Attic space which is converted into occupied space will normally appraise for much more than the same amount of square footage converted in a basement. Although converting basements into leasable area can enhance the project's bottom line, generally the pool of tenants is lower because such space commands lower rents and is often not routinely occupied. Basements can make excellent areas for storage tenants and servant functions of the building. The cost of the work for attic conversions might be about the same, but the return on your investment should be much greater than if you spent your money in a basement. Of course, roofing work is frequently a part of attic conversions, and so is a fair amount of framing. You must be aware, however, that getting into a major roofing change is not going to be cheap. It may be a good value, but it will not be inexpensive.

Cosmetic Improvements

Cosmetic improvements consist of work that makes a property look better. This type of improvement doesn't have any effect on structural elements.

Some people think of cosmetic improvements as inexpensive ways to dress up a building. They are window dressing, but they are not always cheap. In fact, some cosmetic work can be quite expensive. Some examples of costly cosmetics improvements include new siding, new carpeting, new floor or wall tile, new kitchen cabinets, and so forth. Don't get lulled into a false sense of security by thinking that cosmetic work is not expensive. See Figure 10.6.

Cosmetic improvements, on the other hand, can add value to a building. These are improvements that are not needed, but that can enhance the value of a property. With the right plan, a little money can go a long way in making a building more desirable with cosmetic improvements. The types of improvements done depend heavily on the type of building that is being improved. For example, if you were doing cosmetic improvements on an office building, the best improvement might be adding potted plants in the reception area. Sometimes creating a comfortable environment is worth more than a cash increase in value.

There are all sorts of cosmetic improvements that can be done on all types of buildings. Shopping centers, office buildings, houses, and apartments

FIGURE 10.6 A mural covers a concrete parged party wall. When an owner elects to provide public art such as this, they must also make a perpetuating financial arrangement to maintain it. Deteriorating art of this scale contributes to an atmosphere of blight. *Photo: Stephen Culbert*

can all benefit from cosmetic improvements. If you plan to make cosmetic improvements, make sure of your motivation before doing so. Are you doing the work to increase the cash value of your property? Will the improvements be done for the purpose of attracting tenants? Is it your intention for the improvements to make your property sell faster, but not necessarily for a higher price? Ask yourself these types of questions and answer them honestly. Once you have, you can evaluate the cost and the feasibility of doing the work. The photos in Figure 10.7 and Figure 10.8 illustrate how a tight budget was devoted to cosmetic improvements, and still garnered maximum impact for the owner/developer.

Wall and Ceiling Coverings Are Eye Candy for the Passionate Purchase

Wall and ceiling coverings can do a lot to spruce up an old building. Structural work and mechanical systems are quite important to a building, but when it's time to sell or rent, it is often the cosmetic improvements that make the most impact. A buyer will be happy to know that your building has all new copper electrical wiring, but wallpaper in the bathroom

FIGURE 10.7 New windows, infill, and a skim coat of cement plaster protect the envelope of this recommissioned military building.

FIGURE 10.8 The canopy at the recommissioned finance center focused improvement dollars at the principal entry. The canopy visually relieves an otherwise vast ribbon of concrete and windows. *Photo: Stephen Culbert*

and tile in the kitchen may be the pressure points to push the buyer into a decision. Buying strictly on looks is not good business, but it is frequently the way properties are sold and leased. Hard-nosed investors will look past pretty little fix-ups to find flaws in a structure. This group of people is experienced in buying structurally sound buildings. However, veteran investors make up only a portion of the buying power for conversion projects.

Rookie investors are known to act on impulse. If they like the looks of a building, they buy it. Here is a group of people who can be manipulated quite easily with some cosmetic touches. Installing wallpaper and a chair rail in a dining room can help make a sale to this type of buyer. A tile backsplash behind the kitchen range can prove impressive. There are all sorts of ways to stir the emotions of prospective purchasers and tenants.

Inexperienced investors buy properties that they like, not necessarily properties that are good buys. Successful investors learn to overcome this weakness. But, you can sell a lot of buildings to rookie investors as they are working their way through the learning curve. Is this wrong? Probably not. If one is honest and presents properties in a reputable manner, there is nothing wrong with selling to a person's passion. In fact, it's called knowing the market and making sound marketing decisions.

Buying strictly on looks is not good business, but it is frequently the way properties are sold and leased.

Observing Contextual Conformity in Improvement Materials

Conformity can become an issue when choosing exterior materials. Putting vinyl siding on the building is an improvement that might produce a reasonable return on the investment, but this depends on many factors. If your duplex is the only one in the neighborhood that doesn't have maintenance-free siding, you might be well served to make the capital improvement. But if your duplex will be the only one in the area with vinyl siding, the decision for the improvement to be made would probably be a bad one. This is the type of comparison work that is required to make wise decisions. Sometimes reuse requires that owners suppress their creative urges or risk overimproving a property. The owner considered the context of adjacent property when allocating the small budget for exterior improvements on the property shown in Figure 10.9.

Conformity can become an issue when choosing a siding material. Putting vinyl siding on a building might make sense in terms of decreased

FIGURE 10.9 Exhaust for dry-cleaning equipment peeks above the fascia canopy. The canopy was installed when this former bakery outlet was a restaurant.

maintenance, but it could kill the appraised value of your property. Likewise, installing cedar siding could also result in ungained value on an appraisal. Why is this? It is a matter of conformity. When real estate appraisers put a value on a property, they use at least two or three different methods to arrive at a market value. One of these methods involves comparing the subject property to other properties in the area which are similar and which have been sold recently. This is where a non-conforming choice can hurt you.

A duplex covered with vinyl siding in a neighborhood where most others are wood sided would stand out in an unattractive way. Since the surrounding comparable properties are all sided with wood, one should probably use wood siding on the subject building. It may cost a little more and it will present more maintenance requirements, but your property will remain in conformity with the rest of the real estate in the area. Installing vinyl under these conditions could have a detrimental affect on the appraised value of your property. Conversely, an investment in wood might be wasted in another neighborhood where the dominant exterior cover is vinyl.

Major Renovation

Major renovation can create strong equity in a building, but it can also be very risky. Investors who commit to big remodeling jobs can spend tens of thousands of dollars without seeing much of a return on their investment. Conversion projects typically require substantial remodeling. This is to be expected. In the case of a conversion project, the renovation should be factored into the overall project. Not all investors anticipate a major renovation when they buy a typical apartment building or house.

Sometimes putting money into major renovation is very sensible, however, there are investors who get caught up in the excitement of remodeling and just don't know when to stop. For example, an investor may have a kitchen floor covering replaced and like the results so well that a decision is made to replace more flooring. By the time the job is done, all of the flooring might be replaced. This could be a serious monetary mistake. One has to stay focused and make decisions wisely when remodeling your buildings. Major elective improvements on residential rental property are usually money wasted, unless they are renovations to replace elements that are damaged or worn out beyond usability. If the owner is taking the property up-market, the cost-adding amenities need to be compared against the probable payback the higher rent will command. If the property is improved for sale, the benchmark is whether the combined quicker sale and higher offering price will offset the investment. If they won't, let the buyer make improvements to suit.

When considering removing an existing roof and building upwards, understand there are times when one shouldn't do it. Let's say one has found a good single-family residence that can convert into several rental units. With the existing layout of the house, one could create a duplex with only minor interior modifications. However, three units are more desirable. Raising the roof will make room for an extra rental unit. Will one additional rental unit offset the cost of a major roofing remodel? It might, but the odds are not favorable. The monthly profit generated by just one new unit probably won't be sufficient to recoup the investment within a reasonable payback period. This is the line of thinking if the owner/ investor is planning to keep a building, but it also applies if he is looking for a quick flip. In a sales scenario, adding the cost of a new roof line to the sales price of a building can price the project right out of the market. This is clearly a situation where the cost of a major roofing job is not warranted.

There are times when raising a roof is a good move. Let's say, for example, that the owner has stumbled onto a prime conversion property where a residential property can be converted to exclusive office space. We will assume that the location is ideal, the structure is sound, and that the only thing holding you back is a lack of interior space. The price of the property is attractive, but the acquisition cost and the cost of construction make it difficult to produce a positive cash flow. One must generate more floor space to lease out. After assessing all of the options, blowing off the roof and building up makes the most sense. This can double the floor space and create storage space in the attic with the use of attic trusses. The square footage gained from this approach is enough to bring in four extra offices.

The rental income from four offices is more than needed to justify the expense of a major roofing project. Even with a higher-than-average vacancy rate, the increased size of the building makes it possible to perform major roofing changes without unusual risks. This is a situation where you would probably be a fool not to move ahead with the roofing project.

Kitchens and Bathrooms

The kitchen is one of the most important rooms in a residence. Plenty of data compiled from surveys suggests that the kitchen is the one room in house where more buyers are influenced than any other. Kitchens are certainly an ideal location to spend your improvement money.

For example, when you buy an older building, the chances are good that the kitchen will have a window over the sink. And, that one window will probably be the only natural light source in the entire kitchen. This can cause the kitchen to be dark and gloomy.

A kitchen should be bright, cheerful, and inviting. It must also be functional. First impressions are important, and to get a great first impression, you must appeal to people's desires. A functional kitchen will sell a house or rent an apartment, but a fantastic visual aura will sell the house or rent the apartment faster.

Suppose the design goal is to flood a small kitchen with light to make it appear larger and more appealing. How are you going to do it? Storage is a big factor in a functional kitchen, so you shouldn't do away with the wall cabinets. If there is attic space or just a roof over the kitchen, you can turn to skylights. Having skylights installed in the ceiling can do wonders for a kitchen. But, if skylights won't work, you might consider a garden window. These big windows are shaped in a way that allows them to fit nicely in most kitchens, without consuming unnecessary wall space. Country kitchens, for example, are spacious and offer plenty of opportunity for natural light. You will have to assess your project on its own merit, but you should strive to let the light shine in. Another way to get some extra light into a kitchen might be the use of a glazed door. Let's say that the breakfast area is a little cramped. You would like more space, and you desperately need more light. You can solve both of these problems with one improvement. Installing a bay window will give you extra floor space and plenty of light.

Bathrooms are said to be the second most important rooms in residential projects. Houses and apartments need bathrooms for obvious reasons, and the more, the merrier. Bathroom remodeling has historically proved to be profitable. Modern bathrooms are often spacious and bright. This is not the case in older homes. Most bathrooms in older homes are small, dark, and uninviting. This is an issue that you, as a conversion contractor, can change. Some contractors leave existing bathrooms in their present condition, with the exception of new fixtures. This is like shooting yourself in the foot.

It is tempting to avoid enlarging the size of existing bathrooms. When you run the numbers on what it will cost to enlarge and improve a bathroom,

fastfacts

Plenty of data compiled from surveys suggests that the kitchen is the one room in the house where more buyers are influenced than any other.

it is easy to take the path of least resistance. It is not always feasible to enlarge bathrooms. When it is, you should give the option serious consideration. However, when you don't have any growth potential, you have to turn to other means of making existing bathrooms more desirable. When the bathroom is located on an exterior wall, you might be able to accomplish this goal with the use of glass. Skylights may also be possible. Bathrooms situated in interior sections of buildings don't allow many choices for creative improvements. Keep this in mind when selecting projects to convert. Interior bathrooms are not enough of a deterrent to walk away from a deal, but the design options are limited.

Skylights and the Bottom Line

Rooms that develop a lot of moisture, like kitchens, baths, and interior areas on an upper floor, can benefit from the installation of pole-operated skylights or clerestory windows with screens as a source of both light and natural ventilation. Skylights are suitable for attic conversions and to add light into newly carved out two-story space. If they are sized to work with structural spacing (i.e. joist spacing), they can be painlessly installed.

Much of the cost in skylights comes in the light box that must be built when the space being lighted has an attic above it. In weighing the cost benefits of incorporating new skylights into an existing building, the owner will not recoup the full value of the installation in increased appraised value. This is especially true with small unitary skylights and small-scale space. Skylights are relatively expensive but rooms that feel light, open and natural will sell or lease speculatively developed property faster, and that's where the true value may lie.

In industrial settings, removable rigidly framed skylights mounted on curbs can be selected in lieu of large scale roof hatches at lower cost and with the added benefit of natural light.

CONSIDER DEMOLITION AS AN IMPROVEMENT

Demolition is an "improvement" that should not be overlooked. Strategic demolition can reduce the area of a property too large to redevelop. This is often the case with a factory or warehouse.

Demolition alters the character of the space that remains. For example, demolishing floors in a central area of a building with a large floor plate can create new exterior facades for apartments or an interior atrium to let light into offices, retail, or classroom space. Demolition that includes structural elements can also selectively create high bay space for assembly or spatial focus where none existed.

Demolition may be necessary to accommodate new program elements. Depending on the program and the new use, deck demolition may be essential to accommodate a variety of vertical elements: additional exit stairs, elevators for access or circulation, trash chutes, material conveyors, mechanical chase ways, stackable security and communications closets, electrical services, mechanical systems, plumbing risers and vents, roof conductors, and fire suppression systems. Depending on the existing structural bay sizes, existing structure may accommodate stacking these like elements at a core or along the party wall of a multi-story building.

Demolition of existing interior partitions and dated finishes can be the last step in a series that includes structural repair, exterior stabilization, and systems upgrades. It can prime a space for build-to-suit conversions or resale for development because it is easier for the tenant or buyer to visualize the improvements he would like to make.

Operations Improvements

Operations improvements are usually elective improvements made by an owner/developer who will own and operate the property for some time.

Now let's say that the duplex has old electrical wiring in it. The wiring is safe enough, but it is old. The investor would like to upgrade the electrical service and rewire the building. Does this type of improvement make financial sense? Not unless he is going to keep the building for a long time and can afford to make the improvement without much of a return. Tenants will rarely pay more for a unit that has new wiring in it, so long as the older wiring is safe. An appraiser will give a little extra value for the modern wiring, but not nearly enough to pay for its cost of installation. You have to make this type of improvement because you want to, not because it's profitable.

Essential Repairs and Maintenance

Structural repairs rarely add any value to a property. This is because appraisers expect buildings to be structurally sound. If a property is lacking in structural integrity, it should be fixed to meet standard market value. But the money invested will not yield much of a profit percentage.

Installing a new roof could be viewed as an improvement, but really it is maintenance. It's something that must be done at times, but it doesn't raise the value of a property substantially. Don't confuse maintenance with improving a property. When installing improvements in the maintenance category, one must consider that these usually fall into the category of maintaining the base expectations of the tenant or buyer, i.e. a building should be watertight; the HVAC system should be operational. When these invisible elements need attention, the owner can seek to mitigate his costs except where doing so will compromise performance. Figure 10.10 shows how to save a little when installing new rooftop equipment.

Investors are often confused by what they are spending money on. For example, installing a new heating system in a building is an improvement, but it is not one that will be likely to produce a full return on the cost. In many cases, the cost of the so-called improvement is not even closely returned in a sale. The fact is most improvements and maintenance costs cannot be recovered fully.

Maintenance can also stimulate a quicker sale. If an investor did replace an antiquated heating system with a new, energy-efficient model, a prospective buyer might very likely pay more for the property and buy the building more quickly. The total cost of the heating system probably would not be recovered, but the benefits of the work may still be very valuable. How

FIGURE 10.10 Existing roof penetrations can be used to avoid costly cutting and patching. Existing trunk ductwork can often be reused to service reconfigured space. *Photo: Nick Fredericks.*

fastfacts

If a property is lacking in structural integrity, it should be fixed to meet standard market value. But, the money invested will not yield much of a profit percentage.

does this make sense? Well, a capital improvement can effect a faster sale. While money may be lost, in this case on the heating system, money saved in reduced interest cost for carrying a building during the sales process could offset the loss. One must learn to think in different terms as you consider the worth of improvement investments. This is the only way in which you can identify improvements that are wrong for your needs and desires.

It's worth repeating that maintenance is not the same as improvement. Don't confuse replacing a water heater with putting new siding on a building. The installation of siding is maintenance if the existing siding is no longer structurally sound, but putting new siding on merely for appearances is an improvement. It may not be a wise improvement, but it is an improvement. Maintenance is something that must be done to preserve the quality of a structure. An improvement is an enhancement to a property. They are not the same, even though they might both involve the same type of work.

Landlords typically factor in a cost for routine maintenance. Most landlords do this by computing a percentage of their gross rental income to cover expected maintenance. 10 % of the gross income is a typical figure used for calculating spreadsheet numbers. Of course, the amount may not be enough or it may be too much. In any case, 10% is the number used by most people who are projecting numbers for rental property. Rarely is there enough money built into a maintenance budget to cover major expenses, such as a new roof, a new heating system, or major plumbing problems. These big-ticket items are often unbudgeted expenses when they occur.

Smart investors maintain a good amount of money in an operational fund. Investors who are not prepared for unexpected expenses often have to borrow the funds to cover the cost of major maintenance. Having to borrow money for maintenance is not a good practice. The act of maintaining a building doesn't justify a rental increase and rarely creates additional cash value. For these reasons, the money spent on maintenance is hard to recover. When you buy a building, you should have it inspected closely and plan for and schedule major maintenance expenses. In other words,

fastfacts

It's worth repeating that maintenance is not the same as improvement. Don't confuse replacing a water heater with putting new siding on a building.

expect the unexpected and budget money for it when you are working out your cash flow numbers.

Interior Walls and Finishes

Interior finishes are often the first visual cue that separates one class of commercial space from another. An attractive appearance is an essential part of maintenance, regardless of the level of renovation planned.

Walls in older buildings are likely to be covered with plaster. If only minor repairs are needed, it is worthwhile to retain the plaster walls. However, if major destruction is going to take place, as it commonly does with conversion projects, you should plan on replacing the plaster with drywall. Take heed, the stud walls behind the plaster are not likely to be even. Furring strips will be required to bring the walls into a range of evenness that will be acceptable. This is time consuming and adds to the overall cost. If demolition is less selective, it can be more cost-effective to tear out the whole wall and replace it with new lightweight construction at a more desirable location.

Vinyl wall coverings, textured coatings, fillers, and scrims can be used to obscure minor defects in walls that are otherwise sound. They can offer a maintenance advantage in high traffic areas like corridors and lobbies. They can enhance rooms designed to impress visitors. Acoustical fabrics and panel systems can also reduce sound reflections in an otherwise hard surfaced space. Custom papers are used most often in historic installations, or in rooms that seek to evoke a traditional and elegant atmosphere. Combustible finishes like wood, papers, and some fabrics are not permitted in some locations. The available range of wall covering materials is extensive.

In some cases where the existing structural walls are masonry, an exposed finish may be desired. If masonry is stained, it should either be cleaned or painted. It is rarely cost effective to remove old mortar droppings from walls that have been concealed behind other finishes. If they have been covered with lead paint, it should be removed or encapsulated.

Archaic tile and structural glazed tile can be quite attractive in a renovation setting, especially if it has nostalgic or historic ingredients in its aesthetics. Matching and patching such elements can be costly. Material sources and craftsman can be difficult to find. One may be forced to consider combining them with alternative materials or to use a salvage and reinstallation approach.

An attractive appearance is an essential part of maintenance, regardless of the level of renovation planned.

WRONG IMPROVEMENTS

The wrong improvements can cost more than they are worth. There have been many investors who spent hard-earned money to improve a property only to see their money buried in the building. Several investors have stumbled into major investments that produced a loss when the properties were sold. It happens but it can be avoided. With the right research one can avoid most of the problems associated with making bad decisions on which improvements to make.

What constitutes a wrong improvement? It depends on the circumstances. Painting a rental unit is a necessary evil. It is not an improvement that will normally increase a property's value, but it can make a unit easier to rent. Considering the relatively low cost of painting, the improvement can be sensible in most situations. Can the same be said for replacing all of the carpeting in a house? No, usually carpet replacement is not going to increase the value of a house by anywhere near enough to cover the cost of the work. There are times when carpeting must be replaced, but this should be considered maintenance, rather than an improvement. For our purposes, the word improvement means any enhancement to increase property value.

Only a few types of improvements produce a profit during a sale. However, improvements can make a sale occur quicker, and this can save an investor money in carrying cost, so money is made indirectly by the improvement.

Wise investors don't gamble on issues that don't mandate a gamble. Professional investors remove as much risk as they possibly can before making a move. Let's look at an example of what I'm talking about.

In our first example, assume that you have purchased a duplex that is in fair condition. Well, you have to play the odds if you want to win big.

Let's say that the duplex has old wood siding on it that is in need of a fresh paint job. You would like to cover the duplex with vinyl siding, so that it will be maintenance-free in years to come. What's your motivation? If you plan to keep the building for a long time, having a maintenance-free exterior could be a comforting thought. But, if you plan to sell in the next few years, you would probably be much better off to simply paint the existing siding, if the siding is in good repair.

COMMON EXTERIOR ELEMENTS

Renovation projects usually involve maintenance and upgrades to the exterior of the existing building. These will come chiefly in the form of envelope improvements and image altering devices such as signs, awnings, canopies, and building art. Since the second group of items is similar to those used in design for new construction, we will omit discussion of them. Key envelope improvements include repairs to the skin, reskinning, re-roofing, and opening replacement.

An architect was asked, "What is the least quality of aluminum window you would consider yourself responsible in specifying?" "HC- 40," he replied and darted out the door. So why do some developers insist on buying "junk?" It is because they don't have to be there to maintain it five years down the road. As with any investment in an improvement, the intent to keep or sell will determine the client's point of view on values to apply to front-end materials selections.

fastfacts

Key envelope improvements include repairs to the skin, reskinning, re-roofing, and opening replacement.

Repairs To The Skin

Repairs to concrete and masonry skins can be effected with pointing, patching, and cleaning. The key to restoring masonry is that moisture must be removed and controlled at its source. This may involve repair or replacement of roof elements, spalled materials, crack injections, or building flashings.

Spalled materials can sometimes be replaced with salvaged materials from altered areas of the exterior. Sometimes movement in veneers can be stabilized with epoxies and dutchmen. Dutchmen can also be used to give lateral support to structural masonry at floor and rooflines where they can be anchored to structure.

To keep masonry veneer dry, some specialists recommend adding breathable penetrating sealers to masonry that is dry; some can even have a wicking effect on existing moisture. When in doubt about the sealer's ability to exhale moisture from the building cavity or skin material, leave it out. If a change in color is desired, clear penetrating breathable masonry stains should be used on existing masonry, not paints or other coatings.

Sometimes relieving joints must be added and sealed to accommodate years of material creep. Relieving weeps may be added if the originals are clogged or missing. Lime putty mortar is a soft mortar that boils. It is sometimes used to repoint historic masonry, however, it is a specialty contract. Mortar matching in terms of color, texture, and tooling is important when repointing will be unfinished and exposed to public view.

Masonry cleaning can be accomplished with a combination of chemicals, water pressure, or brushing. Sand blasting is not recommended because it may remove the surface of the brick and expose softer, more porous surfaces below. Not all cleaning techniques are compatible with every type of masonry, environment, or stain, so techniques may need to be combined to achieve the desired effect. Typically a test patch will be specified as a benchmark for the standard of cleaning required so that there is an understood answer to the question "How clean is clean?"

Often masonry repair is a specialty contract and may be the subject of allowances or unit prices or proposals. Specialty contractors usually have lower bonding ability because they are smaller companies, so a large project may have to phased or broken into smaller contracts to accommodate this reality.

Reskinning

Reskinning is done for one of two reasons. The original skin is damaged and repair is cost prohibitive or technically impractical, or the original skin is dated and a fresh image is the goal. In the first place, existing veneer masonry may be removed and a new veneer installed. In the second, a new exterior veneer may be installed in its place, or if the masonry is dry and structurally sound, over it. Common material choices for this purpose include: veneer stone, tile, cement plaster, insulated or uninsulated metal panels, EIFS and, where combustible materials are permitted, wood and vinyl siding panels. Aerated autoclaved concrete is being used as a cost effective new material in place of stone and masonry or on non-combustible construction in place of EIFS. These are listed in roughly descending order of initial cost.

Often installing the substrates for these systems will require furring or new anchors. It is important to ascertain whether the existing structure can support the weight of the proposed new skin. Adding or changing layers to the envelope will alter the location of the dew point in the wall assembly. This should be calculated so that it does not occur on the warm side of the vapor barrier.

Replacing an Existing Roof

Replacing an existing roof can be a big job. Depending upon the type of roof one is dealing with, the task could be a moderate expense or a major expense. For example, when working with a typical shingle roof, if the roof has only one layer of shingles, one should be able to install a new layer of shingles right over the old ones. This saves a worthwhile amount of money. However, if the roof has multiple layers of shingles on it, the old shingles should be stripped off before new ones are installed. This is true of most other roof types as well.

Replacing an existing roof can run into an expenditure of thousands of dollars. This is especially true of buildings with large roofs or unusual roofs. When buying a property with a roof that needs replacement, be sure you acquire the building at a price that will allow for the roofing expense without eroding your profit. It may be the single greatest expense in a renovation. Roofs are composed of three components: decks, insulation, and membrane. Roofs come in two basic types: low slope roofs and steep slope roofs.

Factors to consider when selecting replacement roof materials include, in no particular order:

- Building style, aesthetics
- Weight of materials
- Color and heat retention
- Initial cost
- Life cycle cost
- Roof asset management cost
- Durability to anticipated traffic and chemical exposures
- Light exposure
- Compatibility of topping material

- Installation methods
- Tie in to accessories and existing construction
- Compatibility with the substrate and weather
- Compatibility with the insulation system
- Thermal movement of materials
- Common objections
- Stress performance
- Quality of warranty
- Lifespan
- The availability of qualified suppliers and installers
- Roof maintenance requirements
- Seams
- Access
- Quantity
- Sourcing leaks
- Membrane redundancy
- Drainage type and capacity

System components include the following deck types:

- Nail able
- Lightweight concrete
- Wood
- Gypsum
- Non-nail able
- Fiber cement [Tectum]
- Concrete
- Steel
- Plastic panel
- Decks over humid or caustic environments

System components include the following insulation types:

- High thermal
- Isocyanurate
- Foam glass

- Composite (Isocyanurate laminated to facing sheet, gypsum, osb.)
- Tapered
- Low thermal
- Perlite
- Fiberglass
- EPS Expanded Polystyrene
- EPS Extruded Polystyrene
- Rock wool
- Dens deck
- Coated base sheets (vented)

Steep slope membranes include the following choice of materials:

- Asphalt roofing
- Roll
- Fiberglass
- Organic
- Tile
- Concrete
- Metal
- Clay
- Slate
- Wood
- Shake
- Shingle
- Thatch
- Metal
- Architectural
- Structural
- Spray-applied polyurethane foams
- Retrofit over existing roof and parapet surfaces

Low slope roof membranes include the following choice of materials:

- Built-Up (Multi-ply)
- Coal Tar

- Asphalt
- Modified bitumen
- APP
- SBS
- Flexible Sheet (Single-ply)
- EPDM
- TPO's
- PVC's
- Metal
- Standing seam structural
- Spray-applied polyurethane foams
- Retrofit over existing substrate

Installed costs include not only the deck, insulation and membrane, and the coverboard or thermal barrier if required; they also include the cost of the perimeter treatment such as gravel stops, blocking and gutters, flashing, accessories such as curbs, pitch pockets and equipment supports, roof specialties, and warranties. Skylights and lightning protection are usually evaluated as separate systems. Since product selections and combinations are myriad, we will not delve much further into the roof system selection. Most considerations are the same as for new work, however a few items are worth comment.

- The weight of new roof materials and new loads from mechanical and other equipment must be considered with the existing dead load capacity of the structural system.
- Removal and abatement of existing hazardous materials must be addressed in the bid documents or prior to bidding by another contract.
- The effect of surcharge of snow loads must be considered when combining a new roof with an existing roof of a different height. When the lower roof is the existing roof, a structural analysis of the existing system will be required.
- Positive drainage can be achieved on a dead level or minimally sloped roof by using a tapered insulation system or a roof overbuild system that has positive slope. Roof curbs and equipment supports may need to be replaced because of adding a tapered insulation system.
- Existing roof drainage systems may have to be upgraded and overflow drains may have to be added depending on the extent of renovation and the contribution effect of adjacent new areas.

Existing roof drainage systems may have to be upgraded and overflow drains may have to be added depending on the extent of renovation and the contribution effect of adjacent new areas.

Evaluating Window Types

Windows are often needed during conversion projects. Sometimes it is necessary, or at least desirable, to replace all existing windows. Local code requirements may insist that new windows be added as the use of space is changed. When a building is being converted from residential use to commercial space, windows can be a big part of the expense. Fortunately, there is an abundance of window types available.

Double-Hung

Double-hung windows are, by far, the most common type of window used. If you choose this type of window, you will almost always be safe in your decision. The resale value of double-hung windows is good, and so is market appeal. There are, of course, many variations in price and quality when shopping for windows. The type of project you are doing may dictate the class of window needed. For example, if you are creating a triplex in an area of low- to moderate-priced homes, you will be wasting your money to use top-of-the-line windows. However, if you are converting a building into medical space where image is everything, you can justify using more exotic windows. Energy efficiency can be a motivating factor for using more expensive windows. If your prospective buyers will appreciate and pay for more efficient windows, you should be safe in having them installed. Any buildings that you plan to hold for a good while are also prospects for better windows.

Single-Hung

Single-hung windows are not used frequently, but it would not be fair not to mention them. From an appearance point of view, single-hung windows look like double-hung windows. The big difference is that only one sash is movable in a single-hung window. With double-hung windows, both sashes are movable. In low-end projects you might find a time when using single-hung windows is sensible, but you will generally be better off to stay with double-hung windows.

Casement

Casement windows cost more than double-hung windows, but they do offer some special advantages. They are extremely tight in the energy-efficiency department. Since casement windows crank out, it is possible to get full airflow through the window. This is a feature that single- and double-hung windows can't compete with.

There are limited occasions when using casement windows in rental property are justified. Due to their expense, these windows are not normally cost-effective in small rental jobs. However, if you are doing an upscale conversion, casement windows can work out just fine.

Awning

Awning windows are a type of specialty window. The main advantage to an awning window is the fact that it raises up from the bottom. This allows the window to remain open even in heavy rains. Another use for this window is in bathrooms or other areas where privacy is desired. The windows can be mounted high in a wall to allow light and ventilation, while blocking exterior views.

Bay/Bow

Bay and bow windows are expensive and can rarely be justified financially in rental property. Since bay windows can add floor space to a room, such as a small eat-in kitchen, you might be able to make a case for installing one where a breakfast nook is needed. Bow windows are less costly to install than bay windows, and they still provide a lot of light. You will have to assess your personal circumstances, but I doubt if you will find many situations which call for a bay or bow window in a commercial conversion project.

Fixed Glass

Fixed glass is one of my favorite money-saving ways to get extra light into a building. The cost of stationary glass panels is a fraction of operable windows. While no ventilation is gained with fixed glass, an abundance of light can be achieved with it.

Exterior Doors

The choice of doors has a great effect on the budget for development of a property. Carefully determine your exact needs before choosing doors. It is not necessary to skimp on quality but the vast array of types of doors makes evaluation necessary. Once you determine the property's uses, then you'll make an informed decision. The right door can be affordable yet perfectly matched to your property.

Wood Doors

Wood doors have been used for years. They are desirable interior doors, but they do have some disadvantages in exterior applications and humid environments. Solid and rail and stile wood doors don't have great insulating qualities. Wood doors are also subject to swelling and sticking. A wood door can swell to a point where it will not open. A wood door in an area not protected by an awning or overhang can deteriorate rapidly. One good thing about a wood door is that can either be painted or stained, so cosmetic choices are abundant. Stain should be field matched to existing doors if new doors will be combined in the same visual area, or all doors can have an opaque finish or newly applied door face veneers or laminates.

Fiberglass Doors

Fiberglass doors are relatively new. Unlike wood doors, fiberglass units will not swell and stick. The insulating qualities of a fiberglass door are better than those found in wood doors. It is possible, at least with some brands, to stain a fiberglass door. Other fiberglass doors offer a small array of integrally colored doors that do not require a finish. These doors are available flush, embossed, and in custom constructions. They can be made to look like a wood door, but they give longer, better service and resistance to vandalism.

Metal-Insulated Doors

Metal-insulated doors are not only inexpensive, they have good insulating qualities, and they offer good security. Metal doors are available in different styles and designs. Six-panel embossed versions are very popular. While it's true most steel doors will not accept stain, there are now several makers who offer simulated, stainable, steel fire doors and frames and faux finishers who can alter the appearance of existing steel doors in place. In many occupancies, metal doors are an excellent, affordable way to go.

Sliding-Glass Doors

Sliding-glass doors and gliding-glass doors can transform a dark room into a fun place to be. While these doors do allow more heat loss than a standard door, their visual appeal and ventilation qualities make them very desirable in some circumstances. Security, however, is not a strong feature of a glass door, and this may have some bearing on when and where to install an all-glass door. In general, sliding glass doors are not used very often in conversion projects. But, if you have a dark, dismal room that needs help, a glass door can do the job. This type of door cannot serve as a required exit.

Inexpensive doors are often plagued with condensation. In winter, the condensation can turn to frost. You can avoid sweating doors by purchasing high-quality units, but the cost of these doors can be intimidating. A good, clad door can cost three or four times what its low-end competitor will cost. If you decide to install a cheap door, be prepared for problems with condensation.

Inexpensive doors are often plagued with condensation. In winter, the condensation can turn to frost. You can avoid sweating doors by purchasing high-quality units, but the cost of these doors can be intimidating.

Terrace Doors

Terrace doors are very popular. They are often used in place of sliding doors, especially when the opening must function as a required exit. A terrace door has one stationary panel and one panel that swings. Since the door swings, rather than sliding, they are easier to open. This can be a major factor if you are converting a property with elderly residents in mind. Deadbolt locks can be installed on terrace doors, and this give them a security edge over sliding-glass doors.

Frames

Thermally broken frame systems, insulating glass, tinted glass, and low emissivity coatings are all ways to enhance the value and function of a window, door, or skylight. Each enhancement comes at a cost.

Pre-hung frames and pre-finished interior doors can be time savers. Welded frames are, in my opinion, still the best option for intense use. Factory finishes like Kynar Hylar and anodizing are excellent finish choices for low maintenance exterior doors.

For historic applications which are not governed by a covenant that restricts materials to only the original or in kind, there are custom manufacturers for insulated aluminum, metal and fiberglass door and frame profiles which can't be distinguished from original material when viewed from the street.

For historic applications that are controlled by a covenant, window restoration can be expensive, but far less expensive than replication. There are firms specializing in frame and glazing restoration of both wood and steel frames. Glazing can be it's own challenge, since stained glass or other specialty glasses may have to be custom replicated by artisans.

When openings must be protected, listed fire rated frames, doors, hardware and glazing are required. The cost of the listed label can easily add 10-15% to the cost of the assembly. In some jurisdictions, only wire glass is permitted to glaze a rated assembly. In lieu of a rated window, an automatic fire shutter can be used, but now costs for the opening will more than double. Don't leave it out, and don't assume that an existing door complies with the required rating because it is located within an area or occupancy separation wall, unless you can see the label. I have been in more than one existing building where doors through these barriers were cut in after the initial construction and installed without labels because the person who ordered the door and frame didn't understand the significance of maintaining the integrity of the fire separation.

> **Pre-hung frames and pre-finished interior doors can be time savers. Welded frames are, in my opinion, still the best option for intense use.**

Reinforced frames, lined door panels, and bullet resistant glazing should be used where security needs are high, but these materials will likely triple the cost of an opening, so use them judiciously.

VALUE OF TARGETED IMPROVEMENTS MUST BE WEIGHED

The value of targeted improvements can be quantified using the services of the design professional, a professional estimator, or an appraiser, but none of these estimates are as valuable or accurate as the contractor's bid or proposal. They are, however, measures of the fit between the scope, the quality, and the cost. The micro-bidding climate, materials that may not be able to be delivered, and the length and inherent risks of the contract can have an almost unpredictable effect on the competitiveness of the actual bids. That said, estimates would usually predict when value engineering is required.

Value Engineering

Champagne taste, beer budget, is a reality for many owners. The initial wish list and the constructed program are rarely the same. I have met with some clients where the constructed value of the initial wish list was two to three times the initial budget. This is especially true when user input has been sought during the programming phase. Here's a quick reality check:

- Look on the program to find the total area to be renovated, the total area to be added, and the total area to be demolished.
- Get a square foot estimating data source and look up the multipliers for the building type that most nearly resembles the proposed use.
- Apply the factor to the new area, take a fraction of it, and apply it to the renovated area.
- Apply a selective demolition factor for interior demolition.
- Apply a building demolition factor for structures and major portions of existing structures to be removed.
- Add to this the site demolition and development costs including services, or allow about 10-20% of the construction budget.
- Sum these.
- Multiply by the contingency factor. At early stages, 25% is not unreasonable.
- Add about 25-35% to this amount for soft costs like fees, financing, and design-related services.
- Add an inflation factor to the number for each year until construction should be complete.
- Enter the cost of property acquisition.
- Sum these. This will give a pretty good idea of the amount of funds required to execute the project.
- Determine if those funds can be raised, and over what interval.

FIGURE 10.11 Estimators should account for the cost of coring and cutting for new services, and, if applicable, for providing fire stopping in new penetrations. It is easy to overlook the cost of selective demolition. Using a checklist or spec section list may assist in avoiding such an oversight. *Photo: Nick Fredericks*

When the budget is too small for the client's appetite, the problem can be addressed in any two of the three fundamental ways:

- Budget can be increased.
- Quality can be decreased.
- Scope can be reduced or eliminated.

The designer should establish with the owner the order of priority for these three elements at the outset of the project. It will profoundly influence his design approach and material selections from the inception. If value engineering must occur after the design is underway, the owner can work with the design team to revise the design approach to look for construction efficiencies (which are just scope and value reductions by another name) or he can alter the site location and pay for redesign and closing costs. Paying for an estimate at the end of each design phase will keep a budget on track, but this effort is usually sold as an extra service.

Mandated Improvements

The legally mandated category of improvements was not thoroughly discussed in this chapter, because they are not usually optional. The code and regulatory environment trigger construction and design changes when a building is altered, and more so when the use is changed to a use of greater inherent hazard. The designer can optimize the use of regulations applied to the project by seeking equivalencies or variances, applying for the use of alternative provisions found in Chapter 34 of model codes, administrative provisions or sub-codes such as the International Existing Buildings Code. Developing this subject could fill another book.

THE LAST WORD

In *A Change-of-Use*, the authors have looked at the adaptive reuse environment in these contexts: historical, geo-political, economic, community, design, and investment. The intent was to give designers, investors, owners, contractors, and students a better understanding of the forces of change that have made rehabilitation critical to the life and health of our community environment, economy, and culture. With practical advice and observations, we demonstrated the need for revitalization and offered a basic understanding of construction contracts and what is required of the key parties to effect it.

It is our hope that this book delivered sufficient resources, inspiration, examples, plans, and strategic analysis tools for those businesses, redevelopers, designers, and contractors to be motivated to recapture and energize city cores, edge cities, and other areas where existing architecture is under utilized. Examples and warnings have been used to demonstrate that reason must rule passion in making redevelopment choices and where observed deficiency can spell negotiating opportunity. We trust our work has stimulated community and government leaders to seek greater resources and take actions to assist them. We have endeavored to demonstrate the interplay of the roles and agendas of the owner, designer and contractor, government and other parties in achieving the best results in context-specific scenarios.

We hope to have offered some ideas on how to make these efforts sustainable, worthwhile, and successful as measured by the people who live work and own property in the community. Most particularly, we would like to motivate our readers to an enlightened self-interest that can face, unblinking and unflinching, the challenge of bringing back the city for profit.

We have not tried to tell anyone how to design or what is beautiful, how to arrange space or to finish surfaces. These qualities will come from the creativity, cultural understanding, practical knowledge, learned observations, good will, and discourse of people committed to achieve good things together.

Dorothy Henehan & R. Dodge Woodson

June 2003

INDEX

ABOUT THE AUTHORS

Dorothy Henehan is an architect who practices chiefly in the Midwest and lives in Indianapolis with her family. She has served as an officer of AIA Indianapolis and has been an officer of the Indianapolis Chapter of the Construction Specifications Institute. She has degrees in architecture and environmental design from Ball State University where she also undertook Urban Studies. She holds CDT and CCCA certificates from the Construction Specifications Institute. She is a member of the Southern Building Code Congress International. Her wide range of project experience in both public and private sectors includes educational facilities, libraries, environmental service facilities, laboratories, military, justice, urban design, maintenance structures, multifamily housing, commercial kitchens, industrial facilities, corporate headquarters, tenant development, hospitality, medical projects, and interiors services. Her work has included facilities and accessibility assessment reports, code studies, phasing plans, specifications, quality assurance, inter-disciplinary co-ordination, professional development, technical resource and site rehabilitation, and sustainability programs. Two-thirds of those projects involved renovation and about half have involved public money.

R Dodge Woodson is a realtor, developer, builder, and master plumber and gasfitter with over 25 years experience in the conversion market in Maine and Virginia. He has authored over 70 books for major publishers. Woodson contributed his expertise in editing, real estate, building, site evaluation, and improvements strategy for this project.

Photos for this book were primarily provided by Stephen Culbert and Nick Fredericks and the authors. Stephen B. Culbert, P.E. is lead electrical engineer in an A/E firm, a former electrician, and a photographic hobbyist with considerable renovation project experience. Stephen has a keen eye to access projects with original photography that give a man on the street and man on the roof views, illustrating project planning and evaluation concepts discussed. Nick Fredericks is a project manager with a general contractor in Pendleton, Indiana. He has contributed construction and demolition photos that illustrate ongoing work.